American Music in the Twentieth Century

American Music in the Twentieth Century

Kyle Gann

Schirmer Books
An Imprint of Simon & Schuster Macmillan
NEW YORK

Prentice Hall International
LONDON • MEXICO CITY • NEW DELHI • SINGAPORE • SYDNEY • TORONTO

Schirmer Books
An Imprint of Simon & Schuster Macmillan
1633 Broadway
New York, New York 10019

Library of Congress Catalog Card Number: 97-19863

Printed in the United States of America

Printing number

1 2 3 4 5 6 7 8 9 10

Library of Congress Cataloging-in-Publication Data

Gann, Kyle.
    American music in the twentieth century / Kyle Gann..
        p.   cm.
    Includes bibliographical references (p.   ) and index.
    ISBN 0-02-864655-X (alk. paper)
    1. Music—United States—20th century—History and criticism.
I. Title.
ML200.5.G36 1997   97-19863
780'.973'0904—dc21   CIP
                                                               MN

This book meets the requirements of ANSI/NISO Z39.48—1992 (Permanence of Paper)

for Nancy

"I don't think myself confin'd to any Rules for composition, laid down by any that went before me . . . "
—William Billings, 1770

"Can't we get all the art we need from France?"
—Calvin Coolidge, 1927

Contents

Acknowledgments

In addition to all the composers who generously gave me time and information, I would like to thank my wife, Nancy Cook, and my son, Bernard, for their patience and support; Joel Chadabe for help with the electronics chapter; my editor, Jonathan Wiener; Karissa Krenz; and a special thanks to William Duckworth.

Permissions

International Copyright Secured. All Rights Reserved.
Reprinted by Permission.
(mm. 22–32)

Nancarrow STUDY NO. 25
Copyright © 1975 by Conlon Nancarrow
Copyright © assigned to B. Schotts Soehne, Mainz
All rights reserved.
Used by permission of European American Music.
Distributors Corporation, sole U.S. and Canadian agent
for B. Schotts Soehne, Mainz

Nancarrow STUDY NO. 36
Copyright © 1982 by Conlon Nancarrow
Copyright © assigned to B. Schotts Soehne, Mainz
All rights reserved.
Used by permission of European American Music.
Distributors Corporation, sole U.S. and Canadian agent
for B. Schotts Soehne, Mainz

THREE COMPOSITIONS FOR PIANO
© Copyright 1957 by Boelke-Romert, Inc.
Used by Permission.

TIGER
by Henry Cowell
Copyright © 1956 by Associated Music Publishers, Inc. (BMI)
International Copyright Secured. All Rights Reserved.
Reprinted by Permission.
(excerpts as indicated in lettter of August 19, 1997)

THE MOTHER OF US ALL
by Virgil Thomson
Copyright © 1947 (Renewed) by G. Schirmer, Inc. (ASCAP)
International Copyright Secured. All Rights Reserved.
Reprinted by Permission.
(mm. 9, 10. after rh #48, from rh#49 through 50, 1 mm after rh#50)

WALK IN BEAUTY
By Peter Garland
© 1989 by Petroglyph Music (BMI).
Used by permission.

YO SHAKESPEARE
by Michael Gordon
Copyright © 1992 by Red Poppy (ASCAP). Administered Worldwide by G.
Schirmer, Inc.
International Copyright Secured. All Rights Reserved.
Reprinted by Permission.

Prelude:
What Is American Music?

Before 1492, the land that now comprises the United States was occupied only by the people Columbus misidentified as "Indians." Thus, it could be said that the only indigenously American music is the vocal chanting (usually with drums or rattles) of the American Indians. Today that music is taught, however, as part of the field of ethnomusicology, rather than as a shared tradition. Everyone else who lives in the United States is descended from families who came from somewhere else: mostly Europe, Africa, Asia, or Latin America. When we use that speciously simple term "American music," then, whose music are we talking about?

Let us take as our premise that there is such a thing as "American music" and that it results partly from the clash of European, African, Asian, and Latin American influences. Partly, not completely—for it also results from unfettered Yankee inventiveness and from the freedom Americans have had to create their own music without the restrictions (or benefits) of an assumed, shared culture. Every American composition is a dialogue between inheritance and freedom. Unlike the histories of, say, European classical or East Indian classical musics, which deal with individual contributions to a strong, continuing tradition, American music is a history of originality and innovation. It is the paradox of American music, in fact, that it is a tradition of originality.

At this late and sophisticated date, such a concern with what is specifically American in music would seem to have been discredited. The limitations of nationalism as an aesthetic (with its underlying connections to Romanticism) have been apparent for decades. As an antidote, the slogan "American music is whatever is written by American composers" has become widely accepted, valued for its refusal to impose essentialist criteria that would separate "real" American composers from less authentic ones. Laudable as such a motivation is, however, the slogan's seemingly benign transparency has left American music in a vulnerable position.

Today, as musical society gropes about for a situation of fairer representation in the arts under the banner of multiculturalism, the public perception is that Asian, African, European, and Latin American cultures each have their own musical identity, but that aside from jazz and rock, there is no such thing as an American concert music tradition. America is so distrustful of its own musical creativity that it continues to project musical achievement on the rest of the world, preserving its own cultural inferiority complex. So intense is the focus on the dichotomy between Eurocentric tradition on one hand and ethnic musics—by which the Third World is meant—on the other, that "American classical music" is perceived as just a special case of the European tradition.

And yet, every other culture has its formalized, listening-centered, ritual musical tradition as well as its dance music, its theater music, its entertainment music. We have no qualms about speaking of Indian classical music, or Japanese classical music; but applied to our own music, "classical" makes us squeamish, as though it automatically suggests elitism and aristocracy rather than a specific social function and performance situation. Because of this specious, unexamined distinction, American composers, who stood in the shadow of their European counterparts for decades, have recently been expected to step back in favor of musicians from Asia and Africa.

For the sake of our national musical self-esteem, it is urgent to show that America is not an empty vessel into which the musics of other societies may be poured, but a culture with its own genius, innovations, and traditions, now long since capable of influencing other cultures as they have influenced us. (American minimalism, electronic techniques, and the aesthetics of John Cage, for example, have had tremendous impact on Scandinavian, Eastern European, Italian, Japanese, and even Indonesian composers.) The problem is that Americanness in music has been searched for in the qualities of the music itself, music that is far too diverse to generalize about.

More fruitful would be to look for the nature of American music in the social conditions all American composers share, since such conditions determine the expectations and assumptions that go into the creative act. American composers are, of course, free to write anything they wish, and the American public is free to ignore it. Those facts have aesthetic consequences. Given the dearth of professional support for serious music in America, it is possible that a composer who initiates his own radical, personal tradition with himself as sole representative (such as Harry Partch) might conceivably have as much success getting performed and understood as the most academic adherent to European (or other) tradition. An American's acquiescence to tradition is a matter of personal choice, not social compulsion, and therefore takes on a different character. Perhaps America is the only place where traditionalism itself can constitute an act of defiance.

Stylistically, the approach of this book will be reductive, finding Americanness by taking the entirety of what American composers have done and subtracting from it the identifiably European, Asian, African, and Latin American elements. It is impossible to deny American classical music's roots in Europe, just as, later in the century, it becomes impossible to deny African and then Asian roots as well; but there is little point in discussing here what books on European, African, and Asian music discuss at greater depth. Our story will begin with two composers who ignored both the mandates of European tradition and the progression of European fads to invent a new music virtually from scratch: Charles Ives and Henry Cowell. From this fount of native experimentalism an American tradition flowed, a tradition not of procedures and rules but of resources, attitudes, and pragmatic inventiveness.

The book will not explore in any depth the history of rock, jazz, or popular forms, except insofar as they helped shape this tradition. The invention of jazz and rock were supreme examples of American originality, but once established, each genre created its own tradition, each of which deserves its own book.

Consequently, the title becomes an insoluble dilemma. To call the book "American *Art*-Music in the Twentieth Century" would insultingly imply that jazz and rock are not art. "American Classical Music" would create a false expectation that the book covers extensions of European tradition, while that now old-fashioned term "Serious Music" would offend almost everyone. "Concert Music," a term recently favored in some circles, negates the fact that much of this music has spread out into non-concert (loft, outdoor, or ambient) situations, not to mention the obvious complication that there are also jazz concerts and rock concerts. In symphony orchestra circles the terms "experimental music" and even "American eccentrics" have been used to marginalize indigenously American art-music movements. Even if one wanted to disparage the hundreds of composers inspired by John Cage by calling their pieces mere "experiments," to apply such terms to Americans as successful within the establishment as Copland, Babbitt, and Glass would be ludicrous.

This terminological impasse is so symptomatic of cultural conditions in the 1990s that there is little point in decrying it, and less in applying some makeshift solution. Anyone disappointed by the inexact relation of the book's title to its subject matter will simply have to wait for a period of greater musico-terminological clarity than we enjoy at present.

The book is organized roughly by decades, more explicitly by the milieu which seemed to characterize each decade. After 1950, however, one chapter per decade is no longer enough, as the streams of music have proliferated wildly; artrock, postminimalism, and the New Romanticism all developed in parallel during the late 1970s and 1980s, shaped by different sets of forces. Within each decade or milieu I have singled out three to eight composers who seemed to best define that era, even if much of their work was done in decades previous to or following the one I have them representing; most composers' careers span thirty to sixty years, but they commonly become associated with the moment at which they first caught the public ear.

Almost without planning it my criterion has been to emphasize not necessarily the best composers, nor my favorites, nor even the ones best known to the public; but the figures who seemed, in my own view, to exert most influence on the history of American composing (even if in a not-very-public manner, like James Tenney or Conlon Nancarrow), who seemed most responsible for shaping the nature of American music. At the end of each chapter I discuss more briefly as many artists as possible associated with the ideas of the chapter—many of them not minor by any criterion, but arguably less central in defining the chapter's milieu.

It is a cliché that "Jazz is the only indigenous American music," and while the cliché gives due tribute to jazz's importance and authenticity, it conceals a back-handed slap at composers of American classical music, an assumption that all formalized music stems from European tradition. If this book does not help dispel that cliché, it will have failed in its central intention. Only by claiming its creative heritage and relinquishing its macho pose as the world's only "cultureless culture" can America become, as John Cage hoped, "just another part of the world, no more, no less."

CHAPTER 1

Forefathers

American Music in the Eighteenth and Nineteenth Centuries

More than any other art except architecture, music requires a social support system. An artist can finish a painting alone in her studio, but a musical composition usually requires the assembly and rehearsal of performers for its completion, which in turn generally implies the presence of an audience for whom the effort is expended. In African and American Indian societies, the support system for music involves virtually everyone in a village or tribe, each of whom performs music as an essential part of social and sacred ritual. In Europe, where social functions are more specialized, a musician requires a complex network of presenting organizations, teaching institutions, critical venues, and sufficiently sophisticated audiences in order to live a fulfilling musical life.

After 1492, Europeans fleeing religious and political persecution had a strong incentive to emigrate to America. Expert musicians had a strong incentive to stay in Europe, where their music could be performed well and appreciated. The celebrated European composers who toured America in the nineteenth and early twentieth centuries (Busoni, Tchaikovsky, and Scriabin, for example) found such tours, though sometimes lucrative, a burden because of the primitiveness of the musical organizations and the naïveté of the audiences. Thus was America's musical inferiority complex born.

From the beginning the American composer labored under an assumption that crippled his or her creativity: any innovation, any departure from European precedent, would be interpreted as a technical deficiency. In some music circles this is still true today. Europeans like Berlioz, Liszt, and Wagner were free to ignore the past and create their own rules, but American symphonists such as Bristow, Chadwick, and Beach dared not transgress beyond precedents set by even the more conservative Europeans: Mendelssohn, Brahms, Dvořák. As Henry Cowell wrote, "Transplanted to the United States, the rules of harmony and composition took on a doctrinaire authority that was the more dogmatic for being second hand."[1]

The American painter saw in front of him a wilderness that did not look like the paintings of Europe (assuming he even saw the latter), and Nature commanded him, in painting what he saw, to innovate. But the American composer, lacking any such objective correlative, usually felt obliged to ignore the wilderness and write in the urban, psychological style of the European music she could study in the score or hear at concerts. The result, as Wilfrid Mellers put it, was

> a dream-evocation of the Old World as it never was or could have been. . . . Most nineteenth-century American music . . . manifested a passive veneration for the Teutonic, which represented Art; and was usually well written, cheerful, and agreeable: a pretence that the wilderness did not exist, that the heart was not a "lonely hunter."[2]

Mellers's characterization is especially true of the composers who studied in Europe, less so of those who did not. John Knowles Paine (1839–1906) studied in Berlin 1958–1961 with Karl-August Haupt, met Clara Schumann, absorbed German aesthetics, and came home to express the latter in large-scale concert works. George Whitefield Chadwick (1854–1931) studied at Leipzig Conservatory with Reinecke and Jadassohn and enjoyed early success with his string quartets and symphonies. Horatio Parker (1863–1919) studied in 1882–1885 in Munich with Josef Rheinberger and later became known for his grand oratorio *Hora novissima* (1893). Along with John Sullivan Dwight, the "Dean of American music critics"—a Transcendentalist who participated with Bronson Alcott in the ill-fated Brook Farm commune experiment— Paine championed what he called the "modern Romantic movement," meaning Schubert, Schumann, Chopin, and Mendelssohn, as well as Bach (whose works were being rediscovered in Germany during Paine's years there), Handel, Mozart, and Beethoven. The aesthetics of Berlioz, Liszt, and Wagner were considered suspect for moral and sexual reasons as well as musical ones; from the very beginning America has distrusted the bohemian lifestyle of the avant-garde artist.

Paine, Chadwick, and Parker were the leading American musical pedagogues of their day. In the 1870s, Paine convinced Harvard to appoint him America's first university music professor, and he taught many of the composers—John Alden Carpenter, Frederick Converse, Arthur Foote, Edward Burlingame Hill, Daniel Gregory Mason—who in turn taught America's first generation of well-known professional composers. From 1882 until his death Chadwick taught at Boston's New England Conservatory, counting among his students Horatio Parker, Converse, Hill, Mason, and Arthur Farwell. Parker taught at Yale from

1894 on, where his students included Quincy Porter, Roger Sessions, and, most notably, Charles Ives. The power of this triumvirate, then, in imposing an exaggerated awe of European musical standards and practices, was incalculable. One could say that American music has not yet succeeded in completely escaping its grip.

The case of Edward MacDowell (1860–1908) demonstrates how much a European, and specifically German, reputation meant at the time. MacDowell studied at the Paris Conservatory (where Debussy was a classmate) and in Frankfurt with the composer Joachim Raff. As a pianist, he played for Liszt not only Liszt's music, but his own First Piano Concerto, and Liszt had enough faith in him to program his music. MacDowell taught at the Darmstadt Conservatory but was forced to return to America in 1888 by financial difficulties. Upon his return he was celebrated as the one composer to have succeeded in expressing American traits (or perhaps more accurately Celtic ones, through his Scottish descent) through a professional German polish. In 1896 Columbia University appointed him its first professor of music, but syphilis and a cab accident destroyed his mind, and he died in a state of acute mental disability.

Largely because of his continental polish, MacDowell was considered for decades America's greatest composer, and often compared to Edvard Grieg, another nationalist composer (from Norway) who trained in Germany. There is, admittedly, a simple melodicism to MacDowell's music, Lisztian rather than Brahmsian, that makes it more memorable than that of Paine or Chadwick. Eventually, however, the sentimentality and structural weakness of his music became apparent, and his reputation has dropped tremendously, though amateur pianists still play his *Woodland Sketches*. More important to music history, however, is the artist colony MacDowell's wife founded in his name on their eighty-acre estate in the hills of New Hampshire.

On the other hand were composers who did not study in Europe and who made their livings as practicing musicians rather than in the university. The son of a conductor, George Frederick Bristow (1825–1898) played in the violin section of the New York Philharmonic for thirty-six years, though he resigned for several months in 1854 to protest the orchestra's treatment of American composers. If there is, among nineteenth-century American symphonies, a counterexample to Mellers's description above, it may be Bristow's *Arcadian Symphony* (1872), subtitled "The Pioneer," with its first movement growing from a lonely violin solo. Amy Cheney Beach (1867–1944, generally known during her lifetime by her married name, Mrs. H. H. A. Beach), was a child prodigy in Boston who did not visit Europe until 1910, following the death of her husband; the trip was not to study, but to promote her music. Though she curtailed her performing career at her husband's request, her Piano Concerto, her *Gaelic Symphony*, and some of her songs and piano pieces have been revived in recent years.

Studying with Paine at Harvard, Arthur Foote (1853–1937) received the first Master's Degree in music in America, and though he visited Europe as a student, he did not study there formally. He worked as a private piano teacher, teaching piano at New England Conservatory the last sixteen years of his life, and wrote some of the finest chamber music of the American nineteenth century. Charles Martin Loeffler (1861–1935) was born in Alsace on the French and German border and studied in Berlin, but he moved to America in 1881 and eventually became the second concertmaster of the Boston Symphony Orchestra. His music, highly polished and cosmopolitan, leans heavily toward French impressionism in such programmatic tone poems as *La mort de Tintagiles*.

These composers left a neglected body of music that can occasionally be delightful, especially in the smaller forms. Their symphonies, operas, and chamber works often fail, not from misguided innovation but from trying to duplicate too closely the external formal design of their European models, without the sense of inner compulsion from which those models arose in the first place. For instance, the themes of the movements of Chadwick's Second Symphony are all related by melodic contour, after the cyclic thematic form of late French Romanticism, but Chadwick makes the relationships obvious to the point of monotony. Bristow's symphonies are marred by excessive formal repetition. Parker's *Hora Novissima,* highly esteemed in his lifetime because of its grandiose spiritual intentions, today sounds tediously stuffy.

There were, however, other pre-twentieth-century American composers who paid little attention to European models. When their works failed, they failed from genuine ignorance of harmonic and formal solutions. When they succeeded, they achieved an authenticity that holds up, a century later, better than the Europe imitations of the New England symphonists. It is perhaps ironic but understandable that the early American composers who wrote the most sincere and individual music were those who did not feel a debt to Europe and who never felt consigned to force their intuitions into expressive forms foreign to them. In particular, a remarkable trio of American originals felt that their distance from Europe gave them license to sculpt their own forms: William Billings, Anthony Philip Heinrich, and Louis Moreau Gottschalk.

Billings (1746–1800), a Boston tanner by trade, with little musical education, published six books of hymns and secular choral pieces. He has been described as "a singular man, of moderate size, short of one leg, with one eye, without any address [i.e., social adroitness], and with an uncommon negligence of person. Still he spake and sung and thought as a man above the common abilities."[3] Among his innovations were what he called "fuging tunes," a minor form inherited from English music that he claimed was "more than twenty times as powerful as the old slow tunes." In the introduction to Billings's first tunebook, *The New-England Psalm-Singer* (1770, with a frontispiece engraved by no less than Paul

Revere), he wrote the archetypal declaration of American music's independence from Europe:

> . . . all the hard, dry, studied rules that ever was prescribed, will not
> enable any person to form an air. . . . I don't think myself confin'd to
> any Rules for composition, laid down by any that went before me,
> neither should I think (were I to pretend to lay down Rules) that any
> who came after me were any ways obligated to adhere to them . . . I
> think it is best for every Composer to be his own Carver.[4]

The didactic prefaces to his hymn books show that Billings was aware of
the prohibition against parallel fifth intervals in European counterpoint,
but his music shows that he (like Beethoven after him) felt free to use
them anyway. To thumb his nose at his critics and at European authority, Billings wrote one choral song, "Jargon," harmonized entirely in
harsh (though diatonic) dissonances.

For all their occasional naïveté and awkward meter changes, Billings's hymns have a wonderful, vibrant energy. They ultimately became
part of rural America's "Sacred Harp" tradition of shaped-note singing,
a rough-hewn style of psalmody using notes of different shapes for ped-
agogical purposes that survives in rural areas to the present day. (The
second most famous hymn writer in this genre was Supply Belcher,
1751–1836, dubbed "The Handel of Maine.") As late as the 1960s,
Billings's stirring revolutionary war song "Chester" was still taught to
American school children:

> Let tyrants shake their iron rods
> And slavery clank its galling chains
> We fear them not, we trust in God.
> New England's God forever reigns.

Born in Bohemia, Anthony Philip Heinrich (1781–1861) came to
America in 1810 and, self-taught, began to compose in 1818, nevertheless becoming one of America's most prominent musicians in the period
preceding the Civil War. In 1817 he led the first known New World performance of any Beethoven symphony—the First—and in 1842 he was
one of the founders of the New York Philharmonic Society. Starting
with a collection of vocal and instrumental works called *The Dawning of
Music in Kentucky,* he wrote pieces with titles and programs, such as the
Barbecue Divertimento and his grand symphony *The Ornithological Combat
of Kings,* that have occasioned much annotator's humor in this century.
He was the first to use American Indian themes in large works, and
wrote orchestral music of such complexity that the American orchestras
of his day had great difficulty performing it. Certainly Heinrich pushed
the Haydnesque, eighteenth-century language he inherited to extremes
that can seem comic in performance today, but he also strung together
quotations and ideas in a stream-of-consciousness way that anticipated

twentieth-century trends. Though frequently awkward, his music is rarely dull.

Born in New Orleans, Louis Moreau Gottschalk (1829–1869) was exposed early to African, Creole, and West Indian influences, and later made pioneering use of them in his music. A phenomenal pianist, he concertized in France, Switzerland, Spain, and Latin America. He also studied in Paris, but with Berlioz, the Frenchman whose life (he was an opium addict) and musical style the other Americans considered scandalous. Somewhat following Berlioz's example, Gottschalk presented "monster concerts" of ten pianos or 900 musicians and played more than a thousand concerts between 1862 and 1865 alone. Such activities were antithetical to the sober sensibilities of the New England symphonists, and John Sullivan Dwight criticized Gottschalk harshly. At one concert, however, Gottschalk played a work of his own and attributed it to Beethoven in the program; Dwight, as expected, praised the "Beethoven" composition and excoriated Gottschalk's music for its "amateurish inanities," whereupon Gottschalk wrote him to apologize for the unfortunate printing error.

Gottschalk's piano pieces, modeled after Chopin and with sentimentally programmatic titles such as *The Dying Poet, The Last Hope,* and *Souvenir de Porto Rico,* can be superficial, but they also represent a bold and authentic introduction of African and Cuban idioms to the piano repertoire, decades before ragtime would continue the effort. Today, the music of distinguished symphonists such as Paine and Chadwick is exhumed only by specialists, while the less polished music of Billings and Gottschalk has retained considerable popularity, for its own beauty as well as for being a symbol of an inimitably American musical sensibility. The contrast illustrates the enormous conflict in American music between those who believe that great art can only come from following the European tradition and those who feel that America's new situation required starting from a clean slate with an attentiveness to the local environment.

One celebrated incident epitomizes another conflict that the American composer has faced from the beginning. Between 1892 and 1895, the Czech composer Antonín Dvořák served as director of New York's National Conservatory of Music. In 1893, just as he was finishing his own "New World" Symphony supposedly based on Negro themes, Dvořák made a statement to the press, quoted in the *New York Herald:* "I am now satisfied . . . that the future music of this country must be founded upon what are called negro melodies. . . . There is nothing in the whole range of composition that cannot be supplied with themes from this source."[5] The following week, the *Boston Herald* printed replies by Paine, Chadwick, and Beach. Paine's internationalist response was one that would be echoed throughout the twentieth century:

> Dr. Dvorak . . . greatly overestimates the influence that national melodies and folk-songs have exercised on the higher forms of musical art. In the case of Haydn, Mozart, Beethoven, Schubert, and other

German masters, the old folk-songs have been used to a limited extent as motives; but movements founded on such themes are exceptional in comparison with the immense amount of entirely original thematic material that constitutes the bulk of their music. . . .

The time is past when composers are to be classed according to geographical limits. It is not a question of nationality, but individuality, and individuality of style is not the result of imitation—whether of folk songs, negro melodies, the tunes of the heathen Chinese or Digger Indians, but of personal character and inborn originality. During the present century art has overstepped all national limits.[6]

Beach responded with her own opposed nationalist claim:

Without the slightest desire to question the beauty of the negro melodies . . . or to disparage them on account of their source, I cannot help feeling justified in the belief that they are not fully typical of our country. The African population of the United States is far too small for its songs to be considered "American." It represents only one factor in the composition of our nation. . . . We of the north should be far more likely to be influenced by the old English, Scotch, or Irish songs, inherited with our literature from our ancestors.[7]

Here, within one newspaper article, were the two viewpoints between which American music would oscillate for at least a century afterward: Paine, the defender of high art and the extension of European culture, and Beach, the defender of the American's right to choose her own idiom.

Since America is not an ancient country, the relationship of its art music to its vernacular music has never been allowed to evolve gradually or naturally, but always with problematic self-consciousness. In the 1930s, composers would try to create an American music from, if not quotation of actual folk melodies, at least imitation of American inflections. In the 1950s, composers would eschew nationalist characteristics to join Europeans in an international style. And in the 1980s, one of the most bitterly contested philosophic differences among American composers would be the question whether music should flow from a vernacular or whether it should be constructed from pure sonic materials without extramusical referents. The issues of American music were all in place by the mid-nineteenth century and are intrinsic to America's national character and unique social situation. Time has sharpened but not changed them.

Charles Ives

Charles Ives (1874–1954), whom many still consider America's greatest composer, was the first American to step deliberately outside European musical conventions in major works. He is a paradigm of the composer's

Charles Ives. *Photo by Frank Gerratana,* Bridgeport Herald. *Courtesy New York Public Library.*

problematic place in American society: writing music on evenings and weekends, he worked as head of the Ives & Myrick Insurance Agency, a subsidiary of Mutual of New York. Yet Ives's music, most of it written in near-total isolation, contains a list of innovations that anticipates the majority of 20th-century musical trends: unprecedented dissonance, densely heterogeneous textures, instrumental groups set apart from each other in space, unusual means of playing the piano keyboard, classical appropriation of ragtime, quarter-tones, simultaneous tunes played in different tempos, and widespread quotation of folk music, popular music, and hymns.

Ives was born October 20, 1874, in Danbury, Connecticut. His father, George Ives, was the first musician in a prominent family of successful businessmen, and no other composer's father, not even Leopold Mozart, plays so large a role in his son's biography. Charles Ives, who began composing by age 12, attributed his experimental tendencies to his father's open-minded training, and claimed that his father rigged up contrivances with violin strings to experiment with tunings, had the family sing both in two keys at once and in quarter tones, and tried to match the sonorities of local church bells with dissonances on the piano. Ives remembered his father dividing his band into sections and having them play simultaneously from different locations, and again (perhaps unintentionally) having two bands pass each other playing different pieces at once. (Ives's memories, however, are not all confirmable by contemporary press accounts, and he has been charged with glorifying his father's contribution to his spectacular originality.)

Following an Ives family tradition, Ives attended Yale, where he studied with Horatio Parker, who had trained in Munich under Joseph Rheinberger. Parker could not believe that Ives's dissonances and rhythmic experiments were seriously meant, and "asked me," Ives later wrote, "not to bring any more things like these into the classroom."[8] During one of Parker's classes, Parker's teacher Chadwick walked in as Parker was criticizing one of Ives's songs, "Summerfields." According to Ives's *Memos,* Parker had claimed the song had "too many keys in the middle," but Chadwick looked at the song and pronounced, "In it's [its] way almost as good as Brahms! [To Parker:] That's as good a song as you could write."[9] Parker's favored student was David Stanley Smith (1877–1949), who succeeded him at Yale as Dean from 1920 to 1946. Despite Parker's higher regard for it, Smith's music has fallen into oblivion. Parker's influence on Ives is difficult to assess, but there is, in Parker's popular tone poem *A Northern Ballad,* a transition that vividly anticipates one in Ives's *Thanksgiving.*

Unfortunately, George Ives, the only musician prepared to understand his son's experimentalism, died of a stroke in November of Charles's freshman year of college. It would be twenty-three years before Ives would meet another musician sympathetic to his music, twenty-three years in which he would write almost his complete works. Ives's music takes on deeper meaning in relation to his isolation from other professional musicians and to his musical inheritance from his father; it has even been suggested that Ives composed the music his father failed to write.[10] After college, he made only one attempt to go public with his music. On April 18, 1902, he conducted (from the organ) a performance of his cantata *The Celestial Country,* a work patterned after Parker's highly esteemed *Hora Novissima,* and one far more conservative than other pieces Ives had already written. The piece was respectfully reviewed in both the *New York Times* and the *Musical Courier,* yet Ives was apparently disappointed (if not actually afraid of success), quit his organ job, and had no further professional performances of his music until 1921.

Ives suffered the first of a series of heart attacks in 1918, which, along with diabetes, eventually put an end to both his composing and his insurance work. (He retired from business a few weeks after the stock market crash of 1929, which had little effect on him.) Almost all of his music was written by 1921, though he was to live for another thirty-three years. By this time, however, he had become relatively wealthy in the insurance business and could afford to replace his role as composer (however unknown) with that of patron (usually anonymous). In 1920 he had 750 copies of his *Concord Sonata* privately printed and sent to musical figures he thought might be interested. He followed this in 1921 by printing the *Essays Before a Sonata,* literary writings meant to accompany the Sonata as a kind of aesthetic explanation, and in 1922 he published a dazzlingly heterogeneous song collection, *114 Songs.*

The songs and sonata met with general incomprehension, even to the extent of doubts whether Ives could possibly be serious. A few copies, however, fell into sympathetic hands, and in 1927 Ives was contacted by a composer who would do more than anyone else to advance his music: Henry Cowell. Cowell, an indefatigable pianist and music promoter (of whom more in chapter 2), had just begun publishing *New Music,* an important journal in which scores of dozens of progressive American musical works were first published. Cowell made possible the first performances and publications of many of Ives's scores, while, in turn, Ives became the financial mainstay of *New Music.* With Cowell's contacts, Ives's money, and the astounding talent of the Russian-American conductor Nicolas Slonimsky, Ives's *Three Places in New England* was first heard in New York at Town Hall in January of 1931. The concert was to be repeated in coming months in Boston, Havana, and Paris, precipitating Europe's first notice of indigenously American orchestral music.

An even bigger spur to Ives's popularity came with John Kirkpatrick's intrepid New York premiere of the Piano Sonata No. 2, "Concord, Mass. 1840–1860," in 1939. Lawrence Gilman of the *New York Herald Tribune* reviewed the work as "the greatest music composed by an American, and the most deeply and essentially American in impulse and implication." The review sparked public interest in Ives, an interest which (except during the years of World War II) crescendoed into an almost saintlike reputation in the 1960s. In 1947 he was awarded the Pulitzer Prize for his hymn-filled Third Symphony, completed some thirty-six years earlier.

Ives died in 1954. Today his birthplace is marked by a plaque on the side of a Danbury bank on Main Street at Chapel Place, which reads, "On this site was born Charles Edward Ives, one of America's first great composers. Solitary radical in music, pioneer in polytonal harmonies and rhythm, his roots lay deep in his Danbury boyhood." The house he was born in—one of America's rare musical shrines—has been moved from its original site and can be visited on Mountainville Avenue. The composer himself is buried in front of his father in Wooster Cemetery.

Ives's Works and Writings

Ives's important works include four symphonies (plus a visionary, unfinished "Universe" Symphony), two piano sonatas, four violin sonatas, two string quartets, numerous experimental works for mixed ensembles (including *The Unanswered Question*), two orchestral "sets" (one the famous *Three Places in New England*), and more than 160 songs constituting the most important art song repertoire by an American composer.

Ives wrote his Symphony No. 1 (1896–1898), more or less along the Germanic lines of his teacher Horatio Parker, while still in college, yet already it surpassed any earlier American symphony in polish and convincing form. His Symphony No. 2 (1897–1902) is a favorite example of Ives's characteristic quotation technique; the five-movement form is plausibly European, but the themes are loose take-offs on American folksongs such as "Turkey in the Straw," "America the Beautiful," "Camptown Races," "Columbia, the Gem of the Ocean," and even a tune from Brahms's Third Symphony. Ives's Third Symphony, subtitled "The Camp Meeting," is a relatively mild, tranquilly melodic piece, laced with revival-meeting hymns and with a *largo* finale loosely based on the hymn "Just As I Am." The most ambitious work Ives completed is his Fourth Symphony. It requires chorus (singing "Watchman, Tell Us of the Night" in the first movement), two conductors (for the second movement's two competing ensembles), two pianos tuned a quarter-tone apart, and a large percussion battery, symbolizing in the last movement the heavens, or the landscape, against which the melodic action takes place. Characteristically, Ives buried gems of his musical philosophy in a "Conductor's Note" to the score, including the thought:

> How can there be any bad music? All music is from heaven. If there is anything bad in it, I put it there—by my implications and limitations. Nature builds the mountains and meadows and man puts in the fences and labels.[11]

Ives was reportedly a phenomenal improvising pianist, and his piano sonatas occupy a central place in his output. His First Piano Sonata (1902–1909) is remarkable for its static textures of tense cluster chords (adjacent piano keys played with fists or palms) in the fourth movement, its rousing jazz rendition of the hymn "Bringing In the Sheaves" in the third, and its early use of ragtime in three of its five movements. Ragtime, with its jerky syncopations over a back-and-forth bass pattern, had only started gaining public attention at the World's Columbian Exposition in Chicago in 1893, where crowds heard rag pianists like

Scott Joplin, Jesse Pickett, Johnny Seamore, and Ben Harney for the first time. The first pieces specifically called "ragtime" were published in 1896. By the time he graduated from Yale, Ives was sufficiently familiar with this new music to "spell" (take over for) the pianist at Poli's, a local hangout. He used ragtime in the First Sonata at least ten years before Stravinsky, Milhaud, and other art-music composers began to look to it as a serious source. (Debussy, however, based a piece on ragtime's immediate predecessor, the cakewalk, in 1908.)

Ives became especially celebrated, though, for the Second Piano Sonata (1904–1915) when it was recorded by John Kirkpatrick in 1948 and spent several months on the bestseller list. Like much of Ives's music, the Sonata is frankly programmatic, and its subtitle is "Concord, Mass., 1840–1860." The four movements are based on literary figures in the Transcendentalist movement who lived in Concord, Massachusetts, between 1840 and 1860: the essayist Ralph Waldo Emerson, the author Nathaniel Hawthorne, the itinerant philosopher Bronson Alcott and his novelist daughter Louisa May Alcott, and the influential hermit-naturalist Henry David Thoreau. In the 1920s the work became notorious not only for its difficulty and its rhapsodic looseness of form, but for the passages in "Emerson" that required the pianist to play large clusters of notes with a stick of wood.

As if to forestall the inevitable misunderstandings of so unconventional a work, Ives wrote a series of six essays to accompany the "Concord" and published them separately (finding it infeasible to publish the music and words together) as *Essays before a Sonata*. Full of paraphrased philosophic quotations and a salesman's folksy metaphors from everyday life, the book examines the nature of program music and art's complex relation to human character. Ives excuses the helter-skelter complexity of his "Emerson" movement by explaining its subject: "Emerson wrote by sentences or phrases rather than by logical sequence. . . . As thoughts surge to his mind, he fills the heavens with them, crowds them in, if necessary, but seldom arranges them along the ground first. . . . Vagueness is at times an indication of nearness to a perfect truth."[12]

In the epilogue Ives drew a distinction between "substance" and "manner." Substance he defined as "the body of a conviction which has its birth in the spiritual consciousness, whose youth is nourished in the moral consciousness, and whose maturity as a result of all this growth is then represented in a mental image,"[13] i.e., a work of art. "Manner" is the means through which substance is "translated into expression," and Ives found art superficial to the extent to which its manner outweighed its substance. For example, Emerson, for Ives, was almost wholly substance, Edgar Allan Poe almost wholly manner. And beauty, at least in the conventional sense, is not necessarily related to substance: "beauty in music is too often confused with something that lets the ears lie back in an easy chair."[14]

The speculations, in *Essays before a Sonata,* on how music communicates spiritual and moral intuitions point back to a deeper and peculiarly American unease. Ives, who lived the life of an upstanding, successful businessman, defended not only his extraordinary music but his lifestyle as a nonartist. "The moment a famous violinist refused 'to appear,'" he writes, "until he had received his check—at that moment—precisely— . . . he became but a man of 'talent'—incidentally, a small man and a small violinist, regardless of how perfectly he played."[15] No European would have seen any problem with a musician demanding money for his work, nor would any European composer (many of them reputed for shady business dealings, like Wagner, or flagrant extramarital sexual liaisons, like Liszt) have tried to draw a correspondence between personal morality and musical substance.

Paradoxically, within Ives's apologia for complex, unfamiliar-sounding music lies an American businessman's distrust for the artist as a social type, the same distrust that led Ives's teachers to prefer the music of the impeccably churchgoing Mendelssohn to that of the opium addict Berlioz. Yet, in the same writings is a Transcendental optimism that the future is wide open, that we need not compete with European culture. "Music may yet be unborn. Perhaps no music has ever been written or heard. Perhaps the birth of art will take place at the moment in which the last man who is willing to make a living out of art is gone and gone forever. In the history of this youthful world, the best product that human beings can boast of is probably Beethoven; but, maybe, even his art is as nothing in comparison with the future product of some coal-miner's soul in the forty-first century."[16] Ives's *Essays* is a brilliantly enigmatic document of the problem of the composer in American society.

Listening Example: "Concord" Sonata, "Alcotts" movement

Ives was an impressionist, not in the French sense of using lush, coloristic harmonies like Debussy and Ravel (as was true of many other composers of his generation) but in the sense of painting tone pictures of specific scenes, atmospheres, and even intellectual ideas. (One of his college compositions, *Yale-Princeton Football Game,* was a detailed picture of what its title suggests.) Thus the "Concord" Sonata is program music—not simply a musically lucid pattern of themes and harmonic motions, but a portrait of extramusical subjects. The music does not "tell a story" in the manner of Berlioz's *Symphonie Fantastique* or Strauss's *Till Eulenspiegel,* but evinces a series of emotional atmospheres. The work also anticipated, in its free, nonlinear association of motives and quotations, the stream-of-consciousness technique soon to be pioneered in literature by Gertrude Stein and James Joyce. This is the aspect of Ives's music that makes it hardest to approach for devotees of traditional classical music.

The "Concord" Sonata is so dense with ideas, crashing with volcanic harmonies and interwoven with related themes, that the listener can hardly help but be confused on first hearing. However, part of the confusion comes from the reversal of the more expected movement from simplicity to complexity, for the "Concord" begins at its utmost cragginess and moves toward serene clarity. The mountains of notes seem too much to process, but on repeated hearings the work impresses such an aura of sincerity and melodic relatedness that every note comes to seem perfectly in place.

The "Concord"'s "Emerson" movement is dauntingly complex, a dense tone poem alternating between what Ives called passages of irregular "prose" and songlike "poetry." From here the sonata works its way through the ornate playfulness of "Hawthorne" to the much simpler "Alcotts" movement, based on a theme derived from the celebrated opening four notes of Beethoven's Fifth Symphony (example 1.1). This passage suggests, Ives wrote in the "Alcotts" essay, "the little spinet piano Sophia Thoreau gave to the Alcott children, on which Beth played the old Scotch airs, and played at the Fifth Symphony."[17]

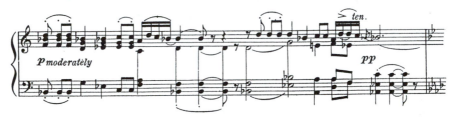

EXAMPLE 1.1 Charles Ives, opening of "The Alcotts," from the "Concord" Sonata.

From this idyllic opening, the Sonata's first truly calm moment, the Beethoven's Fifth theme develops into a climax of dissonances whose unmitigated harshness no other composer had yet attempted (example 1.2). The climax relaxes into the sonata's most important theme, used cyclically in all four movements (example 1.3). The Beethoven's Fifth theme comes back in ghostly quiet, however, accompanied in chords on the whole-tone scale, after which follows a quiet middle section on a new theme. Ives evokes "the memory of that home under the elms—the

EXAMPLE 1.2 Charles Ives, "The Alcotts," from the "Concord" Sonata.

EXAMPLE 1.3 Charles Ives, "The Alcotts," from the "Concord" Sonata.

Scotch songs and the family hymns that were sung at the end of each day
. . . a conviction in the power of the common soul."[18] Here and elsewhere
in his music, Ives loves to toss in pianissimo treble notes dissonant to the
main harmony, as overtones akin to the distant sounds heard in natural
landscapes (example 1.4). This domestic new theme grows restless, and
builds through bitonal dissonances into a recapitulation of the main
theme, ending in a repeat of the Beethoven's Fifth theme in massive
chords of pure C major.

EXAMPLE 1.4 Charles Ives, "The Alcotts," from the "Concord" Sonata.

"The Alcotts" is the Sonata's simplest movement, and usually the
easiest of approach for an unfamiliar listener; "Thoreau," while still
serene, moves toward bitonal mists and ambiguity, ending in C and D-
flat at once. Ives was, if belatedly and not always consistently, a
Transcendentalist, and Transcendentalism was an essentially antiration-
alist movement. For Emerson and Thoreau, logic was an insufficient tool

for gathering ultimate truths, which required the vaster, looser nets of the intuition and the unconscious. Criticisms that have met the "Concord" Sonata in recent decades for its amorphous form and lack of logical clarity exhibit a European, rationalist bias, and totally miss the point. The work is remarkable for its thematic unity, and equally remarkable for the paths it takes from that thematic center into the wild thickets of the musical unconscious.

Listening Example: **Three Places in New England**

Three Places in New England, composed between 1903 and 1914, is Ives's most often-performed orchestral work, a set of three programmatic scenes of Connecticut and Massachusetts. The first movement, "The 'Saint-Gaudens' in Boston Common," refers to a monument by the sculptor Augustus Saint-Gaudens, depicting the Union Army's first African-American regiment under its commanding colonel Robert Gould Shaw. Mostly quiet, the piece exemplifies Ives's pictorial style: ostinatos (repeating bass lines) that carry the music forward with a ghostly tread, melody notes played deliberately offbeat as if by an amateur or exhausted band, upper overtones in the strings and piano representing distant echoes, a hint of ragtime in mid-movement, and quotation of marches and Stephen Foster's "Old Black Joe."

"Putnam's Camp, Redding, Connecticut," the second movement, describes a boy having visions at a Fourth of July picnic, of the Goddess of Liberty encouraging the soldiers of General Israel Putnam. After an explosion of march quotations comes a pause, followed by one of Ives's favorite devices: two ensembles playing different material at different tempos. As strings and winds set up a slow march tempo, piano and percussion begin their own march 4/3 as fast as, in the boy's vision, Putnam arrives with reinforcements (example 1.5). (Slonimsky became famous for conducting this section with one hand beating each tempo.)

Like so many of Ives's instrumental works, movement three, "The Housatonic at Stockbridge," is orchestrated from a song he had written based on a poem by Robert Underwood Johnson (here excerpted):

> Contented river! and yet over-shy
> To mask thy beauty from the eager eye;
> Hast thou a thought to hide from field and town?
> In some deep current of the sunlit brown
> Art thou disquieted.

The music is a rippling continuum of polyrhythms in tempos of 6 against 8 against 10 against $26\frac{2}{3}$. A final climax accompanies the words:

> I also of much resting have a fear;
> Let me thy companion be
> By fall and shallow to the adventurous sea!

EXAMPLE 1.5 Charles Ives, polytempos from *Three Places in New England*.

The impressive calm of this texture, despite all the activity and the complications for the conductor, is a beautiful expression of Ives's philosophy of universal harmony, and one of the most enduring images in American music.

Carl Ruggles

Only one other American of Ives's generation shared his modernist tendencies. While Ives and Carl Ruggles (1876–1971) were both salty Yankee individualists (the latter born in Marion, Massachusetts), they were opposites in creative temperament. Ives was a fertile generalist capable of overlaying diverse musics into a chaotic universe; Ruggles was a single-minded, contrapuntal perfectionist who completed fewer than a dozen works. Yet Ives and Ruggles became friends after 1930 and admired each other's musics more than they did that of any other living

Carl Ruggles, John Becker, and Edgard Varèse.

composer. Ruggles's surviving works (he destroyed whatever did not meet his standards, including an unfinished early opera that he worked on for more than seven years) are tensely dissonant and unremittingly contrapuntal. With no awareness of the tone-row techniques then aborning in Europe, he developed a rigorously atonal method of never repeating a pitch until nine others had been used.

Ruggles was a colorful character who often exaggerated biographical information; accounts of his life claim that he was the grandson of a sea captain and that he attended Harvard, neither of which is true.[19] A talented violinist in youth, he did at one point play for Mrs. Grover Cleveland, though apparently without the President present. He also studied composition privately with John Knowles Paine (who taught at Harvard) and later socialized at the Harvard Club. Dogged by financial difficulties throughout his life, Ruggles worked as a conductor and violin teacher, but he was far too slow and painstaking a composer ever to augment his income through commissions or royalties. After a teaching job in Winona, Minnesota, ended prematurely, he formed the Winona Symphony Orchestra and conducted it from 1908 to 1912, often performing with his wife, the singer Charlotte (née) Snell.

His friend the artist Rockwell Kent described Ruggles as "a strange, intense little man, a bald egg-headed little man, with eyes that were alight with fervor, and a protruding lower lip that could betoken such conceit and arrogance as might defy the world, or tremble with emotion close to tears."[20] Plain-spoken and profane, Ruggles was good at convincing people he was as brilliant as he said he was, but slow to produce. The creative crisis of his life was his work from 1912 to at least 1918 on an opera, *The*

Sunken Bell, a setting in English of a German folklore play by Gerhart Hauptmann, undertaken at the request of the translator. As he labored on the piece, Ruggles's idiom evolved from a rather post-Wagnerian romanticism to an atonal style of angular melodies and harsh dissonance. He even managed to interest the management of the Metropolitan Opera in the work (though they did not agree to produce it, as has been printed), but anti-German feeling during the First World War made the completion of a German fairy opera a discouraging venture.

One last job at the Rand School in New York was Ruggles's farewell experience as a conductor. Hereafter he lived on patronage and what teaching he could find. A crucial step was meeting Henry Cowell and Charles Seeger in 1920, and Edgard Varèse two years later (for these names, see chapter 2); all shared Ruggles's fearlessly modernist tendencies, and Seeger sometimes let the Ruggleses live with him, as did Rockwell Kent in Vermont. In 1922 Ruggles became active in the International Composers Guild and the Pan American Association (of which more will be said in chapter 2), which organized the premieres of many of his works. Then, in 1924, the Ruggleses moved to an old schoolhouse in Arlington, Vermont, so inadequately heated for New England winters that they usually had to live elsewhere during the winter months. Because of a temporary eye problem, Ruggles began composing in large notes drawn on butcher paper with variously colored crayons, and kept up the habit even after his eyes improved. From 1937 to 1943, he taught seminars in modern music at the University of Florida in Miami, where his son went to college. Afterward, however, he devoted himself mainly to painting, a lifelong hobby in which he was both more prolific and more financially rewarded than in his composition.

More insecure than his blustering suggested, Ruggles relied greatly on the musical advice of his professional friends throughout his life, first Seeger and later the pianist John Kirkpatrick and the younger composer James Tenney. Unlike Ives, Ruggles did have some contact with the most advanced European music of his day, on a 1911 trip to London, Paris, and Germany and through performances presented by the International Composers Guild, including the 1923 American premiere of Schoenberg's *Pierrot Lunaire.* Although Ruggles independently arrived at the quasi-Schoenbergian practice of not repeating a pitch until nine different ones had intervened, his compositional practice always remained intuitive, characterized by trial and error, never systematic like twelve-tone music. This fact largely accounts for the snail-like pace of Ruggles's composing, the relatively small scale and number of his works. One of Henry Cowell's stories about Ruggles is a classic anecdote of American music:

> One morning when I arrived at the abandoned school house in Arlington where he [Ruggles] now lives, he was sitting at the old piano, singing a single tone at the top of his raucous composer's voice,

and banging a single chord at intervals over and over. He refused to be interrupted in this pursuit, and after an hour or so, I insisted on knowing what the idea was. "I'm trying over this damned chord," said he, "to see whether it still sounds superb after so many hearings." "Oh," I said tritely, "time will surely tell whether the chord has lasting value." "The hell with time!" Carl replied. "I'll give this chord the test of time right now. If I find I still like it after trying it over several thousand times, it'll stand the test of time, all right!"[21]

The story says something eloquent about the need for security in the bold new world American composers were inventing from scratch.

Ruggles's output, almost all of it written after Ives had already stopped composing, includes three works for full orchestra—*Men and Mountains* (1924), *Sun-Treader* (1926–31), and *Organum* (1944); *Vox Clamans in Deserto* (1923) for mezzo-soprano and chamber orchestra; *Angels* for brass or string sextet (1922); *Portals* for string orchestra (1926); the song "Toys" (1919); and *Evocations* for piano (1945, also in an orchestral version), a series of tone-portraits of four friends, Ives among them. After his wife died, he also wrote in her memory an odd little dissonant hymn setting called *Exaltation* (1958); it was his last work.

Ruggles's masterpiece is unquestionably *Sun-Treader,* its title taken from Robert Browning's address to Shelley: "Sun-Treader, Light and Life be thine forever." Although Nicolas Slonimsky conducted the piece in 1932 in Paris and Berlin, it did not receive its American premiere until 1966, by which time Ruggles was too infirm to attend and virtually too deaf to hear the tape of the performance. The opening theme, whose huge leaps in the French horns bisect series of accelerating timpani strokes, is one of the most famous gestures in American music (example 1–6, which omits some octave doublings). From here the work soars in savage grandeur one moment only to sink in exhaustive despair the next, always in rigorously dissonant counterpoint. The piece is admirably unified, however, by the extensive, immediate repetition of

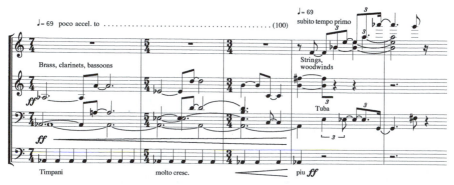

EXAMPLE 1.6 Carl Ruggles, opening measures of *Sun-Treader.*

motives among varying instrument groups, returns of the opening theme, a recurring double canon, and a loosely palindromic form (the second half repeats the themes of the first half in reverse order). Ruggles prided himself on achieving the same freedom of linear counterpoint and seamless consistency of language as the great polyphonic masters of sixteenth-century Europe, only in a dissonant rather than consonant idiom. In *Sun-Treader* he achieved that goal with a technical perfection rare in any era.

Contemporaries of Ives and Ruggles

American composers of the early twentieth century who had public music careers struggled under a plethora of historical and geographical mandates that some found debilitating. On one hand, they were tasked to demonstrate a level of formal and technical polish equal to that of the German romantic school of Schumann and Brahms. On another, they were expected to keep pace with Europe's latest modernist trends. As if that were not enough, they were also challenged by the critical press to make their music sound distinctly "American," even though no one could offer a viable definition for such a quality. Composer Henry Gilbert put the task succinctly: "American music . . . has this problem to face: that it can only become ultimately distinctive by leaving the paths of imitation, and that by leaving the paths of imitation it must temporarily sacrifice both immediate success and the respect . . . of both public and academician."[22]

To help juggle such demands, most studied in Europe. Ives and Ruggles were the only major composers of their generation who did not and whose musical outlook was not oriented toward European idioms. More typically, Americans studied with Rheinberger in Munich (like Parker and Frederick Converse), with Humperdinck in Berlin (like Arthur Farwell and Charles T. Griffes), or with d'Indy in Paris (like Daniel Gregory Mason). In addition, nearly every professional American composer of the period studied at Harvard with either Paine or Chadwick or both.

Despite the continuing tendency to choose Germany over France for one's postgraduate polish, however, the dominant influence on the generation born in the 1870s and 1880s came to be the French impressionism of Debussy and Ravel (evident even in some of the songs Ives wrote in college). Impressionism was a coloristic style given to unresolved dissonances, lush chords with added sixths, sevenths, and ninths, whole-tone scales, and a looser formal organization than the Germanic sonata. For Americans, this formal looseness offered permission to free oneself from German logic, whose formulas had often been followed pedantically. In addition, an opportunity for a definition of Americanness was opened up by the influence of a new music growing up in the cities: jazz. Jazz harmony and impressionist harmony overlapped to some extent, making attempts at fusion attractive. The dialogue between concert music and jazz, enlivened by fertile misunderstandings on both sides, would continue throughout the century.

The best of the jazz-influenced impressionists was John Alden Carpenter (1876–1951), who, like Ives, spent his professional life outside the music business. Born in Park Ridge, Illinois, he worked as vice president of his father's Chicago shipping company, which left him sufficiently free to study in England with Edward Elgar and sufficiently wealthy to retire in 1936 to write music full time. He also studied at Harvard with Paine and in Chicago with Bernhard Ziehn (a German-born contrapuntalist whose harmonic theories, ahead of their time, have never received due acknowledgement). Carpenter's major works, if naive in their attempt at notated jazz rhythm, are nonetheless energetic and memorable. They include, notably, *Krazy Kat* (1921), the first ballet based on a popular comic strip; *Skyscrapers* (1926), a jazzy and self-consciously modernist ballet that attempted to portray the energy of the new urban life; and *Adventures in a Perambulator* (1915), a witty tone poem describing a day in the life of a baby.

Composers who avoided modernist extremes were more widely performed in their lifetimes, though they are largely forgotten today; that pattern has become a constant in America's musical life. Henry Hadley (1871–1937) was more important as a conductor but prolific and frequently performed as a composer of programmatic works with impressionist touches. Frederick Shepherd Converse (1871–1940), dean of the New England Conservatory, flirted with dissonance in *Flivver Ten Million* (1927), a tone poem celebrating the Ford company's 10 millionth car, but generally eschewed modernism's harsher effects. He is better known for his romantic tone poem after Whitman, *The Mystic Trumpeter* (1905). Daniel Gregory Mason (1873–1953), the grandson of the educator and hymn writer Lowell Mason (whose hymns Ives often quoted), took an even more conservative, neoclassic line in emulation of Brahms. Mason was held up to Ives as the model of a "respectable" composer; his String Quartet in G Minor, Op. 19 (1918–1919, revised 1930), is based on Negro songs, but so classicized as to obscure their vernacular origins.

Other composers tried more explicitly to separate from Europe and forge an American style. From 1901 to 1911, Arthur Farwell (1872–1952), a tireless worker for new American musical ideas, operated the important Wa-Wan Press (its name taken from a ceremony of the Omaha Indians) for native music that no other publishers would touch. His own works incorporated melodies of the American Indian, albeit Europeanized by notation and harmonization. Charles Wakefield Cadman (1881–1946) also garnered some small popular success with his sentimentalizations of Indian melodies. (Perhaps the most successful example of the "Indianist" movement is the *Two Indian Sketches* of Charles T. Griffes, who is discussed below.) Likewise, the largely self-taught Henry F. Gilbert (1868–1928) shocked audiences by using Creole slave songs and African rhythms in such works as *The Dance in Place Congo* (1906).

Charles Tomlinson Griffes

One of the great figures of the impressionist movement, along with Debussy and Ravel, was an American: Charles Tomlinson Griffes (1884–1920). Unlike the isolated Ives, Griffes was the first American original to work in the context of international modernism. While he worshipped Debussy, he was also influenced by Scriabin and familiar with the music of Schoenberg and Stravinsky. When the publisher G. Schirmer at first declined to publish Griffes's more "modernistic" compositions, the great Italian pianist-composer Ferruccio Busoni intervened. Griffes's piano works and *Poem for Flute and Orchestra* stand as equals next to the best of Debussy's smaller masterpieces; their popularity has never faded, nor have they needed revival.

Born in Elmira, New York, Griffes borrowed money from his piano teacher, Mary Selena Broughton, to study piano and composition in Berlin, which he did from 1903 to 1907; his composition teachers were Philippe Rufer and Engelbert Humperdinck. He returned to join the faculty at the Hackley School for Boys in Tarrytown, New York. In the last year of his life, the New York Philharmonic premiered his *Poem for Flute and Orchestra* and the Boston Symphony played his tone poem *The Pleasure Dome of Kubla Khan*. Both were greeted with gratifying critical acclaim, sending him well on his way to becoming the most celebrated American composer of his day. But sadly, dogged by poverty (he supported his mother and sister and repaid Broughton on a slim salary), he virtually worked himself to death. Unable to afford having the orchestral parts for *Kubla Khan* copied, he copied them himself in the midst of teaching and other musical projects. Under the strain, pneumonia set in and turned to empyema, which robbed America of its first acknowledged musical genius at the age of thirty-five.

Griffes's works include a tone poem, *The Pleasure Dome of Kubla Khan* (1919, after Coleridge's poem), a *Poem for Flute and Orchestra* (1919), a dance drama, *The Kairn of Koridwen; Two Sketches for String Quartet Based on Indian Themes* (1922); *Roman Sketches* for piano (1915–1916, including *The White Peacock*, which also exists in an orchestrated version); *Three Tone Pictures* for piano (1915); a Piano Sonata in F (1917–1918), and more than forty songs.

Listening Example: The White Peacock

Griffes wrote his *Roman Sketches*, Op. 7, in 1915–1916. Each is associated in the score with a poem by the mystical Celtic poet William Sharp, who published his poems as a woman's, under the pseudonym Fiona Macleod, perpetrating a hoax not discovered until his death. Visiting the Berlin Zoological Garden with Miss Broughton in 1903, Griffes had been struck by an albino peacock, after which he began collecting pictures of white peacocks. Griffes tended to choose titles of poetic allusion, but only after the music was written, and in this case he claimed that the theme came to him while he was watching a sunset. Nevertheless, he kept Macleod's poem *The White Peacock* on the piano while composing the work. Later, he published the piece along with three other tone poems with Macleod affinities as *Roman Sketches*, another Macleod title, and made a version for orchestra in 1919. In part, the poem reads as follows:

> Here where the sunlight
> Floodeth the garden,
> Where the pomegranate
> Reareth its glory
> Of gorgeous blossom;
> Where the oleanders
> Dream through the noontides; . . .
> Moves the white peacock, as tho' through the noontide
> A dream of the moonlight were real for a moment.

Griffes's tone poem opens with a lithe seven-against-three rhythmic figure leading to a chord of the dominant ninth typical of impressionist harmony (idea A, example 1.7). The second motive is a chromatic scale over the harmony of idea A, leading to the work's seminal motive of a rising whole-step in dotted rhythm (idea B, example 1.8). Idea C combines the harmony of A with the final motive of B (example 1.9). Idea C is developed with variations, including a theme in 5/4 meter over arpeggios, marked *con languore* (with languor), leading at last to a playful chromatic motive. After a climax, idea B returns, *subito pianissimo*, sometimes with the chromatic scale in one hand and the dotted-note whole-step motive in the other. Again, a flowingly romantic melody returns to idea B, followed by a recapitulation of idea C with intensified harmonization. At the end, idea A makes a final, mysterious appearance, dying away without resolving.

EXAMPLE 1.7 Griffes, *The White Peacock*, Idea A.

EXAMPLE 1.8 Griffes, *The White Peacock,* Idea B.

EXAMPLE 1.9 Griffes, *The White Peacock,* Idea C.

The White Peacock's harmonies and motives are similar to those of Debussy's style, while its pungent chromatics and the inconclusive ending owe more to the influence of Scriabin. And yet, the piece is perfectly unified, with its own sense of motive and harmonic progression. "One cannot possibly play the new composers much," Griffes wrote, "without being influenced by them in one's own compositions. But I do have a deathly fear of becoming one of the dull imitators of the innovators. There are already enough of those."[23] Griffes was no imitator, but an American master of the impressionist idiom.

Notes

1. Henry and Sidney Cowell, *Charles Ives and His Music,* Oxford University Press (New York: 1955), p. 8.
2. Wilfrid Mellers, *Music in a New Found Land* (London: Barrie and Rockliff, 1964), p. 25.
3. William Bentley, quoted in "William Billings," *The New Grove Dictionary of American Music,* H. Wiley Hitchcock and Stanley Sadie, eds. (London: MacMillan Press, 1988), Vol. I, p. 215.
4. Quoted in the liner notes to *The Continental Harmony: Music of William Billings,* Columbia MS 7277.
5. Adrienne Fried Block, "Dvořák, Beach, and American Music," in Richard

Crawford, R. Allen Lott, and Carol J. Oja, eds., *A Celebration of American Music: Words and music in honor of H. Wiley Hitchcock* (Ann Arbor: University of Michigan Press, 1990), p. 257.

6. Ibid., p. 258.

7. Ibid., p. 260.

8. Charles Ives, *Memos* (New York: W. W. Norton & Company, 1972), p. 48.

9. Ibid., p. 184.

10. Stuart Feder, *Charles Ives: "My Father's Song"* (New Haven and London: Yale University Press, 1992).

11. Charles Ives, Conductor's note from Symphony No. 4 (New York: Associated Music Publishers, 1965), p. 14.

12. Charles Ives, *Essays Before a Sonata* (New York: W. W. Norton & Company, 1962), p. 22.

13. Ibid., p. 75.

14. Ibid., p. 97.

15. Ibid., p. 87.

16. Ibid., pp. 88–89.

17. Ibid., p. 47.

18. Ibid., p. 48.

19. Information on Ruggles's life comes from Marilyn Ziffrin, *Carl Ruggles: Composer, Painter, Storyteller* (Urbana and Chicago: University of Illinois Press, 1994).

20. Quoted in Ziffrin, *Carl Ruggles*, pp. 41–42.

21. Cowell, "Carl Ruggles: A Note," in Lou Harrison, *About Carl Ruggles* (Yonkers, New York: Oscar Baradinsky at the Alicat Bookshop, 1946), p. 1.

22. Henry F. B. Gilbert, "The American Composer," *Musical Quarterly* 1 (April 1915): pp. 94–104; reprinted in Gilbert Chase, ed., *The American Composer Speaks* (Baton Rouge: Louisiana State University, 1966), p. 102.

23. Letter, November 30, 1911, quoted in Edward Maisel, "Griffes and the Piano," liner notes for New World Records NW 310/311, 1981.

CHAPTER 2

Ultramodernism—The 1920s

Each of the World Wars offered the United States, as one of the victors, an opportunity to radically upgrade its self-image. This was as true in music as in any other sphere. After 1918 American composers became less inclined to be intimidated by their European colleagues, and felt freer to invent and apply devices—jazz rhythms, unusual instruments, free dissonances, numerical structures—that Europe had not sanctioned. In fact, in retrospect the period between the world wars, especially before the Great Depression, seems a kind of golden age of musical Americanness. No major European composers were close at hand to exert direct influence (as they were and did after World War II), and Americans felt independent enough to determine their own musical destiny.

As Aaron Copland wrote, "contemporary music as an organized movement in the U.S.A. was born at the end of the First World War."[1] The movement was no sooner born than it split into two camps, making explicit the underlying distinctions between nineteenth-century America's European-trained and self-taught composers. The distinctions were apparent in the organizations that sprang up to promote contemporary music. The Franco-American Musical Society was founded in 1920 by the French pianist E. Robert Schmitz for the purpose of performing contemporary music (primarily European) in several American cities; the name was changed to Pro Musica in 1925. (Among other bold achievements, Pro Musica premiered the first two movements of Ives's Fourth Symphony at Town Hall in 1927.) In 1921 the composer Edgard Varèse and the harpist Carlos Salzedo formed the International Composers' Guild. Members who lost patience with Varèse's egotistic way of running things broke off in 1923 and founded the League of Composers. In 1927, Varèse ended the Guild and formed the Pan American Association of Composers, dedicated to composers of the Western Hemisphere.

Through the late twenties and early thirties, the Pan American Association and the League of Composers found themselves on opposite sides of current musical issues, particularly regarding Europe. Pan

American's members included Ives, Henry Cowell, Ruggles, the Mexican Carlos Chavez, Varèse, Roy Harris, and Wallingford Riegger, the first four of whom had not studied in Europe. The League was typified by composers who had studied in Paris or Fontainebleau, the most important being Aaron Copland. Therefore the Pan Americans concentrated on works by North and Latin Americans, while the League performed European as well as American works. The Pan Americans largely rejected European trends and made their own musical materials from scratch; the League composers, influenced by Stravinsky, supported the new French style of neoclassicism.

There were social as well as musical differences. In general, the League had wealthier patrons; the Pan Americans kept going primarily through Ives's generous financial backing. The League composers were widely supported by two important conductors, Serge Koussevitsky of the Boston Symphony Orchestra and Leopold Stokowski of the Philadelphia Orchestra. The Pan Americans had as their champion Nicolas Slonimsky, who, by 1934, had sabotaged his conducting career by aligning himself too stringently with the avant-garde. (Slonimsky went on to become an important musicologist, editing the indispensable *Baker's Biographical Dictionary of Musicians*.) In these early years a split developed in America's musical personality that continues to the present day. On one side are the composers who believe in extending the European tradition, who have been more widely accepted (if not warmly welcomed) by the classical-music–orchestral establishment. On the other are those who have eschewed Europe to create an indigenous American tradition; they have worked mostly as outsiders and have received recognition only late in life, if at all.

Quaint as the term may seem at this historical distance, the American avant-gardists associated with the Pan American association called themselves "ultramodernists." The first announcement of Henry Cowell's New Music Society in 1925 referred approvingly to "the works of the most discussed composers of so-called ultra-modern tendencies, such as Stravinsky, Schoenberg, Ruggles, Rudhyar, etc." George Antheil always ended his recitals, he said, "with a modern group, preferably of the most 'ultra' order."[2] If Strauss, Mahler, and the late romantics were still considered "modern" by audiences of the day, then the new advocates of free dissonance and rhythmic complexity would call themselves ultramodern. And the ultramodernists, disdainful of any mandate imposed by Europe or tradition, shrank from no musical effect that occurred to their imaginations.

Henry Cowell

No one in the first half of the century did more for the dissemination, support, and self-definition of American music than Henry Dixon Cowell (1897–1965). Born March 11, 1897, in Menlo Park, California,

Cowell left school in third grade but chanced upon a number of sup-
portive mentors and patrons. The composer Henry Hadley found spon-
sorship for the young man to study at Berkeley with Charles Seeger.

Charles Louis Seeger Jr. (1886–1979) was a remarkably forward-
looking theorist and ethnomusicologist. Cowell visited Seeger in 1914
and played him his Opus 108—his 108th composition. Already, at the
age of 13, he had written a piano piece using tone clusters—chords made
up of adjacent pitches, often played on the piano with the fist or forearm, and notated as in example 2.1, Cowell's *Tiger* (1928). By the time
Cowell discovered them, they were not unprecedented, but Cowell was
the first to justify them theoretically as further, upward extensions of the
basic triads via the overtone series.

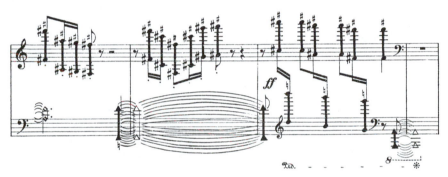

EXAMPLE 2.1 Henry Cowell, *Tiger.*

During Cowell's period of study with Seeger, he wrote one of the
seminal books of twentieth-century music: *New Musical Resources,* written
in 1917–1918 and published in 1930. "The purpose of *New Musical
Resources,*" he asserted, was " to point out the influence the overtone
series has exerted on music throughout its history, . . . and how, by
applying its principles in many different manners, a large palette of
musical materials can be assembled."[3]

To demonstrate the overtone series, play any note on a grand
piano. If you stop the string exactly in the center with your finger and
strike the key again, you will obtain a pitch one octave higher, corresponding to vibrations that are twice as fast. Each smaller fractional
length of the string will provide a higher note in the overtone series. For
example, if we approximate a low G as vibrating at 100 cycles per second, the overtone series on G will rise as in example 2.2. What interested
Cowell was the harmonic implications of the overtone series. For
instance, take the fourth, fifth, and sixth overtones and one has a major
triad, the most basic musical chord of the sixteenth through nineteenth
centuries. Continue up the overtone series, through the seventh, eighth,
ninth, tenth, eleventh overtones and so on, and one finds a tone cluster

Henry Cowell performing directly on the strings of the piano. *Courtesy BMI Archives.*

Cowell's genius was even more apparent in the revolutionary section on rhythm. Here he applied the same ratios as are heard between pitches to different beats going at the same time. For example, the pitches of a G-major triad, G–B–D, vibrate at frequency ratios of 4:5:6. Why not express this relation rhythmically as well, by dividing a measure into six equal parts in one voice, five in another, and four in another? Cowell invented a rhythmic notation capable of specifying divisions of a whole note up to fifteen equal parts (example 2.3). Such a notation,

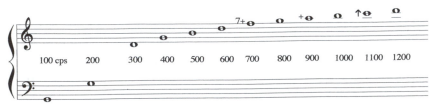

EXAMPLE 2.2 The overtone series. (Symbols indicate that the seventh overtone is a third of a half-step flat and the eleventh is a quarter-tone sharp. The notation is Ben Johnston's, discussed in chapter 4.)

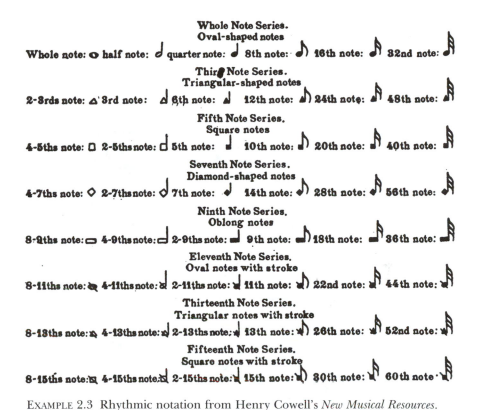

EXAMPLE 2.3 Rhythmic notation from Henry Cowell's *New Musical Resources.*

Cowell argued, would make passages such as those in example 2.4 clear in intent, if not easier to play. Cowell used this rhythmic notation in a handful of works, such as the *Quartet Romantic* for two flutes, violin, and viola (1915–1917; see example 2.5).

At age twenty-six Cowell went to Europe on a daring concert tour, performing his own music in Germany and Austria. He returned to Europe several times in the next decade, and in 1928 he became the first American composer invited not only to tour Russia but to have his music published there. Amazed at how effective European composers were at getting their music performed and published, Cowell came back determined to organize American composers for their own benefit. In 1927 he began the quarterly *New Music,* and from 1929 to 1933 he directed the Pan American Association while Varèse was in France. Between 1927 and 1958, *New Music* published dozens of new, radical American works. For most of his tenure as editor, Cowell did all the magazine's correspondence, packaging, mailing, and bookkeeping without compensation. For many years only Charles Ives's contributions kept it solvent.

Under Cowell's tenure, the Pan American Association made a courageous bid to gain publicity for the orchestral works of radical Americans.

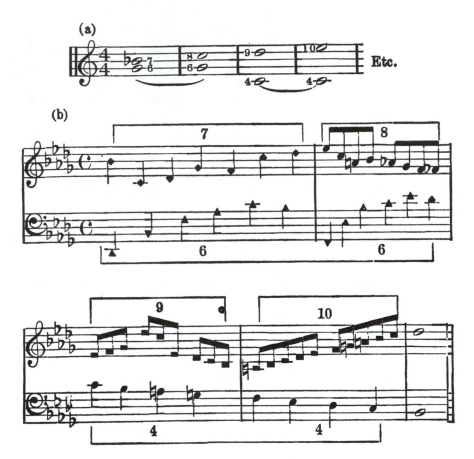

EXAMPLE 2.4 Rhythms from Henry Cowell's *New Musical Resources.*

In Boston, Cowell had met a brilliant young conductor, a Koussevitsky protégé and Russian immigrant named Nicolas Slonimsky (1894–1995). Slonimsky was a colorful figure whose unique musical talents included the ability to conduct ambidextrously in two meters at once. With Ives's financial backing, Slonimsky conducted the Chamber Orchestra of Boston (which he had founded, using members of the Boston Symphony) in a concert at New York's Town Hall on January 10, 1931. The program included the world premieres of Ives's *Three Places in New England,* Ruggles's *Men and Mountains,* and Cowell's Sinfonietta.

While the Town Hall concert attracted little attention, Cowell and his allies realized what each new generation has realized since: that in order to conquer America, an American artist must first conquer Europe. Slonimsky quickly repeated the program in Havana and then conducted similar concerts in Paris (June 6 and 11). The following year,

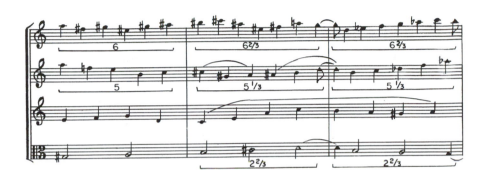

EXAMPLE 2.5 Henry Cowell, *Quartet Romantic*.

1932, Slonimsky conducted the Orchestre Symphonique de Paris in the premier of Ruggles's *Sun-Treader,* plus pieces by Ives, Cowell, and Rudhyar; he next led the Berlin Philharmonic in Cowell's *Synchrony,* Varèse's *Arcana, Sun-Treader,* and *Three Places in New England.*

European critics were intrigued by American rhythmic complexity and dissonance but mistakenly assumed that the composers had been influenced by Schoenberg and Hindemith; surely Americans could not arrive at such innovations on their own. Ives's thickly layered rhythms, they wrote, must stem from Stravinsky's *Le Sacre du Printemps*, although actually *Le Sacre* was written in 1913 and *Three Places in New England* in 1903–1904. Characteristically, Philip Hale of *The Boston Herald* wrote:

> If Mr. Slonimsky had chosen a composition by Loeffler, [Edward Burlingame] Hill, one of Deems Taylor's suites, Foote's suites, or music by some who, working along traditional lines have nevertheless shown taste, technical skill and a suggestion at least of individuality, his audience would now have a fairer idea of what Americans are doing in the arts.[4]

The Cowell-Slonimsky-Ives concerts in Paris and Berlin in 1931–1932, which cost Ives thousands of dollars, had little ultimate effect. Slonimsky was widely admired for his genius at negotiating such a repertoire's unprecedentedly complex rhythms; upon his return to America, however, similar programs in Los Angeles were denounced as too radical. Hitlerism soon swept across Germany, wiping out any sympathetic German response to the American modernists. Nevertheless, the Pan Americans had, for the first time, set a new American music on a world stage.

One of the saddest episodes in American music began in May, 1936, when Cowell was arrested on a homosexual morals charge involving a minor.[5] Incarcerated at San Quentin, where he continued writing music, Cowell was paroled in 1940 at the urgings of many prominent musicians, and pardoned in 1941, a pardon requested by the prosecuting attorney, who had decided Cowell was innocent. Upon his release, Cowell entered into heterosexual marriage in 1941, with the ethnomusicologist Sidney Robertson.

By this time, Cowell's music had taken a conservative turn, informed less by acoustical research and experimentation than by the influence of various ethnic musics from around the world. One indicator of this change is that the symphony became his preferred medium. His career turned toward teaching, at New York's New School for Social Research from 1940–1962, and also in California and at Columbia University. His *Ongaku* (1957), written in Tokyo and Kyoto, is based on the style of Japanese Gagaku and Sankyoku musics, and his *Persian Set* (also 1957) was premiered in Tehran. He did not abandon American sources, however. Among his most popular works are his sixteen *Hymns and Fuguing Tunes,* instrumental adaptations of a form invented by William Billings.

Listening Example: **The Banshee** *(1925)*

As a young man Cowell became notorious for his pianistic style, which included strumming and plucking the piano strings and playing clusters of keys with his palm or forearm. The piano pieces he toured with, mostly written between 1917 and 1930, are still the works with which he is most identified. One of the most original of these, *The Banshee,* was written around 1923–1925 (example 2.6).

Cowell based many of his works on Celtic mythology and Irish songs. In Irish folklore a Banshee is, in Cowell's words, "a woman of the inner world . . . who is charged with the duty of taking your soul into the inner world when you die. So when you die she has to come to the outer plane for this purpose, and she finds the outer plane very uncomfortable

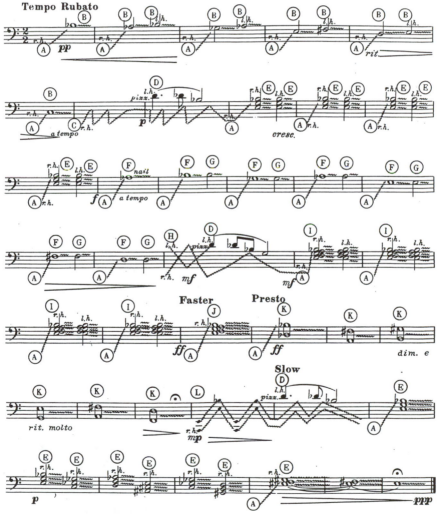

EXAMPLE 2.6 Henry Cowell, *The Banshee.*

and unpleasant, so you will hear her wailing at the time of a death in your family."[6] The Banshee's wailing, produced by scraping the coils of the piano's lower strings, is eerie indeed.

The Banshee, a one-page score lasting two and a half minutes, falls into three sections with similar endings, a form that could be diagrammed as AAB, or even AB AB CB. The first six gestures feature a sweep with the flesh of the finger up to the notated pitch (marked A in the score), ending in a sweep lengthwise along the string (B). After a series of up-and-down sweeps (C), a motive is plucked on the strings (D). Seven gestures similar to the first six follow, but with the string swept with the fingernail (F) and then partly damped by another finger (G). As the notation clearly shows, H is a sweep of the strings in two directions at once, leading to the return of motive D.

The third section begins with the piece's climax, in which chromatic clusters are swept fortissimo. Following a decrescendo, sweeps up and down the strings lead to a final repetition of the D motive, followed by a dying series of diminished triads. No piece more clearly indicates the ultramodernist sense of freedom from European tradition.

Edgard Varèse

Two of the American ultramodernists were born in Paris: Edgard Varèse (1883–1965) and Dane Rudhyar (1895–1985). Both seemed to leave European aesthetics so far behind them upon their arrival that they are generally figured into the stream of American musical life. Varèse is widely considered the century's foremost genius in the area of timbre. His music seems to hover in air, reemphasizing sonorities without progressing or developing, and evoking the machine age with its rough edges and explosions of percussion. His colorful sonic images, often couched in repeated notes and harsh sonorities, are irreducible and unforgettable.

Varèse grew up in Burgundy and then Turin, Italy, before moving back to Paris. Groomed for a career in engineering, he trained in mathematics and science. (Later, his works would often take their inspiration from the concepts of molecular physics.) Over the intense opposition of his father, however, he entered the Schola Cantorum in 1904 to study with Vincent d'Indy and Albert Roussel, also studying at the Conservatoire with Charles-Marie Widor. He met Debussy in Paris and Richard Strauss and Feruccio Busoni in Berlin; all three of them took an interest in his music. His other friends included Picasso, Cocteau, Malraux, and Henry Miller, and he also discussed theories of noise and new instrumental resources with the Italian Futurist Luigi Russolo. An early marriage to an actress ended in separation, and he later married the American writer Louise Norton. Receiving a medical discharge from military service in 1915, he came to New York, leaving behind, to be lost forever, a series of at least nine orchestral works.

Varèse's life in New York was marked by poverty. For a while he sold pianos, and his attempts at a conducting career were not successful. In 1921 he and harpist Carlos Salzedo formed the International Composers' Guild. Then, in 1927, Varèse abruptly dissolved the Guild and formed in its place (along with Cowell, Ruggles, and Chavez) the Pan American Association. However, while Varèse had no sympathy for the neoclassical style that swept through Parisian music in the twenties and thirties, he was not happy about his fortunes in America and returned to Paris for the years 1928 through 1933. He was in Paris, then, when Slonimsky and Cowell, with Ives's financial backing, gave their 1931 concerts of American music, and was able to arrange press interviews and introductions.

Varèse returned to New York in 1933 to retake the reins of the Pan American Association, angering Ives with his gratuitous criticisms of Cowell's administration. Actually, Cowell's leadership of the Association was more efficient and less egotistic than Varèse's, and under Varèse the organization fell apart quickly, becoming inactive in 1934.[7]

Following the composition of *Density 21.5* in 1936, Varèse entered a period of depression and unproductivity, writing no more music for over a decade; largely because his sonic visions had so far outstripped what ensembles of conventional instruments were able to offer, and he had failed to interest either Bell Telephone, the Guggenheim Foundation, or the Los Angeles film companies in his visions of "organized sound" for new electronic instruments. He struck up a friendship with Leon Theremin (1896–1992), the Russian physicist and musician who invented the early electronic instrument named after him, an instrument Varèse later used in his *Ecuatorial*. The Theremin is played by moving the hands in space at varying distances from a fixed bar, the movements varying the pitch and timbre. The inventor, who had demonstrated his instrument to Lenin in 1927, presented a concert with ten Theremins at Carnegie Hall in 1930 and lived for awhile in America. Varèse worked with Theremin on ideas for electronic musical instruments and, in 1941, wrote to him, "I no longer wish to compose for the old instruments played by men, and I am handicapped by a lack of adequate electrical instruments for which I conceive my music."[8]

During World War II, thanks to the demands of espionage, great improvements had been made in the process of recording sounds on electronic tape. Soon after the war, an anonymous donor sent Varèse an Ampex tape recorder, and in 1958, at the age of seventy-five, he completed one of the first and most impressive works for electronic tape, *Poème électronique,* to be played through 240 speakers scattered throughout Le Corbusier's pavilion at the Brussels International and Universal Exposition. A collage of church bells, eerie voices, and simple synthesizer tones, the piece sounds naïve compared with today's digital acoustic wizardry, yet its communicative power remains firm.

Varèse's compositions are few in number, and uniformly dazzling. They include *Offrandes* for voice and orchestra (1922); *Hyperprism* for nine winds and percussion (1923); *Octandre* for septet (1924); *Intégrales* for small orchestra and percussion (1925); *Amériques* for orchestra (1921); *Arcana* for orchestra (1927); *Ionisation* for percussion ensemble (1931); *Ecuatorial* for bass voice, brass, piano, organ, percussion, and Theremin (1933–1934); *Density 21.5* for flute (1936); *Etude pour espace* for chorus, pianos, and percussion (1947); *Deserts* for winds, percussion, and electronics (1954); and *Poème électronique* (1958) for electronic tape.

During his life Varèse became the symbol of ultramodernism's most nihilistic excesses. His sonic concepts were simply too abstract and too unprecedented to find critical understanding. Ernest Newman's comments about *Intégrales* in the *New York Post* will serve as a typical example:

> It sounded a good deal like a combination of early morning in the Mott Haven freight yards, feeding time at the zoo, and a Sixth Avenue trolley rounding a curve, with an intoxicated woodpecker thrown in for good measure.[9]

References to zoos were almost obligatory. By 1960, however, Varèse began to be honored with concerts and recordings of his music, and his genius, with its pervasive influence, was recognized worldwide. As Milton Babbitt said of him, "His mind's ear changed not only the sonic surface but the very anatomy of musical structure."[10]

Listening Example: Ionisation

Bursting into existence in the years 1931–1933, percussion music was an exciting, experimental new genre, pursued by Varèse, John J. Becker, Lou Harrison, Johanna M. Beyer, and the young John Cage. Written in 1931, *Ionisation* has the distinction of being the first piece by a Western composer written solely for percussion, and it remains the classic work for percussion, widely performed by university ensembles across the country.

Scored for thirty-nine instruments played by thirteen percussionists, *Ionisation* uses an exotic array of noisemakers: anvils, sleigh bells, slapstick, castanets, bongos, lion's roar (a drum through whose head a string is pulled), güiro (a serrated block of wood across which a stick is rasped), high and low sirens, triangle, maracas, cymbals, drums, tam-tams, chimes, glockenspiel, and piano. Note that only the last three instruments are capable of discreet pitches, and they appear only on the piece's climactic, final seventeen measures. As much as *Ionisation* sounds like a random noise-fest on first hearing, it has a carefully worked-out form with recurring motives and themes.

The listener to *Ionisation* must acclimate him- or herself to listening for timbral ideas and rhythmic motives rather than melody or harmony. Varèse helps this process by beginning with a motive—three beats in the bass drums, a cymbal tremolo, and a snare drum roll—immediately repeating it, then repeating it with timbral variation. (Meanwhile the sirens crescendo menacingly.) He then proceeds directly to the main theme, a snare drum rhythm with contrapuntal accompaniment in the bongos and maracas, which will recur (example 2.7). The theme begins to start over but is interrupted and then more fully restated and expanded with variations.

EXAMPLE 2.7 Edgard Varèse, *Ionisation*, main theme.

A sudden burst of fortissimo drumming prepares the way for the secondary theme, stated in unison quintuplet patterns in the Chinese wood blocks, maracas, bongos, and snare drum (example 2.8). A triangle announces a section in which all of the metal instruments are struck, as the sirens begin again. After a fermata which allows the sirens to decrescendo from their highest pitch, the main theme returns. A brief reference to the second theme heralds the work's climactic coda: the entrance of the chimes, glockenspiel, and piano (the latter playing huge forearm clusters), accom-

EXAMPLE 2.8 Varèse, *Ionisation*, second theme.

panied by gongs, cymbals, and sirens. The unvarying sonorities of the pitched instruments can be seen in example 2.9.

Slonimsky conducted the world premiere of *Ionisation* in New York on March 6, 1933. As he recounts it, percussionists from the New York Philharmonic could not handle the quintuplets, and he had to recruit composers. Cowell played the piano, Wallingford Riegger the guiro, and William Schuman the lion's roar.[11]

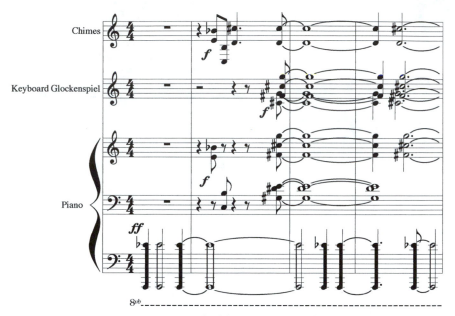

EXAMPLE 2.9 Varèse, *Ionisation*, pitched instruments at climax.

Ruth Crawford

Arguably history's first major woman composer, Ruth Crawford (1901–1953) was born in East Liverpool, Ohio. Though her composing career was interrupted and abbreviated, she was precocious and left a dozen major works impressive in their structural integrity and warm in their lyricism.

In 1920 Crawford left home to attend the American Conservatory in Chicago, where she found a heady atmosphere. She studied harmony with an open-minded German, Adolph Weidig, and piano with Djane Lavoie-Herz. Lavoie-Herz lived in the center of a stimulating circle. John Alden Carpenter sponsored her soirées; Cowell visited her as he traveled between California and New York; Rudhyar dropped in on his pilgrimages in the opposite direction, spreading the new gospel of

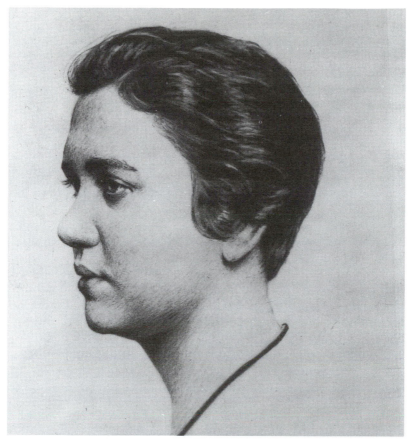

Ruth Crawford. *Courtesy New York Public Library.*

Scriabin. In addition, Crawford taught piano to the daughters of the poet Carl Sandburg; the music critic Alfred Frankenstein fell in love with her; the Chicago Symphony conductor Frederick Stock took an interest in her music; and she studied with and eventually married Charles Seeger. Chicago's new-music scene, before it was dispelled by the Great Depression and World War II, was a lively one.

In 1930 Crawford became the first woman to win a Guggenheim fellowship, and left for Europe, visiting London, Berlin, Vienna, Budapest, Munich, and Paris and meeting Berg, Ravel, Hindemith, Bartók, Boulanger, Varèse, Roussel, and Josef Hauer. (She amused Berg by telling him that she preferred Schoenberg's music prior to Op. 25, and he advised her "to study German music more and to write something in a larger form demanding more coordination and development of ideas."[12]) When Slonimsky conducted his Paris concerts of American music, Crawford was in the audience. Her return to America was not to Chicago, however, but to the more exciting scene of New York, where she and Seeger set up housekeeping together. In 1932, on the day Seeger's divorce from his first wife became final, they were married.

Crawford quickly absorbed Seeger's theories of dissonant counterpoint and was soon writing more ambitious works in the style than he had. If her early piano works show that Rudhyar's Scriabin-preaching had found a target, her first chamber works—the String Quartet (1931) with its remarkable palindromic finale, and the *Music for Small Orchestra* (1926)—show an astonishingly original handling of form and texture for someone so young. Her *Three Songs on Poems of Carl Sandburg*, scored for alto, oboe, percussion, and piano, are remarkable for their smooth fusion of a lyrical atonal style with an ultramodernist emphasis on percussive noise.

In 1936, however, Crawford gave up composing. The Depression had replaced the new-music patronage of the twenties with a concern for America's vanishing rural culture, and Crawford moved with Seeger to Washington, D.C., where she transcribed and wrote piano accompaniments for thousands of American folksongs. Another impediment to further composing may have been the four children she bore during the thirties. She broke her silence to write a small orchestra piece (*Risselty Rosselty*) in 1941 and returned to composition in the fifties with a fine Suite for Wind Quintet (1952), but she died at the age of 53.

Listening Example: **Music for Small Orchestra,** *first movement*

Written in 1926, Crawford's *Music for Small Orchestra* was first performed in 1975—a delay that symbolizes the difficulties women composers have had in getting heard. Considering that it is one of her earliest works, the piece's smooth fusion of diverse influences is astonishing. The melodic intervals suggest Scriabin or Berg, the rhythms come from the theories of Cowell and Seeger, yet the piece does not sound like anyone else's music; it is an impressively self-assured unveiling of Crawford's mature style.

Scored for flute, clarinet, bassoon, four violins, two cellos, and piano, the first movement is an atonal continuum remarkable for its limpid calm. Crawford divides the measure freely into three, four, five, or six equal beats for each instrument. The piano begins quietly playing an F in unchanging rhythm, $2 + 3 + 3 + 2$. Soon the F becomes a steady half-note, the piano adds a bass chord every ten beats, one cello plays an open fifth every five beats, and the other cello begins a quintuplet ostinato within the measure, over which woodwind melodies enter in triplets (see example 2.10). Aside from Ives, Cowell, and Stravinsky, few composers had written music of this rhythmic complexity, yet the repeating ostinatos and bass drone chords allow an overall feeling of effortless gliding.

EXAMPLE 2.10 Ruth Crawford, *Music for Small Orchestra,* Movement 1, mm. 21–26.

The American Five and Other Ultramodernists

Within the Pan American Association, Cowell particularly championed the work of four older composers who eschewed European methods: Ives, Ruggles, Wallingford Riegger, and John J. Becker. So frequently were these five figures associated on concerts that the important American musicologist Don Gillespie has dubbed them "the American Five," analogous to the French "Six" and the Russian "Mighty Five."

Wallingford Riegger (1885–1961) was the only one of the Five to acquire a European polish. Born in Albany, Georgia, he studied in Berlin with Max Bruch and became one of the first Americans to experiment with the twelve-tone method invented by Arnold Schoenberg; his use of the twelve-tone row can be lightly tuneful in a very un-Schoenbergian way. His *Study in Sonority* (1927) for ten violins, written in the height of the ultramodern years, is a remarkably well-crafted and original work inhabiting the chromatic language of Bartók and even late Schoenberg, with an endlessly inventive array of textures. Riegger's Variations for Two Pianos (1952) and Fourth Symphony (1956–1957) are among his best works.

The least known of the Five, John J. Becker (1886–1961) was born in Henderson, Kentucky, studied in Chicago, and spent his career in the midwest, frustrated by geographic isolation and hampered by an acerbic personality from making inroads into New York musical society, despite generous personal support from Ives. A Catholic, Becker was drawn to church polyphony, quoted Gregorian chant in his *Soundpiece No. 1,* and modeled his dissonant counterpoint after the polyphony of Bach and Palestrina. Becker's most notable work is his Third Symphony, *Symphonia Brevis* (1929). The brief first movement is a savage scherzo of harsh dissonances, the second a calmer, more long-lined contrapuntal movement, its stately chorales in 5/2 meter interrupted by percussion. His series of chamber works titled *Soundpieces* are serious and well-crafted, and occasionally receive the revival they deserve.

Johanna Magdalena Beyer (1888–1944) is one of music's most shadowy figures. Born in Leipzig, she emigrated to New York in 1924 and, coming to composition in her forties, studied with Cowell, Seeger, Ruth Crawford, and Dane Rudhyar. Beyer's percussion and electronic works, such as *Three Movements for Percussion* (1939), made daring use of noise and anticipated minimalism with their rhythmic cycles and static textures. Nearly forgotten, she is being newly appraised and seems to have been in many ways decades ahead of her time.

Dane Rudhyar (1895–1985) has remained one of the lesser-known ultramodernists because his career got sidetracked into the improbable field of astrology. Born Daniel Chennevière in Paris, he was present at the world premiere of *Le Sacre du Printemps.* He came to America in 1916; two of his orchestral works were premiered in New York in 1917. Through a disciple of Scriabin, he became involved with the Theosophical movement begun by Madame Helena Blavatsky—a mystical philosophical movement based in Hindu scriptures—with which Scriabin was also tangentially connected. Though the first of Rudhyar's more than three dozen books was on Debussy, and the second on Hindu music, Rudhyar turned to astrology in 1930 and became one of the world's leading astrologers.

Rudhyar's music seems very much a continuation of Scriabin's aesthetic, though unhindered by the timid formalism that makes Scriabin's cut-and-dried forms a poor match for his mystic thematic materials. Rudhyar's music falls into two widely separated periods, 1915 to 1930 and 1976 to 1985, for he resumed composing when performers began taking an interest in his early music. Yet, aside from a notable Debussy influence in the earliest compositions, differences in style over that seventy-year range are nearly imperceptible. Most of his works are brief or else composed of a series of brief movements, such as *Pentagrams* (1924–1926), *Paeans* (1927), and *Syntony* (1968), all for piano.

For a few years in the 1920s, it looked as though America's great composer was going to be George Antheil (1900–1959). Bad career management, though, combined with an inability to live up to his own hype, reduced him to the status of a minor film composer. Antheil, the son of a shoe-store owner in Trenton, New Jersey, studied privately with the Swiss émigré Ernest Bloch (1880–1959), the composer of the popular *Schelomo* (1915–1916) for cello and orchestra, who had come to America in 1916. In 1922 Antheil set off, like Cowell, on a European piano tour, living in Berlin and Paris until 1933. In Berlin he became friends with Stravinsky; the most obvious influences on Antheil's modernist works, *Ballet Mécanique* included, are Stravinsky's *Les Noces* and *Le Sacre du Printemps*. He next became involved in Paris's heady literary and artistic life, befriended by James Joyce, T. S. Eliot, Ernest Hemingway, and Pablo Picasso and championed by Ezra Pound. The machinelike dissonance of Antheil's piano works shocked audiences.

Antheil's most notorious work—in fact, almost the entire basis of his reputation—is his *Ballet Mécanique* of 1924–1925, which represented, as he later wrote, "the anti-expressive, anti-romantic, coldly mechanistic aesthetic of the early twenties."[13] The work was scored for two pianos, player piano, three xylophones, drums, wood and steel airplane propellers, electric bells, siren, and other percussion. The work's jangling, perpetual motion is drawn from variations of a tiny number of figures, subjected to constant displacements of accent à la Stravinsky, as audible in the opening measures (example 2.11, pianos only). In its attempt to "out-Stravinsky Stravinsky," the *Ballet* not only extended the Russian

EXAMPLE 2.11 George Antheil, *Ballet Mécanique*.

master's work with short, interchangeable modules and repeating ostinatos and imitated the instrumentation of Stravinsky's *Les Noces*, but
anticipated the minimalist works of the 1960s, especially in Antheil's
description:

> Some time in the future we will have forms which will not last a half
> hour, nor an hour, but eight hours, sixteen hours, or two days. This
> is not romancing. The reason lies in the fact that we have discovered
> the new and true dimension of music and its basic principles which
> insure larger and almost endless forms.[14]

And, anticipating John Cage, Antheil included long silences in which
"time itself acts as music." In his musical evocation of the dynamic, inhu-
man precision of machines, Antheil was preceded, though not influenced,
by the Italian futurists Francesco Balilla Pratella and Luigi Russolo.

The premiere of *Ballet Mécanique*, June 19, 1926, was a well-pre-
pared riot, the audience shouting, whistling, and opening umbrellas as
Pound stood and yelled "Vous êtes tous des imbéciles!"[15] In 1927, however, Antheil's overheated career took a nosedive. Paris found his works
after the *Ballet* (such as the *Symphonie en Fa* and Piano Concerto) neoclassic and derivative of Stravinsky, while the *Ballet* itself had a disastrous,
overhyped, error-ridden New York premiere at Carnegie Hall, prompt-
ing the newspaper headline "Mountain of Noise Out of an Antheil."

Suddenly out of fashion, and finding that worldwide economic difficulties had disintegrated Paris's vivacious milieu, Antheil turned to
operas on American subjects (*Transatlantic, Helen Retires, Volpone*) and
then film scores, living out the remainder of his life in Hollywood. His
greatest subsequent success was his Symphony No. 4 (1942), written in
the patriotic style of the 1940s, one of the many symphonies inspired by
the horrors of World War II (including Shostakovich's Seventh and
Harris's Sixth). Antheil's later life is an amazing hodgepodge of unrelated ventures: besides film music, he wrote a syndicated column of
advice to the lovelorn, wrote articles for *Esquire*, developed a patented
torpedo with the actress Hedy Lamarr, and contributed to the field of
glandular criminology.

Another, less eccentric enfant terrible who did not sustain his career
was Leo Ornstein (b. 1892). He made a splash starting in 1915 with his
concerts of modernistic works employing tone clusters, such as *Three
Moods* and *Suicide in an Airplane*, and his name was associated with
Cowell, whom he met in New York. In 1920, however, he retired from
the concert stage, and he disappeared from public view around 1930.
Thereafter, until 1953 he ran the Ornstein School of Music in
Philadelphia with his wife. Like Antheil, he turned his back on the pro-
gressivity of his early music and assumed a more romantic idiom.

Like Cowell, Colin McPhee (1901–1964) represented American music's turn toward Asian rather than European sources for new techniques. He was, in fact, the first American whose aesthetic was formed by his experience with Balinese music; there have been many more in recent decades. Born in Montreal, McPhee graduated from Baltimore's Peabody Conservatory, studied in Paris (with Paul LeFlem), and settled in New York. Around 1929 he chanced to hear a rare recording of a gamelan, the Balinese orchestra consisting of gongs, suling flutes, and metallic mallet instruments played in hypnotic repeating cycles. Fascinated, he realized that Balinese rhythms and melodic patterns represented a new direction his early neoclassic music (such as his Concerto for Piano and his Wind Octet of 1929) had been pointing in anyway. He embarked for Bali in 1934 and stayed for most of the next six years.

McPhee's Balinese studies culminated in the composition of his most famous work, *Tabuh-Tabuhan* for two pianos and orchestra (1936). The title is from the Balinese word *tabuh,* meaning a percussion mallet, or by extension a rhythmic beating. The piece's mallet-percussion textures, exotically modal melodies, and static permutation of pitch cells mark the first (and an engaging) example of Balinese rhythmic cycles applied to the Western orchestra, an anticipation of minimalism more than three decades early. However, he wrote little else besides a *Nocturne* for chamber orchestra (1958) and Second Symphony (1957).

The music of Peggy Glanville-Hicks (1912–1990) also evinces ethnomusicological influences. Born in Melbourne, Australia, she studied with Vaughan Williams and Boulanger, but in 1939 she became an American citizen, and she served under Virgil Thomson on the remarkable critical staff of the *New York Herald-Tribune.* She used aspects of Hindu music in her 1953 opera *The Transposed Heads.* Her *Etruscan Concerto* (1954) for piano and orchestra shares with *Tabuh-Tabuhan* a delightful and highly original exoticism.

Notes

1. Aaron Copland, *The New Music* 1900–1960 (London: MacDonald, 1968), p. 102.
2. Quoted in Linda Whitesitt, *The Life and Music of George Antheil* (Ann Arbor, Mich.: UMI Research Press, 1983), p. 9.
3. Henry Cowell, *New Musical Resources* (New York: Something Else Press, 1969), pp. xvi–xvii.
4. Philip Hale, "Mr. Slonimsky in Paris," *Boston Herald,* July 7, 1931, p. 14.
5. Nicolas Slonimsky, admittedly one of Cowell's closest friends but also a meticulous historian, writes that Cowell was arrested "on largely contrived and falsified evidence, on charges of homosexuality (then a heinous offense in California) involving the impairment of the morals of a minor.

Lulled by the deceptive promises of a wily district attorney of a brief confinement in a sanatorium, Cowell pleaded guilty to a limited offense, but he was vengefully given a maximum sentence of imprisonment, up to 15 years." From *Baker's Biographical Dictionary of Musicians,* seventh edition (New York: Schirmer Books, 1988), p. 368.

6. Interview with Cowell, recorded on *Henry Cowell: Piano Music,* Smithsonian Folkways CD SF40801.

7. Frank R. Rossiter, *Charles Ives and His America* (New York: Liveright, 1975), p. 254.

8. Virgil Thomson, *American Music Since 1910* (New York: Holt, Rinehart, and Winston, 1971), p. 44.

9. Ernest Newman, *New York Evening Post,* March 2, 1925.

10. Milton Babbitt, in "For Edgard Varèse on the Celebration of his 80th Year," Carnegie Hall program, March 31, 1965, p. 14.

11. Nicolas Slonimsky, *Perfect Pitch: A Life Story* (Oxford and New York: Oxford University Press, 1988) p. 138.

12. Matilda Gaume, *Ruth Crawford Seeger: Memoires, Memories, Music* (Metuchen, N.J., and London: Scarecrow Press, 1986), p. 83.

13. Quoted in Whitesitt, *The Life and Music of George Antheil,* p. 12.

14. Antheil, Letter to Ezra Pound, Yale University; quoted in Whitesitt, *The Life and Music of George Antheil,* 1983), p. 104.

15. Ibid., p. 25.

CHAPTER 3

Populism—The 1930s

Other things being equal, musical innovation and economic insecurity ebb and flow in inverse ratio. The 1920s, in America and Europe, were an era of free-wheeling avant-gardeness too hot to sustain. In October of 1929 the stock market crashed, precipitating the Depression. In the 1920s, Cowell, Ornstein, and Antheil had been considered the notorious great pianist-composers of the future; by the mid-1930s all three had abandoned their early innovations for an undistinguished conservatism. As money dried up after the Crash, so did patronage and a viable scene of musical intelligentsia, in short order. The Depression demanded of the American composer an end to self-indulgence and a turn to larger social issues. In the 1940s, Antheil quoted folk songs in his Third String Quartet and Becker wrote a patriotic *Symphony of Democracy*.

No longer able or willing to indulge "art for art's sake," artists turned their sights outward, to political objectives. Marxism was a pervasive influence on many artists during the thirties. Wallingford Riegger, Marc Blitzstein, and Conlon Nancarrow were Communist Party members, and the last (see chapter 4) fought with the Lincoln Brigade in the Spanish Civil War. Crawford wrote leftist songs and collected folksongs as part of her concern for the proletariat. One Communist-oriented musical organization in New York, the Composers' Collective, included Charles Seeger, Elie Siegmeister, Blitzstein, Cowell, Riegger, and Stefan Wolpe (for whom see chapter 5). Political progressivism walked hand in hand with musical conservatism, as composers abandoned modern dissonance and complex textures in a democratic attempt to reach a mass audience.

Parallels between American and Russian music during this period are full of irony. Under the Soviet regime, composers were expected to eschew "decadent Western formalism" and write music easily accessible to a wide public, with nationalist programs. At various times in the thirties and forties, the Soviet Politburo removed Shostakovich, Prokofiev, Khachaturian, and other composers from their teaching and administrative positions and banned some of their works from performance. The Russians retained their livelihoods only by renouncing perversions such as dissonant counterpoint, complex harmonies, and jazz rhythms and returning to national subjects and singable tunes. The Americans placed themselves voluntarily under the same social-realist stylistic limitations, under the influence at first of Marxism, and later of World War II patriotism. Prokofiev and Shostakovitch, Copland and Harris all simplified their harmonic and rhythmic languages and turned to writing patriotic music for the people, though from vastly different motivations.

A not inconsequential force in determining the musical direction of the late thirties was the Works Progress Administration, created in the summer of 1935 during the "second hundred days" of Roosevelt's New Deal legislation. The WPA created jobs building bridges, highways, and parks, but also created public art projects to give employment to writers, artists, actors, and musicians. At a cost of $11 billion, the WPA gave jobs to about 8½ million people at an average monthly wage of $54.33. Aside from commissioning 2,500 murals in public buildings, it supervised a Composers' Forum-Laboratory, which sponsored concerts and radio broadcasts and made it possible to get paid for composing. Many of the composers who worked for it (Virgil Thomson, Marc Blitzstein, Charles Seeger, John Becker) found their music naturally moving in a more populist, *Gebrauchsmusik* direction due to the nature of the projects they were involved in. Difficult to justify during wartime, the WPA was discontinued in 1943.

The story of American music from the 1920s onward is incomplete without an account of an extremely influential Frenchwoman: Nadia Boulanger (1887–1979). A student of Gabriel Fauré, she gave up composing when her sister Lili, a talented composer, died at the age of twenty-four, and she subsequently became one of history's most celebrated composition teachers. American students were her particular specialty; she taught several generations of them, including Aaron Copland, Roy Harris, Walter Piston, Virgil Thomson, Elliott Carter, Douglas Moore, David Diamond, Marc Blitzstein, George Walker, Elie Siegmeister, and, most recently, Philip Glass. As Thomson explained her appeal,

> What endeared her most to Americans was her conviction that American music was just about to "take off," just as Russian music had done eighty years before.[1]

Boulanger was famous for her strict discipline and her insistence on counterpoint exercises. As Copland said,

> Nadia Boulanger knew everything there was to know about music, pre-Bach and post-Stravinsky, and knew it cold. All technical know-how was at her fingertips: harmonic transposition, the figured bass,

score reading, organ registration, instrumental techniques, structural analysis, the school fugue, the Greek modes and Gregorian chant.[2]

She was a devoted apostle of Stravinsky, not terribly sympathetic to the twelve-tone school.

Boulanger was also a holy terror as a teacher. Her last famous American student, Philip Glass (see chapter 8), recounted one of his lessons as follows:

> She saw an error in something called hidden parallel fifths. She studied the page in silence and then turned toward me. With a look of understanding and compassion she asked how I was feeling. I said, "I'm feeling fine, Mademoiselle." She asked, "Do you have a fever? Do you have a headache?" And I didn't know what was going on. "I know of a good psychiatrist. Seeing a therapist can be very confidential, and one need not be embarrassed at all." I explained that I didn't need that kind of help. Finally she said, "Well, I don't understand." . . . Then she wheeled around and pointed at the mistake I had made. "How else do you explain the state of mind that produced this error?[3]

Aaron Copland

The most visible and celebrated American composer during the middle decades of the century was Aaron Copland (1900–1990). In fact, the folk-song-based style of his ballets of the 1940s so perfectly fit the popular conception of an American classical idiom that, for general audiences, he has become the symbol of American music. As a performer, concert organizer, conductor, educator, writer, and critic, he assumed a position of leadership among American composers early in his career. Copland's early works shared the interests of many of his contemporaries: jazz rhythms, dissonance, a preference for Parisian over German influences. It was in the ballets of his Americana period that he took preeminence among the composers of the new, nationalist idiom.

Copland's parents were Lithuanian Jews (original name Kaplan) who emigrated to escape persecution and military conscription. He persuaded his parents to pay for piano lessons and began composing at thirteen. When Copland saw an advertisement for the Summer School of Music for American Students at Fontainebleau, he applied, and, accepted, sailed for France in 1921. He quickly gravitated toward Boulanger and studied with her, becoming part of the same heady Parisian milieu as Antheil and Thomson.

In an attempt to create a recognizably American music, Copland used elements of jazz in two works of the mid-1920s, *Music for the Theatre* (1925) and his gritty, two-movement Piano Concerto (1926), which won him a reputation as one of the most shocking modernists. Avid at keeping abreast of new musical movements, Copland lectured on twelve-tone music at the New School as early as 1928, and in 1930 based his *Piano Variations* on a quasi-serial five-note row; spare, thorny, and muscular, the piece is considered one of the classics of modern piano literature.

By the mid-1930s, however, Copland began to question the American composer's isolation from the broader public. Voicing sentiments that would reappear among American composers throughout the last third of the century, he wrote,

> It seemed to me that composers were in danger of working in a vacuum. Moreover, an entirely new public had grown up around the radio and phonograph. It made no sense to ignore them and continue writing as though they did not exist. I felt it was worth the effort to see if I couldn't say what I had to say in the simplest possible terms.[4]

After visiting Chavez in Mexico in 1932, Copland wrote *El Salón México*, his first piece based on folk themes, with which he suddenly achieved a wide public success. Other folksong-based pieces, mostly ballets, followed: *Billy the Kid* (1938), *Rodeo* (1942, for Agnes de Mille), *Appalachian Spring* (1943–1944, for Martha Graham), and *A Lincoln Portrait* for narrator and orchestra (1942). His Symphony No. 3 (1946), in some respects his masterpiece, was an attempt to fuse his Americana style with a more dissonant, developmental idiom. Its final movement incorporates a separate, brassy, triad-filled work that has achieved tremendous commercial success: *Fanfare for the Common Man*.

Copland's fellow composers, dismayed at his apostasy from modernism, begged him to go back to writing "real" music, but one need only glance at the motivic transformations between his modernist and Americanist works to see that Copland did not really change his musical thinking when he simplified his style; he simply pared down his materials for easier recognition. The method of immediately developing an opening motive by altering its rhythm is essentially the same in Copland's "severe" style of the *Piano Variations* (example 3.1) as it is in *Billy the Kid* (example 3.2). Unlike Cowell and Antheil, Copland did not

EXAMPLE 3.1 Aaron Copland, *Piano Variations*, mm. 1–6.

EXAMPLE 3.2 Aaron Copland, *Billy the Kid*, mm. 1–4.

have to weaken his style to simplify it, which is why his music shone in the social situation of the 1930s while theirs fell into neglect.

In 1953, Copland's tone poem *A Lincoln Portrait* (with texts from Abraham Lincoln) was scheduled to be performed at President Eisenhower's inaugural concert, but was abruptly cancelled because an Illinois congressman, Fred E. Busbey, had protested Copland's Communist connections of the 1930s. Copland had never actually been a Party member, but he had written a prize-winning song for the Communist Composers' Collective and given musical lectures for Communist organizations. Within months a telegram arrived from Senator Joseph McCarthy, calling Copland to appear before the House Committee on Un-American Activities. The Committee's trumped-up charges failed to convict Copland of wrongdoing, but in their search for suspicious musical figures, HUAC also investigated Elie Siegmeister, Wallingford Riegger, and David Diamond. (A similar cancellation occurred in 1973, when another work for narrator and orchestra, Vincent Persichetti's *A Lincoln Address*, was omitted from Richard Nixon's inauguration ceremony because Lincoln's text seemed to imply criticism of the Vietnam War. Apparently the words of Abraham Lincoln are too inflammatory for today's politicians.)

By the late 1940s, Stravinskian neoclassicism was taking a defensive posture under the onslaught of twelve-tone music, with its intimidatingly

EXAMPLE 3.3 Aaron Copland, *Appalachian Spring*.

intellectual cachet. Copland introduced an eleven-tone row in his Piano Quartet (1950), and continued exploring serial technique in two large orchestra works, *Connotations* (1962) and *Inscape* (1967). Due to a sharp decline in his mental abilities, however, his composing career was over by 1973. Copland achieved a national fame denied to many more original composers whose music exercised longer-lasting influence. Despite his fame, though, some of this best works—including his populist opera *The Tender Land,* discussed below—have been unaccountably neglected.

Listening Example: **Appalachian Spring**

Asked for a dance score by the great choreographer Martha Graham, Copland responded with *Appalachian Spring* (1943–1944), the celebration of a new farmhouse by a pioneer farm couple in the hills of Pennsylvania. The piece opens to fifty tranquil measures of pure A major. A dancelike motive bursts in, igniting a series of "wrong-key" rabbit chases. As the motive broadens into a theme, it combines with a slower chorale that is the ballet's real main theme (example 3.3). A third

EXAMPLE 3.4 Aaron Copland, *Appalachian Spring.*

section, a duo for the newlywed couple, begins as a tentative dance, but quickly turns poignant and then melancholy, its motives taken from the main theme. Before long, though, as a revivalist and some country fiddlers enter, the flute and clarinet announce a perky dance that sounds unmistakably like spring, and which turns into a square dance, accenting the final beat of every 4/4 measure. The dance then unsquares itself, skewing the rhythm's symmetry by throwing in extra beats (example 3.4). This technique of repeating the same pitch image over and over while varying the rhythm unpredictably is a Copland trademark, a trick he picked up from Stravinsky's early neoclassic works.

The square dance is followed by a solo for the bride in the form of a playful quasi-fugue, leading to more Stravinskian machine-gun-fire staccato rhythms. As the fireworks dissolve, the piece quietly restates its introduction, as though it is coming to a close. Instead, however, the clarinet breaks into the popular Shaker hymn "Simple Gifts." In Copland's earlier style, the theme might have been broken up into motives and tricky rhythms; here it is simply stated six times in succession, with varying orchestration and figurations, the last statement a climax. An extended coda then recaptures the opening quiet, leading back to the opening motives.

Roy Harris

Although Copland's fame with mass audiences has been more enduring, in the 1940s it looked as though Roy Harris (1898–1979) would emerge as the "great American symphonist" the world had been waiting for. The contrast between Brooklyn (Copland's birthplace) and Oklahoma Territory (Harris's) is apparent in the energy and scale of their respective works. Copland's ballets show a lean economy of means, with detailed motivic rhythms. Harris's symphonies evolved an original sense of rolling, majestic, "auto-generating" melody, enlivened by characteristic harmonic traits based on the superimposition of triads. Copland's music points to the jazzy pace of the cities, Harris's to endless vistas and a sense of limitless expectations.

Born on a homestead in Oklahoma Territory, Harris made much of the fact that he was born not only in a log cabin, like Abraham Lincoln, but on Lincoln's birthday; several of Harris's works are programmatically linked with the Great Liberator, including his Sixth and Tenth Symphonies and his chamber work *Abraham Lincoln Walks at Midnight*. In 1903 Harris's family moved to California's San Gabriel Valley, where Harris played clarinet in the school band. Working as a dairy deliverer and truck driver, he studied with the sympathetically Americanist Arthur Farwell.

Harris's career took flight via what he later called a lucky chain of events. He sent a small orchestra piece to Howard Hanson, who conducted it in New York. This led to a residency at the MacDowell Colony, where Harris met Copland, who advised him to study with Boulanger. Harris left for Paris in 1926. His egotism led to a tempestuous student-teacher relationship; the story is famous that when Boulanger asked him to write 20 melodies, he returned with 107. The conductor Serge Koussevitsky became Harris's most influential champion and premiered his First Symphony (called *Symphony 1933*), a critical success. Harris's Third Symphony (1938) quickly became popular, receiving more than seventy performances in its first decade.[5]

Harris's extraordinary natural talents, however, were accompanied by crudeness of technique in certain respects, and his stellar early success gave way to charges of self-repetition. He sometimes borrowed themes and even entire sections from earlier works for later ones, and his favorite devices can become irritating tics: folk song quotations, melodies of major-minor ambiguity, polytonal chorales, rollicking brass textures, all punctuated by what biographer Dan Stehman has called "the Harris gamelan" of piano, harp, vibraphone, and chimes.[6] If it can be said that any one symphony became "the great American Symphony," that title must go to Harris's Third. Unfortunately, his most beautiful later works contain flaws too patent to ignore.

Following his success with the Third, Harris led a restless and adventurous life, uprooting his family every other year or so to teach at a new school or organize a new music festival, finally settling in 1961 at the University of California at Los Angeles. He was embittered in his last years by the lack of recognition given his late works and toyed with the idea of moving to the Soviet Union, where his ideal of symphonies depicting the life of the proletariat was more in vogue. Nicolas Slonimsky records an anecdote that sums up both Harris's ambitions and his decline:

> Harris was having lunch with Virgil Thomson. He looked tired and dejected. "I am fifty years old," said Harris, "and I don't think I'll make it."
> "Make what?"
> "Beethoven."[7]

Harris's works include thirteen symphonies (he triskaidekaphobically numbered the last one No. 14), three string quartets, a violin concerto, two piano concertos (one for "amplified piano"), a piano sonata, and two piano suites, along with tone poems such as *Kentucky Spring*.

Listening Example: Symphony No. 3
The Third Symphony is in a one-movement form that Harris sometimes found more congenial than multimovement division. It falls into five sections that Harris characterized as follows:

1. Tragic
2. Lyric
3. Pastoral
4. Fugue (dramatic)
5. Dramatic-tragic

The work opens with a long, meandering melody in the lower strings. As if recapitulating the history of music from Gregorian chant on, the line is at first monophonic (without counterpoint), then breaks successively into octaves, fourths and fifths, and finally, after forty measures, a triumphant major triad. Three mournful notes in the French horn signal the entrance of a new melody in the violins, which will recur in later sections (example 3.5). The melody is then repeated by the entire woodwind section.

EXAMPLE 3.5 Roy Harris, Symphony No. 3. Theme from section I, "Tragic."

Section 2, "Lyric," opens with a change of mood and an alternation of two varied figures between the strings and woodwinds (example 3.6). These figures will recur motivically in later sections.

EXAMPLE 3.6 Roy Harris, Symphony No. 3. Theme from section II, "Lyric."

The "Pastoral" section is one of Harris's most famous moments, one of his static passages in which time seems to stop as the orchestra floats (not without energy) between seventh chords and polytonal chord combinations. Overlapping arpeggios in the strings create a kind of field in which woodwind melodies are tossed lightly from key to key (example 3.7). At

EXAMPLE 3.7 Roy Harris, Symphony No. 3 (some string parts are omitted).

last the momentum turns more anxious, with darker harmonies punctuated by the vibraphone.

A crescendo of activity leads to the dramatic fugue, one of the most
famous themes in American music (example 3.8). The middle of this
fugue section develops some of the motives from section 2, over a shifting polytonal background reminiscent of section 3. The fugue climaxes
in a rhythmic idea that will dominate section 5 (example 3.9).

This last section, "Dramatic-Tragic," brings back the violin melody
from section 1 (example 3.5), in canon between the strings and woodwinds as a background for the rhythmic motive in brass and timpani. At
last the music strips down to a dirgelike repeating stroke in the timpani,
which runs through the final chorale. One of Harris's finest passages,
this chorale spins out motives from sections 1 and 2 before a timpani-
articulated final cadence of tragic grandeur. Like a novel by John Steinbeck or one of Carl Sandburg's longer poems, the work flows through an
epic series of emotions in a single, sweeping gesture.

EXAMPLE 3.8 Roy Harris, Symphony No. 3. Fugue subject (IV: Fugue-
Dramatic).

EXAMPLE 3.9 Roy Harris, Symphony No. 3. Motive from section V, "Dramatic-Tragic."

William Schuman

Harris's symphonic aesthetic has been brilliantly extended by his most important student, William Schuman (1910–1992), who stands with Copland and Harris as one of the three finest midcentury American symphonists. Born in New York, Schuman began as a jazz band musician and published some popular songs. After hearing a symphony orchestra for the first time, however, he abruptly quit business school and enrolled in the Malkin School of Music, studying afterward with Harris at Juilliard. He taught at Sarah Lawrence College (1935–1945) and subsequently became one of America's leading arts administrators, first as president of the Juilliard School (1945–1962), then as president of the Lincoln Center for the Performing Arts. Throughout a demanding administrative career, he kept himself prolific through an unyielding discipline that is audible in his every work.

Schuman withdrew his earliest works, and jokingly called himself "the composer of eight symphonies, numbered three through ten." His earliest extant symphony, the Third, shows a strong Harris influence in its long, nonrepeating melodies, polytonal harmonies, muscular orchestration, and even its movement titles: "Passacaglia; Fugue" for the first, "Chorale; Toccata" for the second. From the outset, though, Schuman's music has a more disciplined sense of structure than Harris's, and he never resorts to the Americana clichés and quotations which can make the worst of Harris's music tiresome. Less tuneful than Harris's, Schuman's symphonies have not found as wide a following, but they are generally more solid in their workmanship.

The Symphony No. 8 (1962) is one of Schuman's finest, and despite its brooding atonalism, Harrisian touches are still evident, from the richly poignant major-minor triad with added dissonances that opens the work through the striking and well-used ensemble of glockenspiel, vibraphones, piano, and two harps. Repeated brass chords in asymmetrical rhythmic patterns of crescendoing nervousness are an unmistakable Schuman trait. Like Harris, Schuman usually avoids true development; instead he builds up textures through gradual accretion and passes themes from one section of the orchestra to another. His best-known works, however, are not his symphonies, but his *American Festival Overture,* his *New England Triptych* (1956), based on hymns by William Billings, and his orchestration of Ives's *Variations on America.* He also gave vent to his love of sports in a baseball opera, *Casey at the Bat* (1951–53), and won the first Pulitzer Prize ever given for music, for his cantata after Whitman *A Free Song* (1943).

Other Symphonists

The esteem accorded the seven symphonies of Howard Hanson (1896–1981, born in Wahoo, Nebraska) has fallen drastically in recent decades, the curve of his reputation paralleling that of MacDowell. In midcentury he was considered the Vaughan Williams or Sibelius of America, our leading large-scale romanticist. Hanson's career had gotten off to a rousing start: he was, in 1921, the first American to go to Rome (where he studied with Respighi) on the Prix de Rome. In 1924 he was appointed director of the Eastman School of Music, where he taught for forty years, improving the school's orchestra and conducting pioneering recordings of American works. The motivic logic of his symphonies is clear almost to a fault, and to post-1960 ears their limited impressionist harmony, timid next to even Debussy, has brought them a reputation for dullness, perhaps one not wholly deserved. In addition to his seven symphonies (ranging from the "Nordic," 1922, to *A Sea Symphony,* 1977), he wrote an opera *Merry Mount* (1933, from which he arranged a popular suite), a Piano Concerto (1948), and many choral works.

David Diamond (b. 1915 in Rochester, New York) is another composer whose career fell on hard times, though he dealt with it by becoming an expatriate; from 1953 to 1965 he lived in Florence. He studied with Bernard Rogers and Roger Sessions and, starting in 1936, with Boulanger in Paris, where he also met André Gide, Ravel, Roussel, and Stravinsky. Since 1973 he has taught at Juilliard. His nine symphonies, championed by composers such as Koussevitsky, Munch, and Bernstein, form the core of his output, but in the fifties he was best known for his suite from incidental music to *Romeo and Juliet* (1947). He has also written ten string quartets, three violin concertos, and concertos for piano and cello. The tentative revival of his popularity in the 1980s seemed to be due to a general return to tonality and the values of romanticism.

Elie Siegmeister (1909–1991, born in New York) closely resembles Copland in output and philosophy, though with more overt ideological leanings. A politically outspoken leftist during the thirties, he made heroic efforts to perform his music for audiences of working-class people unfamiliar with new or even classical music. Like Copland, he wrote music of dissonant, modernist abstraction (Theme and Variations No. 1

for piano, 1932; String Quartet No. 2, 1960), orchestral works of jazzy American flavor (Third Symphony, 1957), lighter orchestral works that use American folk material (*Ozark Set*, 1943; *Western Suite*, 1945), and even musicals and operas with popular songs (*The Plough and the Stars*, 1969). He also wrote eight operas, eight symphonies, several concertos, five piano sonatas, and six violin sonatas.

Born a little too late for the populism of the thirties, a little too early to embrace twelve-tone technique, Peter Mennin (1923–1983) wrote symphonies that were more austere and abstract than those of the other composers in this chapter, but without the chromaticism or complex counterpoint of the twelve-tone school. His music bristles with nervous energy and broods with dark, angular, dissonant melodies, but follows the general guidelines of classical form. Mennin's teachers at Eastman were Hanson and Bernard Rogers (1893–1968). Mennin taught at Juilliard from 1947 to 1958, directed the Peabody Institute from 1958 to 1962, and served as president of Juilliard from 1962 until his death. He wrote the usual nine symphonies, concertos for cello (1956), piano (1958), and flute (1983), a string quartet (1951), a piano sonata (1963), and a Concertato based on *Moby Dick* (1952).

If there is a "Copland figure" among black composers of nonjazz music, it is William Grant Still (1895–1978), who wrote music basically romantic in idiom but with strongly American rhythmic accents. Though brought up by a bandmaster father who loved opera, Still had many connections to the jazz world. He worked extensively with the seminal blues bandleader W. C. Handy and played oboe for vaudevillian Eubie Blake, but also studied with Chadwick and Varèse. Of his five symphonies, No. 1, his charming *Afro-American Symphony* (1930), was the first work by a black composer to be played by a major orchestra: the Rochester Philharmonic under Howard Hanson. His works, many of them written for public occasions and memorials, sometimes quote black spirituals but more often, as in the *Afro-American Symphony*, use original themes with jazz- or spiritual-derived characteristics.

Another black composer whose music followed a mostly diatonic, Americanist aesthetic is George Walker (b. 1922), who studied with Menotti and in Paris with Boulanger. While his idiom has always been highly lyrical, his works of recent decades, such as the Piano Concerto of 1975 with its beautifully pensive adagio lamenting the death of "Duke" Ellington, have moved in a more complex, near-atonal direction. He has also written much chamber music, a symphony (1961), and concertos for trombone (1957), cello (1982), and violin (1984). In 1996, he became the first black composer to be awarded the Pulitzer Prize for music.

Though Still is a patriarchal figure for black composers, he was not the first, having been notably preceded by R. Nathaniel Dett (1882–1943, composer of spiritual-inspired piano music), Clarence Cameron White (1880–1960), Samuel Coleridge-Taylor (1875–1912, half-African, half-

English, living in London), and Louis Moreau Gottschalk, whose mother was of Haitian Creole descent. In addition, Scott Joplin (1868–1917), the most successful of ragtime composers, wrote an opera, *Treemonisha* (1911), which was revived with much publicity in 1972.

To say that black composers who work outside jazz had tremendous difficulty becoming accepted in the first two-thirds of this century would be putting it mildly. Not only did they run up against a tacit assumption that they would be unable to master larger musical forms, they have also sometimes been criticized by jazz musicians for writing "white man's music." Prevented from taking part in the usual new-music networks, black composers built a less visible network of their own, usually based in local communities and church performance. The ultra-liberal Oberlin Conservatory in Ohio attracted black composers; Still, Dett, Walker, White, and Carman Moore all studied there, and Olly Wilson taught there. In recent years the situation has improved for many; Alvin Singleton, Wilson, and Moore, among others, have had considerable success in the performance of large ensemble works, including frequent orchestra commissions.

Leonard Bernstein

America's first generation of talented symphonists might have gone largely unnoticed without brilliant interpretive champions, and, luckily, one of the best arrived. Leonard Bernstein (1918–1990) never fully reached the goals he aimed for as a composer in either the serious or popular realms of music, but as a total musician he had an impact unparalleled in his era. He was born in Lawrence, Massachusetts, son of a father who left the Ukraine at 16, took a job in the Fulton fish market, and later opened a beauty supply business, which he expected Leonard to join. Against his father's wishes, Leonard gravitated naturally to the piano.

In 1935 Bernstein entered Harvard, studied with Edward Burlingame Hill and Walter Piston, and, while still a student, declared his leftist political leanings by directing a production of Marc Blitzstein's *The Cradle Will Rock* (of which more below). Here he met Copland, eighteen years his senior, just as the latter's career was taking off with *El Salón México*; he also met Schuman, Diamond, Harold Shapero, Irving Fine, and the conductor Dimitri Mitropoulos. Soon after he became friends with Ned Rorem (b. 1923), who would become one of the century's most prolific writers of art songs, and Paul Bowles (b. 1910), better known now as a novelist and short-story writer, but then a budding composer. After graduation Bernstein studied conducting with Fritz Reiner at the Curtis Institute, writing popular songs under the pen name Lenny Amber (Amber being a translation of Bernstein). He also became Koussevitsky's protégé at Tanglewood. In August of 1943 he obtained

Leonard Bernstein conducting the New York Philharmonic. *Photo © 1986 by Steve J. Sherman.*

the position of assistant conductor of the New York Philharmonic, and, on November 14, fate placed his destiny in his lap. Conductor Bruno Walter fell ill, and Bernstein took his place in a concert aired over national radio. The reviews of Bernstein's flamboyant, emotive conducting technique were superb, and he was suddenly famous.

A rare American serious-music celebrity, he was to prove a valuable ally to the Americanists. As Leopold Stokowski's successor at the New York City Symphony Orchestra (1945–1948), head of the orchestra department at the Berkshire Music Center (1951–1958), and finally the first American-born conductor of the New York Philharmonic (1958–1969), he plunged the orchestra into a world of modern music. He was a champion of the Americana symphonists, giving wide exposure to works by Copland, Harris, Schuman, and Diamond. He had little affinity for the ultramodernists; he also deeply distrusted twelve-tone music and the avant-garde that followed, though he eventually premiered works by Carter, Feldman, Babbitt, and Cage. For decades he was the only major conductor who could do American music justice, who knew how to make jazz rhythms swing, who knew how to time an American syncopation. By the time his conducting career took off, he had already written his first two symphonies, *Jeremiah* (1944) and *The Age of Anxiety* (1949), the latter programmatic (though nonvocal) after a poem by W. H. Auden. During the fifties he wrote two light operas—*Trouble in Tahiti* and *Candide*—and a musical, *West Side Story* (1957), the greatest composing triumph of his career.

In 1958 Bernstein began presenting his "Young People's Concerts" on television, which ran for fifteen years and offered significant musical pedagogy for the first generation growing up on television. For such activities Bernstein has often been dismissed by intellectuals. It is enough to answer that his Norton lectures at Harvard (1973, published as *The Unanswered Question*, 1976) are among the finest ever given by a musician, more provocative and better thought out than those of either Sessions or Stravinsky. Bernstein's overriding point in the lectures is that music possesses a universal deep structure analogous to the universal transformational logic that the linguist Noam Chomsky had found in the world's spoken languages. To demonstrate, Bernstein rewrote passages by Mozart, Stravinsky, and others, at greater length, showing how the composers had whittled out redundancy and condensed their ideas to make them more poetic. The essays are a stunning feat of wide-ranging musical literacy and explication.

Except for *West Side Story,* with its Coplandish infusion of Latin American rhythms into a Broadway pop style, Bernstein never completely developed a distinctive compositional voice, and such works as *The Age of Anxiety,* though attractive in parts, borrow from too many diverse styles to project a unified impression. Bernstein's Third Symphony, *Kaddish* (1963), uses twelve-tone techniques only to resolve them into tonality, as a way of moving from "the agony of 12-tone music" to the release of tonality. The hegemony of twelve-tone music during the sixties sent him into a creative crisis. In 1971, his *Mass* was commissioned to open the Opera House at Washington's sparkling new Kennedy Center, even though Bernstein had already created his own political scandal two years earlier by hosting a fundraising party for the Black Panthers, a militant black political organization. Bernstein's *Mass* was an eclectic hodge-podge of popular and high art styles, centered on a guitar-strumming priestly celebrant who goes through a mad scene that looks like an LSD trip. Richard Nixon was supposed to attend, but FBI director J. Edgar Hoover sent Nixon's Attorney General John Mitchell a memo detailing Bernstein's radical background and mentioning that the subversive Daniel Berrigan had been one of the consultants on the text of *Mass*. Nixon, who could play piano but whose record for appreciating modern composition is pretty poor, did not attend.

With the advent of minimalism and the return to tonality it offered, Bernstein found faith in contemporary music again. Nevertheless, he spent his last years conducting standard repertoire with the Vienna Philharmonic, and he greatly increased his stature as a conductor before he died.

American Opera and Its Composers

If critics of the 1930s and 1940s were waiting to hail the Great American Symphony, they were also waiting for the Great American Opera, which, somehow, never quite seemed to materialize. Often an opera would be given a highly publicized premiere, only to be critically condemned and forgotten about owing to a poor production, or to faults that revision could have easily effaced. The first wave of American opera in the twentieth century consisted chiefly of Americanist composers, who tended to incorporate some flavor of national folk idioms in an attempt to create an opera that sounded American. (A later operatic wave would emerge in the mid-1970s, derived from minimalism and multimedia.) The major operas of this first period include the following:

Virgil Thomson:	*Four Saints in Three Acts* (1934)
	The Mother of Us All (1947)
George Gershwin:	*Porgy and Bess* (1935)
Aaron Copland:	*The Second Hurricane* (1936)
	The Tender Land (1952–1954)
Marc Blitzstein:	*The Cradle Will Rock* (1937)
	Regina (1949)
Gian Carlo Menotti:	*The Old Maid and the Thief* (1939)
	The Medium (1946)
	The Telephone (1947)
	The Consul (1950)
	Amahl and the Night Visitors (1951)
	The Saint of Bleecker Street (1954)
Douglas Moore:	*The Devil and Daniel Webster* (1939)
	The Ballad of Baby Doe (1956)
	Carrie Nation (1966)
Bernard Herrmann:	*Wuthering Heights* (1941–1950)
Leonard Bernstein:	*Trouble in Tahiti* (1952)
	Candide (1956)
Carlisle Floyd:	*Susannah* (1955)
Samuel Barber:	*Vanessa* (1958)
	Antony and Cleopatra (1966)
Robert Ward:	*The Crucible* (1961)

Except for *Amahl and the Night Visitors,* which became a Christmas television tradition, not one of these operas has passed into a permanent repertory; this fact may say more about the machinations of the opera world than about the quality of the operas concerned. In particular, newspaper reviews carry enormously more weight in theater than they do in music, and the tremendous expenditure of money and manpower opera requires makes it more vulnerable to critical dismissal than concert music.

The American composer most closely associated with opera has been, predictably, an Italian, Gian Carlo Menotti, born 1911 in Cadegliano, Italy. He attended the Milan Conservatory at age thirteen, already having written two operas, then moved to Philadelphia in 1927 to attend the Curtis Institute, where he met Samuel Barber, who would become his traveling and living companion for many years. Menotti's operatic success is largely due to his talent for writing librettos; his music, despite modernist touches, rarely strays far from its model in Puccinian verismo. Menotti has written about two dozen operas, the most successful of which are listed above.

The Tender Land should have been a star candidate for Great American Opera. Not only was it by Copland, but it took a story out of the American heartland, with a plot reminiscent of John Steinbeck, inspired by a famous American book: James Agee's *Let Us Now Praise Famous Men,* a description of the Depression South. The libretto by Erik Johns tells the story of Laurie, a girl on a rural farm, who falls in love with a migrant farmworker and abandons her uncomprehending family to search for him. The music, some of the best of Copland's Americana style, contains a noble farmland quintet "The Promise of Living," a rousing square dance, and a passionate love duet. But the opera was originally intended for two purposes that jinxed it in the opera house: it was written for television (before NBC's Television Opera Workshop rejected it), and it was meant to be simple enough for young people to perform. The work was never intended as "grand" opera, to stand next to Verdi. Despite revisions after the 1954 production, *The Tender Land* was hurt by bad reviews.

For many, George Gershwin's *Porgy and Bess* is the greatest American opera, though its reputation as such has been dogged by ultimately pointless charges that it is a musical, rather than an opera—a distinction based on little more than the fact that it was premiered on Broadway rather than in an opera house. Gershwin (1898–1937) was a genius of New York's songwriters' strip Tin Pan Alley, the equal of songwriters such as Irving Berlin, Jerome Kern, Richard Rodgers, and Cole Porter; he was the only one to succeed also as a composer of concert music. The son of Russian immigrants in New York, Gershwin took to the piano naturally, and at fifteen got a job as a song plugger, a pianist who promoted a publisher's new songs by playing and singing them for customers. His swiftness of inspiration was spectacular: at nineteen he wrote the song "Swanee," later made famous by Al Jolson, in fifteen minutes. Much of his success was owed to the lyricist with whom he worked so well: his brother Ira.

George Gershwin graduated to the Broadway stage, turning out sixteen musicals in the early twenties alone. In 1924 he scored a spectacular hit with his first instrumental work of major length, *Rhapsody in Blue*. Gershwin's later works, such as his Piano Concerto in F (1925), *Cuban Overture* (1932), and Second Rhapsody (1932), are more sophisticated than *Rhapsody in Blue*, but the latter was the first large concert work in a jazz idiom, and its opening clarinet glissando is an American aural icon. (The piece also brought him a quarter million dollars in the next ten years.) The late twenties brought his most successful musicals, *Strike Up the Band* (1927) and *Of Thee I Sing* (1931), the latter a hilarious satire of presidential elections in which the First Lady is chosen via a beauty contest.

Gershwin's rise from song plugger to orchestral composer took place with little benefit of formal training. He never overcame his insecurity about compositional matters, even though he had enriched the Broadway song form, with its rhythmic basis in African-American dance, by an impressive range of impressionist harmony. He asked to study with the French composer Maurice Ravel, and the story is that Ravel asked him, "How much do you earn a year from your compositions?"

"Between one hundred and two hundred thousand dollars."

"Then," Ravel replied, "it is I who must ask you to teach me to compose."

In 1932–1936 Gershwin did, however, study the compositional method of Joseph Schillinger (1895–1943), a Russian-born theorist who devised a musical technique based on the mathematical superimposition of pitch and rhythmic patterns according to what he felt were the underlying laws of nature. Tin Pan Alley composers, under pressure to turn out songs at incredible speed, flocked to Schillinger's method when inspiration dried up; besides Gershwin, he counted Tommy Dorsey, Benny Goodman, and Glenn Miller among his students. Schillinger also attracted attention from experimental composers, including Cowell and John Cage.

Gershwin used Schillinger's techniques in certain parts of his magnum opus, the opera *Porgy and Bess* (1935), based on DuBose Heyward's 1924 novel of the same title. The opera takes place in Catfish Row, a Charleston tenement. Porgy, a cripple, and Crown are both in love with Bess. Drunk at a crapshoot, Crown kills Robbins and tells Bess to wait for him while he hides out, but Bess goes to live with Porgy. Crown returns for Bess and fights with Porgy, Porgy stabs him, and the police eventually arrive to take Porgy away to view Robbins's body. While he is gone, Sportin' Life convinces Bess that Porgy will be locked up for good and persuades her to accompany him to New York. Porgy does return, however, and finding Bess gone he sets off for New York on his little cart to bring her back. To write the opera, Gershwin immersed himself in the songs of the Gullah language in South Carolina, a mixture of English and Creole spoken among Blacks descended from slaves from the west coast of Africa.

It is difficult in hindsight to understand why *Porgy and Bess* was not critically or financially successful in its first run, but posterity has rehabilitated its reputation, and the Metropolitan Opera finally presented it in 1985. The opening song, "Summertime," has become one of the most famous songs ever written, recognizable throughout the world, and the opera's leitmotiv technique, echoing the contours of significant phrases in the orchestra at important dramatic moments somewhat in the manner of Berg's *Wozzeck,* is sophisticated for its time. Soon after the opera's premiere, however, at the height of Gershwin's career, a brain tumor cut his life short at thirty-eight.

"Composers fall into two categories," Copland has said; "those who are 'hopelessly' opera composers, such as Rossini, Wagner, and Puccini— and those who debate whether and when to write an opera. . . . The urge has to be so strong that because of some inner drive, little else in music attracts you—and then you are an honest-to-God opera composer. I am not such."[8] Besides Menotti, however, America has produced several composers known only for their many operas. Douglas Moore (1893–1969), who taught at Barnard and Columbia from 1926 to 1962, wrote seven major operas, of which *The Ballad of Baby Doe* was most successful. The true story of a Vermont stonecutter who strikes it rich as a silver miner and divorces his wife to marry Baby Doe, the piece makes effective use of such nineteenth-century American genres as parlor ballads and dance-hall tunes. Carlisle Floyd (b. 1926), like Menotti, writes his own librettos, and has made operas from both Emily Brontë's *Wuthering Heights* (1958) and John Steinbeck's *Of Mice and Men* (1969). *Susannah,* his most popular work, relocates the apocryphal story of Susannah and the Elders to rural Tennessee, in a setting full of tuneful folk song references.

Bernard Herrmann (1911–1975), an early champion of Charles Ives's music, was extremely successful as a composer for films. His scores for Orson Welles's *Citizen Kane* and Alfred Hitchcock's *Psycho, Vertigo, North by Northwest,* and *The Birds* as well as *Journey to the Center of the Earth, Fahrenheit 451,* and *Taxi Driver* are considered classics of the genre. He found less success in concert music, and his *Wuthering Heights* did not receive a stage performance until 1982. Robert Ward (b. 1917), a student of Hanson, achieved some success with his operatic treatment of Arthur Miller's play about the Salem witch trials of the 1690s, *The Crucible.* Ward's five other operas, including *Minutes till Midnight,* a warning about nuclear apocalypse, have not been as widely performed.

The Crucible, or rather Miller's eponymous play, used the Salem witch hunts to criticize the McCarthy-ite communist hunts of the 1950s. Despite the political upheaval of the times, however, most of these composers did not deal directly with political subjects. One major exception was Marc Blitzstein (1905–1964, born in Philadelphia). After studying with Boulanger in Paris and Schoenberg in Berlin, he began as a composer in dissonantly neoclassic style. In 1935, however, he heard the Marxist film composer Hanns Eisler lecture on "The Crisis in Music" at the New School for Social Research. Eisler convinced Blitzstein of the Marxist idea that one could not analyze music without considering the social conditions of its production. A meeting with Bertolt Brecht reinforced this train of thought, and Blitzstein began writing works of musical theater with a pointed social purpose, including, in 1952, an extremely popular English adaptation of Brecht's and Weill's *Die Dreigroschenoper, The Three-Penny Opera.*

Blitzstein's most famous work was *The Cradle Will Rock,* an opera about the organization of a union in Steeltown, USA. The Federal Theater Project, which had originally planned to produce it, found it too controversial, and it was produced independently by Orson Welles and British actor John Houseman. Blitzstein also based an opera, *Regina* (1949), on Lillian Hellman's popular novel *The Little Foxes;* it has been revived with some success. An opera about the political martyrs Sacco and Vanzetti remained unfinished when Blitzstein was killed at a Martinique bar in a political altercation.

One of the most disappointing operatic premieres in American history was Barber's *Antony and Cleopatra,* for Samuel Barber (1910–1981) had enjoyed considerable popularity as an American representative of high Romanticism. Born in West Chester, Pennsylvania, Barber entered Curtis Institute in 1924 (along with Blitzstein) as part of its first graduating class. A trained baritone singer capable of recording his own songs, he developed a neoromantic style based in singable melody, a quality that resulted in one of the few popular hits in American classical music: the second movement of his First String Quartet (1936), orchestrated as the *Adagio for Strings,* a tearjerker of a piece filled with poignant melodic suspensions. His Piano Concerto (1962) and *Prayers of Kierkegaard* (1945) remain prized for similar qualities.

Of Barber's two operas, *Antony and Cleopatra,* based on the Shakespeare play, was commissioned to open the Metropolitan Opera House at Lincoln Center. It was a critical failure largely because of a clumsy production by its librettist, Franco Zeffirelli, and Barber responded by retreating to the Italian Alps and composing little in the following five years. A revised production, with the libretto redone by Menotti, was insufficient to reverse the opera's fortunes. Barber's thoroughgoing traditionalism did not prevent him from using an electronic synthesizer (originally an Ondes martenot, a French electronic instrument) to express the "music i' the air" outside Antony's battlefield in Act II of the opera, nor from experimenting with a twelve-tone row in his Piano Sonata of 1949.

Virgil Thomson

Two of the most remarkable American operas were the result of collaborations between a plain-spoken music critic from Missouri and a seminal expatriate author. Virgil Thomson (1896–1989) was a composer of music whose surface simplicity, indebted to the eccentric French composer Erik Satie, hid an elegant sophistication. Gertrude Stein (1874–1946) was the most experimental American writer of the early twentieth century, a fantastically original stylist whose obsessive repetition of short words and disregard for punctuation created a style of great cumulative emotional power. Her major works include *The Making of Americans, The Autobiography of Alice B. Toklas,* and *Tender Buttons.* Born in Pennsylvania, Stein presided over the unbelievably fertile literary, artistic, and musical scene of 1920s Paris. When Thomson wandered into that scene, the two formed the century's most perfect American operatic team.

Thomson was born in Kansas City, Missouri, on November 25, 1896. In adolescence he played the organ in churches and the piano in movie halls. Though he enlisted in a field artillery unit, World War I ended before his departure for France became necessary. At Harvard, Edward Burlingame Hill introduced him to modern French music, and after his glee club toured Europe in 1921, Thomson stayed behind in Paris. Here he studied organ and counterpoint with Boulanger, met Cocteau, Satie, and the circle of composers known as Les Six, and wrote his first music reviews as foreign correspondent for the *Boston Evening Transcript.* He returned to America long enough to give the American premiere of Satie's masterpiece, *Socrate.* Thomson's next stay in Paris, in 1925, would last for fifteen years.

Thomson met Gertrude Stein in the winter of 1925–1926. "Gertrude and I," he later wrote of their first meeting, "got on like Harvard men. As we left, she said to him [George Antheil] only good-by, but to me, 'We'll be seeing each other.'"[9] Early in 1927 they began talking about plans for an opera about saints, preferably Spanish ones of an earlier century. Stein had a libretto written by June, Thomson finished a piano score in 1928, and *Four Saints in Three Acts* had its world premiere February 8, 1934, in Hartford, Connecticut, with an all-black cast dressed in cellophane costumes. (Because of fire hazards, the New York Fire Department subsequently passed a law banning cellophane from any New York stage.) Copland, Gershwin, Roger Sessions, Toscanini, and a crowd of luminaries were in attendance.

Thomson's best works of the thirties were film scores for documentaries by Pare Lorentz, a WPA project. *The Plow that Broke the Plains*

Virgil Thomson. *Photo by George Platt Lynes. Courtesy Virgil Thomson Papers, Yale University Music Library. Used by permission.*

(1936) and *The River* (1937), successful as concert works, quote folk and cowboy songs as extensively as Copland's *Rodeo,* but unlike Copland, Thomson had no need to change his style. In 1928 he had already written his *Symphony on a Hymn Tune,* a four-movement work based on the Protestant hymn "How Firm a Foundation," and formed a quotation-filled style of deceptive banality. He also took up the habit of making musical Portraits of his friends, mostly for piano or small chamber combination, written quickly while the subject sat, as for a painting.

In 1940 Thomson fled the crisis in Europe and obtained a post as critic for the *New York Herald Tribune.* For fourteen years he served as the best music critic in the English language, with an elegant, terse, inimitable style. "Nouns," he wrote, delineating his critical philosophy, "are names and can be libelous; the verbs, though sometimes picturesque, are few in number and tend toward alleging motivations. It is the specific adjectives that really describe and that do so neither in sorrow nor in anger." Thomson raised hackles by denigrating such sacred cows of the classical establishment as violinist Jascha Heifitz and the New York Philharmonic, but his charm and humor turned away wrath. To a reader who protested his positive review of a soprano, he replied,

> If Miss S— had committed grave misdemeanors about pitch, I am sure I should have waked up. At musical performances I sleep lightly, and only so long as nothing in any way abnormal, for good or ill, takes place on the stage.[10]

When Thomson suggested to Stein an opera about nineteenth-century America, using quotations from historical speeches, she quickly wrote *The Mother of Us All*, sending it to him in March of 1946. It was her last completed work, for in July she died of cancer. Thomson lived the rest of his life in an apartment in New York's Chelsea Hotel. His third opera, *Lord Byron* (1961–1968), to a libretto by Jack Larson, lacks the audacious charm of the operas he wrote with Stein.

Listening Example: The Mother of Us All, *Act One, Scenes Two and Three*

Of the two Stein-Thomson operas, *Four Saints in Three Acts* has become more famous for its audacious non-sequiturs and humor. Divided into four acts rather than three, it contains many more than four saints and is steeped in the nonsense of the Dada movement Thomson encountered in Paris. Charming as *Four Saints* is, *The Mother of Us All* is a more profound, more human, more moving opera. In the course of Stein's nonlinear, lightly punctuated libretto, she makes several points that she obviously felt deeply, and the manner in which those points work their way repetitively through what seems like nonsense on the surface makes them all the more powerful. A constant theme is that men, especially powerful men, do not listen; hearing becomes a metaphor for receptiveness, for a willingness not to dominate others. The importance of names, and what it does to a thing to name it, is touched upon frequently. *The Mother* delivers one of Stein's most fervent feminist, humanist messages.

And Thomson, stepping out of the way, lets the message through beautifully. Scene 2 of *The Mother* quotes "London Bridge Is Falling Down" and contains marches (symbolizing men) that are humorous in their immobile lack of variety; Scene 3 features waltzes and a veiled love duet in which nothing is actually communicated. Both scenes exhibit Thomson's subtle method of intercutting back and forth between recurring textures and tonalities, as though he had translated *Le Sacre du Printemps* into polite, nineteenth-century American. Except for eerie bitonal (or whole-tone) passages such as the beginning of scene three, the music stresses a specious simplicity, every chord drawn from the vernacular.

There is no real plot to *The Mother of Us All*, though there are situations that change throughout the course of the opera. As Act I opens, a conversation between Susan B. Anthony and her companion Anne is being narrated by two characters suspiciously named Gertrude S. and Virgil T. Susan is already complaining about the behavior of men: "That is to say politeness is agreeable. That is to say it could be if everybody

EXAMPLE 3.10 Virgil Thomson, *The Mother of Us All*, Act I, scene 2.

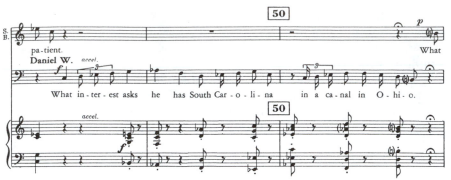

EXAMPLE 3.10 *(continued)*

were polite, but when it is only me, ah me." In scene two, Daniel Webster begins his politicking in the company of fellow politicians John Adams, Andrew Johnson, and others. Much is made of names: "Susan B. Anthony is my name, to choose a name is feeble," our heroine sings. But choosing a name will turn out to be a crisis for Indiana Elliott, for when she marries Jo the Loiterer, he will demand that she change her name. Susan B. and Daniel W. debate (see example 3.10), but while she answers his comments, he does not listen to a word she says.

Daniel Webster is in love with Angel More. John Adams loves Constance Fletcher, but in scene three has trouble expressing his love:

> Dear Miss Constance Fletcher, it is a real pleasure that I kneel at your
> feet, but I am an Adams, I kneel at the feet of none, not anyone.

In Scene 4, Susan B. dreams of people who will not help her: a Negro man who will vote even if she cannot, and a chorus of three Very Important Persons.

As Act II begins, the men are trying to persuade Susan B. to speak at a meeting. Jo arrives, upset because Indiana Elliott refuses to change her name. Susan agrees to speak, but Scene 2 reveals that her only effect was that the men have, for the first time, written the word "male" into the suffrage clause of the United States Constitution. The final scene is an epilogue. Susan B. has died, and the other characters are paying homage to her statue. Women now have the vote, and although nothing has really changed for the better, Susan B.'s statue sings: "We cannot retrace our steps."

There is no conclusive proof that, somewhere within this rich repertoire, the Great American Opera has not already appeared. That possibility granted, *The Mother of Us All* has as solid a claim to that position as any of them.

Notes

1. Virgil Thomson, *Virgil Thomson: An Autobiography* (New York: Alfred A. Knopf, 1966), p. 54.
2. Aaron Copland, *On Music* (London: Andre Deutsch, 1961), p. 86.
3. Quoted in K. Robert Schwarz, *Minimalists* (London: Phaidon Press, 1996), p. 114.
4. Aaron Copland, *The New Music 1900–1960* (London: MacDonald, 1968), p. 160.
5. Nicolas Slonimsky, "Roy Harris: The Story of an Oklahoma Composer Who Was Born in a Log Cabin on Lincoln's Birthday," in Crawford, Lott, and Oja, eds., *A Celebration of American Music: Words and Music in Honor of H. Wiley Hitchcock* (Ann Arbor: University of Michigan Press, 1990), p. 314.
6. Dan Stehman, *Roy Harris: An American Musical Pioneer* (Boston: Twayne Publishers, 1984), p. 107.
7. Nicolas Slonimsky, "Roy Harris: The Story of an Oklahoma Composer Who Was Born in a Log Cabin on Lincoln's Birthday," in Crawford, Lott, and Oja, eds., *A Celebration of American Music: Words and Music in Honor of H. Wiley Hitchcock*, p. 317.
8. Virgil Thomson, *Virgil Thomson: An Autobiography* (New York: E. P. Dutton, Inc., 1985), p. 89.
9. Virgil Thomson, *A Virgil Thomson Reader*, p. 181.
10. Tim Page and Vanessa Weeks Page, eds., *Selected Letters of Virgil Thomson* (New York: Summit Books, 1988), p. 216.

CHAPTER 4

Experimentalism

The years of World War II marked a general hiatus in European music. For American composers the period was hardly better, even though the fighting was overseas. In their state of war-aroused patriotism, American audiences were uncomfortable about enjoying music by Germans and Italians. And yet, rather than program more American music as might have been expected, orchestras turned toward the repertoire of non-Germanic Europe, increasing their proportion of Norwegian, French, and English works. During World War I, the presence of American music (measured as percentage of the total number of works performed) on the programs of the New York Philharmonic and Boston Symphony Orchestras had risen slightly as German offerings dipped, then returned after the war to approximately the original levels:[1]

	AMERICAN		**GERMAN/AUSTRIAN**	
	NYPO	BSO	NYPO	BSO
1916–17	3.2%	9.8%	60%	62%
1917–18	8.7%	4.8%	47%	42.6%
1918–19	10.5%	7.9%	32%	29.7%
1919–20	4.2%	7.2%	51%	43.3%
1920–21	4.4%	12%	67%	44%
1921–22	5.5%	6.3%	65%	49.5%

(So popular was Wagner that his participation in the revolution of 1848–1849 was widely adduced to prove that, were he still alive, he would have been as opposed to the Kaiser as the Americans were; therefore it was all right to listen to his music.) World War II evinced a similar pattern: patriotic interest in home-grown art did not survive the cessation of hostilities. Despite attempts by American composers throughout the thirties to reach out to a wider public, they found that neither the patriotism of the war years nor their own simplification of their language led to increased opportunities. In the long run, in fact, the effect was quite opposite, and not only because of the termination of the WPA.

Hundreds of European musicians as well as untold thousands of European music-lovers found themselves exiled to America (including Europe's greatest composers, who will be discussed in chapter 5). With their presence, the classical music establishment veered drastically away from American music. In the prewar period, conductors had felt some obligation to program American works. Under the American conductor Frederick Stock, for example, the Chicago Symphony, which he directed until 1942, normally performed one American work per concert, except for the occasional all-Beethoven or all-Wagner program. After World War II, partly because of the influx of Europeans (especially conductors) who had no faith or interest in American composers, that rate dropped down to about two or three American works per orchestra per year. From the standpoint of American music's presence in classical music programs, the influx of European émigrés was a disaster.

Naturally, the war interrupted all but a few musical careers. Some composers, such as Ben Johnston and Ulysses Kay, played in the Navy band. Blitzstein, fighting in the 8th Army Air Force in England, took the opportunity to collect songs of the French resistance. Barber was drafted into the Army Air Force, which commissioned him to write his Second Symphony on the base at Fort Worth; he later withdrew the work. Milton Babbitt, with his mathematical expertise, did military research on code-breaking. Piston was a civilian air raid warden. Ross Lee Finney served for the American Office of Strategic Services, stepped on a land mine, and survived to receive a Purple Heart. Roger Sessions left Europe and found a teaching job because he saw the war coming. Even Colin McPhee in Bali could not escape the war; he beat a hasty retreat to America in 1939 partly because the Japanese were scrutinizing Bali for strategic military purposes (also because the hard-pressed Dutch were beginning to crack down on homosexual activity in their island territories). Once home, composers encountered a scene in which there was little further interest in their music, nor any way to get it performed. No American composers of any reputation died fighting, but one, Charles Naginski (1909–1940), committed suicide at Yaddo in his depression over the dearth of professional opportunities.[2]

Depending on how you look at it, America's disenfranchisement of its composers has been a freeing influence as well as an alienating one. A statement by Henry David Thoreau could be taken as the philosophic basis of American music. After Thoreau published *Walden,* the great majority of the copies, unsold, were returned to him by the publisher; Thoreau put them in a coffin and mused, "It makes me feel so good that no one is interested in my work, because it leaves me free to go in any direction that is necessary." The composers in this chapter are not really associated with each other, nor with the war years (although the careers of Partch, Nancarrow, Brant, and Harrison did begin more or less in war time, and each was forced by the absence of societal support to find a new way to make music). What they have in common is that they all worked outside the mainstream of American musical life. By not providing what a composer needs to have a rewarding career, America has turned many of its best musical minds into experimentalists. Each composer here followed his own course and created his own tradition.

Harry Partch

Of all America's nonconformist composers, none has valued independence more than Harry Partch (1901–1974). From the first moment of his musical life, he growled in a late interview, "I was not going to be straitjacketed by anyone. I was going to be completely free."[3] He achieved that aim to an astonishing extent. He invented new, whimsical instruments. He abandoned Europe's twelve-pitch scale and devised a new one with forty-three pitches to the octave. From the surviving shards of ancient Greek drama, Chinese theater, and American Indian ritual, he forged his own style of performance, incorporating dance, costumes, and theater. If originality is the essence of American music, Partch was the most American composer of all.

Born in Oakland, California, on June 24, 1901, Partch was the son of Presbyterian missionaries who fled China after the Boxer Rebellion. The family later moved to Tucson, Arizona, and then Albuquerque. The boy's early impressions, then, were a mixture of Chinese (including his mother's lullabies), Mexican, and Yaqui Indian influences. In his teens he became proficient on the piano, wrote piano music, and made money by providing musical accompaniment at silent movie theaters. Partch dated the beginning of his apostasy from European music to 1923, the year in which he ran across Hermann Helmholtz's classic volume on acoustics, *On the Sensations of Tone.*

What Partch found in Helmholtz convinced him that European music had been based on, as he called it, an acoustic lie. He began experimenting with stringed instruments, tuning them differently, and in 1930, living in New Orleans, he made his break vividly symbolic: he burned all the music he had written up to that point, including a piano concerto, in a big, pot-bellied stove. He invented his first instrument, the adapted viola, and began performing by himself. Traveling to New York, he met Copland, Harris, Cowell, Seeger, Hanson, Piston, and Otto Luening, interesting them in his work.[4] In 1934, he received a $1,500 grant from the Carnegie Corporation that allowed him to visit the British Museum to research the history and theory of tuning. On a side trip to Dublin he also visited the poet W. B. Yeats (1865–1939), to play him sketches he had made for an opera based on Yeats's *Oedipus.* The great man gave Partch some much-needed encouragement.

When the grant ran out, Partch returned to an America in the grip of Depression. For the next eight years, he lived as a hobo: stealing rides

Harry Partch performing on two of his instruments: the gourd tree and the cone gongs. *Courtesy BMI Archives.*

in train boxcars, living in transient shelters and hobo camps, picking grapes, cleaning latrines, and—as an absolute last resort—begging for food. As he lived this way, he transcribed the speech patterns of the bums he lived among, recording them in a diary later published under the title *Bitter Music.* Because of this experience, and his ear for speech patterns, Partch in his later theater works became the voice of the highway in art music, our operatic Jack Kerouac.

What was the "acoustic lie" that Partch rebelled against? He inherited, as we all have, an octave containing twelve equally spaced pitches. An octave is defined as the pitch space between two pitches, one of which vibrates twice as fast as the other. If, for example, an A vibrates at 440 cycles per second, the A an octave higher vibrates at 880 cycles per second. Therefore, the ratio of an octave is 2:1. Any musical interval that can be expressed by a ratio between small whole numbers is, by definition, considered consonant—that is, simple and intelligible to the ear. A. J. Ellis (Helmholtz's translator) established a perceptual unit for measuring the size of intervals: the cent. By definition, an octave is 1,200 cents large.

2/1	3/2	4/3	5/4	5/3	6/5	8/5

EXAMPLE 4.1 A just-intonation scale in ratios, cents, and frequencies.

Most pianos are tuned today by a system known as equal temperament, wherein the twelve pitches divide the octave into twelve equal steps:

	C	C♯	D	E♭	E	F	F♯	G	A♭	A	B♭	B	C
CENTS:	0	100	200	300	400	500	600	700	800	900	1000	1100	1200

However, equal temperament contains only one pure consonance: the 2:1 octave. Other pure consonances are shown in example 4.1. The approximate sizes of these pure intervals in cents are as follows: octave (2/1), 1,200; fifth (3/2), 702; fourth (4/3), 498; major third (5/4), 386.3; major sixth (5/3), 884.4; minor third (6/5), 315.6; and minor sixth (8/5), 813.7. As you can see, apart from the octave, none of these pure consonances can be found in the equal-tempered scale of the modern piano.

The pure tuning of intervals according to their mathematical ratios is called "just intonation." For example, a twelve-pitch keyboard might be tuned as in example 4.2 (ratios and cents given with reference to C as a starting point). The tuning given here will be perfect if one wants to play in the key of C. The moment one wants to play in the key of D, however, the perfect fifth on D (D to A) is only 680 cents instead of 702, a dissonant, unusable interval with a ratio of 40:27. Equal temperament shifts all of the intervals a little out of tune to make all keys equally viable.

Partch, however, insisted on having his musical intervals perfectly consonant and also on having access to consonances that European

PITCH:	C	C♯	D	E♭	E	F	F♯
RATIO:	$\frac{1}{1}$	$\frac{16}{15}$	$\frac{8}{8}$	$\frac{6}{5}$	$\frac{5}{4}$	$\frac{4}{3}$	$\frac{45}{32}$
CENTS:	0	112	204	316	386	498	590
CPS:	264	281	297	316.8	330	352	371.25

PITCH:	G	A♭	A	B♭	B	C
RATIO:	$\frac{3}{2}$	$\frac{8}{5}$	$\frac{5}{3}$	$\frac{9}{5}$	$\frac{15}{8}$	$\frac{2}{1}$
CENTS:	702	814	884	1018	1088	1200
CPS:	396	422.4	440	475.2	495	528

EXAMPLE 4.2 Ratios of common intervals, tuned in just intonation.

music had never used, intervals that slipped between the keys of the piano, such as 7:4 (969 cents) and 11:8 (551 cents). He developed a scale of forty-three pitches to the octave, given in example 4.3, with G as its tonic. Ratios of small numbers are consonances; those of larger numbers (such as 40:27 or 160:81) are dissonant over the tonic G but allow consonance over other steps of the scale for purposes of modulation to different keys. There is nothing acoustically sacred about the number forty-three; Partch often used scales of fewer pitches and arrived at forty-three by aiming for a fairly even distribution across the octave.

Clearly, to play this forty-three-pitch scale, Partch had to invent new instruments. His first, the "adapted viola," is a viola with a fingerboard extended six inches longer than normal, which is held between the knees while playing and has tiny brads nailed into the fingerboard as frets. The Chromelodeon I is a harmonium, or reed organ, with its reeds tuned to the forty-three-tone scale. The keys are painted with blocks of different colors, so that the eye can quickly recognize which tonality each pitch is consonant in. Partch's kithara, based on the ancient Greek instrument of the same name, is a tall, harplike instrument with seventy-two strings grouped in twelve vertical rows of six each. The strings are plucked with a plectrum, and smooth glissandos are made possible by sliding Pyrex glass rods that act as movable bridges. The Surrogate Kithara has sixteen horizontal strings. The diamond marimba places thirty-six wooden marimba blocks over resonators in a diagonal, diamond-shaped pattern. The pitches are arranged in a criss-cross pattern so that a sweep in either diagonal direction remains within a single tonality. The most heavenly timbre in many of Partch's compositions comes from the cloud-chamber bowls, which are sawed-off sections of twelve-gallon Pyrex glass bottles, played—lightly, lest breakage occur—with a mallet.

The Partch instruments, over two dozen in all, are beautiful to look at as well as to hear, for he felt that music should be not only an aural but also a visual and theatrical experience. His performers wear costumes, and playing his instruments requires dancing.

Partch's hobo years ended when a friend offered him a place to live and work in Chicago; he immortalized the freight-train trip to Chicago in his music-theater piece *The Wayward*. The next thirty years saw him establish and abandon a series of studios in Wisconsin, California, Illinois, and Ohio. Despite continuing hostility from several university music departments, he presented his music at Bennington and Eastman, enjoyed a three-year residency at the University of Wisconsin, performed *Oedipus* at Mills College, and started an ensemble at the University of Illinois. In Sausalito he recorded his works on a private record label called Gate 5.

During these years Partch wrote several major theater works, including the dance-drama *The Wayward* (1941–1943), *Oedipus* (1951), *The Bewitched* (1955), *Revelation at the Courthouse Park* (1960, an adapta-

Ratio	Cents	Interval Name
1/1	0.0	
81/80	21.5	syntonic comma
33/32	53.3	
21/20	84.5	
16/15	111.7	half-tone
12/11	150.6	undecimal "median" second (1.5 half-steps)
11/10	165.0	
10/9	182.4	minor whole-tone
9/8	203.9	major whole-tone
8/7	231.2	septimal whole-tone
7/6	266.9	septimal minor third
32/27	294.1	Pythagorean minor third
6/5	315.6	minor third
11/9	347.4	undecimal "median" third
5/4	386.3	major third
14/11	417.5	
9/7	435.1	septimal major third
21/16	470.8	septimal fourth
4/3	498.0	perfect fourth
27/20	519.6	
11/8	551.3	undecimal tritone
7/5	582.5	septimal tritone
10/7	617.5	septimal tritone
16/11	648.7	
40/27	680.4	
3/2	702.0	perfect fifth
32/21	729.2	
14/9	764.9	septimal minor sixth
11/7	782.5	undecimal minor sixth
8/5	813.7	minor sixth
18/11	852.6	undecimal "median" sixth
5/3	884.4	major sixth
27/16	905.9	Pythagorean major sixth
12/7	933.1	septimal major sixth
7/4	968.8	septimal minor seventh
16/9	996.1	minor seventh
9/5	1017.6	minor seventh
20/11	1035.0	
11/6	1049.4	undecimal "median" seventh
15/8	1088.3	major seventh
40/21	1115.5	
64/33	1146.7	
160/81	1178.5	
2/1	1200	octave

Example 4.3 Harry Partch's 43-tone scale.

tion of Euripides's *The Bacchae*), *Delusion of the Fury* (1965–1966), and *The Dreamer that Remains* (1972, a mini-opera protesting the proliferation of "No Loitering" signs). Instrumental works, usually for dance, include *Castor and Pollux* (1952), *Daphne of the Dunes* (1958), and *And on the Seventh Day Petals Fell in Petaluma* (1963–1966). Partch's ensemble style is based in percussion, and his music is propulsively rhythmic, often dividing the beat into five quick pulsations and grouping beats into meters of five, seven, or nine.

The infectious rhythms and exotic timbres of this music are matched by its wisdom and humor. *The Bewitched* contains scene titles such as Scene 1: "Three Undergrads become Transfigured in a Hong Kong Music Hall"; Scene 4: "A Soul Tormented by Contemporary Music Finds a Humanizing Alchemy"; and Scene 9: "A Lost Political Soul Finds Himself Among the Voteless Women of Paradise." At the end of *Delusion of the Fury,* a mime opera based on the Japanese Noh theater, a deaf hobo gets in an argument with an old woman over a goat. At the trial, the superbly near-sighted judge says to the hobo (as the old woman holds the goat), "Young man, take your beautiful young wife and your charming child and go home, and never let me see you in this court again!" The chorus responds with a joyous refrain: "Oh how would we ever get by without justice!"

Like so many radical American experimentalists, Partch has often been dismissed as an amateur. He was not. His major book, *Genesis of a Music* (1949), its delightful vernacular tone notwithstanding, remains the best, most insightful one-volume history of tuning available. Many of Partch's instruments have been duplicated (the originals are at the Smithsonian Museum), and performances of his music, usually under the direction of people who performed with him, are becoming fairly common. The composer Dean Drummond, whose Newband ensemble uses Partch instruments, has commissioned new works from other composers for those instruments. The music Partch created from scratch has become a continuing tradition.

Listening Example: **Barstow**

"It's a mighty long stretch," wrote Partch, "to Needles, or to Las Vegas. . . . Barstow from the west is easy. But east it turns into a hitchhiker's bottleneck." This explains why, on the highway railing of U.S. 66 at Barstow, as he headed toward Chicago and a place to live, Partch found such (comparatively) long and elaborate hitchhiker inscriptions:

> It's January 26. I'm freezing.
> Ed Fitzgerald. Age 19. Five feet, ten inches.
> Black hair, brown eyes.
> Going home to Boston, Massachusetts.

It's 4:00, and I'm hungry and broke.
I wish I was dead.
But today I am a man.

Fascinated, Partch set eight such inscriptions to music in 1941, revising them with an expanded instrumentation in 1954. *Barstow,* a section of *The Wayward,* is scored for "Speaking and/or Singing Voice," "Chorus Voice," surrogate kithara, chromelodeon I, diamond marimba, and boo. Each inscription begins with the same introduction. That introduction is given in example 4.4, first in Partch's notation (indicating what notes to play to get the required pitches), then in Ben Johnston's microtonal notation (explained below), which, if one ignores the unfamiliar accidentals, will give an approximate idea of the pitches intended. The numbers in the Diamond Marimba part show what row to play the notes on, and one can get a sense of how physical Partch's writing is.

EXAMPLE 4.4 Harry Partch, *Barstow,* in original and transcribed notations.

Ben Johnston

Ben Johnston (b. 1926) has been a seminal compositional figure in the American Midwest, less well-known on the coasts. Most of his music, despite its wide variety of idioms, is united by its use of just intonation. Johnston is particularly important for his ten (so far) string quartets, the most thoroughgoing and beautiful exploration of that genre since Schoenberg and Bartók. Though he belongs to a later generation than the other composers in this chapter, he was for years Partch's only protégé to develop his own brand of just intonation, and his work in this area is so closely related to Partch's that they are more easily discussed side by side. In addition, although Johnston was central to the exciting scene that occupied the midwestern universities in the 1960s and 1970s, his music is not typical of that scene. He is a loner whose path lies far away from the trends of recent decades.

Born March 15, 1926, in Macon, Georgia, Johnston heard, at age 11, a lecture about Helmholtz's influence on Debussy, giving him his first taste of the acoustical truths he would pursue for the rest of his life. As early as 1944, following a recital of his compositions, an interview with Johnston in the *Richmond Times-Dispatch* referred to his view "that with the clarification of the scale which physics has given to music there will be new instruments with new tones and overtones."[5] Graduating from the College of William and Mary, Johnston attended graduate school at Cincinnati Conservatory, where, in 1949, a musicologist who knew of his interest in acoustics gave him a copy of Partch's *Genesis of a Music* hot off the press. Johnston wrote to Partch, who invited him to come live and work at his studio at Gualala. Johnston and his wife stayed for six months of 1950.

Though not handy with tools, Johnston possessed from the beginning a remarkable ear. As he later wrote, Partch

> could have wished for a carpenter or for a percussionist. . . . But he had one thing he had not counted on: someone who understood his theory without explanation, and who could hear and reproduce the pitch relations accurately.[6]

Johnston and his wife appear as performers on Partch's early recordings of his music. He wanted to study composition further, though, and Partch, who refused to teach, suggested he study at Mills with Darius Milhaud. Upon finishing his master's at Mills, Johnston was soon hired by the University of Illinois at Urbana, where he taught until his retirement in 1983.

From the outset, Johnston used tuning differently from Partch. For one thing, being neither a carpenter nor inclined to build his own instruments, he waited until 1960 to write in just intonation. (His first such piece was *Five Fragments*, a vocal piece based on texts from Thoreau.) Under Milhaud's influence he first went through a brief neoclassic phase, typified by his rather Stravinskian Septet (1956–1958). When the iconoclastic John Cage gave an inflammatory performance in Urbana at a 1952 Contemporary Arts Festival, Johnston was the only music faculty member who would talk to him afterward, and he later studied with him briefly in New York. Cagean elements such as chance and quotation appeared in Johnston's *Gambit* of 1959, along with neoclassic and jazz elements. However, he had already used a twelve-tone row in his *Etude-*

Toccata for piano of 1949, and twelve-tone technique would appear inter-mittently in his music all his life, even in his just-intonation works.

Theoretically, just intonation and twelve-tone music are diametri-cally opposed. Just intonation implies a central, tonic pitch, while twelve-tone music explodes pitch hierarchy. Johnston, however, wanted his chromaticism purely tuned and came up with several different solutions to well-tuned atonality. His *Sonata for Microtonal Piano* (1964) expressed a crisis both personal and creative. (Johnston has suffered mental health difficulties following a period spent in the cult around Gurdjieff in the early 1960s.) The work's tuning involves purely tuned fifths and triads radiating out from the center of the keyboard, a complex plan in which there are virtually no purely tuned octaves; chords within any small reg-ister will be purely consonant, but anything involving different registers is dissonant in the extreme. The *Sonata* is a complex, fragmented piece based on twelve-tone rows abstracted from pop tunes ("I'm in the Mood for Love" and "What Is this Thing Called Love?"). A later, calmer work is Johnston's *Suite for Microtonal Piano* (1978), in which the piano is tuned to the 16th, 17th, 18th, 19th, 20th, 21st, 22nd, 24th, 26th, 27th, 28th, and 30th harmonics above C. The outer movements, in the key of C, contain a strong sense of tonic. One movement is twelve-tone, however, and the remaining two are in D and E, respectively, in which the C over-tones create a strangely exotic scale.

One thing Johnston had inherited from Partch was a concern for both overtones and "undertones," the latter being the overtone series inverted; in Johnston's usage, overtones suggest a major tonality, under-tones a minor one. His rows often consist of six overtones of one pitch combined with six undertones of another, with perhaps a seventh over-tone as their common pivot note. For example, the row of his Sixth String Quartet (1980) consists of an overtone series on D and an under-tone series below D♯ (given in Johnston's notation, explained below):

	OVERTONES	UNDERTONES
1	D	D♯
3	A	G♯
5	F♯	B
7	C7+	E♯∠
9	E+	C♯
11	G7+	A♯∠

Rather than being limited to a forty-three-pitch scale like Partch's music, Johnston's works may potentially include hundreds of distinct pitches. To negotiate this sea of endless pitches, Johnston invented an elegantly specific notation of new accidentals, as follows:

+	raises a pitch 81:80, or 21 cents
–	lowers " " 80:81 or –21 cents
♯	raises " " 25:24, or 71 cents
♭	lowers " " 24:25, or –71 cents
7	lowers " " 35:36, or –49 cents
⌐	raises " " 36:35, or 49 cents
↑	raises " " 33:32, or 53 cents
↓	lowers " " 32:33, or –53 cents
13	raises " " 65:64, or 27 cents
Ɛ̣1	lowers " " 64:65, or –27 cents

and so on.

The ♯ and ♭ change major thirds into minor ones and vice versa. The 7 indicates a seventh harmonic, the ⌐ (7 upside-down) a seventh under-tone. The arrows denote either the 11th harmonic- or undertone, and the 13 a 13th over- or undertone. In addition, for consistency's sake, the major triads on F, C, and G are purely tuned, in a 4:5:6 pitch ratio:

F	A	C	E	G	B	D
16	20	24	30	36	45	54
				4	5	6
		4	5	6		
4	5	6				

Further in the circle of fifths in either direction, plus (+) and minus (-) are necessary to compensate for the syntonic comma; for example, D- to A is a perfect fifth (3:2), as is D to A+, but D to A is 40:27, a bad perfect fifth 21 cents flat. With such a system, Johnston has been able to notate any overtone of any pitch up to the 31st harmonic (which appears in his String Quartet No. 9).

In 1988, Johnston left Illinois to live in North Carolina.

Listening Example: String Quartet No. 4, "Amazing Grace"

Only part of Johnston's output is twelve-tone. Much of it is tonal, based in folk song and Southern hymnody. The extreme consonance (though in a twelve-tone context) of his Second and Third Quartets led back to tonality, and his String Quartet No. 4 (1973) was one of the first works to return to a new, non-European tonality after the years of twelve-tone hegemony. The Quartet is a set of variations on the popular hymn "Amazing Grace," in the key of G minus.

The theme is first stated sweetly in a purely tuned pentatonic (five-pitch) scale. The scale's tuning is Pythagorean, meaning that all the intervals are based on perfect 3:2 fifths: G- D- A E B. The interval G- B in this tuning is not 5:4 but 81:64, a sonority dating from the medieval era that has a rustic, folk-fiddler's quality (example 4.5). Each successive variation expands both the number of pitches used and the rhythmic complexity, treating pitch and rhythm in an analogous manner. In variation 1 the first violin states the melody using the entire G- major scale. Variation 2 adds seventh harmonics and triplet and quintuplet rhythms. Variation 3 is horrendously complex in its rhythmic notation (see example 4.6), with a rhythm of 35-against-36 running between the viola and cello and with crashing chords for all four players providing an overriding articulative pattern. The difficulty, however, is only for the performers, as the listener's ear never loses the relationship of the melody to the original theme. Variation 4 plays with the inversion of the theme as an excuse to introduce the seventh undertone.

EXAMPLE 4.5 Ben Johnston, theme from String Quartet No. 4, "Amazing Grace," in Pythagorean tuning.

(*Continued*)

EXAMPLE 4.6 Ben Johnston, String Quartet No. 4, variation 3.

+) *(cont. from previous page)* The notes so marked, like all notes not so marked, form with each other intervals available on triadic just intonation.

EXAMPLE 4.6 *(continued)*

Variation 5 is a ghostly continuum of minimalist repetitions, the quartet playing rhythms such as 7 to 8 to 9 to 10 in scale patterns derived from the ancient Greek modes Partch also used. In the middle, "Amazing Grace" can be clearly heard in cello harmonics. The passionate final variation expands the language to both major and minor microtonal scales, twenty-two pitches in all. *Amazing Grace* is one of the most difficult string quartet scores in the repertoire, yet despite its complexity, the theme is never far from the surface, and its development is emotionally satisfying even on first listening. Few works of the so-called "avant-garde" have been so warmly embraced by general audiences.

Conlon Nancarrow

Conlon Nancarrow (1912–1997) is one of the strangest cases in the entire history of music. A recluse, he lived in Mexico City from 1940 on, and the world began discovering his music only in 1977. Over three-fourths of it is written for one instrument, and that an eccentric one: the player piano, which he has used to produce the most rhythmically complex body of music ever written. Yet his roots are in jazz and blues, and his music, its complexity notwithstanding, is joyous, bracing, and thrillingly tumultuous.

Conlon Nancarrow. *Photo by Sabine Matthes.*

Nancarrow was born in 1912, in Texarkana, Arkansas. A fiery and rebellious teenager, he played trumpet and went into music against his father's wishes. He moved to Boston after an abortive period of study at Cincinnati Conservatory, and studied privately with Slonimsky, Walter Piston, and Roger Sessions.

A communist, Nancarrow went to Spain in 1937 to fight the fascists as a member of the Abraham Lincoln Brigade. Upon Nancarrow's return, he found that the U.S. government was denying passports to those with communist affiliations. He moved in 1940 to Mexico City. Just before he left, he picked up a copy of Cowell's *New Musical Resources*.

In his section on rhythm, Cowell admitted that the rhythms he notated were too complex for human performance, but suggested that a player piano could achieve them easily. In 1948, receiving a small inheritance, Nancarrow traveled to New York and bought a player piano; then located a roll-punching machine, and found an instrument maker who would build one for him to the same specifications. Long interested in complex rhythmic techniques, he let his rhythmic imagination run wild in a series of about fifty Studies for Player Piano. Study No. 1, which shows the influences of both Bartók and jazz, uses two basic tempos of 4 against 7. Study No. 3, a Blues Suite, is based on jazz riffs strung across a series of lightning-fast ostinatos. Other early Studies (Nos. 7 and 11) revived the medieval practice of isorhythm, a technique wherein a rhythm of several notes is repeated over and over, going out of phase with a repeating pitch series with a different number of notes.

Starting with Studies Nos. 14 through 19, Nancarrow revived another technique with ancient roots: the tempo canon. A tempo canon takes a line or section of material and plays it against another version of itself at a different tempo. For instance, in the greatly simplified example 4.7 (using the pitch row from Study No. 21), the higher voice moves 4:3 as fast as the lower one. Nancarrow based the early canons on the tempo ratios 4:5:6. Study No. 37 is a masterpiece, a huge twelve-voice canon. Study No. 48 is perhaps Nancarrow's magnum opus, a massive canon in three movements at a tempo ratio of 60:61. At the beginning of each movement the canonic voices are only 6 seconds apart, and the slower one catches up with an extreme gradualness that brings a fantastic tension to the final climax.

EXAMPLE 4.7 Tempo canon technique.

The tremendous variety of form in Nancarrow's Studies comes partly from the deployment of convergence points, whose placement is as structurally inventive as that of the cadences in the Beethoven sonatas. The most famous convergence point is that of Study No. 36, in which the voices ripple on a diminishing series of chromatic runs before plunging down the keyboard (see example 4.8).

EXAMPLE 4.8 Conlon Nancarrow, Study #36, climax.

(Continued)

Yet another device Nancarrow experimented with is perfectly gradual acceleration. Studies Nos. 21, 22, 23, 25, 27, 28, and 29 explore every possible permutation: acceleration against a steady beat, deceleration against a steady beat, acceleration and deceleration at the same time, all three at once. Study No. 21 is subtitled "Canon X" because as one voice gradually speeds up, the other, playing the same notes (transposed), slows down.

Peter Garland began publishing Nancarrow's scores in his *Soundings* journal in 1977, the same year Charles Amirkhanian began making them available on record. Aside from his fifty-odd player piano studies, Nancarrow wrote a handful of works for human players in the 1930s and 1940s, and wrote a few more in the eighties after performers began expressing interest in his work. After decades of isolation, Nancarrow became much in demand for festivals in Europe and the West Coast after receiving the MacArthur "genius" award in 1983.

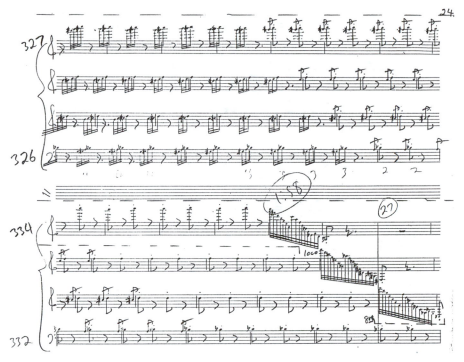

EXAMPLE 4.8 *(continued)*

Listening Example: Study #25

Study No. 25, written sometime in the late 1950s (Nancarrow has never dated his Studies), is one of his most popular works. This is the Study in which he first discovered how to write idiomatically for the player piano.

Though many of the studies contain thousands of notes each, making them seem like huge, substantial works, only seven of them run over seven minutes. No. 25 lasts under six minutes, yet is divided into eight sections:

> Section 1: Glissandos and arpeggios, ripping by at about 175 notes per second, are laid over a single line, then over a series of chords. One remarkable eighty-five-note figure (at 0:37, shown in example 4.9) alternates glissandos in both directions at once.

> Section 2: This section contains three layers. The first to appear is a feathery series of four-note arpeggios marking a steady beat. Above it floats a series of longer arpeggios, sustained rather than staccato.

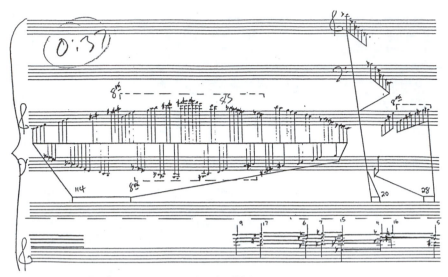

EXAMPLE 4.9 Conlon Nancarrow, Study #25.

Section 3: Next comes a rhythm canon at a tempo ratio of 7 against 10, but while one voice is a series of widely-spaced ten-note chords, the slower is a series of down-up arpeggios.

Section 4: The next part is a tempo canon at ratio 21:25. Each voice of the canon actually consists of two contrapuntal lines.

Section 5: Use of the sustaining pedal is very rare in Nancarrow's canons, but here he uses it to let ring the notes of complex glissando and arpeggio patterns. Each is cut off by a big seven-note chord.

Section 6: Section 6 returns to the feathery arpeggios of section 2, superimposing four layers of them in a tempo canon.

Section 7: The texture here consists of two layers, one of seven-note chords (grouped in phrases with the last chord staccato), and one of arpeggios. Halfway through, an acceleration canon begins, with the chords accelerating twice as fast as the arpeggios.

Section 8: The final explosion is a maelstrom of figures, 1,028 notes within 12 seconds (88 per second), blurred into a swirl of noise by the sustaining pedal. There is nothing analyzable about this arpeggiated cacophony: major triad arpeggios, scales, broken octaves, sudden leaps in register, twistings and turnings of key, every quick note figuration used up until now combined in one blitzkrieg climax.

Study No. 25, incidentally, is Nancarrow's only work to use a twelve-tone row, which governs the succession of harmonies throughout. (He frequently used rows of more than thirty notes.) Nancarrow claims he never met Schoenberg, whose year in Boston coincided with Nancarrow's stay there, but Nancarrow's first wife remembers them attending a party at Schoenberg's apartment. Otherwise, this is one of Nancarrow's freest studies in terms of technical controls, a chaotic climax to his middle period. In the way it brings together, for the first time, all the techniques he had used in previous studies—isorhythm, canon, acceleration—it anticipates his great, massive Studies of the 1970s and '80s, Nos. 40, 41, 45, 47, and 48.

Lou Harrison

Composers born on the West Coast have often felt less compelled to follow European models than their East Coast colleagues. Cowell, growing up, heard more Chinese, Japanese, and Indian music than European, and never became conversant with the European repertoire. Partch felt free to throw the entire baggage of European culture overboard. Lou Harrison (b. May 14, 1917) came from Portland, Oregon, and he, too, more often looked to Asia than to Europe for his inspiration. While Colin McPhee was the first to transcribe Balinese gamelan patterns for the European orchestra, Harrison has become the leading American composer for the Balinese gamelan itself.

Harrison studied with Cowell in 1934–1935, and also with Schoenberg in Los Angeles. In the forties he worked as a florist, a records clerk, a dancer, a dance critic, and a music copyist (his elegant calligraphy is famous), and he also organized, with John Cage, some of the first concerts of percussion music. He also became close to Ives, deciphered several of Ives's illegible pencil scores, edited the score of Ives's Third Symphony, and conducted its world premiere with the New York Little Symphony in 1946. Ives showed his gratitude by assigning the royalties of some of his works to Harrison; these eventually amounted to a significant financial help. At last Harrison found a niche as a music critic, and, under Virgil Thomson's patronage, wrote reviews for the *New York Herald-Tribune* in 1945–1948. He subsequently suffered a nervous breakdown, but thereafter held several teaching positions, at Black Mountain College (1951–1952), San Jose State University (1967–1980), and Mills College (1980–1985).

A prolific composer of exceptional versatility, Harrison has written in many styles, partly because his work as a composer for dance in the forties required diverse techniques. Some of his early music has the craggy ferocity and dissonance of Ives's piano music. His *Symphony on G* (1948–1961) is largely written in twelve-tone technique, though with G as a consistently central note, and uses a subsidiary ensemble of piano, harp, and tack piano, an instrument he invented by placing tacks in the hammers of a piano for a Nancarrovian, brittle sound. Harrison is a staunch advocate of the invented language Esperanto, using it for many of his titles and texts. His *Koncherto por la Violono Kun Perkuta Orkestra*—"concerto for violin with percussion orchestra" (1940)—includes flower pots, wind bells, brake drums, coffee cans, and washtubs in its ensemble. The violin part exhibits an interesting technique, an alternative to the twelve-tone system, of using only three possible intervals: a minor second, a major third, and a major sixth. Dance forms of the Middle Ages and Renaissance appear in Harrison's music; the String Quartet Set (1978–1979) and Piano Concerto (1985) each contain a medieval dance, the *estampie.*

When he writes for European orchestra, Harrison says, his model is Brahms; one can hear echoes of the Brahms D-minor Piano Concerto in the dramatic opening trills of Harrison's own Piano Concerto. In studying Balinese music, however, (and also Korean court music, which he did in Korea in 1961–1962), Harrison became interested in pure tunings; his Piano Concerto is written for a keyboard tuned eighteenth-century style, with pure perfect fifths on the black keys and sweeter major thirds on the white keys. Some of his music for Western instruments uses Balinese tuning, such as the *Concerto in Slendro* (1961) for violin, tack pianos, celesta, and percussion, which uses the Balinese *slendro* scale (requiring a retuned celesta). Beginning in 1972, he collaborated with William Colvig on building the bronze and wood metallophones (something like oversized xylophones) and nipple gongs of the Balinese gamelan; they created the gamelan si darius (named after French composer Darius Milhaud) at Mills College. Several of his works combine a Western solo instrument with gamelan, such as the *Double Concerto for Violin and Cello with Javanese Gamelan* (1981–1982). *La Koro Sutro* (1972) is an ecstatic 100-voice choral setting, with gamelan, harp, and organ, of the *Heart Sutra* from the Buddhist scriptures, translated into Esperanto.

Harrison's style ranges from the high Romanticism of the *Symphony on G* and Piano Concerto to the folklike joie de vivre of his chamber music to the imperturbable stasis of his percussion and gamelan works. His larger works (for example *Symphony on G* and Symphony No. 4, "Last") sometimes threaten to become disunified because of the extreme heterogeneity of ensembles used from movement to movement. But all of his music is marked by accessibility, humor, and inspired experimentation.

Henry Brant

Henry Brant (b. 1913), a visionary of Ivesian imagination, is the leading pioneer of spatial music, music played by ensembles separated by wide distances. If he remains a rather obscure name, it is only because his

Henry Brant.

music, for huge ensembles placed at wide distances, is so difficult to organize and record that few have a chance to experience it.

Born September 15, 1913, in Montreal, Brant moved with his family to New York in 1929. Though he studied at the Institute of Musical
Art (later renamed Juilliard), his primary composition teaching came
from private lessons with Riegger and Antheil, and he also learned conducting from Gustav Mahler's nephew, Fritz Mahler. He received considerable practical experience writing popular music for radio and films,
which imparted fluency to his compositional technique. He later taught
at Columbia University from 1945 to 1952, at Juilliard 1947–1954, and
at Bennington 1957–1982.

From the beginning, Brant demonstrated an unusual sensitivity to acoustic sound. His early works use nonmusical objects to create sound; for example, *Music for a Five and Dime* (1932), scored for E-flat clarinet, piano, and kitchen hardware. *The Marx Brothers* (1938, three portraits titled "Chico," "Groucho," and "Harpo") accompanies Brant's own instrument, the tin whistle, with chamber ensemble. In 1938 he had an opportunity to perform with Partch's ensemble. Accordingly, Partch included tin whistle and double flageolet, instruments Brant could play, in his *Yankee Doodle Fantasy.*

Brant has frequently written for multiples of one instrument, and when he does so, he tries to vary the range in size smoothly; thus, his delightful 1931 flute concerto, *Angels and Devils*, uses as its orchestra three piccolos, five normal flutes, and two alto flutes. Despite such monolithic instrumental groups, heterogeneity and contrast are the keys to Brant's style. He turned to spatial music because of the perceptual problems of trying to hear so many contrapuntal lines at once. As he later said,

> I tried writing eight or ten simultaneous, contrasted, contrapuntal lines, still in bars or with the musicians all placed together, as usual. I found that I was running into trouble: The musicians could play the notes all right, but you really couldn't identify the details in the compound result. . . . But there didn't seem to be a necessary reason why music should be limited to even twelve horizontal events at once. Why not more than twelve? The ear never said, "I refuse to listen."[7]

Looking for an answer, he studied Ives's *The Unanswered Question* and found that Ives had solved his contrapuntal problems by widely separating the performing groups. (Brant's long-lined, dissonant conception of melody was also influenced by Ruggles.) In 1953, Brant wrote *Rural Antiphonies*, his first antiphonal (spatial) composition. Pointing out that "all music is spatial music," Brant insists that the physical position of the players is an unavoidable compositional decision. "Spatial separation is essentially a contrapuntal device," he says. "It makes counterpoint more distinct."[8]

His *Orbits* (1979) is scored for eighty trombones (including not only tenor and bass trombones but the much rarer soprano, alto, and contrabass kind), organ, and "sopranino" voice. The piece uses quarter tones, common in Brant's music, and the trombones sometimes play eighty different lines, creating eighty-note chords with clusters of twenty-four pitches per octave. *Fire on the Amstel* uses four boatloads of twenty-five flutes each, four jazz drummers, four church carillons, three brass bands, three choruses, and four street organs. Brant's performances, which often take place outside from necessity, sometimes run up against irrevocable forces. In 1972 his *The Immortal Combat* for different instrumental groups, performed on the outdoor plazas and balconies of Lincoln

Center, was totally drowned out by traffic noise, a fountain, and a thunderstorm. A 1992 performance of *500: Hidden Hemisphere,* written for the Columbus quincentennial, combined three military bands and steel band outside Lincoln Center with much better results. Nevertheless, Brant has worked to develop acoustic instruments with the power of tugboat whistles, loud enough to drown out even an urban environment.

The ultimate generalist, Brant envisions musical universes even vaster than Ives's, incorporating music of different national styles. His *Meteor Farm* (1982) combines orchestra, jazz band, Indonesian gamelan ensemble, African drummers, and Indian soloists. One of his pet projects of recent years is a concert hall with movable plywood walls, which can be moved during a performance to make the acoustics of the room one of the changing components of the composition; in his *Voyage 4* of 1963, performers occupy not only the floor but the vertical wall space as well.

Brant's legacy has been carried on in New York by Wendy Mae Chambers (b. 1953), who has written a Mass for seventy-seven trombones, *Ten Grand* (1983) for ten grand pianos and laser lights, *The Grand Harp Event* (1984) for thirty harps, *Marimba!* (1986) for twenty-six marimbas, and *Music for Choreographed Rowboats* (1979) for twenty-three musicians in rowboats. In her *Symphony of the Universe* (1989) for choir, organ, jazz band, digital tape, and 100 timpani, rhythmic motives rip up and down the entire length of a cathedral with tremendous effect.

Alan Hovhaness

Like McPhee and Harrison, Alan Hovhaness (born March 8, 1911, in Somerville, Massachusetts) is one of the Americans who took his inspiration from cultures other than that of Western Europe. He is also one of the most prolific of American composers, with more than 400 compositions to his credit, including more than sixty symphonies. His music—simple, melodic, and inspired by ancient church hymns—is pervaded by an air of mysticism. It went utterly against the flow of the complexity of forties and fifties music but gained considerable audience following.

Hovhaness's interest in mysticism was evident early in life. He studied with Frederick Converse at New England Conservatory in the early thirties and with Bohuslav Martinů at Tanglewood. In 1936 he discovered Indian music, when several Indian virtuosi performed in Boston. Under the criticism of Bernstein and Copland at Tanglewood, Hovhaness destroyed many of his early works, which had been influenced by Renaissance music, and studied the music of his ancestral Armenian heritage. Lou Harrison was present at the New York premiere of Hovhaness's *Lousadzak* (1945), a piano concerto. Harrison's recollection provides a vivid snapshot of the American scene of the 1940s:

The intermission that followed was the closest I've ever been to one of those renowned artistic riots. In the lobby, the Chromaticists and the Americanists were carrying on at high decibels. What had touched it off, of course, was the fact that here was a man from Boston whose obviously beautiful and fine music had nothing to do with either camp and was in fact its own very wonderful thing to begin with. My guest John Cage and I were very excited, and I dashed off to the lamented *Herald Tribune* [lamented because by the time Harrison was speaking the paper had ceased to exist] and wrote a rave review while John went back to the Green Room to meet Alan.[9]

In 1959 Hovhaness traveled to India and Japan on a Fulbright fellowship, collecting folk songs for future use. He became the first Western composer invited to participate in the music festival at Madras, where he played his *Madras Sonata* for piano.

Hovhaness developed a style of modal, exotically inflected melody, with an impressionistically static harmony sometimes colored with ultramodernist touches such as tone clusters. In some works (for example, Symphony No. 46, *To the Green Mountains,* of 1980) performers in an ensemble play at independent, unsynchronized speeds. Of his sixty-plus symphonies, the Second, subtitled *Magic Mountain* (1955), became quite popular, at least in part for its vigorous double fugue in the second movement, also because it was championed by conductor Fritz Reiner. Further celebrity came with *And God Created Great Whales* (1969), an orchestral essay that included the taped songs of humpback whales. As one would expect of so prolific an output, Hovhaness's music varies considerably in quality, though the amount of work he's destroyed shows that he does not lack self-criticism. The best of his music, however, is deeply inspired and rooted in ancient traditions, with a deliberate naïveté propelled by an ecumenical spirituality.

Notes

1. Barbara Tischler, *An American Music* (Oxford and New York: Oxford University Press, 1986), pp. 74 and 85.
2. Carol Oja, *Colin McPhee: Composer in Two Worlds* (Washington and London: Smithsonian Institution Press, 1990), p. 176.
3. Harry Partch in *The Dreamer that Remains* (Eugene, Ore.: New Dimension Media, 1974).
4. Harry Partch, *Bitter Music: Collected Journals, Essays, Introductions, and Librettos,* Thomas McGreary, ed. (Urbana and Chicago: University of Illinois Press, 1991), p. xix.
5. Heidi von Gunden, *The Music of Ben Johnston* (Metuchen, N.J., and London: Scarecrow Press, Inc., 1986), p. 5.

6. Ibid., pp. 11-12.
7. Cole Gagne and Tracy Caras, *Soundpieces: Interviews with American Composers* (Metuchen, N.J., and London: Scarecrow Press, 1982), p. 57.
8. Ibid., p. 60.
9. Quoted in liner notes, *Mysterious Mountain,* Music Masters MMD 60204.

CHAPTER 5

Atonality and European Influence

The nadir of the American Depression was 1933, the year Roosevelt took office and had to close the banks, the year the only thing we had to fear was fear itself. In Germany, on January 30, Adolf Hitler was named chancellor. On March 1, the Nazis declared their intention to remove Jews from all university posts. The Jewish composition teacher of the Prussian Academy of the Arts, Arnold Schoenberg, fled Berlin in May, and arrived in New York on October 31. He taught at Boston's Malkin Conservatory for one miserable year (his health unequal to the New England weather), then moved to Hollywood. By 1935 he had obtained a position at the University of California at Los Angeles, where he would teach until 1944. He died in Los Angeles in 1951.

European artists scattered. Igor Stravinsky began touring America in 1937 and applied for American citizenship in 1939. Stravinsky also lived in Los Angeles (he and Schoenberg met only once, at a mutual friend's funeral), and moved to New York shortly before his death. Paul Hindemith, denounced by the Nazis as a "cultural Bolshevik," emigrated to America in 1940 and taught at Yale from 1940 to 1953. Béla Bartók moved to New York in 1940.

This means that, within a seven-year period, the world's four most famous composers all abandoned Europe to converge on the United States. From 1940 to 1945, all four lived here. Schoenberg's presence extended to 1951, Hindemith's to 1961, and Stravinsky's until 1971. (This does not even take into account many slightly less important émigrés, such as Kurt Weill and Ernst Krenek.) American classical music had always exhibited a strong bias toward European composers, but until the 1930s, those composers lived far away. Now, they were suddenly among us, and the complexion of American music altered tremendously. As Milton Babbitt put it in 1975,

> It was not merely that we could learn from the Schoenbergs and the
> Hindemiths and the Bartóks; it was that suddenly we were no longer
> in any sense irrelevantly awed by them. We suddenly realized they
> had their failings.[1]

This attitude can be contrasted with that of Ives, Cowell, and Partch, who
felt no such awe of Europeans in the first place.

If the twenties were a decade of carefree avant-gardism and the
thirties one of social responsibility and reaching out to the masses, the
postwar years were a period of absorption of Continental aesthetics. The
composers covered in this chapter felt, as Edward T. Cone (b. 1917) put
it, "that the American past is the European past and that the foundation
provided by the great line [meaning Beethoven, Brahms, and so on] is
basic to the development of music in the United States as well as
Europe."[2] At first, that absorption had to do with Stravinsky's neoclassicism. But soon the only important issue would be twelve-tone technique.

The twelve-tone method is a method of composing that relates the
twelve pitches of the equal-tempered chromatic scale to a basic twelve-
tone *row* rather than to a single tonic *pitch*. The row is an ordering of the
twelve pitches. In general theory, every pitch relationship in a work is to
be derived from the row, which can be transposed, reversed, or inverted
(so that ascending intervals now descend the same amount). In *serial*
music, the row concept is further extended to include other aspects of
sound besides pitch.

Use of twelve-tone method is flexible, and composers vary widely
in how they apply the principle. Most simply, some use a melody containing all twelve pitches with little or no duplication, as Wallingford
Riegger does in his Concerto for Piano with Wind Quintet (1953) (example 5.1). Others, like Roger Sessions, are less intent on the order of the
row but instead use it as a means of partitioning the chromatic scale.
Milton Babbitt uses it as the field for a background structure articulated
by register, tone color, and dynamics.

It became a cliché in the 1950s to classify twelve-tone composers
according to how "lyrical" their music was. Thus, music that relied more
on stepwise melodic motion was on the "lyrical" side, closer to the music
of Schoenberg's popular student Alban Berg than to that of his other student Anton Webern. Ben Weber and most of Sessions's music fit this

EXAMPLE 5.1 Wallingford Riegger, row from Concerto for Piano with Wind
Quintet.

characterization. Babbitt's music represents the opposite extreme in which notes are registrally scattered. Still other composers (Copland in his Piano Quartet, for example) use a row within a freely atonal texture and some (Carter and Perle) develop their own structuralist pitch systems analogous to but different from twelve-tone method.

In July of 1921, after crafting his first twelve-tone row, Schoenberg had written, "Today I have discovered something which will ensure the supremacy of German music for the next hundred years." By the late 1950s, Schoenberg's claim had come to seem prophetic, for from that point twelve-tone music dominated what was "acceptably modernistic" in American music for a full quarter-century. Sessions and Copland, both Stravinskyites, both turned to twelve-tone writing in the early fifties, as did Stravinsky himself, sounding the death knell for neoclassicism. The dichotomy between Stravinsky and Schoenberg had been that between musical image and musical language, between irreducible sonic inspirations and the search for a note-to-note intelligible syntax. Later in the century, in the 1980s, composers would swing back toward Stravinsky and toward image, partly through the influence of Morton Feldman. But for the composers discussed in this chapter, the quest was to inherit and perfect a musical language.

The postwar years also brought about a 180-degree shift in the way composers were expected to make a living. With millions of veterans returning to college, enrollments began to swell. Professors were greatly in demand, advanced degrees not always necessary. Before World War II, a full-time university position was considered an eccentric livelihood for a composer. By the mid-sixties, it became the expected career path. Ultimately, this trend reinforced the turn toward twelve-tone music. At first, universities put up a horrified resistance to twelve-tone technique, calling it mathematics rather than music. But, once inside the door, the twelve-tone composers found their work so well-suited for classroom explication that the university became their haven. Given the dearth of major performance opportunities and critical discussion of new music, American composers who teach often depend on their students for the dissemination of their work and reputation.

The Neoclassicists

America's neoclassic movement, the wing that followed Stravinsky rather than Schoenberg, had a short-lived success, its achievements all but obliterated by the hegemony of twelve-tone music after 1955. Although many Americans had been propelled into musical careers by the centrifugal force of *Le Sacre,* around 1922 Stravinsky abandoned the asymmetric rhythmic ferocity of his early music and began reinterpreting the formal articulations of eighteenth-century music, in works such as *Pulcinella,*

Capriccio, Symphony in Three Movements, and *Oedipus Rex.* Following this new phase, the neoclassicists tended to write nonprogrammatic music in the abstract, traditional forms of the Baroque and Classical eras: symphony, serenade, sonata, partita, divertimento, wind quintet, string quartet, concerto. As opposed to twelve-tone music's chromatic atonality, their music represented the diatonic tonality of the 1940s and 1950s, a tonality not rooted in folksy American tunes like Copland's and Harris's, but impersonal, rhythmically straightforward, and highly contrapuntal. The movement was associated not only with Stravinsky and Boulanger, but with New England and Harvard's composition professor, Walter Piston.

The composer who, more than any other, came to symbolize America's hard-core neoclassic movement with its devotion to Stravinsky was Harold Shapero (b. 1920 in Lynn, Massachusetts). Though he had studied with Slonimsky, Krenek, and Piston, and would soon work with Hindemith and Boulanger, Shapero fell under the spell of Stravinsky when the latter was Harvard's Norton Professor in 1939–1940, delivering the lectures later collected in *The Poetics of Music.* Copland, writing in the *New York Times Magazine* in 1949, called Shapero's subsequent music "baffling," describing it in terms that could have applied to the neoclassicists in general:

> Stylistically, Shapero seems to feel a compulsion to fashion his music after some great model. Thus his five-movement Serenade for string orchestra . . . is founded upon neoclassic Stravinskian principles, his *Three Amateur Piano Sonatas* on Haydnesque principles, and his recent long symphony is modeled after Beethoven. For the present he seems to be suffering from a hero-worship complex.[3]

Shapero's magnum opus, his *Symphony for Classical Orchestra* (1947), does end in a finale of Beethovenian bombast, and has been revived in recent years with considerable success. A pianist and conductor, Shapero taught at Brandeis from 1952 on. Another neoclassicist on the Brandeis faculty was Irving Fine (1914–1962), who studied with Piston and Boulanger. Not prolific, he wrote a Symphony, a Violin Sonata, a String Quartet, and some choruses for *Alice in Wonderland.*

Quincy Porter (1897–1966, born in New Haven to a family of Yale professors) studied with Horatio Parker and David Stanley Smith, in Paris with d'Indy, and back in America with Bloch. Porter's most important works include his ten string quartets, *Concerto Concertante* for two pianos and orchestra (1952–1953), *New England Episodes* for orchestra (1958), and Harpsichord Concerto (1959). The return of the harpsichord after a 150-year hiatus is a dead giveaway of neoclassic concerns, and Porter's charming concerto alludes to Baroque textures not only in its choice of solo instrument but its melodic ornamentations as well. A violist, Porter became dean of the New England Conservatory in 1938, then taught at Yale from 1946 to 1965. That he was as much neoromantic as neoclassic is made clear by the Brahms quotations in his lovely "Elegiac" Oboe Quintet of 1966.

In fact, as a descriptive category, neoclassicism is forced to cover a wide range. If one generalizes it to extend to the filling of classical forms with new materials, then Walter Piston, Vivian Fine, and Vincent Persichetti must be included, even though their works are lyrically romantic and emotively expansive, devoid of Stravinsky's ironic emphasis on rhythmic surprise. Piston (1894–1976) studied with Boulanger and Dukas in Paris and became the leading compositional figure at Harvard from 1926 to 1960. His music is almost all instrumental, including eight symphonies and five string quartets, and almost all in abstract, classical forms; although one programmatic ballet, *The Incredible Flutist* (1938), remained his most popular work for decades. While he never joined the Americanists in quoting folk tunes, his music is melodic and highly accessible, yet also dedicated to New England ideals of polished polyphony. In 1965, he, too, gave up fighting the spirit of the times and turned to twelve-tone composition.

Vivian Fine (b. 1913) was Ruth Crawford's most notable student and also studied with Cowell and Sessions. Her compositions are classical as to form and romantic as to feeling. She taught at Bennington from 1964 to 1987. Persichetti, who taught at Juilliard from 1947 on, is an extremely versatile composer whose facility in modern styles is evident in his influential book *Twentieth-Century Harmony,* a virtual catalogue of every possible harmonic tendency. Though his music is romantic in feeling and stylistically difficult to pin down, his devotion to classical forms is evident in the genres of his output: he wrote nine symphonies, twelve piano sonatas, six piano sonatinas, eight harpsichord sonatas, and fourteen serenades.

Roger Sessions

Once considered a European composer by Americans and an American by Europeans, Roger Sessions (1896–1985) consciously grafted his own music onto the European tradition. In youth he was a follower of Stravinsky; as his style developed, though, he gravitated naturally toward twelve-tone technique and wrote his first twelve-tone works in nearly the same year as Stravinsky's own conversion to dodecaphony (1951).

Born December 28, 1896, in Brooklyn—on the same street, in fact, as Aaron Copland—Sessions came from a musical and literary family. After entering Harvard at fourteen, Sessions transferred to Yale, where, like Ives, he studied with Horatio Parker. He would have studied in Europe had not World War I been raging at the time. Instead, he worked privately with the Swiss émigré Ernest Bloch, who became his most important musical contact. When Bloch took a job as director of the Cleveland Institute of Music, Sessions followed him there.

While in Cleveland Sessions wrote his first major work, which would remain his most popular for several decades: *The Black Maskers,* incidental music written in 1923 and arranged into an orchestral suite in 1928.

In 1924, with his father footing the bill, Sessions and his wife began a stay in Europe—Paris, London, Geneva, Florence, Berlin, Rome—that would occupy most of the succeeding eight years. A 1931 grant brought him to Berlin; his recognition of the growing Nazi menace hastened his return to the United States, where he resumed his teaching career. His sixty-year pedagogic career included positions at Smith College, Cleveland Institute of Music, Boston University, Princeton, Berkeley, Harvard (for the Norton Lectures), and Juilliard.

Sessions had no qualms about drawing his techniques from the European masters, saying, "I have no sympathy with consciously sought originality."[4] His music after *The Black Maskers* leaned closer to the chromatic, contrapuntal idiom of Berg or Schoenberg. Sessions disagreed with a common perception that one had to choose between tonal and atonal composition. "The borderline between tonality and atonality," he once said, "is a very, very wide one. You don't step over the threshold from one to another. You have to go down a long, long, long corridor."[5] Sessions made the transition so gradually that there is no break in style, nor does the music sound twelve-tone in the sense that all twelve pitches are constantly in use. A lovely example is the *Andante* from the Third Symphony (1957). A twelve-tone row floats languidly in the clarinet while other lines derived from it are slowly built up in the harp and horns (see example 5.2).

Sessions's orchestral style is easily characterized. The most noticeable element is soaring melodies in the violins, accompanied by closely spaced counterpoint in the woodwinds and brass, with climaxes punctuated by drums and mallet percussion. A slow, painstaking composer, he was sometimes unable to finish a work by a concert deadline. Composition of his Violin Concerto required the years 1930–1935, his opera *Montezuma* took from 1947 to 1963; the latter has never been a critical success. Such slowness delayed the rise of his reputation, which did not fully begin until the fifties, with the appearance of his Third through Ninth Symphonies, and later his orchestral Rhapsody (1970) and Concerto (1979–1981), and his cantata after Whitman, *When Lilacs Last in the Dooryard Bloom'd* (1964–1970).

Listening Example: Piano Sonata No. 3

Sessions's music is easier to approach than that of many later twelve-tone composers because his compositional building block always remained, not the individual note or interval, but the gesture. Few of his works demonstrate this principle so concisely as the Third Piano Sonata (1965). The work's three movements reverse the usual fast–slow–fast classical

EXAMPLE 5.2 Roger Sessions, Symphony No. 3, third movement.

pattern; the outer movements are relatively subdued, while the second is a violent "scherzo." The third movement was written as an elegy for John F. Kennedy.

Typical of the Sonata is its continual, and changing, division of the twelve pitches of the scale into four trichords (three-note chords). This process is visible at the beginning (example 5.3). The top line of these opening chords—A-flat, G-flat, F-flat—spells out a mi–re–do motive which will become more important in the third movement. The exposition of this movement moves slowly through groups of sonorities back to

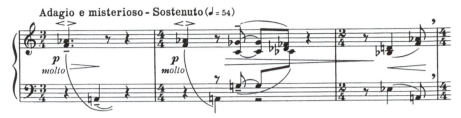

EXAMPLE 5.3 Roger Sessions, Sonata No. 3, opening.

a transposed version of the first. Then, after a pause, a development follows (example 5.4). The development's violence gradually focuses on intense streams of midregister clusters. The recapitulation then enters *subito piano* (suddenly quiet), leading to an ending that almost states the opening backwards (example 5.5).

EXAMPLE 5.4 Roger Sessions, Sonata No. 3, first movement, development.

EXAMPLE 5.5 Roger Sessions, Sonata No. 3, end of first movement.

The second movement is a violent rondo; the Schoenbergian opening theme recurs no fewer than five times, though in a sense its intervals are always present. A quieter center section, *piu tranquillo*, restates the theme in a favorite Sessions texture, as a wide-ranging melody over a set of recurring bass sonorities (example 5.6). The third movement opens with the melody that came to Sessions upon hearing of Kennedy's death (example 5.7). The mi–re–do motive and its inversion/retrograde per-

15320-32

EXAMPLE 5.6 Roger Sessions, Sonata No. 3, second movement.

EXAMPLE 5.7 Roger Sessions, Sonata No. 3, opening of third movement.

vade the texture, and the movement dies away to end on the same pitches that began the entire piece.

Stefan Wolpe

Though born in Berlin, Stefan Wolpe (1902–1972) wrote the works for which he is best known in the United States. He was not a twelve-tone composer; when he did use a serial row it was likely to have more than twelve notes (as in the Passacaglia of 1936, with its twenty-two-note row). Instead, he developed a playful idiom which contrasted sets of pitches in fluid and surprising textures.

Wolpe's life divides into three stylistic periods, corresponding to geographical location. He started out, in Berlin, as a composer of Hindemithian *Gebrauchsmusik* and theater music, but of explicit political sympathies. His music of this period is dissonantly tonal, and densely textured. The ascension of the Nazis drove him to Vienna, where he studied with Webern (1933–1934), and to Palestine the following year. In Palestine his music began to absorb Hebrew influences and a more exotic tonality. His *Ten Songs from the Hebrew* (1936–1939) is more texturally fluid than the music of his German period and remarkable for its individualistically ambiguous tonalities.

In 1938 he moved to New York, and thereafter he lived in Greenwich Village except for a four-year stint at Black Mountain College (1952–1956). Here his style underwent another drastic change. The tight, spare, atonal works of his American period give the impression of Webernesque pointillism freed from the twelve-tone row to pursue unpredictable asymmetry. He headed the music department at C. W. Post College of Long Island University from 1957 to 1968, but he developed Parkinson's disease in the mid-sixties. His motor abilities degenerated, and by decade's end his writing was an illegible scrawl.

The early masterpiece of Wolpe's American period was *Enactments,* a massive, densely pointillistic work for three pianos that sounds like the aural analogue of a late Jackson Pollock canvas. Such late works as *Form* (1959) and *Form IV: Broken Sequences* (1969) for piano, the Trio for flute, cello, and piano (1964), *Piece for Two Instrumental Units* (1962–1963), the String Quartet (1969), and *Piece for Trumpet and 7 Instruments* (1971) illustrate Wolpe's method of moving from one field of pitches to another, sometimes gradually, sometimes suddenly, always with vivid imagination.

Listening Example: Form

Wolpe's *Form* (1959) is a tiny, three-minute masterpiece, a perfect example of his pitch-set contrasts in miniature crystalline clarity. The piece divides the twelve pitches of the scale into two hexachords (sets of six pitches each). The first is blankly stated in the first six quarter notes: A♭, F, B♭, A, G, E. Immediately, those pitches are transformed into brittle, arrhythmic configurations for three and a half measures, until suddenly the other six pitches—F♯, C, D, C♯, E♭, B take over (example 5.8). For the rest of the

EXAMPLE 5.8 Stefan Wolpe, *Form,* opening.

piece, Wolpe fixates on one or another of these pitch areas (or transpositions of them), articulating the same pitches in myriad rearrangements (example 5.9). It is reported that Wolpe enjoyed watching fish in an aquarium to get his inspirations, which helps explain why his notes shimmer, freeze, then dart in a new direction with such spontaneity.

EXAMPLE 5.9 Stefan Wolpe, *Form.*

Elliott Carter

Starting out in neoclassicism and ending up in atonality, Carter has had a musical career parallel to that of Sessions, but with significant differences. Carter wrote many more neoclassic works than Sessions; and although he abandoned neoclassicism, Carter never turned to twelve-tone technique. Another difference is that Carter's emphasis has long been on rhythm, tempo contrasts, and dramatic characterization, concerns very different from Sessions' pitch-centered European musicality.

Born December 11, 1908, in New York, Carter studied at the Horace Mann School with Clifton Furness, who, as luck would have it, was one of the handful of people who had realized the importance of, and were in touch with, the reclusive Charles Ives. Furness introduced Carter to Ives in 1924, and Carter helped decipher several of Ives's messy pencil manuscripts. The two were frequently in touch until 1932, and Ives wrote Carter a recommendation to Harvard.

Then, in 1932, Carter went to Paris and studied with Boulanger, who offered an aesthetic outlook very different from that of the circle around Ives. His early ballets *Pocahontas* (1936–1939) and *The Minotaur* (1947) are neoclassical, suggesting Milhaud, Hindemith, or Prokofiev. It perhaps shows how much Europe had pushed Carter toward neoclassic

Elliott Carter, shown with Pierre Boulez. *Courtesy BMI Archives.*

concerns for logic and formal clarity that, in a 1939 review, he excoriated Ives's *Concord Sonata* upon its premiere by Kirkpatrick:

> In form and aesthetic it is basically conventional, not unlike the Liszt Sonata, full of the paraphernalia of the overdressy sonata school. . . . Behind all this confused texture there is a lack of logic which repeated hearings can never clarify. . . . The esthetic is naive, often too naive to express serious thoughts, frequently depending on quotation of well-known American tunes, with little comment, possibly charming, but certainly trivial.[6]

In addition, Carter abused his earlier friendship with Ives by suggesting that the latter added dissonances to his scores decades after they had been written in order to make them sound more up-to-date. The charge has since been refuted by musicologists specializing in Ives's manuscripts.

In 1948 Carter began composing the work that marks the beginning of his mature musical personality: the Sonata for Cello and Piano. In this work, for the first time, Carter tackled the problem of creating a drama of two instruments as two different personalities. He achieved this most interestingly through rhythmic means; for example, in the first movement, keeping a steady, metronomic beat in the piano, against which the cello plays a rhapsodic, accelerating and decelerating line. Carter's most celebrated rhythmic device has become known as metric modulation, or tempo modulation. By analogy with harmonic modulation from one key to another, metric modulation shifts from one tempo to another via a notatable rhythmic ratio. One of the clearest and most effective such shifts is found in a passage from the Cello Sonata (example 5.10), in which the

EXAMPLE 5.10 Elliott Carter, Sonata for Cello and Piano, metric modulation.

dotted sixteenth-note of the old tempo becomes the eighth-note of the new tempo.

Nancarrow met Carter in New York in 1948 and soon after sent him the score of his Rhythm Study No. 1; it spurred Carter's interest in textures in which several tempos run at the same time. Carter wrote his String Quartet No. 1 in 1951. In the opening measures, the cello plays four equal beats per bar, the viola six, the second violin $3\frac{1}{5}$, and the first violin $\frac{1}{5}$, for a total tempo resultant of 10:15:8:3. Such tempo contrasts continue throughout the work. As an homage to the composers who preceded him in such explorations, Carter quotes Ives's Violin Sonata No. 1 in the cello in the first movement, and the Nancarrow Study No. 1 in the third movement.

Carter's First String Quartet was his first major critical success, the work that brought him to public attention. From here on his works would increase in their variety of simultaneously contrasting characterizations. The Sonata for Flute, Oboe, Cello, and Harpsichord (1952) retains hints of Carter's neoclassic style in its instrumentation and cadences; in the first movement the harpsichord acts as metronomic timekeeper against the other instruments' more varied rhythms. In the mid-fifties Carter visited the new-music center of Darmstadt, Germany, where he found the composers around Boulez and Stockhausen scaling new heights of notational and conceptual complexity, and still getting expert performances of their music. This convinced him that he could transcend previous limits of performance difficulty.

The systems of characterization in Carter's late works are ingenious, though sometimes so complex and so based in minute distinctions as to become difficult to distinguish by ear without analysis of the score. The Double Concerto (1961) pits a harpsichord on the left side of the stage against a piano on the right, each with its own chamber orchestra behind it. The two groups are distinguished by, among other things, the pitch intervals in their vocabularies. The harpsichord orchestra plays minor 2nds, minor 3rds, perfect 4ths, tritones, minor 6ths, and minor 7ths; the piano orchestra plays major 2nds, major 3rds, perfect fifths, major 6ths, and major 7ths.

The continuous form is divided into a seven-part, symmetrical arch:

1. Introduction   7.Coda

    2. Harpsichord cadenza   6. Two piano cadenzas

      3. Allegro scherzando   5. Presto

          4. Adagio

Carter's Symphony of Three Orchestras (1976) divides a large orchestra into three parts, each of which has its own four movements. Each orchestra moves to the next movement independently, so that the second movement of one orchestra will overlap with the first movement of another, and so on. His *Night Fantasies* for piano (1979–1980) is based around a large-scale tempo contrast, 175 against 216 (10.8 beats per minute against 8.75), the beats coinciding only in the third measure and the final one.

Carter has never explored his complex systems in the spirit of pure sonic experimentation, like the ultramodernists and experimentalists, but always in the service of a wider, philosophic programmatic speculation, often with literary associations. In this respect he is reminiscent of Ives—a physics-driven, abstract Ives, that is, with no use for marching bands, hymn tunes, or references to the everyday world.

Listening Example: Second String Quartet

Carter's Second Quartet (1959) is the most widely analyzed of his works for a good reason: it's the most classically clear example of his dramatic characterization of members of an ensemble as contrasting like characters in a play. Each instrument has its own adjectival characterization, its own time sense, and even its own dominant intervals, seen in example 5.11. Though continuous, the twenty-minute piece divides into nine

INSTRUMENT	CHARACTER	RHYTHMIC TYPE	INTERVALS
Violin I	fantastic, ornate, mercurial	fragmented fast/slow	minor 3rd perfect 5th
Violin II	laconic, orderly, humorous	metronomic	major 3rd major 6th major 7th
Viola	expressive	rubato	tritone minor 7th
Cello	impetuous	accelerando ritard	perfect 4th minor 6th

EXAMPLE 5.11 Elliott Carter, instrumental characterization in String Quartet No. 2.

sections, as outlined in example 5.12.[7] The *Allegro fantastico, Presto, Andante,* and *Allegro* represent the four movements of the classical string quartet. The horizontal center axis of this plan represents a midpoint between independence and cooperation; the higher above that center line the more the instruments cooperate, the lower, the more independent they act. The *Presto* includes tempo modulations that revolve around the second violin's pizzicato metronome, which marks off time even though its beat is not shared by the other instruments (example 5.13). In the final Allegro the instruments begin to exchange characters and build up common structures, accelerating in a series of waves. Just at the point of their potential merging, everything explodes, leading to a fragmented conclusion.

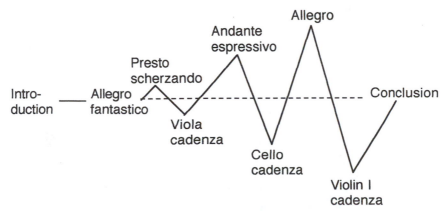

EXAMPLE 5.12 Elliott Carter, nine sections of String Quartet No. 2.

EXAMPLE 5.13 Elliott Carter, String Quartet No. 2, Presto scherzando.

Milton Babbitt

When Schoenberg arrived in New York, he was met at the boat by Lehman Engel (1910–1982), who had grown up in Mississippi with another composer, Milton Babbitt (b. 1916). Engel secured Babbitt an introduction to Schoenberg. And Babbitt would become, more than anyone else, the composer who carried out the ultimate implications of Schoenberg's twelve-tone method in American music.

Born in 1916, Babbitt grew up in Jackson, Mississippi, where his world revolved around the twin poles of mathematics (his father's profession) and popular music. He could later boast, "I know the lyrics of every popular song between '26 and '35,"[8] and one of his first large-scale musical efforts was a musical comedy (*Fabulous Voyage,* 1946) intended for Mary Martin; the project fell through. Babbitt studied at Washington Square College with Marion Bauer (1887–1955) because she was one of the few composers in the country with an interest in twelve-tone music.

Milton Babbitt seated at the RCA Synthesizer in the late 1950s. *Courtesy BMI Archives.*

He later studied privately with Sessions, though in the years when Sessions was still "fundamentally anti-Schoenberg." Babbitt taught mathematics at Princeton (1942–1945) before he taught music there (1948–1984), and he additionally taught at Juilliard from 1973 on.

In 1947–1948, Babbitt wrote two pieces—*Three Compositions for Piano* and *Composition for Four Instruments*—in which, for the first time, the idea of the row was applied not only to pitch, but to rhythm. For a simple example, in the first *Composition for Piano,* two forms of the row are played at once, one in the left hand and another, transposed up a major third, in the right. Within each hand the rhythmic grouping of pitches also follows a row of four values (5–1–4–2) which is also retrograded (2–4–1–5), "inverted" (1–5–2–4), and retrograde-inverted (4–2–5–1) (example 5.14). Olivier Messiaen achieved a similar feat a few months later, drawing correspondences between pitch and duration in his *Modes et valeurs d'intensitées* of 1949, the work that launched the serialist movement via his students Boulez and Stockhausen. For once an American composer had discovered an innovation, working within the European tradition, that the Europeans would soon follow.

Babbitt's application of the row to note groupings did not exhaust his experiments in serial rhythm. In 1962 he published a method of "time-point sets," by which a measure could be divided into twelve equal beats analogous to the twelve pitches of the chromatic scale. A row of twelve pitches could then be mapped onto a series of time points within

EXAMPLE 5.14 Milton Babbitt, use of rhythmic row 5–1–2–4 in *Three Compositions for Piano.*

EXAMPLE 5.15 Milton Babbitt, *Post-Partitions.*

a bar of 3/4 or 12/16 meter. One of the clearest configurations of Babbitt's time-point system is his piano piece *Post-Partitions* (1966). This work also demonstrates a further step in Babbitt's pitch thinking, the concept of the *all-partition array*. A conceptual advance beyond the tone row, the array is an intricate overlay of several forms of a twelve-tone row in such a way that twelve-tone sets are formed not only by each individual horizontal line, but moment-to-moment by the combinations of tones from different rows.

Example 5.15 shows the first page of *Post-Partitions*. Example 5.16 shows the section of the array from which the first section of the piece is built. Note that, within each stave, the staccato notes (notated here as 16ths) spell out one form of the row, the sustained (whole) notes another. Example 5.17 gives the six underlying divisions of the measure to which the time-point system is applied, respectively 12, 16, 20, 24, 28, and 32 divisions per measure. Within each implied tempo, time-points are picked out analogously to the pitches of the row. Here they are numbered in the twelve-tone analysis style that substitutes "t" for 10 and "e" for 11.

Babbitt's compositional efforts center around the role of the specific properties of a twelve-tone row in determining the overall structure of a composition. He defined and thoroughly developed the concept of combinatoriality, which is the property of one segment of a row being identical with a transposition of another segment (or its inversion).

EXAMPLE 5.16 Milton Babbitt, all-partition array from *Post-Partitions*.

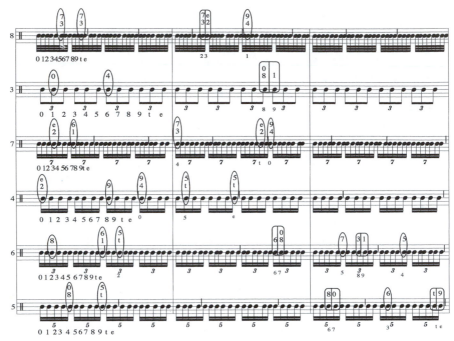

EXAMPLE 5.17 Milton Babbitt, rhythmic array from *Post-Partitions*.

Combinatoriality determines what forms of a row will combine well with what other forms. Babbitt uses a wide variety of register and dynamics to articulate the divisions and dispensations of his tone-rows.

In 1959 Babbitt published an article in *High Fidelity* magazine that was intended to be entitled "The Composer as Specialist"; instead the editors altered it to a more inflammatory "Who Cares If You Listen?", giving a negative spin to Babbitt's career that he's never completely shaken off. In the article Babbitt compares the situation between composer and audience to that between physicist or mathematician and layman. If the layman cannot follow the latest developments in theoretical physics without extensive training, why should music be otherwise? Given this allowance, the isolation of the composer, presumably within the university, becomes unavoidable.

> Why should the layman be other than bored and puzzled by what he is unable to understand, music or anything else? It is only the translation of this boredom and puzzlement into resentment and denunciation that seems to me indefensible. After all, the public does have its own music, its ubiquitous music.[9]

"I dare suggest," Babbitt continues,

> that the composer would do himself and his music an immediate and
> eventual service by total, resolute, and voluntary withdrawal from
> this public world to one of private performance and electronic
> media, with its very real possibility of complete elimination of the
> public and social aspects of musical composition.[10]

Babbitt is music's ultimate rationalist. He does not believe in
music's ability to communicate on an emotional level, and he once chas-
tised a critic in print for stating that the music of Mendelssohn lacks real
depth; not because Babbitt disagreed, but because he found such a statement literally meaningless.[11] He feels that a composer who claims to
compose "intuitively" is simply choosing to remain ignorant of the
restraints that he unconsciously imposes on his musical materials.
Babbitt is determined to be conscious of every minute compositional
decision and to know the reason in each case.

Listening Example: **Philomel**

The other side of Babbitt's activity besides his advancement of the
twelve-tone language is his work in electronic music. He found that with
synthesizer and tape he could achieve the precision for his detailed
scores that, at that time, no performers were able to provide. *Philomel*
(1964) was written for the soprano Bethany Beardslee and incorporates
her voice into the tape part, so that we hear her singing in counterpoint
with a fractured, distorted version of herself. Babbitt asked the poet John
Hollander to write him a text specifically for the piece, and Hollander
responded with a text narrating the ancient Greek myth of Philomel.

Philomela and Procne are sisters, daughters of Pandion, king of
Athens. After her marriage to Tereus, king of Thrace, Procne misses her
sister and sends Tereus to go bring her back. Tereus, however, rapes
Philomela in the woods and tears out her tongue to prevent her from
telling anyone. Procne finds out, however, and in revenge kills her and
Tereus's son and serves him to Tereus for dinner. When Tereus realizes
what Procne has done, he pursues the women into the woods, but before
any more harm can be done, the gods turn all three into birds.

The strategy in the taped sounds concerns the transformation of
voices when Philomela first loses her tongue, then finds her voice transformed into that of a bird. The first section of Hollander's poem is plays
on the protagonists' names:

Philomel: I feel
            Feel a million trees
            And the heat of trees

Tape: Not true trees—

Philomel: Feel a million tears

Tape: Not true tears—
           Not true trees—

Philomel: Is it Tereus I feel?

Tape: Not Tereus: not a true Tereus—

The second section (which begins at 5:02, five minutes and two seconds into the piece) is called the "Echo Song":

Philomel: O Hawk in the high and widening sky,
           What need I finally do to fly,
           And see with your unclouded eye?

Tape: Die, die, die. . . .

In the third section (beginning at 11:29), Philomel is reflecting on her pain. The voices on tape no longer answer, though the taped music sometimes follows her voice in unison. Her words become birdlike, syllables broken into two-note motives. The Webernesque angularity of the vocal line, a cliché in so much twelve-tone music, here perfectly suits Philomel's anguish and her increasingly birdlike character. More direct and more dramatic than many of Babbitt's works, *Philomel* exists at a beautiful moment in which the resources of electronic music and the technique of the twelve-tone language mesh perfectly with the poetic expression.

Other Atonal Expressionists

Some composers attempted a fusion between the pitch methods of twelve-tone music and Stravinsky's propulsive rhythms. Chief among these was Arthur Berger (b. 1912 in New York), who studied with Piston (at Harvard), Boulanger (in Paris), and Milhaud (Mills College). Though Schoenberg was his early influence, Boulanger's training turned him toward Stravinsky. His *Duo for Cello and Piano* (1951), for example, combines Stravinskian diatonicism with Webernesque pointillism. Often working as a music critic, Berger has taught at Brandeis and New England Conservatory, and, in 1962, with the composer Benjamin Boretz (b. 1934), he founded the important and ongoing journal *Perspectives of New Music*. The rhythmically spiky yet melodic charm of his best music—such as his orchestra piece *Ideas of Order* (1953)—managed to fuse the best of both worlds.

One of the most attractive, though highly idiosyncratic, alternatives to twelve-tone technique has come from George Perle (b. 1915, Bayonne, New Jersey), who developed his own personal, flexible brand of serialism through a happy misunderstanding. In 1937 he happened on a score to Berg's *Lyric Suite* and discovered through it Schoenberg's twelve-tone system. Instead of regarding the row, however, as an inviolable ordering of the twelve pitches, he considered it a modified scale within which the composer could move around at will. He later discovered his mistake (in the course of becoming the world's leading authority on Berg), but by that time he had discovered so many possibilities in his own system that, as he put it, "Schoenberg's idea of the series seemed so primitive compared to mine." Perle calls his own method "twelve-tone tonality."

If Perle's language is atonal, however, his form often tends toward the neoclassic. His major works include the Concertino for Piano, Winds, and Timpani (1979), *A Short Symphony* (1980), *Ballade* for piano (1983), four Woodwind Quintets (1959, 1960, 1967, 1984), and Serenade No. 3 for piano and chamber orchestra (1983). This last piece in particular has a mercurial, lyric charm that very little atonal music can match. Perhaps because Perle does not adhere to strict twelve-tone practice, his harmony offers more variety of mood and is capable of great sweetness.

Ben Weber (1916–1979) is one of the most accessible (and sadly neglected, perhaps because he held no university position) of twelve-tone composers, his sturdy music characterized by dynamic rhythmic momentum. Although he studied music theory at Chicago's De Paul University, he was basically an autodidact. However, a meeting with Schoenberg (who lectured at the University of Chicago in 1946) convinced him to learn twelve-tone technique. His works include a *Symphony on Poems of William Blake* (1950), a Violin Concerto (1954), and a Piano Concerto (1961) that is finely melodic and, though twelve-tone, not terribly dissonant.

Ulysses Simpson Kay (1917–1995), one of the century's leading black composers, was the nephew of well-known jazz cornetist Joseph "King" Oliver (1885–1938), who encouraged his studies. Kay studied with Hanson and Bernard Rogers at Eastman and with Otto Luening at Columbia, and attended Paul Hindemith's classes at Tanglewood. His output includes five operas, a symphony (1967), an oboe concerto (1940), and three string quartets (1953, 1956, 1961). He is best known, though, for his symphonic essay *Markings* (1966), based on the book by the Swedish statesman Dag Hammarskjöld. *Markings* is an atonal tone poem with an impressively romantic sweep, aided by the expert orchestration that is Kay's trademark.

Ralph Shapey (b. 1921 in Philadelphia) has always been something of an outsider, largely because of his relative isolation in Chicago. Though he's taught at the University of Chicago since 1964, he spent his life up to that point in relative poverty, as a free-lance conductor and violin teacher in New York. He is one of the composers (the other major one is Morton Feldman) associated with the abstract expressionist painters of the 1940s. A wonderfully cantankerous personality, he became embittered in the sixties over lack of sympathetic treatment of his music, and in 1969 declared a moratorium on performances and publication—not, however, one that was strictly enforced. In 1976 he officially relented, and in 1982 he received the MacArthur "genius" award ($288,000 over a five-year period).

Shapey's music is neither twelve-tone nor systematic. His paradigms are the classical forms—he is especially proficient at variation technique—but his methodology is to work with large blocks of dissonant harmony, transforming them with an abundant imagination, an attribute he shares with his primary teacher, Stefan Wolpe. A section is often made up of a few simple but thorny sound images, shifted and shuffled against each other for a chaotic variety. His chamber and piano works are superb, especially the *Fromm Variations* (1966–1973, dedicated to the Chicago music patron Paul Fromm), *21 Variations for Piano* (1978), *Three for Six* (1979), and the Sixth and Seventh String Quartets (1963, 1972), the last of which he calls his answer to Beethoven's *Grosse Fuge*.

Notes

1. Cole Gagne and Tracy Caras, *Soundpieces: Interviews with American Composers* (Metuchen, N.J.: Scarecrow Press, 1982), p. 46.
2. Edward T. Cone, "In Defense of Song: The Contribution of Roger Sessions," in *Critical Inquiry* Vol. 2, No. 1, Autumn 1975, p. 97.
3. Aaron Copland, "The New 'School' of American Composers," *New York Times Magazine*, March 14,1948.
4. Andrea Olmstead, *Roger Sessions and his Music* (Ann Arbor, Mich.: UMI Research Press, 1985), p. 51.
5. Ibid., p. 49.
6. Elliott Carter, *The Writings of Elliott Carter* (Bloomington: Indiana University Press, 1977), p. 51.
7. From David Schiff, *The Music of Elliott Carter* (London: Eulenberg Books, 1983), p. 198.
8. Cole Gagne and Tracy Caras, *Soundpieces: Interviews with American Composers* (Metuchen, N.J.: Scarecrow Press, 1982), p. 46.
9. Milton Babbitt, "Who Cares If You Listen?", reprinted in Gilbert Chase ed., *The American Composer Speaks* (Ann Arbor: Louisiana State University Press, 1969), p. 239.
10. Ibid., p. 242.
11. Milton Babbitt, "The Structure and Function of Musical Theory," in Boretz and Cone, eds., *Perspectives on Contemporary Music Theory* (New York: W.W. Norton & Company Inc., 1972), p. 11.

CHAPTER 6

John Cage and the New York School Revolution

August 29, 1952, was a landmark date in American music history, as important here as the premiere of *Le Sacre du Printemps* was for Europe in 1913. On that date, at the Maverick Concert Hall in Woodstock, New York, pianist David Tudor sat at a piano in front of an audience for four minutes and thirty-three seconds without playing a single note or even making an intentional sound. During that period, as quietly as possible, he closed the keyboard lid and opened it again three times to indicate the beginnings and endings of three movements. This was the premiere of *4'33"* by the almost-forty-year-old John Cage (1912–1992), who would subsequently become the most influential and controversial, well-loved and widely ridiculed composer of the second half of the twentieth century. As a piece of music, *4'33"* did not consist of silence, nor of the audience's disgruntled reaction, as has sometimes been claimed; it consisted of whatever unintentional and ambient sounds the audience heard during the framed time period. It requested a new attitude toward listening, and toward the concept of music itself.

As a work in which the composer chose to exercise no control whatever (except for the arbitrary, chance-determined length of the four-and-a-half-minute time frame), *4'33"* represents the antithesis of the personality-centered, self-expressive, European concept of art. Cage often acknowledged the influence of Zen Buddhism on his work, and he is cited as an example of the influx of Eastern thought into American art. Yet, presumably no Asian composer had ever before made a musical work entirely of unintended sounds. In reality, *4'33"* was a supremely American gesture. Consider: the nineteenth-century painter, in order to begin a new art movement grown authentically from the American soil without European interference, had to block out the European capitals from his mind and trace the image of the American wilderness, gauge the contours of the American landscape, observe the color of the

American sky—had to take a hard, unbiased look at America itself. What did the composer need to do who wanted to create an American music?

Listen to what America actually sounded like.

If Ives was music's Emerson, dense with meanings drawn from older cultural references, Cage was its Thoreau, a naturalist of sounds who could afford to flout the conventions of human habit and society. For many musicians (though their number is rapidly shrinking), Cage was simply a charlatan, a charming joker who sold the world nonsense packaged as art. Given that Cage was in his fifties before his music began to earn him anything more than the most meager income and that his music was typically vilified in most serious music circles for an even longer time, those detractors are hard put to specify what such charlatanism was meant to achieve.

No matter what opinion one arrives at, however, Cage was one of music history's turning-point figures, like Monteverdi or Haydn or Stravinsky, after whom the course of music shot off at a new angle. He is the sole figure in twentieth-century music whose influence has also been widely felt in visual art, literature, and dance. He was an adored father figure to hundreds of young composers in America, Europe, Asia, and around the world. Controversial as he is, Cage has become the closest thing American music has to a saint, and it will be necessary to go through his life in considerable detail, if only because certain events in it have taken on a mythic status, with deep implications for music's subsequent direction.

Cage's Early Life

Born September 5, 1912, in Los Angeles, John Milton Cage Jr. was the son of an inventor, and all his life pointed to his father's vocation as a precedent for the audacious innovativeness of his own work. In youth Cage was torn between music, writing, art, and architecture. Studies at Pomona College did not inspire him, and he abandoned college to travel in Europe. Studying architecture in Paris, Cage heard his teacher say that in order to become an architect, one must devote one's entire life to it. Unable to make such a commitment, Cage returned to Los Angeles and began studying composition. When he sent a Sonata for Clarinet (1933) to Henry Cowell, the latter took an interest in his music, and advised him to study with Schoenberg, who was then teaching at UCLA.

First, however, to fill some gaps in his musical training, Cage went to New York to study for a year with Schoenberg's first American student, Adolph Weiss. In 1935 Cage returned to Los Angeles and asked Schoenberg to teach him, admitting that he had no money to pay him. Schoenberg asked Cage if he was willing to devote his life to music. Cage now answered an unequivocal "yes." Despite Schoenberg's autocratic

John Cage. *Photo by Bob Cato.*

and ruthless classroom manner, Cage worshipped him, he later said, "like a god." Schoenberg complained that Cage had no feel for harmony and warned him that without such an affinity he would never be able to write good music; it would be as if he had come to a wall through which he could not pass. In a now-famous reply, Cage answered, "In that case I will devote my life to beating my head against that wall."

Also in 1935 Cage married Xenia Andreevna Kashevaroff from Juneau, Alaska. The marriage lasted ten years, ending when Cage became homosexually involved with the innovative American choreographer Merce Cunningham (b. 1919), originally in the company of the famous Martha Graham. The Cage-Cunningham collaboration became one of the century's most dynamic artistic pairings.

Cage's earliest works, written before his studies with Schoenberg, are mathematical in nature, using methods analogous to twelve-tone construction. From reading Cowell's *New Musical Resources* and *Towards a New Music* by the Mexican composer Carlos Chavez, he had become interested in noise and new rhythms.

Starting with a 1935 quartet for unspecified instruments, Cage began to write purely rhythmic works for nonpitched percussion. On a trip to San Francisco in 1938, he was offered a job at the Cornish School in Seattle making music for the dance department, since for dancers, rhythmic structure was sufficient.

For Cage's early percussion works he developed a form in which each phrase had the same proportions as the whole, which he called "micro-macrocosmic" form. For example, his *First Construction (in Metal)* of 1939 was built up of phrases whose sixteen-measure units were divided 4 + 3 + 2 + 3 + 4. Likewise, the entire work is divided into five sections: there are four such phrases in the first section, three in the second, two in the third, three in the fourth, and four in the fifth. Cage's use of rhythm to define structure had a tremendous impact on the course of American music, influencing many younger composers.

The rise of talking films and radio dramas had brought a wide range of electronic and nonelectronic sound effects into widespread use, and Cage was among the first composers to use them. In 1939, he used variable-speed turntables in his *Imaginary Landscape No. 1* (perhaps the first-ever electroacoustic composition). *Credo in Us* (1942) asks for a recording of a symphony by Dvořák, Tchaikovsky, or some other romantic favorite, which is then interrupted collage-style by piano and percussion. In 1938 Cage organized a percussion orchestra at the Cornish School, in whose performances Lou Harrison was a frequent collaborator. Cage embodied his ideas on percussion music in a famous credo:

> I believe that the use of noise to make music will continue and increase until we reach a music produced through the aid of electrical instruments which will make available for musical purposes any and all sounds that can be heard. . . . Whereas, in the past, the point of disagreement has been between dissonance and consonance, it will be, in the immediate future, between noise and so-called musical sounds.[1]

In March of 1940, the dancer Syvilla Fort asked Cage to create an accompaniment for her dance *Bacchanale*. The Cornish School's small stage wouldn't accommodate a percussion orchestra, and Cage had only a piano to work with. In desperation, he began placing newspapers, ashtrays, keys, and pie plates on the piano strings to alter the sound; he liked the results, but the objects bounced off. Finally it occurred to him that bolts and screws could be securely screwed between the strings without falling out, and he also placed weather-stripping between the strings. The "prepared piano," as it was subsequently called, places a virtual percussion orchestra in the hands of one player, and allows a variety of unpredictably tuned tones with the striking of a single key. In subsequent years he wrote his greatest early works for the invention: *The Perilous Night* (1943–1944), *Root of an Unfocus* (1944), Three Dances for Two Amplified Prepared Pianos (1944–1945), and especially the wide-ranging, Eastern-inspired, twenty-movement cycle *Sonatas and Interludes*.

After several months in Chicago, Cage moved to New York in 1942. A 1943 concert of his percussion music at the Museum of Modern Art was accompanied by a feature story in *Life* magazine, which noted, with an odd mixture of naïveté and philosophical insight, that

> percussion music goes back to man's primitive days when untutored savages took aesthetic delight in hitting crude drums or hollow logs. Cage believes that when people today get to understand and like his music, which is produced by banging one object with another, they will find new beauty in everyday modern life, which is full of noises made by objects banging against one another.[2]

Though welcome, such exposure failed to lead to fame and career stability. Around 1945, concomitant to his breakup with Xenia, he endured something of a nervous breakdown and consulted a Jungian analyst. Put off by the analyst, he instead began studying Indian music and philosophy with a student who had come to him from India, Gita Sarabhai. This marked the beginning of his involvement with Asian ideas. Sarabhai told Cage that, in India, the considered purpose of music was "to quiet the mind and render it susceptible to divine influences." When Harrison showed Cage a similar statement from a seventeenth-century English musician, Cage felt he had reached some kind of musicophilosophical bedrock.

Listening Example: **Sonatas and Interludes (1946–1948)**

Restful yet primitive-sounding, noisy yet delicately classical as to form, *Sonatas and Interludes* is unlike anything else in Cage's output and is perhaps his most famous work aside from *4'33"*. With its sinuously ornamented melodies, the work is intended to express the nine emotions acknowledged by Indian aesthetics: the heroic, the erotic, the mirthful, the wondrous, fear, anger, sorrow, disgust, and tranquillity, toward which the others ultimately move. Cage never specified, however, which of the piece's twenty movements correspond to which emotions. All that seems clear is the move toward repetitive tranquillity.

The piano's strings are altered by screws inserted at given distances from the dampers, by bolts, nuts, pieces of rubber, and erasers, or some combination of these elements. As a result, some keys emit more than one tone; some thump with no definite pitch; adjacent tones have contrasting sounds (an interesting effect on trills); a chromatic scale played upward may bounce up and down erratically in register.

Most of the sixteen sonatas are in binary form, like the simple sonatas of the early eighteenth century (those of Domenico Scarlatti, for example): divided into two parts, with each part repeated verbatim. Sonatas IX through XI, though, expand this form with a nonrepeated section (resulting in a form such as ABBCC, AABBC, or AABCC instead of AABB). Cage often smooths melodies across the repeat sign so that the listener is usually unaware of the repetition. Each movement is composed according to Cage's micro-macrocosmic form and can be divided into rhythmic units whose structure is duplicated by the form of the movement as a whole.

Sonata II, one of the more rhythmically complex movements, is built in a unit of $7\frac{3}{4}$ measures of $\frac{4}{4}$ (31 beats), divided in proportions of $1\frac{1}{2}$, $1\frac{1}{2}$, $2\frac{3}{8}$, $2\frac{3}{8}$ (example 6.1). Looking at the score, one can find that the movement divides into 31-beat sections, these further divided mostly into phrases of either 6 or $9\frac{1}{2}$ quarter-note beats (6 having the same ratio to $9\frac{1}{2}$ as $1\frac{1}{2}$ does to $2\frac{3}{8}$). With half-beats accounted for by inserted measures of 3/8, the phrases within each repeated half work out as follows (phrase-lengths given in quarter-note beats):

$$||: 6\ 6\ 9\tfrac{1}{2}\ 9\tfrac{1}{2}\ 6\ 9\tfrac{1}{2} :||: 21\tfrac{1}{2}\ 9\tfrac{1}{2}\ 21\tfrac{1}{2}\ 9\tfrac{1}{2}\ 11\tfrac{1}{2} :||$$

EXAMPLE 6.1 John Cage, *Sonatas and Interludes,* Sonata No. 2.

(Continued)

EXAMPLE 6.1 *(continued)*

The $21\frac{1}{2}$-beat phrases of the second half are equal to $6 + 6 + 9\frac{1}{2}$. Therefore, the movement's basic 31-beat phrase structure—$6 + 6 + 9\frac{1}{2}$ $+ 9\frac{1}{2}$—occurs one and a half times in the first half of the piece and two and three eighths times in the second half, the final $11\frac{1}{2}$ (23 8th-notes) approximating $\frac{3}{8}$ of the 31-beat unit. Cage sometimes draws contrast from use of the pitches that are not prepared; note for instance the low E and F in measures 28 through 31, marked *fz* and *f*.

The rhythmic proportions of the Third Interlude (example 6.2) are much simpler. The rhythmic proportions of the form are $1\frac{1}{4}$, $1\frac{1}{4}$, 1, 1, $\frac{3}{4}$, $\frac{3}{4}$, $\frac{1}{2}$, $\frac{1}{2}$. Multiplying each number by 28, we have 35 quarter-note beats for each of the repeated first sections, 28 for the second section, 21 for the third section, and 14 for the final section. The opening triad of measure 17 (G–B-flat–D) uses only unprepared notes, giving it a character much different from that of the other triads following it. The overall impression of *Sonatas and Interludes* is a wealth of lively, timbrally unpredictable percussion melodies within a free, tranquil aural space.

EXAMPLE 6.2 John Cage, *Sonatas and Interludes,* Third Interlude.

Cage's Late Aesthetic

Had Cage died in 1949 after writing *Sonatas and Interludes,* his music would form a picturesque backwater in the course of American music. Even those affronted by Cage's late writings admit some charm to his prepared-piano works, some of which anticipate the even-surfaced moods of minimalism and New Age music by several decades. Following the composition of *Sonatas and Interludes,* however, he underwent a radical transformation of style and artistic philosophy.

The change in Cage's compositional attitude took place between 1949 and 1952, the year of *4'33".* His lovely *String Quartet in Four Parts* of 1949–1950 is still in micro-macrocosmic form. The subsequent Concerto for Prepared Piano (1951) is similarly meditative but transitional and heterogeneous, with a much wider palette. Conflicted about the role of expressive freedom in music, Cage contrasted the roles of piano and orchestra; the piano part is written in accordance with the usual rhythmic structure, but according to Cage's taste, while the orchestra part is written in a strict and impersonal technique. Sounds for the orchestra were arranged in charts patterned after magic squares. For the third movement, however, Cage filled in the spaces in the rhythmic structure with a new technique: chance procedures.

One day, Cage's precocious seventeen-year-old composition student, Christian Wolff, brought him a new edition of the ancient Chinese book of oracles, the *I Ching,* or *Book of Changes.* The *I Ching* is a book of indeterminable antiquity, one of the foundations of Chinese philosophy. One consults the oracle by throwing sticks—or one can toss six groups of three coins each, the more common method today—to obtain six binary results, together called a hexagram. Because 2 to the 6th power is 64, there are 64 possible hexagrams, each with its own divinatory explanation.

The intended use of the *I Ching* oracle is to be consulted to direct one's actions. The underlying philosophy is that each moment of the universe is a unity, and so the number that comes up on the *I Ching* cannot help but be the appropriate number to that moment of one's life. Cage, though, used the *I Ching* more as a random-number generator to make decisions for pitches, durations, dynamics, and so on in his music. In the third movement of the Prepared Piano Concerto, he made charts of sounds for both piano and orchestra and used the *I Ching* numbers to help select which sound aggregates went where.

Music of Changes (1951) is Cage's first work in which the *I Ching*'s influence is pervasive. He first made up charts with composed pitch or harmonic images in one chart, rhythms in another, dynamics in a third. Then he tossed coins to determine where in his rhythmic structure each sonority or figure would occur and what rhythm or dynamics it would have. *Music of Changes* is one of the most complex, fragmented, and fiercely difficult keyboard works of the entire modern era. Yet it offers rare moments of lucidity, because some of Cage's intuitively written pitch images recur over and over, modified by tempo and dynamic gesture.

Writing his music according to chance was the hardest fact for Cage's detractors to swallow. It flies in the face of the European conception of art, wherein the supreme mark of the artist is his ability to make artistically meaningful choices. And yet, the philosophy of the *I Ching* is founded on an absolute faith in the rightness of the moment. The very concept of chance can be seen as the negative result of a Western scientific view. In Eastern thought, on the other hand, as in the thought of Carl Jung, there are no accidents and chance does not exist.

In addition, there is no such thing as leaving *everything* to chance. Were Cage's compositions entirely the result of chance, it would be impossible or meaningless to tell them apart, and yet his chance compositions—*Études Australes, Atlas Eclipticalis, Hymnkus, Europeras*—are easily distinguished by texture, instrumentation, range, behavior. The intuitive aspect of a late Cage work is how he set up the parameters within which chance operates. When Cage has been dissatisfied with global results of his chance processes, he has revised them, as he did in the case of his *Hymns and Variations* (1979).

Chance was not an endpoint for Cage's aesthetic, however. Partly spurred on by the music of his protégés Morton Feldman and Earle Brown (of whom more below), he moved in the late fifties toward an even more radical concept he called indeterminacy. In a chance work some randomness goes into the composition of the work; in an indeterminate work, the notation itself is ambiguous, so that different performances could arrive at quite different sonic manifestations. Cage's first major structurally indeterminate work was his Concert for Piano and Orchestra of 1957–1958. In composing this piece, he used the *I Ching* not only to make note choices but to tell him when to develop a new *method* of notation. The result is a Pandora's box of eighty-four different types of notation among the fragments of music scattered across the sixty-three pages of the solo part (example 6.3).

Many people are frustrated by the attempt to listen to a late Cage work, by the absence of linearity or any meaningful continuity, the inability to predict anything. Yet his chance music is not difficult to listen to in the same sense as Babbitt's or Carter's musics, because it does not ask you to listen for deeply buried or complicated musical structures. In fact, it is difficult because it negates musical structures, refusing to lead the ear any place in particular.

In 1960 Cage published *Silence,* a book of essays and experimental writings interspersed with non-sequitur stories; it became the most influential book written by a musician in the late twentieth century. While

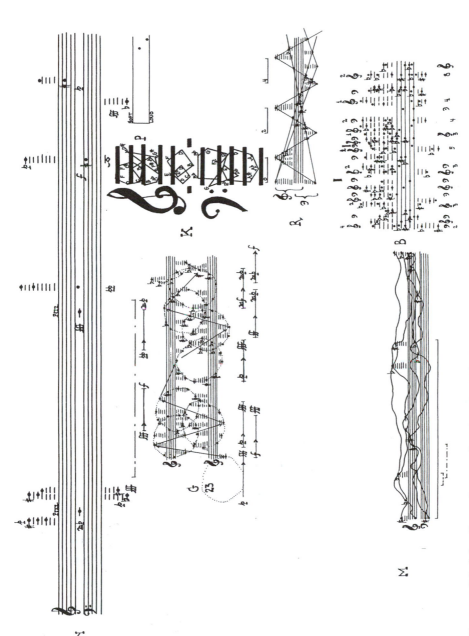

EXAMPLE 6.3 John Cage, Concert for Piano and Orchestra.

Cage's statements—humorously paradoxical, surprising in their counterintuitive common sense, gentle even when deliberately provocative— justify his composing means and prepare one to listen sympathetically, they also lead to a whole new set of interpretive problems. Refreshing as Cage's viewpoint is, his writings do not make up a consistent or interlocking system of thought, nor does he avoid self-contradiction. As a result, the artists inspired by Cage have plenty to argue about, and all can support their views by quoting him.

One aspect of Cage's thought that many people have trouble with is that he came to regard value judgments—distinctions between good and bad—as unnecessary and even harmful. His response to something he didn't like was to use it in his work and see if he could come to like it. He hated the sound of the radio, so he wrote his *Imaginary Landscape No. 4* for twelve radios to try to learn to appreciate the sound. And yet, even Cage's own words cannot be taken too literally. Although he eschewed judgments of relative value, that does not mean that he had no preferences or couldn't recognize a good piece of music when he heard one. As he once explained, "I am actually an elitist. I always have been. I didn't study music with just anybody; I studied with Schoenberg. I didn't study Zen with just anybody; I studied with Suzuki. I've always gone, insofar as I could, to the president of the company."[3] Many composers have used Cage's ideas as an excuse to make bad art, but as Cage reminded an interviewer, "Just because my name comes up doesn't make a failure a success."[4]

Cage felt that art was a victim—as indeed we are all victims—of a business-oriented, commodity-driven society in which something has value only insofar as we can trade it for something else: for example, a great piece of music for fame. A corollary to this is that our rationalism has gone so far in allowing us to understand art in an intellectual sense that we have ceased to derive from art the mystery or direct, sensuous experience which is its prime function. Therefore, Cage often claimed, whenever he understood something, he tried to go beyond it to something that he didn't understand.

Therefore he created situations that frustrated our habitual tendency to "get" something from art. In his lecture-concert *Indeterminacy*, he told one story each minute while pianist–electronic artist David Tudor made electronic noises; occasionally the noises drowned out part of the stories, which Cage considered acceptable. The stories, deadpan and sometimes humorous, often illustrate Cage's worldview:

> I went to a concert upstairs in Town Hall. The composer whose works were being performed had provided program notes. One of these notes was to the effect that there is too much pain in the world. After the concert I was walking along with the composer and he was

telling me how the performances had not been quite up to snuff. So I said, "Well, I enjoyed the music, but I didn't agree with that program note about there being too much pain in the world." He said, "What? Don't you think there's enough?" I said, "I think there's just the right amount."[5]

Invited in the early fifties to visit an anechoic chamber at Harvard—that is, a room in which virtually all sound is absorbed so that one could experience complete silence—he heard two sounds anyway, and asked the engineer what they were. "The high one," the engineer replied, "is your nervous system in operation; the low one is your blood in circulation." Cage was elated at finding that silence doesn't really exist. "We need not fear," he wrote, "about the future of music."

Cage's insight about silence resulted in *4'33"*. Cage had mused about writing a work devoid of intended sounds several years earlier and finally made such a move when he saw the totally white canvases of his friend, the painter Robert Rauschenberg. In his lectures as well as his music Cage began incorporating silence, represented on the printed page as empty spaces:

> I have nothing to say
>
> and I am saying it   and that is
>
> poetry   as I need it . . .

> Our poetry now
>
> is the realization   that we possess   nothing
>
> Anything   therefore   is a delight
>
> (since we do not possess it)   and thus   need not fear its loss. . .[6]

There is no denying the stunning creativity of Cage's best late music. His *Hymnkus* (1986) is his answer to minimalism, a quietly rustling continuum of pitches all within a small register. *Variations IV* (1963) is the grandfather of electronic record collages, widely imitated since. *Songbooks* (1970) is a vastly entertaining free-for-all of imaginatively varied theatrical actions. *Four* (1989) is a string quartet of delicately transparent textures, as natural as the wind over Walden Pond. Commissioned by the Frankfurt Opera to write "an opera to end all operas," he responded with *Europeras I & 2* (1985–1987). In this work, the singers all sing chance-selected fragments of arias from the operatic repertoire. Several minutes into the work, one singer after another begins to rise and fly across the stage, suspended from invisible wires. A giant wheel rolls across stage with a performer inside. At two points, the orchestra pit rises and lowers again, giving the audience a brief look at the perplexed orchestra. And later, a radio-controlled, helium-filled blimp floats off the stage and around the balcony.

In 1987 Cage's music entered a new phase, that of his so-called "number" pieces, or "time bracket" pieces. These include dozens of quiet, muted compositions in which the instruments play single notes or chords at any point within notated time brackets; for example, the player, watching a stopwatch, can begin a note any time between 3'00" and 3'45" into the piece, and end it any time between 3'33" and 4'15". These pieces, titled by the number of instruments plus an exponent indicating how many works Cage had written so far for that number—such as *Four⁴*, *Seven²*, or simply *103*—have something of the sustained quality of Morton Feldman's music; the first such piece, *Two* for flute and piano, appeared in 1987, the year Feldman died.

Perhaps Cage's greatest significance was that, by example, he demonstrated to thousands of young composers that they did not have to take European techniques as their starting point, that they could rely on their own individuality rather than try to tie into a tradition whose centers were on a distant continent. Paradoxically, despite Cage's rejection of self-expression in his music, he opened up a new, freer attitude toward self-expression for composers who came after him. A cheerful lecturer who could deflect anger and incomprehension with humor and calm, Cage became a father figure to younger generations.

Morton Feldman

During the 1950s, Cage was associated with three composers and a pianist who shared his view of music: Morton Feldman (1926–1987), Earle Brown (b. 1926), Christian Wolff (b. 1934), and pianist David Tudor (b. 1926). Feldman relates that for five years in the 1950s he and Cage and sometimes the others met every night at six o'clock at New York's famed Cedar Bar, the same bar where the Abstract Expressionist painters hung out, including Jackson Pollock, Philip Guston, and Willem de Kooning. In recent years it has become customary to refer to Cage, Feldman, Brown, and Wolff as "the New York School."

Although Feldman started out as simply one of Cage's "school," his own independent reputation began a rapid rise during the 1970s, until by century's end he has become probably the single most widely imitated composer of the 1990s. Feldman's music sidesteps many of the dichotomies that have bedeviled modernist aesthetics. His music projects an instantly recognizable image, and yet he wrote freely and intuitively with a deep appreciation for sound. His compositions are nearly all pointillistic, with single notes and small flourishes applied with painterly feeling for detail, and—most recognizably of all—usually played "as soft as possible." He repeats melodic figures and chords over and over, but with a rhythmic freedom that prevents the repetition from becoming obvious. In his later years, Feldman became impatient with the standard

Morton Feldman. *Courtesy New York Public Library.*

twenty-minute length of most modern works, and wrote pieces stretching out to seventy-five minutes, two hours, four, even six hours.

Born in 1926, in Queens, New York, Feldman studied with Wallingford Riegger and Stefan Wolpe. In the winter of 1949–1950 he attended a performance of the Webern Symphony at Carnegie Hall at which the audience responded antagonistically. Recognizing Cage, he introduced himself, and the two became close friends. Soon afterward, Feldman brought Cage a string quartet he had written, and Cage asked,

"How did you make this?" Feldman, accustomed to having to defend and justify his musical structures, replied weakly, "I don't know how I made it." Unlike his other teachers, who still thought in European structural terms, Cage was delighted.

After an early piano piece of Wolpe-esque angularity and dissonance—*Illusions* of 1950—Feldman turned immediately to the quiet, delicately introverted, almost mournful aesthetic he would cultivate the rest of his life. Impatient with the music world's Schoenberg-Stravinsky polarity, which revolved around petty arguments of consonance versus dissonance, he began leaving pitches unspecified, notating sounds as points on graph paper in a series called *Projections* (1950–1953). Typically, these pieces divide the pitch range into general areas of high, medium, and low, leaving the specific notes to the performer. From the beginning, dynamics were kept soft.

Feldman was not satisfied with trusting the performer's taste, however, and his next strategy, in works such as *Last Pieces* for piano (1959), was to notate pitches as note-heads without stems, allowing the performer freedom in the timing of each chord. Especially in works for piano, mallet percussion, and pizzicato strings, this slow-paced rhythmic freedom led to highly original textures that focused on the decay of each note. In his *Piece for Four Pianos* (1957), four pianists read from the same music, each at his or her own rate; the enchanting result is a slow, irregular canon at the unison, in which every note played on the fastest piano is eventually echoed by the other three. (The piece has often been cited as a precursor of minimalist process music.) Such an interest in performance process led to what Feldman called his "race-course" notation, in which each instrumentalist would proceed through his part at his own rate, with no attempt at synchronicity.

To call Feldman a minimalist, as some have, is misleading, for his intuitive attention to each sound is a far cry from minimalism's motor-driven, mass-produced repetitions (described in chapter 8). But it is true that Feldman anticipated many of minimalism's concerns with process, stasis, and repetition. As early as his *Structures* for string quartet (1951) he repeated chords and two-note figures over and over again, often limiting himself to a handful of pitches for long passages. In the sixties the minimalists would turn to similar repetitions, but never with Feldman's delicate feel for balance and timing.

Until his mid-forties, Feldman made a living working in his uncle's dry-cleaning plant each morning; he then composed in the afternoon and hung out at the Cedar Bar at night. In 1972, though, he was appointed to the faculty of the State University of New York at Buffalo. Here, his style expanded in length and depth. In 1969 he had returned to conventional notation, with an orchestral work titled *On Time and the Instrumental Factor*. In a series of pieces called *The Viola in My Life* (1970–1971), and then further in *Rothko Chapel* (1972), he began writing chamber orchestra works in which the continuity consisted of recurring sonic images: a bittersweet chord, a viola arpeggio, a vibraphone ostinato, a descending minor seventh in the pizzicato bass. His pieces became longer; his First String Quartet of 1979 was 100 minutes long. During the seventies he hounded the great playwright Samuel Beckett for a libretto so he could write an opera. Finally Beckett gave him a sentence scrawled on a piece of paper. It was enough for Feldman's seventy-minute opera, *Neither* (1977).

Feldman had perhaps the late twentieth century's most impressive ear for tone color. Once, discussing his method of composition at June in Buffalo, he described how he would choose the instruments he wanted to work with. Then he paused. "But Morty," Earle Brown said, "just because you've chosen the instruments doesn't mean the piece is finished." Feldman replied quietly, "For me it is."

As a writer and thinker, Feldman was as impressive and stylish as Cage, and even less systematic. His thoughts about music and painting are almost unparaphraseable.

> Of course the history of music has always been involved in controls, rarely with any new sensitivity to sound. Whatever breakthroughs have occurred took place only when new systems were devised. The systems extended music's vocabulary, but in essence they were nothing more than complex ways of saying the same things. Music is still based on just a few technical models. As soon as you leave them you are in an area of music not recognizable as such.[7]

He composed at the piano, saying, "Those 88 keys are my Walden." He resented the fact that in America, innovative composers not influenced by Europe are not taken seriously in professional circles.

> [T]he real tradition of twentieth-century America, a tradition evolving from the empiricism of Ives, Varese, and Cage, has been passed over as "iconoclastic"—another word for unprofessional. In music, when you do something new, something original, you're an amateur. Your imitators—these are the professionals.[8]

> All his life [Ives] was branded an amateur. An amateur is someone who doesn't stuff his ideas down your throat.[9]

Feldman was adamant that music was about sound, not about ideas. "Unfortunately for most people who pursue art," he said, "ideas become their opium."[10]

Feldman died in 1987 of pancreatic cancer, soon after completing what was perhaps his masterpiece: a forty-five-minute surface of dark, glistening chords dotted with single notes on harp, piano, and vibraphone, titled *For Samuel Beckett*. More than twenty compact discs of his music appeared in the next few years. And in 1996 Lincoln Center in New York mounted a three-day retrospective of Feldman's music. It was overdue but welcome recognition of the great musical poet of our age.

Listening Example: Why Patterns?

Feldman wrote *Why Patterns?* in 1978, one of three works for flute (doubling with alto flute and/or piccolo), piano (doubling with celesta), and percussion (mostly glockenspiel). The notation of the opening page of *Why Patterns?* (example 6.4) exhibits devices characteristic of both Feldman's early and late attitudes toward notation. No attempt is made visually to synchronize the three parts. If all three performers play at the notated tempo, the percussionist will reach the end of the page first, the pianist last. The rhythms seem arbitrarily complex in places. In a 5/4 measure, for example, the pianist faces a dotted-half rest and a dotted-half-note chord with a "6" bracket over them, each representing half a measure. Within its constantly changing meters, the flutist begins every note just before a bar line, with never a downbeat. Feldman was fascinated by the ability of notation to influence the psychology of performance; the flutist will likely play every note here unaccented, with a slight crescendo onto the next beat. As he once wrote, "The degree to which a music's notation is responsible for much of the composition itself is one of history's best-kept secrets."[11]

The repetition of sonic images is the basis of Feldman's late music. Each instrument plays with a certain kind of chord, a certain trill figure, an alternation between two notes or chords, but then each instrument will suddenly, without reason, switch to a different kind of figure. One thing that persists throughout Feldman's music, he wrote, is that "I did not develop my ideas, but went from one thing to another. 'Negation' was how Wolpe characterized this."[12]

Feldman adds a coda in which the three players synchronize their final notes all in dotted quarter-notes. The flute rocks slowly back and forth between a high E and F, the piano between a low E-flat and D, and between them the glockenspiel slowly descends a chromatic scale. The

EXAMPLE 6.4 Morton Feldman, *Why Patterns?*, opening measures.

gently synchronized effect, coming as it does after a half-hour of independent gestures, sums up the chromatically sliding harmonies that characterize the entire piece. Once when German composer Karlheinz Stockhausen pressed Feldman to tell him what his "secret" was, Feldman replied: "I don't push the sounds around."[13] These pensive tones do not sound pushed around.

Earle Brown

In 1951, Cage and Cunningham toured America, stopping in Denver to give performances and master classes. There Cunningham was impressed by a terrific dance student named Carolyn Brown, whose husband, it turned out, was a composer. Earle Brown (b. 1926) was born in Massachusetts and took an engineering degree at Northeastern University, though he also played jazz trumpet. By 1951, he had become interested in composing, and studied the Schillinger system.

Brown was intently involved in studying contemporary art—the mobiles of Alexander Calder, the drip paintings of Jackson Pollock—in search of analogous methods for music when Cage stepped into his life and changed it. Soon afterward, Brown and Carolyn moved to New York and began working with Cage and Tudor on their electronic music projects. In 1952, Brown gave up the extremely complex, serial style of his piano piece *Perspectives* (1952) in favor of groundbreaking graphic scores, some of which did not even use notes. These scores were collectively called *Folio,* each member of which represented a new step in a search for a freeing notation.

November 1952, subtitled "Synergy" (example 6.5), consisted of fifty parallel lines on which notes were placed, without bar lines but with accidentals and specific durations; the players are expected to supply whatever clefs they wish to interpret the ambiguous notation. *December 1952* goes even further, dropping staff lines and notes both in favor of vertical and horizontal lines and rectangles reminiscent of a painting by Mondrian. The next step was open form, pioneered in a piano work entitled *Twenty-five Pages* (1953) and consisting of that many sheets of clefless, barline-less music that could be played in any order, either right-side-up or upside-down.

Open form is the attribute with which Brown has been most identified. The technique reached its mature state in his first open-form works for orchestra, *Available Forms I* (1961) and *Available Forms II* (1962). A great concern in the early fifties was to catch music up with the exciting developments going on in visual art. Brown was particularly interested in creating a mobile musical form analogous to the large steel mobiles of Alexander Calder: a form in which the content was predetermined but in which the (temporal) relationships between the different

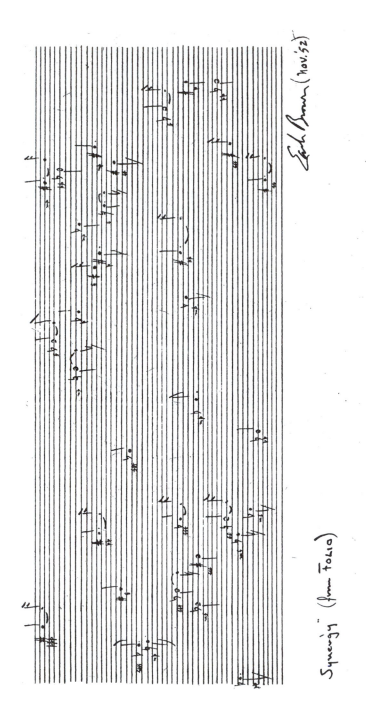

EXAMPLE 6.5 Earle Brown, *November 1952* ("Synergy").

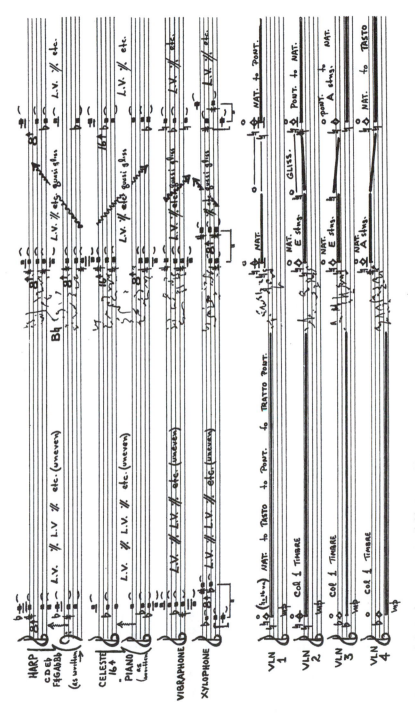

EXAMPLE 6.6 Earle Brown, *Available Forms II.*

parts would be different at each performance, and even within one performance. His solution was to write different passages of music (often using graphic notation, rhythmless noteheads, or even squiggles) in large rectangles, with a number by each one. *Available Forms II* (part of a page is given in example 6.6) contains thirty-eight such musical units to be cued by two conductors, whose sound-sculptures overlap in ways unpredictable prior to the performance. The role of the conductor, then, becomes crucial in shaping the raw materials and prechosen colors into an emotionally meaningful shape.

From 1953 on, the basic strategies of Brown's music change little. Unlike the other three figures of the New York School, he never underwent a style change in his mature years. His music remains more dependent on intelligent performer interpretation, and thus comes closer to improvisation, than the music of his colleagues—not a surprising fact, given his jazz experience. If his reputation has not kept pace with those of the other composers here, it may be largely because his music's brilliance is so tied to his own performing skills. He is a superb conductor and shaper of his own works, with an eloquent language of hand gestures and an elegant way of sculpting sound on the spur of the moment into tactile forms. While his performances can be exciting, his pieces do not take on as well-defined a personality as do those of Cage or Feldman.

In 1995 Brown wrote a piano piece, *Summer Suite '95,* by improvisatorily realizing a predetermined scheme of ranges and densities at a computer-connected piano, allowing notation software to notate the results. This partially solved the problem of transferring his own performing sensibility to another musician.

Christian Wolff

The youngest member of the New York School by eight years (b. 1934), Christian Wolff was the one who brought Cage his first copy of the *I Ching.* Cage later said of the precocious teenager, "He was quite remarkable, and I believe I learned more from him than he did from me."[14] Born in Nice, France, to American parents, Wolff moved to the U.S.A. in 1941 and studied classics at Harvard. Aside from a few informal lessons with Cage, he remained self-taught in music. He taught at Harvard for eight years and then at Dartmouth from 1971 on, where he teaches not only music but also classics and comparative literature. His specialty in classics is Greek tragedy, and he has published papers on the plays of Euripides.

Wolff's earliest music, influenced by Webern, was pointillistic but static in the extreme, stripped down to a few pitches in a way that would have later been called minimalist. His Trio for Flute, Trumpet, and Cello of 1951 uses only three pitches, E, B, and F sharp, two perfect fifths apart; no two measures are alike, and the music runs through what seems like all possible permutations of rhythm, timbre, and pitch combinations. Between 1957 and 1964, he changed to an unconventionally notated style of music based on performers cueing each other according to sometimes elaborate rules. The score for *Duet I* for pianos (1957) contains a few indications for allowable pitches and then a series of hollow and filled dots connected by lines, occasionally accompanied by numbers and dynamic markings (example 6.7). Two dots connected by a vertical line, for example, direct the pianists to

> Coordinate as closely as possible both attack and release without however any intentional signals. I.e. somebody has to make the first move and somebody the last and the other react as quickly as possible. Needless to say, the one who attacked first need not be the initiator of the release.

If one of the dots is preceded by another dot with a tie (slur mark), then the appropriate pianist begins a sound and holds it until the other enters; and so on. This aspect of Wolff's music, which makes the performance into a kind of game among the players, became influential in improvisatory music of the 1980s, with younger performers such as John Zorn and Nic Collins crediting Wolff for ideas they had borrowed from him.

Just as Cage found his music turning into theater, Wolff became more interested, after 1971, in the political significance of the performer situations he was setting up than in the sounds produced. A democratic socialist, he became involved with a transcontinental group of composers whose music was motivated by political concerns: among them, Frederic Rzewski (for whom see chapter 9), John Tilbury of the British AMM trio, Frank Abbinanti of Chicago (b. 1951), and Cornelius Cardew, the founder of the British Marxist-Leninist Party. Wolff began writing works less as experiences for the audiences than as models for social interaction. One of the most ambitious of these works is *Changing the System* (1972–1973), in which the performers must collaborate on group decisions about when and what to play. One premise of Wolff's middle-period music, like that of many of the political composers, is that it is performable by nonmusicians as well as by professionals. This often means that the instruments are not specified and that conventional instruments may not even be involved.

With *Accompaniments* (1972), Wolff turned to text as a way of making his political commitment more concrete. Playing a note or chord on the piano simultaneously with each syllable, and also hitting percussion as well, the pianist is to read a text written by a midwife during the Chinese cultural revolution:

> Formerly many women were always pregnant. Most now understand that this is bad. But we must go on spreading information. . . .

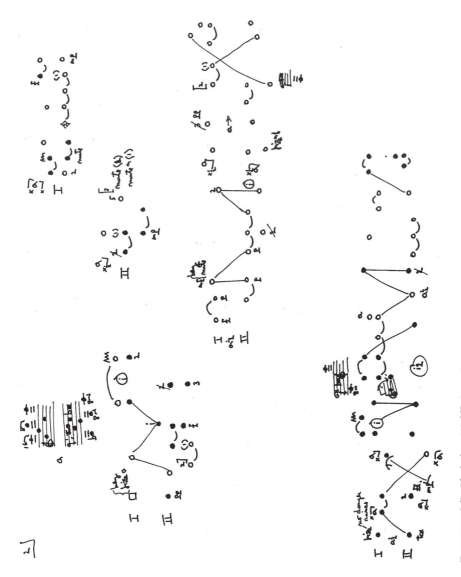

EXAMPLE 6.7 Christian Wolff, *Duet I.*

> Hygiene is a political question. The old bad habits are deep-rooted, but we're fighting them all the time. . . . This work we do during study meetings. To study and apply Mao Tse-Tung Thought is a good method.[15]

The performance technique is striking and quite original; later, however, Wolff decided that the ideas behind the Cultural Revolution had been discredited, and that the politics of *Accompaniments* were no longer valid.[16] Subsequent pieces such as *Hay Una Mujer Desaparecida (after Holly Near)* (1979) and *Bread and Roses* (1976, one version for piano, another for violin) used political folk songs as musical material for variations, in a thorny, but basically tonal style. While he often starts with a politically significant song as a nucleus, Wolff has lowered his expectations of raising political awareness through music:

> . . . [O]ne way to try to convey something political is with a text. That's the guaranteed way, theoretically; actually, it's not at all guaranteed. . . . But at least it's a start, because people will say, what do you mean? or what does this title mean? or where is that text from? You create an occasion in which political questions can be raised, or a little bit of modest education can take place.[17]

Like Cage, Wolff has always been a chief apostle of freedom in his music, including a freedom that will free the performer from his or her habitual reflexes; unlike Cage, however, he has often mixed composed materials with chance (or at least unpredictable) procedures. For example, his *Snowdrop* of 1970 for harpsichord and any number of other keyboards randomly superimposes insouciant melodies over one another in cheerfully disorderly counterpoint. Some of his instruction pieces, such as *Stones* (from *Prose Collection*, 1968–1971), indicate methods of producing sound but not what sounds are to be made. In solo pieces like *Bread and Roses*, the performer is occasionally required to make extraneous noises, such as whistling or striking the piano. More recent ensemble works, such as *Bowery Preludes* (1985–1986), *For Si* (1990–1991, based on songs by the activist-songwriter Si Kahn), and *Spring* (1996, written for an orchestra of seven trios), mix conventional notation with verbal instructions designed to elicit unpredictable textures. Wolff's music never fails to convey an aura of joyous surprise.

David Tudor

The New York School contained four composers and a performer. Were it not for the obsessively precise and relentlessly disciplined pianism of David Tudor, much of the music by the composers in this chapter would never have come into existence. A disproportionate amount of music in the 1950s—not only by Cage, Feldman, Wolff, and Brown, but also by Boulez, Stockhausen, Bussotti, and several other Europeans—is for solo piano, and Tudor had as much to do with that fact than the ubiquity of the piano did.

Born in Philadelphia, Tudor (1926–1996) fell in love with the keyboard music of Messiaen at the age of eleven and began his career as an organist. He studied composition with Stefan Wolpe and piano with Wolpe's daughter, Irma Wolpe Rademacher. Feldman, also a Wolpe student, introduced Tudor to Cage, who had just received the score to his friend Pierre Boulez's *Deuxième Sonate*. Tudor made a splash by giving the highly demanding work its U.S. premiere in New York in 1950.

Stories of Tudor's perfectionism strain the imagination. He did much of his preparation away from the piano, practicing mentally. Avant-garde music of the 1950s indulged an unprecedented ambiguity, and Tudor's relentless persistence made the music possible to play. In Cage's and Brown's aleatoric scores he would measure every note-duration with a milimeter ruler; the composers might leave much to chance, but not the performer. To play the violent tone clusters in the *5 Piano Pieces for David Tudor* by Italian avant-gardist Sylvano Bussotti, he donned leather gloves. Cage tells, in *Silence*, a story of himself and Tudor receiving in the mail two boxes of spices in which the caps had come off, so that the spices were all mixed up. Tudor spent the better part of three days separating out his spices grain by grain and offered to help Cage with his. Argentine composer Mauricio Kagel's comment about Tudor is typical: "He could play the raisins in a slice of fruitcake."[18]

In the early fifties, however, Tudor had begun making his own electronic music; the noises that accompany and sometimes interrupt Cage in his recording of the lecture *Indeterminacy* are Tudor's. By 1970 Tudor had given up playing the piano, allowing his pianistic legend to live only on records. Thereafter he devoted himself to composition, becoming a pioneer in the newly growing field of live electronics. Tudor's magnum opus was a series of works begun in 1968 under the collective title *Rainforest*. In these works, assemblages of suspended cast-off objects— lawn sprinklers, car windshields, bicycle rims—were made to vibrate with transducers, bringing the detritus of civilization to acoustic life. Tudor's solo electronic works, like *Hedgehog* and his *Neural Synthesis* series, chirped and whistled with the warmth of a swarm of insects or distant flock of birds and were presented with a sense of mystery that made him shy away from technical explanation. His circuits themselves were the scores, and he would set them up in such a way that he himself couldn't predict how the resulting sound would behave.

Tudor's unrelenting purity made him a difficult figure for audiences to understand and approach. But he became a father figure to several younger electronic composers, especially those who worked with him on *Rainforest*, such as Linda Fisher and John Driscoll.

Notes

1. Cage, *Silence,* pp. 3–4.
2. *Life* magazine, March 15, 1943.
3. Quoted in William Duckworth, *Talking Music: Conversations with John Cage, Philip Glass, Laurie Anderson, and Five Generations of American Experimental Composers* (New York: Schirmer Books, 1995), p. 21.
4. Ibid., p. 15.
5. *Silence,* p. 93.
6. John Cage, "Lecture on Nothing," in *Silence,* pp. 109–110.
7. Morton Feldman, "The Anxiety of Art," in *Essays,* Beginner Press (Cologne, 1985), p. 91.
8. Ibid., p. 87.
9. Morton Feldman, "Conversations without Strawinsky," in *Essays,* Beginner Press (Cologne, 1985), p. 61.
10. Quoted in Robert Ashley, *Morton Feldman Says,* a 1964 interview turned into a performance theater piece.
11. Morton Feldman, "Crippled Symmetry," in *Essays,* Beginner Press (Cologne, 1985), p. 132.
12. Ibid., p. 134.
13. Ibid., p. 131.
14. Quoted in David Revill, *The Roaring Silence: John Cage: A Life,* Arcade Publishing (New York: 1992) p. 129.
15. Quoted in the liner notes to *Music by Christian Wolff,* CRI SD 357.
16. Cole Gagne, *Soundpieces 2: Interviews with American Composers* (Metuchen, N.J.: Scarecrow Press, Inc., 1993), p. 461.
17. Ibid., p. 464.
18. Quoted in David Revill, *The Roaring Silence: John Cage: A Life* (New York: Arcade Publishing, 1992), p. 102.

CHAPTER 7

Post-Cage Conceptualism

The 1960s were a period of intense questioning of virtually every cultural assumption. What is art? What is music? What authority do governments have to send young men to war? Why are wars really fought—for legitimate principles or economic interests? Why "should" men have shorter hair than women? Why should people wear clothes? Why should they wait until marriage to have sex? Why shouldn't people relieve the monotony of their existence with psychedelic drugs? No assumption, it seemed, was so basic that the young people of the sixties couldn't call it into question. To some extent, the explosion was a reaction to the overwhelming conformity of the postwar era, an era in which stabilization and restoration of economic growth had been paramount priorities. President Eisenhower, a five-star general who commanded the U.S. forces in Europe during World War II, had represented the uniformity of military discipline; John Kennedy (served 1961–1963), at forty-three the youngest man ever elected U.S. president, seemed to usher in an era of youth and new possibilities.

The immense spectrum of answers opened up by the question "What is art?" makes the sixties an especially difficult decade to summarize. Anything you could imagine being presented as a work of art *was* presented as such, along with many more things almost no one could imagine. The conventions of musical performance were overhauled. One of the more radical gestures was a series of "pieces" called *Listen* (1966–1968), in which composer Max Neuhaus took an audience, each person with the word "LISTEN" stamped on his or her hand, through found-sound environments such as power plants and subway stations. In another "piece," *Homage to John Cage*, Nam June Paik poured shampoo on Cage's head and cut off his tie. One 1969 piece by Phillip Corner has yet to be performed: "One anti-personnel type-CBU bomb will be thrown into the audience." Annea Lockwood burned pianos amplified by asbestos-covered microphones and followed one such performance in 1968 with a séance at which Beethoven's spirit was allegedly aroused. We can only wonder what he thought of the milieu he found.

Partly as a consequence of the ephemerality and nondocumentability of many conceptualist works, it seems likely that less music will survive in performance from the sixties than from any other decade of the century, because to the question, "Hey, can *this* be art?", the answer is frequently, "Yeah, you can *call* it art, but so what?" Yet the decade was a fascinating learning experience, yielding an enormous supply of musical anecdotes if nothing else. Spurred on by Cage, it cleared the stage of the last vestiges of European high-art obligations and freed composers to start again from zero.

It also initiated a radical split in American music's self-image. In 1961 in Manhattan, an Asian-American pianist named Yoko Ono—at first the wife of the Cage-influenced composer Toshi Ichiyanagi, later famous for her marriage to the rock star John Lennon—began a new trend by opening up her downtown Manhattan loft for performances of experimental music. Ono's move, and the concert series curated at her loft by La Monte Young and Richard Maxfield, initiated a downtown tradition of presenting new music informally in rough, unconventional spaces. This geographic dislocation resulted in an entire new body of work, so-called "Downtown music," though in many respects it continued the experimental tradition inherited from Ives, Cowell, Partch, and Cage. In 1979, Downtown music—mostly conceptualist and minimalist—made its first public collective splash at New York's experimental arts space The Kitchen in a widely-attended festival called New Music New York. From this moment, the music that traced its inheritance back to Cage's *4'33"* had a new, overly vague but widely used name: New Music.

Despite this downtown Manhattan identification, the sixties and seventies were the period in which music decentralized and spread across the nation. The Midwest scene, in many ways more innovative and less doctrinaire than the coasts, centered loosely around college towns along Interstate 80: Ann Arbor, Oberlin, Champaign-Urbana, Iowa City, Bloomington. Activities in Ann Arbor were particularly intense between 1958 and 1969 because of the ONCE festivals. By the 1980s, though, the Midwest scene was moribund, several of the protagonists having moved to New York, and the universities involved having discontinued the practice of hiring radical composers.

The sprawling group of tendencies gathered together here under the rubric of conceptualism is not a unitary phenomenon. One might delineate several points of crystallization within which the music of this chapter can be fluidly located. One endpoint came directly from John Cage: since sounds were considered more interesting when freed from having to express the composer's ego, any process or concept or activity that caused sounds might well result in something interestingly unforeseen to listen to. The sonic result of the piece would be a side effect of the actual activity, and thus outside the "composer"'s control. Such a thought process lay behind a piece such as Larry Austin's *Accidents*, in which the pianist tries to avoid making sounds, or Alvin Lucier's *Vespers*, in which performers explore a space using echolocation devices.

Another endpoint, related but different in emphasis, was the insight that a concept itself could be a work of art, that the appreciation of a work of art could take place entirely within the imagination without having any manifestation in the physical world at all. This attitude led to the creation of hundreds of word-pieces, brief descriptions striking for their whimsicality, paradoxical nature, or impossibility of realization. Thus La Monte Young's *Composition 1960 #15*: "This piece is little whirlpools out in the middle of the ocean." Or Takehisa Kosugi's *Music for a Revolution*: "Scoop out one of your eyes 5 years from now and do the same with the other eye 5 years later." Or Nam June Paik's *Danger Music No. 5*: "Creep into the vagina of a living whale." In between these two poles were verbal-instruction pieces that could be carried out or at least attempted, the bizarre nature of the attempt serving to entertain the presumably hip audience. For instance, Young's *Composition 1960 #5*: "Turn a butterfly (or any number of butterflies) loose in the performance area."

Beyond this is still another conceptualist paradigm (and these given by no means exhaust the possibilities). Especially in the Midwest, conceptualism evolved partly as an expansion of serialism. Midwestern composers took their cues from Europeans like Stockhausen, Kagel, Bussotti, and others who had started with Anton Webern's music (*not* Schoenberg's) and taken it several steps further. If twelve pitches or twelve durations or twelve timbres could be organized with a row, why not twelve quotations? Twelve styles of music? Twelve actions? And so Salvatore Martirano's *Ballad* (1966) organizes several popular songs sung by an amplified singer within a serialist instrumental texture. This brand of conceptualism, found in the works of James Tenney, Roger Reynolds, Larry Austin, Dary John Mizelle, and others, translated concepts by analogy and metaphor into musical scores of often extreme complexity. Many of the notated-music conceptualists share with the minimalists (for whom see chapter 8) a love of gradual and systematic processes. What they do not share is any concern for the more accessible and atmospheric aspects of minimalism, such as a steady beat, repetitions, and diatonic tonality.

As if in deliberate fulfillment of Cage's statement that "all music is theater," conceptualism erased the line between music and theater, and often those between the other arts as well. Theatrical "happenings" occurred throughout the sixties, sometimes planned in detail and sometimes spontaneously, with little documentation, and often with painters, actors, and musicians trading roles. Such happenings often attempted "information overload," the piling up of activity and information until the listener-observer is no longer able to keep track of everything that's happening. The conceptualist word-pieces were equally opaque to understanding and ambiguous as to medium. Is "little whirlpools out in the middle of the ocean" a piece of conceptualist music, after all, or a conceptualist painting, or conceptualist theater? Conceptualism allowed artists to dabble in arts other than their own and was in part a reaction against the virtuosity and expertise of the European classical establishment.

As a result, the roster of artists who could be included in this chapter is enormous. And yet, because of the short-lived nature of much conceptualist work, this era is less well-known to the general public today than any other in American music. If the era was a wild free-for-all, it was also austere, peopled by composers who wanted no trace of nostalgia in their music, no reminder of what music had been. The conceptualist era was an extremely important one, nevertheless, marking a turning point in the definition of music.

Robert Ashley

Electronically innovative, socially provocative, and incorrigibly theatrical, Robert Ashley epitomizes the conceptualism of the 1960s, yet more than any other figure he has also transcended it. No other composer is so associated with, or recognizable by, his own voice: mellow, nonchalant, and invitingly husky, he has used it in almost every work.

Born in Ann Arbor, Michigan, on March 28, 1930, Ashley studied at the University of Michigan and the Manhattan School of Music, studying acoustics and composition with Wallingford Riegger, Ross Lee Finney, Leslie Bassett, and Roberto Gerhard. Though he never taught at the University of Michigan, he participated in a heady scene revolving around the famous ONCE festivals of contemporary music, which ran from 1958 to 1969. These festivals, organized by the ONCE group (including Ashley, Gordon Mumma, Roger Reynolds, filmmaker George Manupelli, Donald Scavarda, and George Cacioppo), had nothing to do with the University of Michigan, whose music department, in fact, frowned on such seemingly frivolous music. With three other electronic composers—David Behrman, Gordon Mumma, and Alvin Lucier—Ashley formed the Sonic Arts Union, a group that toured America and Europe to perform electronic theater music by its members.

Ashley's most oft-cited early work was a notorious theater piece for his own voice and noisy tape collage: *Wolfman* (1964). A 1968 *Source* magazine review describes the piece as follows:

> It depicts that moment in time known to anyone who has ever attended a crowded restaurant, night club or bar—that moment when the sound becomes unbearable. . . . The piece begins with a tape collage of restaurant-bar sounds and is immediately recognized as such. After about a minute of the collage, the vocalist [Ashley]

walks into the spotlight. He begins to project long, continuously altered (by the vocalist) sounds, each duration consisting of one full breath. Gradually the relatively articulate collage is transformed into an inchoate mass of electronic sound, the voice overcoming the holocaust of feedback in the circuit and becoming more and more indistinguishable from the tape. The volume level is extremely high; the audience is literally surrounded by a wall of sound that is comparable to and even surpassing that of today's rock music.[1]

In another, equally provocative nightclub-ambiance piece, *Purposeful Lady Slow Afternoon* (1968), a woman hesitantly, without using any explicit words, describes being forced to give oral sex, over a disarmingly innocent accompaniment of bells.

By the late seventies Ashley was known as a kind of "bad boy" of the avant-garde, whose provocative theatrical works were highly conceptual. Then, around 1978, he began experimenting with automatic speech, and found himself building up a long poem which would become the libretto for an opera, *Perfect Lives*. He developed *Perfect Lives* in stages, originally performing it as a solo text, with piano and tape, and ultimately with other singers and video. Ashley loves to slowly pile layer upon layer of text and music onto a work until the listener is hard put to decipher all the meaning, thus achieving information overload.

Since *Perfect Lives,* Ashley has written several more operas evolved from the same set of characters: first *Atalanta,* then a tetralogy of four operas grouped together as *Now Eleanor's Idea*: *Improvement: Don Leaves Linda, Foreign Experiences, El Aficionado,* and *Now Eleanor's Idea* (the "title opera" of the tetralogy). However, Ashley's operas are not at all operas in the conventional, European sense: they're made for television, with video as a primary component. "I put my pieces in television format," he has said,

> because I believe that's really the only possibility for music. I hate to say that. But I don't believe that this recent fashion of American composers trying to imitate stage opera from Europe means anything. . . . We don't have any tradition. If you've never been to the Paris Opera, never been to La Scala, never been to the Met more than once, we're talking primitivism. How can you write the pieces if you've never been there? It's like Eskimos playing baseball.[2]

Ashley's approach to art is highly collaborative. While he creates the text and rhythmic structure, his musical accompaniments and video images are often the handiwork of the brilliant artists he's surrounded himself with: pianist "Blue" Gene Tyranny (stage name of Robert Sheff), baritone Thomas Buckner, soprano Jacqueline Humbert, the well-known vocal virtuoso Joan LaBarbara, and several others.

With so many people involved, there is rarely a score to the opera in any complete sense. In some of the operas the singers perform with headphones that cue them as to rhythm and pitch, allowing for a stunning precision of speaking in perfect unison. Being for television, the operas are divided into 22-minute segments, 22 minutes being defined in the TV world as a commercial half-hour. Unfortunately, however, because of their innovativeness, most of Ashley's operas have not yet been produced on television. *Perfect Lives* has been aired only in Great Britain.

Listening Example: **Perfect Lives**

Perfect Lives is structured in seven television-length episodes. Each movement of the opera is based on a different cyclic rhythm scheme, all at a tempo of 72 beats a minute. The rhythmic patterns are as follows:

The Park (Privacy Rules)	13 beats (8 plus 5)
The Supermarket (Famous People)	5 beats
The Bank (Victimless Crime)	9 beats (5 plus 4, 4 plus 5)
The Bar (Differences)	7 beats (4 plus 3, 3 plus 4)
The Living Room (The Solutions)	4 beats (in triplets, 12/8)
The Church (After the Fact)	4 beats (duple)
The Backyard (T' Be Continued)	triplets in 5-beat and 6-beat lines

Ashley speaks the text of each opera more or less in rhythm over a background of taped music augmented by live speakers and musicians in an abstracted rock vernacular.

The libretto of *Perfect Lives* wanders on the periphery of the actual story, referring to it obliquely and digressing into metaphysics and visual images. Raoul and Buddy ("The World's Greatest Piano Player") come to a small Midwestern town to play at the Perfect Lives Lounge. There they fall in with two locals, Isolde and her brother Donnie, captain of the football team. The four form a plan: to steal all the money from the local bank for one day and then return it. Buddy's dogs create a diversion at the bank, and they take the money off with friends Ed and Gwyn, who are eloping. Isolde's father, the sheriff, figures out the plot, but too late. Ed and Gwyn are married at the church, after which the friends meet in Isolde's backyard to celebrate the twilight.

This surreal plot becomes a pretext for Ashley's stream-of-consciousness monologue made up of bits of Midwestern speech patterns. As the music opens with exotic calm, and Buddy ("Blue" Gene Tyranny) starts tickling the ivories, we picture Raoul ("a slightly seedy older man") in his motel room:

> He takes himself seriously.
> Motel rooms have lost their punch for him.

The feeling is expressed in bags.
    There are two and inside those two there are two more.
It's not an easy situation, but there is something like
    abandon in the air....
One of the bags contains
    a bottle of liquor.
A sure sign of thoughtfulness
    about who one might have been.
He pours himself a small drink in a fluted
    plastic glass sans ice.
He thinks to himself, if I were from the bigtown,
    I would be calm and debonair.
The bigtown
    doesn't send its riffraff out.[3]

Three episodes later, Raoul and Buddy enter the Bar, where Buddy sits down at the piano and begins a monologue to entertain the other patrons:

Hi, my name is Buddy. If I could help you make the
    Load a little lighter, it would be my pleasure.
We've all felt that it's hard, at least harder than
    We think it should be, and we look for change.
It's my way—it's been given me—to move among
    The people, and to know our nature.
So, I should not hesitate to share my thoughts
    And my experience with you.
For instance, to begin from the beginning, as it
    Should be:

There is only one Self. That Self is
    Light. The Self is ageless.
The body has four forms, times,
    Eras, four ages.
But the Self the one and only Self is ageless,
    Without age and without aging.[4]

Ashley patterned *Perfect Lives* after the *Tibetan Book of the Dead,* an ancient scripture that is intended to be read into the ear of a dying person to guide him through the afterlife, to help him stay permanently in Nirvana and avoid reincarnation. Ashley's protagonists move with a kind of Zen calm, as if operating from the standpoint of a higher Self, stepping back to view everyday things in terms of metaphysics. Whether one is attuned to such esoteric meanings or not, *Perfect Lives* is an entertaining work in a mild rock vernacular whose verbal images, as one character puts it, "massage the brain."

Pauline Oliveros

If Cage could be said to have a female counterpart, it would have to be Pauline Oliveros, whose activities have been similarly universal in their attempt to alter human behavior in spiritually beneficial ways. It is fitting to her role as the avant-garde's premier female artist that she has molded her work to the supremely feminine archetype of receptivity, specifically a radical receptivity to sound. Like Cage, she has been among the hardest figures for the classical music establishment to take seriously. Her performances frequently involve the audience making sounds of their own choosing, with directions that leave much to the imagination.

Born in Houston in 1932, Oliveros grew up playing the accordion. As it turned out, no choice could have been more felicitous, for Oliveros's aesthetic grows from the slowly repeating and tapered envelope of the human breath, a shape that the accordion replicates precisely. Studying at the University of Houston and then San Francisco State College, she spent the first phase of her career on the West Coast. In 1957 in San Francisco she began improvising with Terry Riley and Loren Rush when it was unheard of for classically-trained, nonjazz musicians to improvise. From this trio, the art of free improvisation spread to hundreds of other musicians.

Oliveros started out composing in a style of quasi-serial atonal textures. In 1961, however, she abandoned conventional notation in a choral work called *Sound Patterns,* in which the singers cluck their tongues, hiss white noise, and smack their lips in rhythm. (*Sound Patterns* won the Gaudeamus Prize in Europe for best foreign composition; within a couple of years, European composers like Stockhausen and Ligeti were also using similar vocal noises in such pieces as *Momente* and *Aventures.*) As codirector (with Ramon Sender and Morton Subotnick) of the San Francisco Tape Music Center from 1961 to 1967, she became one of the first composers to experiment with tape delay, which would later lead to the development of minimalism. Two of the better-known results of her early tape-delay efforts are *Bye Bye Butterfly* (1965), which works an aria fragment from Puccini's *Madame Butterfly* into a continuum of sawtooth waves, and *I of IV* (1966), an improvisation in real time (no splicing or overdubbing) with criss-crossing electronic glissandos.

The qualities of *I of IV* can be generalized as characteristic of Oliveros's entire output, whether meditational, improvisatory, electronic, solo, or group-oriented. Her music is slow, sustained, and gradual in its development, like that of early minimalism; yet unlike the minimalists, she allows tension, dissonance, and noise. Every piece by Oliveros can be considered a meditation on sound, and the sounds are more often than not dark, rich, and complex. She was the foremost pioneer in what has become a common genre: the *sound continuum.*

Pauline Oliveros. *Photo © Becky Cohen.*

Oliveros has been deeply concerned with the problems women composers face. In an essay published in 1984, "The Contribution of Women Composers," she distinguishes two modes of creativity:

> (1) active, purposive creativity, resulting from cognitive thought, deliberate acting upon or willful shaping of materials, and (2) receptive creativity, during which the artist is like a channel through which material flows and seems to shape itself.[5]

She complains that this society accords value only to the first mode, which is identified with aggression and masculinity. "Artists who are locked into the analytical mode with little or no access to the intuitive mode are apt to produce one-sided works of art. Certainly many of the totally determined, serial works of the post-war years seem to fit that category."[6] Women's liberation represents, for Oliveros, the recognition and re-evaluation of the intuitive mode as being equal to and as essential as the analytical mode for an expression of whole-ness in creative work. Oppression of women has also meant devalua-tion of intuition, which is culturally assigned to women's roles.[7]

And while both analysis and intuition need development in any complete creative artist, the devaluation of intuition has meant that brilliant women composers are not recognized as such because their dominant creative mode is devalued. Those critics who ask "Where are the great women composers?" define their terms in such a way that anyone who manifests the intuitive creative mode more strongly is ineligible.

The problem Oliveros pinpoints here is just as crucial for male artists as it is for women. The mid-twentieth-century exhibited an over-whelming imbalance in favor of analytic creativity, in its preference for twelve-tone music and other idioms characterized by quasi-scientific sys-tems and complicated structures. Only recently has intuition's rightful place in artistic creation been slowly restored. Even so, it remains symp-tomatic that the classical and academic establishments have clung to ana-lytically-written serialist music and tried to suppress more audience-friendly, intuitive movements such as minimalism and post-minimalism. Oliveros's focus on women's values and contemplation con-stitute a radical attempt to correct a musical world badly off balance.

A contemplative 1970 work became one of the best known of Oliveros's audience participation pieces: *Meditation on the Points of the Compass*. In this, the listeners sit in a circle, surrounding a chorus and surrounded in turn by eight percussionists. The audience is invited, dur-ing the piece, to perform the kind of meditative improvisations Oliveros had been doing herself, humming, buzzing, and whistling long tones. The essence of Oliveros's aesthetic is evident in a series of *Sonic Meditations* she wrote in the seventies, of which No. 1 is titled *Teach Yourself to Fly* (1974):

> Any number of persons sit in a circle facing the center. Illuminate the space with dim blue light. Begin by simply observing your own breathing. Always be an observer. Gradually allow your breathing to become audible. Then gradually introduce your voice. Allow your vocal cords to vibrate in any mode which occurs naturally. Allow the intensity of the vibrations to increase very slowly. Continue as long as possible, naturally, and until all others are quiet, always observing your own breath cycle. Variation: translate voice to an instrument.

Oliveros has become better known, though, for her solo meditations which she performs singing with accordion. *Horse Sings from Cloud* (1977), for example, is a meditation in long tones sustained the entire length of a breath or an accordion squeeze, the instruction being to "sus-tain a tone or sound until there is no longer any desire to change it.

When all desire to change the tone or sounds has subsided, then select a new tone or sound."[8]

In recent years Oliveros has collaborated with Panaiotis and David Gamper on a computer-controlled sound system that can alter the apparent acoustics of a room during a performance. Perhaps the most dramatic demonstration of the system was in the context of a music-theater piece, *Nzinga the Queen King* (1992), based on a story about a sixteenth-century princess of Ndgono (present-day Angola) who took over as king when her father died. Overall, however, Oliveros has not been known so much for specific works as for the steady and intense outpouring of her musico-social activities: making audiences more receptive to and aware of the sensuousness of sound and raising consciousness about what women specifically have to offer through music.

Alvin Lucier

A brilliant conceptualizer of acoustic phenomena, Alvin Lucier is a sculptor of sound, almost more conceptual artist than conventional musician. Born in New Hampshire in 1931, he studied at Yale and Brandeis with Arthur Berger, Irving Fine, and Harold Shapero, and privately with Quincy Porter. As these names suggest, his original style of composing was neoclassic. After two years at Rome on a Fulbright Fellowship, he was hired to teach at Brandeis (from 1962 to 1969), who were under the impression they were gaining a rather conservative composer.

But then, in either 1958 or 1959, Lucier met Cage at Tanglewood. He was walking along the road and Cage, driving past, gave him a ride. The older man asked Lucier what kind of music he wrote, and Lucier, cowed by Cage's avant-gardeness, replied, "My music is way back in the twentieth century." Cage grinned his famous grin and responded, "Our music is timeless."[9] Soon afterward, in Rome, Lucier wrote a string quartet, *Fragments,* in thorny post-serial style, with glissandos and various noises. No sooner had he been hired at Brandeis than he began evincing Cagean influences in *Action Music for Piano* (1962), a theatrical work that required the pianist to play notes in difficult and unconventional ways (for example, with both knees at once). The first piece, though, that represents the mature Lucier was *Music for a Solo Performer* (1965), in which he attached small electrodes to his scalp in order to amplify the alpha rhythms of his brain—that is, the low-voltage brain wave signal that appears during nonvisualizing phases of mental activity.

In 1970, Lucier took a job at Wesleyan University. Lucier's most famous work appeared in 1971, a tape work called *I Am Sitting in a Room* whose text is virtually self-explanatory:

Alvin Lucier in a realization of his *Music for Solo Performer*, supplying brain waves as input for electronic devices and percussion instruments. *Photo by Phil Makanna.*

> I am sitting in a room different from the one you are in now. I am recording the sound of my speaking voice and I am going to play it back into the room again and again until the resonant frequencies of the room reinforce themselves so that any semblance of my speech, with perhaps the exception of rhythm, is destroyed. What you will hear, then, are the natural resonant frequencies of the room articulated by speech. I regard this activity not so much as a demonstration of a physical fact, but more as a way to smooth out any irregularities my speech might have.

This text, read by Lucier, is what one hears at the beginning of *I Am Sitting in a Room*. The tape is then repeated, and each time becomes a little fuzzier, a little hollower with resonance until, by only the fifth repetition, the tunnel-like ringing of the room is more apparent than Lucier's voice. After several more repetitions, the words are no longer intelligible at all, and one listens for the remainder of the work to the sustained frequencies reinforced by the room he recorded in.

I Am Sitting in a Room is very popular, one of the easiest works to use to attract people to listening to music based on acoustic phenomena. The idea that each room contains its own chord, its own sonic fingerprint, so to speak, is a pleasant one, and to hear that fact become audible through clear repetitions (Mimi Johnson calls the piece "Alvin's *Bolero*") is surprising and delightful. The in-joke to the piece, though, is its basis in Lucier's speech, for he was famous for a pronounced stutter that the Sonic Arts Union composers made occasional use of. (On the recording, Lucier stutters over the "r" of the word "rhythm" and the "s" in "smooth.")

All of Lucier's subsequent works have made some hidden but common acoustic phenomenon audible. In *Music on a Long Thin Wire* (1977), he used an oscillator to vibrate an eighty-foot wire, allowing the movement of air in the space to alter volume, timbre, harmonic structure, rhythm, and cyclic patterning. In several pieces—the most ambitious is *Crossings* (1982–1984), for orchestra—he directed instruments to sustain a series of very soft notes as a sine-wave oscillator slowly swept across the frequency spectrum from 32 to 4,186 cycles per second. As the sine wave approaches each held note, acoustic beats appear which become slower, flatten out at unison, then speed up again and disappear.

In *Music for Piano with One or More Snare Drums* (1990) a pianist plays single notes whose resonant frequencies cause different snare drums surrounding the piano to vibrate unpredictably.

In a way, Lucier's music completes the program begun by John Cage. Where Cage wanted to draw people toward listening to sound as sound, divorced from human intentions or expression, Lucier's music can only be heard as sound to experience it at all. It takes considerable concentration to focus on the acoustic beats in his music, but once one is tuned in, one becomes mesmerized, lost in tracking phenomena that cannot be sustained or analyzed. Lucier's performances are usually so delicate that they are at the mercy of hall acoustics, outside noise, and so on. But when they work well, they are among the most meditative and aurally engrossing experiences in contemporary music.

Lucier's impact on younger composers has been so enormous as to have given birth to virtually a separate genre of acoustically-aware electronic music, typified by the work of Ron Kuivila, Nic Collins, and Ben Manley.

James Tenney

When John Cage, who studied with Schoenberg, was asked in 1989 whom he would study with if he were young today, he replied: "James Tenney." Largely hidden from the general public, Tenney has been called (by his student Larry Polansky) "America's most famous unknown composer." In a way he stands at the center of American music, a kind of focal point: he studied and worked with seminal figures such as Varèse, Partch, Ruggles, Cage, Kenneth Gaburo, and Lejaren Hiller; he performed in the ensembles of his contemporaries Philip Glass and Steve Reich; and he has taught some of the leading young composers, including John Luther Adams, Polansky, and Peter Garland. No other composer is so revered by fellow composers, and so unknown to the public at large, as James Tenney.

Born in 1934 in Silver City, New Mexico, Tenney took an engineering scholarship to get into the University of Denver, where he switched over to his first love, music. A phenomenal pianist whose renditions of the *Concord Sonata* are reportedly enlightening, Tenney then went to Juilliard and worked there with Chou Wen-Chung; more importantly, he met Varèse in New York and became a close friend. Juilliard being not to his taste, he switched to Bennington and became friends with Ruggles. Tenney later went to the University of Illinois and worked in Harry Partch's ensemble, but Partch fired him after six months for "arrogance"; apparently Tenney would ask the great man's opinion of various composers and argue with him when he disagreed.[10]

A turning point came when Tenney was hired by Bell Laboratories in New Jersey to do psychoacoustic research. In a department run by the pioneering computer musician Max Mathews (for whom see chapter 10), Tenney helped develop sound generating systems, urging the labs to add random generators, envelope generators, and band-pass filters, devices that he had discovered while working with Hiller at Illinois. After this program ended in 1964, he played in the ensembles of Reich and Glass and formed an ensemble called Tone Roads with composer-pianist Phil Corner (b. 1933, a conceptualist-minimalist who later became involved with Balinese gamelan) and the improvising violinist Malcolm Goldstein.

Cage later claimed that, if Feldman hadn't insisted on "a closed group," the Cage-Feldman-Wolff-Brown school would have expanded to include Goldstein, Corner, and Tenney.[11]

In the seventies Tenney taught at California Institute of the Arts (1970–1975) and the University of California at Santa Cruz (1975–1976), where he had his largest impact on students. His work at Bell Labs had been with large mainframe computers, but at CalArts he found himself in a studio full of analogue synthesizers such as the Moog and Buchla. "I'm not a knob turner," Tenney comments, and he wrote virtually only instrumental music thereafter. In 1976 he accepted a job at York University in Canada, where he has remained ever since.

Tenney's musical output is difficult to characterize as a whole. One thread that has continued throughout his output since his days at Bell Labs is his interest in music as a structural process. Many of his pieces follow some gradual process from beginning to end, a process that may be clearly audible or may take considerable attention to discern. As he puts it,

> I conceive of form as not a result of a rhetorical process, not, as Schoenberg described it, as a means for ensuring comprehension, but rather as an object of perception itself.[12]

Sometimes the form can be extremely clear and the process austere, as in *For 12 Strings (Rising)* (1971), where repeated glissandos throughout the

(Continued)

EXAMPLE 7.1 James Tenney, *Chromatic Canon.*

entire range of a string orchestra create the illusion of endless upward motion. Elsewhere the process results in various degrees of complexity and clarity, as in *Chromatic Canon* for two pianos (1980–1983), which runs through a slow additive canonic process around a twelve-tone row made up of major and minor triads (example 7.1). As the row is built up note by note, the music is first consonant, then dissonant once the entire row is present, then consonant again at the end. In *Tableaux Vivants* of 1990, Tenney gradually brings about evolutions of melodic contour and tonality within a generally postminimalist tonal language. The resulting textures are lovely and gentle, yet perceptually challenging.

Musical activity in the twentieth century, Tenney feels, became splintered because the resources of harmony were exhausted, and further developments can only be brought about through a move toward microtonality. His *Bridge* for two pianos, eight hands (1984) uses twenty-two pitches per octave in a just-intonation, five-limit system. *The Road to Ubud* for prepared piano and Indonesian gamelan (1986), written after a sabbatical in Indonesia, approximates a Balinese *pelog* scale with a nine-equal-tones-to-the-octave tuning. Works such as *Spectral Canon for Conlon Nancarrow* (1974) and *Critical Band* for the Relache ensemble (1988) slowly unfold the harmonic series like a flower opening up in the ear. The consistency of Tenney's vision and the consistently rigorous quality of his music have created an output of which much remains to be joyously explored.

EXAMPLE 7.1 *(continued)*

Roger Reynolds

The prime paradigm of a composer whose conceptualism translated to detailed musical scores is Roger Reynolds. Born in Detroit in 1934, Reynolds electrified the music world with the drastically innovative look of his score *The Emperor of Ice Cream* (see example 7.2). The score not only indicates the volume and rhythm of the spoken text (Wallace Stevens's eponymous poem about death), it even shows by position on the page where each performer should stand at any given point; the score's diagonal dotted lines indicate performers walking from one station to another. While Reynolds's later notation became more conventional and has always been quite detailed, much of his notation exhibits innovative approaches to getting the textures he wants.

Reynolds developed in a direction quite antithetical to that of Ashley, Mumma, Behrman, and the other ONCE composers, towards greater and greater abstraction and complexity. One could say that, just as Elliott Carter came from neoclassicism and became Europeanized, Reynolds became Europeanized from the direction of experimentalism, perhaps especially after his residencies at IRCAM (Pierre Boulez's electronic music institute in Paris) in 1981–1982. Like Tenney, Reynolds had first trained as an engineer (at the University of Michigan) before switching to music. In keeping with this split background, Reynolds refers to other disciplines constantly, and his music is the most relentlessly literary of the period. Many of his titles are literary quotations: *Quick Are the Mouths of Earth* (1964–1965) is from Thomas Wolfe; *Ping* (1968) is from Beckett; "*. . . from behind the unreasoning mask*" (1975) and "*. . . the serpent-snapping eye*" (1979) are from Melville.

In 1972 Reynolds founded the Center for Musical Experiment at the University of California at San Diego, where he still teaches. On a note-to-note level, his music is full of serial technique, though since the Center added computers in 1978 he has also used frequent computer algorithms. Metaphoric transformation lies at the heart of Reynolds's conception of music. His *Archipelago* for thirty-two instruments and computer sound (1982–1983) became the source work for a number of smaller "island pieces," such as *Summer Island* for oboe (1984), each of which accompanies an instrument with computer-processed versions of its own timbres. In *Transfigured Wind II* (1983), a concerto for flute, tape, and orchestra from a series of such concertos, computer-altered echoes of the flute lines waft through the orchestra like a ghost flute chorus. *Whispers Out of Time* for string quartet and string orchestra (1989, its title from a John Ashbery poem) transforms quotations from Beethoven and Mahler in curved slow motion, as if in a convex mirror. Reynolds's magnum opus to date is a 75-minute opera, *Odyssey* (1989–1993).

Reynolds could be thought of as America's closest parallel to Pierre Boulez. Both use serial techniques to create transparent textures of sta-

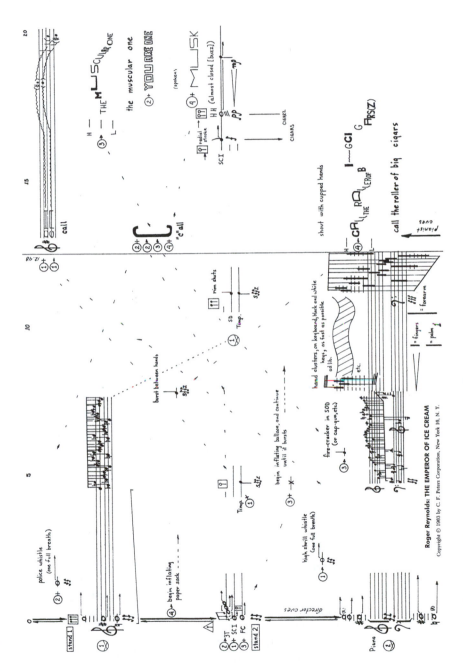

Roger Reynolds: THE EMPEROR OF ICE CREAM

EXAMPLE 7.2 Roger Reynolds, *The Emperor of Ice Cream.*

sis and flurried gestures; both derive music from literary associations; each founded an experimental music center; and each wrote an early theoretical book—Boulez's *On Music Today* (1963) and Reynolds's *Mind Models* (1975)—outlining musical possibilities in what seemed at the time an unlimited high-tech future. The main differences are that Boulez shied away from electronics in his own music while Reynolds has welcomed it with open arms, and Reynolds has been tremendously more prolific. It is a telling detail of Reynolds's career that he became, in 1989, the first composer since Ives from an experimentalist background to win the normally conservative Pulitzer Prize for music.

Fluxus

One of the more stunning phenomena of the sixties was a movement of artists from across several disciplines who became grouped together under the name Fluxus. The movement was the invention of George Maciunas (1931–1978), a graphic artist from Lithuania who came to New York in 1948. He opened a gallery in 1960 and within a few months met La Monte Young (who will be discussed more fully in chapter 8) and Richard Maxfield, two composers who shared Maciunas's interest in the ideas of John Cage. The same year, Young and Maxfield curated a concert series at the downtown Manhattan loft of a Japanese failed concert pianist named Yoko Ono (b. 1933 in Tokyo), who was at the time married to Toshi Ichiyanagi (b. 1933 in Kobe), a pianist and protégé of Cage. Once Young, Maxfield, Ono and several other artists began to form a group identity, Maciunas crystallized the movement by giving it a name: Fluxus, with connotations of impermanence and variability. Some saw the naming as a transparent marketing ploy, but if so, it worked beautifully. Dozens of artists worked under the Fluxus imprimatur, and many of them are remembered today only for that association.

Quite self-consciously, Fluxus was a resurgence of Dada, the French and German art movement of the 1920s that had reacted to the horror of World War I by plunging into nihilism and meaninglessness with often hilarious aplomb. Like Dada, Fluxus was an anti-art art movement, a violent renunciation of the art world's elitist claims to profundity and expertise. Maciunas summed this up clearly in a 1965 manifesto:

FLUXMANIFESTO ON FLUXAMUSEMENT—VAUDEVILLE-ART? TO ESTABLISH ARTISTS NONPROFESSIONAL, NONPARASITIC, NONELITE STATUS IN SOCIETY, HE MUST DEMONSTRATE OWN DISPENSABILITY, HE MUST DEMONSTRATE SELFSUFFICIENCY OF THE AUDIENCE, HE MUST DEMONSTRATE THAT ANYTHING CAN SUBSTITUTE ART AND ANYONE CAN DO IT. THEREFORE THIS SUBSTITUTE ART-AMUSEMENT MUST BE SIMPLE, AMUSING, CONCERNED WITH INSIGNIFICANCES, HAVE NO COMMODITY OR

INSTITUTIONAL VALUE. IT MUST BE UNLIMITED, OBTAINABLE BY ALL AND
EVENTUALLY PRODUCED BY ALL. THE ARTIST DOING ART MEANWHILE, TO
JUSTIFY HIS INCOME, MUST DEMONSTRATE THAT ONLY HE CAN DO ART.
ART THEREFORE MUST APPEAR TO BE COMPLEX, INTELLECTUAL, EXCLU-
SIVE, INDISPENSABLE, INSPIRED. TO RAISE ITS COMMODITY VALUE IT IS
MADE TO BE RARE, LIMITED IN QUANTITY AND THEREFORE ACCESSIBLE
NOT TO THE MASSES BUT TO THE SOCIAL ELITE.[13]

Fluxus events and artifacts, then, tended to be little slices of life, actions
or objects that one wouldn't ordinarily view with an aesthetic interest,
though usually these were twisted into gags, puns, and wry paradoxes.

The movement was international, since Maciunas was curating
exhibits in Germany from the earliest years. Many of the music or theater pieces—a distinction was rarely possible—were realizations of brief
text instructions, what Young called "short forms," and effective performances depended on following the instructions in a clever, unexpected
way. For example, George Brecht's (b. 1926) *Drip Music* simply states, "A
source of dripping water and an empty vessel are arranged so that the
water falls into the vessel." In *Distance for Piano,* by Takehisa Kosugi (b.
1938 in Tokyo), the pianist (originally David Tudor) is separated from
the piano by a number of obstacles, and is tasked to make sounds on the
piano from a fixed distance. In her *Song No. 1, "Onion Skin"* (1972),
Alison Knowles (b. 1933) pressed bits of onion skin between cellophone
wrap, placed them over musical staves, and asked a pianist to perform
them.

Occasionally preparations would be more elaborate. In George
Brecht's *Motor Vehicle Sundown (Event),* drivers sit in their cars and follow
directions written on instruction cards, including honking horns, turning headlights off and on, opening and closing doors, and so on. Young's
Poem for Chairs, Tables, and Benches, Etc., or Other Sound Sources (1960) sets
up a random time scheme within which sounds are to be made by dragging, scraping, and pushing the objects named. One of the most elegantly poetic Fluxus works is Benjamin Patterson's *A Dozen for Carmen*
(1990): as a recording of Bizet's *Carmen* plays, a dozen performers enter,
each dropping a red rose into a blender half-full of water. After the last
rose is added, Patterson turns on the blender, pours the liquidated flowers into a glass, and, after a skeptical look, drinks them.

Quite quickly, Fluxus pieces turned toward the whimsically non-
performable, the absurd, the irredeemably conceptual. Young's *Piano
Piece for David Tudor #3* reads only, "most of them were very old grass-
hoppers." His Piano Piece for David Tudor #1 gave the instruction,

> Bring a bale of hay and a bucket of water onto the stage for the piano
> to eat and drink. The performer may then feed the piano or leave it
> to eat by itself. If the former, the piece is over after the piano has
> been fed. If the latter, it is over after the piano eats or decides not to.

Tudor got off easy; the instruction for *Piano Piece for Terry Riley #1* requires him to push the piano through a wall. And some Fluxus pieces that have been performed were probably allowed against the presenters' better judgment; a case in point being *Trace for Orchestra* (ca. 1963) by Robert Watts, in which an orchestra sets fire to their music.

If Young tended toward whimsicality, other Fluxus artists tended toward violence and danger, the master of this mode being Nam June Paik (b. 1932 in Seoul, Korea), who saw the future in television and later took up a career in video installations. Besides cutting off several neckties, on John Cage and off, in *One for Violin* (1961) he slowly and menacingly, over a period of several minutes, raised a violin over his head, finally ending the suspense by indeed smashing it on a table. Paik was also one of Fluxus's main advocates for sex in art; in 1967, the cellist Charlotte Moorman was arrested for indecent exposure in the middle of performing Paik's *Opera Sextronique,* playing cello with her bare breasts covered only by two of Paik's small TV screens. Dick Higgins (b. 1938 in Cambridge, England) created an orchestral score by attaching sheets of blank manuscript paper to a board and having a friend fire bullets into them.

Fluxus purists (if that is not an oxymoron) feel that the movement died with Maciunas in 1978, if not a few years earlier; others feel that the spirit of Fluxus is as unquenchable as it is undefinable. Besides providing a near-endless supply of anecdotes, Fluxus performances often proved that, once pretensions are kicked out the door, beauty often slips in the window.

Source Magazine and Other Conceptualists

The spirit of sixties music is preserved nowhere better than in *Source* magazine, a bulky, anything-goes journal that was published and edited by Larry Austin and Stanley Lunetta. It ran to only eleven issues, from 1966 to 1974, but included at least a dozen composers in each volume, and the names include virtually all of the era's most radical musicians. Few pages contained anything recognizable as musical notation: there are charts of dots and dashes, wild scribblings, cartoons, electrical circuit diagrams, photographs, clear acetates marked with inscrutable graphics, even patches of fur glued to the pages, and in each issue a ten-inch vinyl recording of two or more of the pieces discussed. If it is difficult to look through *Source* and figure out what the composers actually did, the picture it provides is probably an accurate one.

The guiding force behind *Source,* Larry Austin, was and is a tireless inventor of abstract but lively music systems, born in Oklahoma in 1930. Like so many of the conceptualists, he was identified for years with one early work: *Accidents* (1967), in which the pianist is required to play fast

Annea Lockwood.

and violent gestures and forearm clusters, but depressing the keys silently so as not to make a sound. In other words, if the pianist succeeds, the piece is silent, and the only sounds are accidental. Sea-shell wind chimes are placed on the piano strings and amplified with contact microphones, so that the pianist's slightest mistakes will be heard through loudspeakers. On the faculty at North Texas State University since 1978, Austin has based works on the sketches of Charles Ives's *Universe Symphony,* and his aesthetic shares Ives's transcendent beauty of naturally generated, calm complexity. An example is *Canadian Coastlines* (1981), an eight-part canon at eight different tempos for instruments and computer-sequenced tape, its lines based on a mapping of Canada's coastlines by means of mathematical fractals.[14]

Few artists made a more dashing appearance in *Source* than Annea Lockwood, who was born in New Zealand in 1939 and whose burning piano made the cover of Volume 9. After a period of study in Europe (1961–1973), she came to New York, where she has taught at Vassar ever since. The instructions to her *Piano Burning* (1968) direct the performer (arsonist?) to "overtune the strings as high as possible so as to get maximum sound when they snap with the heat. Cover two . . . microphones with asbestos and fasten inside of piano. . . . Splash small amount of kerosene on back of the piano. . . ." Balloons and firecrackers are listed as optional accoutrements. In another 1972 performance, *Piano Drowning*, Lockwood rolled an upright piano into a cow pond near Amarillo, Texas, where it is presumably still sinking.

However, Lockwood subsequently mellowed out as the era did, and most of her works are meditative, compassionate, universal in their empathy. Her most arresting early work is a tape piece called *Tiger Balm* (1970), which begins with a highly amplified cat's purr and continues with heartbeats and muffled bell tones in a lovely, meditative continuum. For *Delta Run* (1981), Lockwood interviewed a sculptor dying of throat cancer only hours before he died, and used the interview as background for a quiet theater piece about completing the circle of life. To create her *Sound Map of Hudson River* (1982), a symphony of rushing liquid in various speeds and densities, Lockwood recorded the water at different points along the Hudson River. More recently she has turned to ensemble works, the most ambitious and beautiful being her *Thousand-Year Dreaming* (1990): a haunting, primitive tone poem inspired by Paleolithic cave paintings and framed by four pulsing didgeridoos played by performers moving around the hall.

One of the strangest figures to haunt the pages of *Source* didn't emerge as a major influence until the 1990s. Jerry Hunt (1943–1993) was a thin, angular, nonstop talker who kept up his tremendous energy by imbibing enormous quantities of coffee. He lived in a barn some miles outside Dallas, Texas, and his performances were entertaining but inexplicable. His equipment, which could fill an entire stage, consisted of video machines, dozens of wires, board after board of electronic circuitry, electronic keyboards, toys, amulets, even suitcases. As he hit things with sticks, waved wands, and played the keyboard with sound-producing devices on his wrists, these machinations would somehow trigger changes in the electronic sound and video displays.

Hunt grew up fascinated by the mysteries of religion. At the age of thirteen, he started his own church, sending out literature and asking for donations. His parents discovered what was going on and put a temporary stop to Hunt's evangelism when two devotees traced his address and showed up asking to see "The Master." Hunt's ambiguous interest in religion survived in his music-video performances. His aim, he said, was to allow enough perceptible correspondences between his actions on stage and the video-aural results to reinforce the faith of those who believed there was some connection, but not enough to convince skeptics. He also used in his works the angelic alphabet of the sixteenth-century magus John Dee, who supposedly spoke with angels through his shyster-skryer Edward Kelley. *Lattice (stream): ordinal* (1991) is an example of Hunt's incredibly manic piano style, which involved a complex notation for uneven tremolos with simultaneous crescendos and decrescendos. The end of Hunt's life seemed of a piece with the rest of it. Incurably ill from cancer, he took his death into his own hands, rigging up an apparatus from which he breathed carbon monoxide.

Little known to the public but admired by younger composers, Dary John Mizelle (born 1940 in Oklahoma) combines the earthy sensuousness of Lockwood's music with the conceptualist complexity of Austin's. Mizelle plays the *shakuhachi*, a Japanese wooden flute, and much of his music is for percussion ensemble, structured around theories he derived from working with Stockhausen in the sixties. Although the perceptual parameters of the music are often arranged along simple lines—growth versus decay, metal percussion versus skin, free rhythm versus cycles and cross-rhythms—the actual working out in a piece such as *Soundscape* (1976) can be extremely complex. Many pieces, including the mammoth *Lake Mountain Thunder* for English horn and percussion ensemble (1981), are proportioned in accordance with a mystical mathematical formula that Mizelle found in a book on the ancient Egyptian pyramids:

$$\pi = \tfrac{6}{5} \times \phi^2$$

or

$$\mathrm{pi} = \tfrac{6}{5} \text{ times phi squared}$$

pi being, of course, the ratio of the circumference of a circle to its diameter, phi being the golden section: 1.618. . . . Pi might equal the whole duration of a work, for example, and important structural points be marked off by ratios of phi and rhythms of five-against-six. There is an other-worldly quality to Mizelle's music, primitive in sound, meditative in shape, yet intricate, as though it were made from scratch by a shipwreck victim stranded on a lush, tropical island.

Alvin Curran is quite opposite: suave and sophisticated with fluent jazz piano chops. Born in Providence in 1938 and a student of Elliott Carter and Mel Powell at Yale, he is best known as the expatriate keyboardist of the Italian live-electronics ensemble Musica Elettronica Viva, which he founded in Rome in 1965 with Richard Teitelbaum and

Frederic Rzewski. However, he relocated to America in the late eighties. His early work, such as *Song and Views from the Magnetic Garden* (1973–1975) combined electronic tape with live voice and occasional instruments in quiet, meditative soundscapes. His magnum opus is probably *Crystal Psalms* (1988), a radio collage for the fiftieth anniversary of the Nazi *Kristallnacht* pogrom, incorporating tapes of the sounds of Jewish life (a shofar ram's horn, Yemenite Jews praying at the Wailing Wall, his father singing Yiddish) along with six ensembles; with its Jewish chants juxtaposed with crashes of shattering glass, the piece is chilling. He is also known for conventionally notated works such as *For Cornelius* (1981), a chromatic slow waltz for piano with a near-minimalist middle section of angry tremolos.

Another superb pianist who improvises in his conceptual pieces is "Blue" Gene Tyranny, creator of some of the musical characterizations in Ashley's operas. Born Robert Sheff in San Antonio in 1945, he and a fellow composer Philip Krumm started their own new-music scene in their home town. Juilliard tried to entice Tyranny, but, repelled by the stifling atmosphere, he headed instead for Ann Arbor and became part of the ONCE group, later moving to Mills College and finally New York. Tyranny's germinal work is *Country Boy Country Dog* (1967), a conceptual piece which has given birth to many quite disparate realizations. He has a way, in pieces like *We All Watch the Sun and the Moon (For a Moment of Insight)*, of taking a single page of abstractly notated harmonies and expanding it into ethereal textures of ostinatos, circuitous arpeggios, melodies reharmonized over and over. His downtown-style "opera" *The Driver's Son* (1990–1993) uses a somewhat Ashley-esque vocal technique and is tangentially about Benjamin Franklin, or at least about electricity. Few conceptualists have the ability to create such sensuous beauty from such abstract concepts.

Originally a member of the Sonic Arts Union, David Behrman (born 1937 in Salzburg, Austria) has specialized in interactive computer systems that respond to live performers. He studied with Riegger, Piston, Henri Pousseur, and Stockhausen before becoming codirector of the Mills College Center for Contemporary Music; he later moved to New York. His first electronic improvisation work was *Runthrough* (1967), a setup of inexpensive circuitry (sound generators, modulators, and photoelectric cells) on which three or four people perform by turning knobs and shining flashlights. Behrman's pieces give the impression of being "verbs" rather than "nouns"; that is, the identity of each piece emerges from the process of performing it as a set of possibilities, rather than as a structure that will recur with each performance. Within such freedom, the music nevertheless has its own distinct personality, mellow, ambient, and timbrally exotic. In *Unforeseen Events*, the trumpeter (and composer) Ben Neill first plays nine pitches, which the computer will then use as a kind of harmonic "spine"; henceforth only those pitches will trigger changes in the synthesizer. Behrman has recently built a text work, *My Dear Siegfried, . . .* (1996), around letters exchanged between his father, the playwright S. N. Behrman, and Siegfried Sassoon during the First World War.

The fourth member of the Sonic Arts Union, Gordon Mumma (born 1935 in Framingham, Massachusetts) was also a cofounder of the ONCE festivals. Along with Behrman and Tudor, he was one of the pioneers of live electronics, designing circuitry that would assist in compositional design through electronic and later computer logic. His best-known early work is *Hornpipe* (1967), in which a French horn player (Mumma) plays into what's termed a cybersonic console, a kind of analog computer which modifies the sound of the horn in ways that are triggered by the horn itself.[15] At first one hears the natural horn sound, then the sounds become more and more raspily electronic. Many of Mumma's early pieces involved multimedia and were quite theatrical, notably *Megaton for William Burroughs* (1963), in which the performers surrounded the audience, communicating via headphones like members of a bomber crew, as quotations from old British World War II movies slowly seeped through the electronic texture. In the eighties, Mumma began to use computers, as in *Than Particle* (1985) for percussion and digitally synthesized percussion. Since 1986, however, he has mostly written chamber and solo instrumental music, such as *Piano Sets* (1986–1996).

In addition to *Source* magazine and the ONCE festivals, the University of Illinois in the sixties and early seventies was an exciting musical world full of faculty—Ben Johnston, Salvatore Martirano, Kenneth Gaburo, Lejaren Hiller, Herbert Brün—and students whose interests included jazz, serialism, Cage, open form, graphic scores, theater, sound poetry, and anything else that might come up. No one blended jazz, serial techniques, and electronics with less regard for boundaries than Salvatore Martirano (1927–1995, born in Yonkers, New York). A student of Bernard Rogers at Eastman and later of the Italian twelve-tone composer Luigi Dallapiccola in Florence, his eclecticism first became evident in *O, O, O, O, That Shakespeherian Rag* (1958), a serialist choral setting of passages from Shakespeare's plays with a chamber orchestra that includes a jazz ensemble.

The piece that made Martirano notorious was *L'sGA* (1967–1968), a classic sixties theater piece requiring three movie projectors and two-channel tape. In *L'sGA*, an actor wearing a gas mask recites Lincoln's Gettysburg Address while breathing helium, resulting in a surreally high-pitched squeal. The earnestness of Lincoln's text is further subverted by films mixing occasionally obscene images of war and sex (such as toy tanks driving along a nude woman's body), while deafening noises play in the background. The piece concludes with Muzak in a postholocaust world, as a Ronald-Reaganesque spokesman insists nothing is wrong. From the late seventies on, Martirano became almost exclusively involved with his invention, the Sal-Mar Construction, an electronic machine that could perform along with an instrumentalist, responding to, altering, and interrupting his or her sounds; with it he made pieces such as *Robot* and *Sampler: everything goes when the whistle blows.*

It is symptomatic of that Midwest scene that Stuart Saunders Smith calls himself a jazz musician, though the sound of his music has much in common with twelve-tone music, and his scores are often charts of enigmatic symbols. Born in Portland, Maine, in 1948, he studied with Brün, Martirano, and Johnston at Illinois and teaches at the University of Maryland at Baltimore. He often composes in words chosen for their sonic values; his solo opera *By Language Embellished: I* (1983–1984) contains passages like:

> Hush the Cull Snivet.
> Hush the Cull Snivet.
> Carburetor cuts off air
> and Clog-hinder-stroke
> baffles the exhaust.
> Silent flute
> Fired sleeper's nostrils!

While jazz lies at the heart of his aesthetic, he has also, since 1971, composed mobiles, structures in which the musical content could be reordered by the performers. His *Notebook* for any musicians (1980) uses melodies derived from famous jazz tunes within a mobile form. *Return and Recall* (1976–1977) is a set of grids filled with circles, letters, numbers and arrows to be interpreted according to elaborate rules in an exercise in group composition. The format of Smith's music is often political in intent; his *Songs I–IX* (1981) is a mini-opera in which the actor-singer-percussionist performs with spoons, bowls, a jug of water, frying pans, and a similarly "poverty-stricken" array of instruments as an ecological protest against the exorbitant means required by conventional opera. Other works, like *Pinetop* for piano (1976–1977) are notated with a complexity meant to preserve the spontaneity of jazz.

Two figures were especially well loved on the West Coast as teachers, though their music has not had much recent impact: Kenneth Gaburo and Robert Erickson. Gaburo (1926–1993) pioneered electronic collage and a fusion of composition with linguistics; he ran interdisciplinary workshops and quit teaching at San Diego to run the experimental Lingua Press. His most ambitious essay in speech music was *Maledetto* (1976) for seven "virtuoso speakers" who theatrically recite texts exploring all possible connotations—some learned, others obscene—of the word "screw." Erickson (b. 1917), who taught at San Diego from 1966 on, abandoned twelve-tone writing to take up a fanatical interest in timbre, including that of taped natural sounds. Most characteristic of this interest is *Pacific Sirens* (1969), in which an instrumental ensemble accompanies a tape of the California surf which has been filtered to emphasize various pitches.

Perhaps it was Petr Kotik who, more than almost anyone else, absorbed Cage's methods into the act of composition, and with idiosyncratic results. Though born in Prague in 1942, he came under Cage's spell early, and came to America in 1969; soon afterward the Russians invaded Prague, making a return disadvantageous, so he formed the S.E.M. Ensemble and moved it to New York in 1983. In 1971, Kotik discovered a box, being thrown away, of graphs that charted the results of experiments measuring the reaction times of rats to ingested alcohol. Pleased with the gently undulating shapes, Kotik used these graphs as the basis of several major works up through 1982: including *There Is Singularly Nothing* (1971/1973), *John Mary* (1973–1974), and his early magnum opus, *Many Many Women* (1975–1978), all based on texts by Gertrude Stein. The most distinctive aspect of Kotik's music is the parallel fourths and fifths he uses as harmony. In more recent works such as *Wilsie Bridge* (1986–1987) and *Quiescent Form* (1995), he has added vibrant percussion to his music, tambourines, cowbells, cymbals and such. If Kotik's methods are eccentric, his music possesses a peculiar beauty, like Gregorian chant randomly sung by monks in different keys, sometimes with a hot rhythmic background.

Improvisation and the New Virtuosity

One of the most pervasive currents of the seventies was a new fascination with instrumental virtuosity, a new approach to musical instruments that considered them as physical objects to be used in every way imaginable, rather than simply as producers of musical tone. A choir of composer-virtuosos sprang up: Joseph Celli on the oboe, Malcolm Goldstein on the violin, Joan LaBarbara and David Moss on voice, Stuart Dempster on trombone, Bertram Turetzky on double bass, and Harvey Sollberger and Robert Dick on flute. Celli (born in Bridgeport, Connecticut, 1944) often writes works for a solo instrument combined with multiples of itself on tape or video; for example, *Sky: S for J* for quintuple English horns (1976) and *Video Sax* for saxophones of all sizes with the five nonlive instruments played via video (1993). Celli's music is marked by resonant sonic images pursued with relentless, almost minimalist intensity. When improvising, he often takes apart the oboe and performs on just the reed, the mouthpiece, and so on, and has won by so doing an active place in the free improvisation scene that sprouted up in the 1980s.

Malcolm Goldstein (born in Brooklyn in 1936), codirected the Tone Roads series with Tenney and Corner and improvised with Celli and Moss. Because of the decidedly nonurban nature of his personality, he moved to rural Vermont in the early seventies, and his music has become concerned with the sounds and aesthetics of nature and natural environments. His violin improvisations, called *Soundings,* emphasize rough, scratchy, breathy tones on the violin, and his unconventional scores take advantage of his skills as a calligrapher. *The Fragility of Line* (1982), for example, consists of horizontal penned lines whose uneven thickness is to be reflected in terms of bow and finger pressure. Some of Goldstein's best works, though, are for large ensemble; his *The Seasons: Vermont* (1980–1982) surrounds the audience with a large array of percussion, which is deployed in textures of delicate chaos.

The other performer-composers listed here have been heavily involved with improvisation, but Joan LaBarbara (born 1947 in Philadelphia) has more often sung with a prerecorded tape background. Singing in the ensembles of Steve Reich and Philip Glass in the seventies, she began to develop her own repertoire of vocal effects—trills, whispers, cries, sighs, inhaled tones, and multiphonics (singing more than one pitch at a time)—and wrote her own pieces to exploit them. The taped backgrounds of her "sound paintings" consist mostly of her own voice, with occasionally a percussion instrument or synthesized timbre, with which she blends in sometimes illusionistic ways. She has remained active in performing other composers' music; Feldman wrote his *Three Voices* for her, and Ashley wrote her the lead role in his opera *Now Eleanor's Idea.*

Finally, if an era can be summed up better in satire than description, the conceptualist sixties and seventies can have no better epitaph than the multimedia theater works of the duo [THE], which consists of the trumpeter Edwin Harkins and the vocalist Philip Larson. Both on the faculty of the University of California at San Diego, the pair specialize in precisely choreographed works that spoof conceptualist conventions. With astonishing comic timing, they throw pencils at each other, explicate meaningless complex diagrams, show films of themselves playing golf on craggy mountains, dip ringing finger cymbals in teacups of water to supposedly alter the pitch, shout nonsense syllables in perfect unison, and justify the whole mess with pseudoscientific statements. If the conceptualist era sometimes degenerated into absurdity, [THE] has taken exquisite revenge on its excesses.

Notes

1. Will Johnson, "First Festival of Live-Electronic Music 1967," in *Source,* Issue Number 3, p. 54.
2. Quoted in Kyle Gann, "Shouting at the Dead," *Village Voice,* October 8, 1991, pp. 89–90.

3. Robert Ashley, *Perfect Lives: An Opera* (New York: Archer Fields and Burning Books, 1991), pp. 5–6.

4. Ibid., pp. 68–72.

5. Pauline Oliveros, "The Contribution of Women Composers," in *Software for People* (Baltimore: Smith Publications, 1984), p. 132.

6. Ibid., p. 134.

7. Ibid., pp. 135–36.

8. Liner notes, Pauline Oliveros, *Accordion & Voice*, Lovely Music VR 1901.

9. Interview with the author, July, 1996.

10. Interview with the author, September 19, 1996.

11. Quoted in William Duckworth, *Talking Music* (New York: Schirmer Books, 1995), p. 16.

12. Interview with the author, September 26, 1996.

13. Quoted in Jon Hendricks, *Fluxus Codex* (New York: Harry N. Abrams, Inc., 1988), p. 133.

14. Quoted in an interview with the Canadian Broadcasting Corporation Radio, included on *The Composer in the Computer Age IV: A Larry Austin Retrospective: 1967–94*, Centaur CRC 2219.

15. I am indebted for this characterization to Michael Nyman, *Experimental Music: Cage and Beyond*, p. 86.

CHAPTER 8

Minimalism

No other single aspect of twentieth-century music seems so central as the celebrated and oft-trotted-out "gap between composer and audience." If the name hadn't already been appropriated by a popular clothing store chain, one might expect that future music historians will refer to this century simply as The Gap. It is our defining neurosis. We pretend to lament its existence, but actually, we have become so proud of it that, when music doesn't put up barriers to the audience's comprehension or patience, we accuse it of not being authentically twentieth-century. There's something tough and puritan about living with The Gap, like doing without running water or television.

How else to explain the controversy surrounding minimalism, the first musical movement in a hundred years that has threatened to close The Gap? Why has there been so much head-shaking over a repertoire of music that has brought audiences scurrying back into record stores and opera houses by the thousands?

Actually, if we take a larger perspective on music history, minimalism appears to be the latest instance of a recurring phenomenon. The theorist Leonard Meyer has pointed out that "styles have generally moved in the direction of reduced redundancy."[1] In his scenario, each historic style period—Renaissance, Baroque, Classical, and so on—has moved through three identifiable phases:

- Preclassic: the beginning of the style, in which the musical language is extremely redundant, repetitive in its formulas and devices (or at least more so than the music that preceded it historically), and the music provides little compositional information; i.e., it is quite simple, and may "often appear to later generations to be somewhat naive and even tedious";

- Classic: the mature period of a style, in which the language has evolved to a point of optimum balance between compositional redundancy and information, so that the "audience must be experienced, but prodigious feats of integrative memory are not required" for comprehension; and

- Mannerist: the decadent or moribund phase of a style, in which the rate of compositional information is greatly accelerated and redundancy very low; "Schemata are elliptically suggested rather than explicitly presented. . . . Sensitive, accurate appreciation demands considerable experience and training."[2]

During each period, Meyer claims, the level of perceived information remains pretty much constant, since at the birth of a new style the information, though not dense, is new and unknown, while at the end, it is extremely familiar but highly dense.

Seen through this grid, one can look at minimalism as the latest in a series of preclassic phases, with predecessors that include the opera of the Florentine Camerata (Baroque) and the early symphonies of Sammartini and the Mannheim school (Classical). In each case, the preclassic phase followed an era of complex polyphony, so saturated with musical meaning that further developments or elaboration seemed impossible:

- Palestrina polyphony gave way to the Florentine Camerata

- Bach polyphony gave way to the early symphony

- Babbitt serialism gave way to minimalism

In each case, the academic masters of the older style went into an uproar. The new style always seems—and is, actually—so simpleminded, so redundant, so naïve, whereas the old style was so elaborate, so evolved, so dense, so perfect. But new composers come along, and just as Monteverdi could not have written more perfect masses than Palestrina, and C. P. E. Bach could not have written more elegant fugues than J. S., the minimalists could not have surpassed Babbitt in elegance and complexity. They had to do something else.

This is an *a posteriori* explanation. No one was thinking along these lines in 1964. Although only Babbitt is mentioned above to simplify the parallel, the early sixties were awash in complex, austere music that denied personal choice and subjectivity, whether from Babbit's and Boulez's viewpoint of twelve-tone technique, Stockhausen's of global structure, or Cage's of rigorous chance processes. In the welter of structures, methods, and mandates, there was no room to use one's God-given musicality, no allowance made for putting a phrase down merely because one liked it. Even conceptualism was pretty dry territory, little whirlpools in the ocean notwithstanding, but at least it offered a sense of humor, an unpretentiousness, and a way out. Minimalism grew quietly from the premises of conceptualism: it wasn't very far from verbal instructions like "make a sound until you no longer want to change it" to "play a tape loop of a sound over and over."

So Terry Riley started playing with tape loops and repetition, Steve Reich applied the effect to live pianists, and poof! a new aesthetic existed. It was several years, however before anyone realized a new movement had started, many more before a new historical tendency seemed imminent. Given the unpredictable direction of modern culture under the influence of electronic technology and the increasing confluence of diverse ethnicities, there may never be a classic phase to follow minimalism (though I believe that postminimalism and totalism represent the stirrings of such a classic phase). But the impulse to start over with the simplest materials after a period of complexity and confusion seems a recurring one, and the outcry against minimalism among academic composers and classical music mavens seems based in an ignorance of history.

There has even been a disproportionate amount of controversy about the term minimalism, which was coined around 1968 or 1971 by either, depending on whom you believe, Tom Johnson, a composer and music critic for the *Village Voice* in New York, or the British composer Michael Nyman, who wrote a groundbreaking book called *Experimental Music*. Other terms have been advanced with less staying power: "trance music," "hypnotic music," "process music" (which has a slightly different connotation discussed below), "modular music," and, more pejoratively, "wallpaper music" and "going-nowhere music." "Minimalism" has won out, however, even though quintessential minimalists Steve Reich and Philip Glass both impatiently disavow the term (just as Debussy disavowed "impressionism").

How, critics argue, can you apply the term "minimal" to works like those of Steve Reich or Philip Glass that last from one to four hours with thousands of notes going by? Well, easily, if you're comparing the quasi-geometric linearity and predictability of those notes with the geometric lines and simple optical illusions of the visual art style that had been known as minimalism since the early sixties. One visual-art definition of the word refers to art that is "barren of merely decorative detail, in which geometry is emphasized and expressive technique avoided."[3] It's hard to imagine minimalist music described more precisely. It's true that hours of arpeggios by Philip Glass seem far more involved than a pairing of red and black panels by Ellsworth Kelly, but since music is extended in time, it generally requires a continuous influx of energy and thus a large number of notes. Since Philip Glass produced some of his early concerts in collaboration with the minimalist painter Sol LeWitt and the minimalist sculptor Richard Serra, and since everyone with much cultural literacy by now knows that minimalism in music refers to the work of Young, Glass, Reich, and Riley, it seems pedantic to deny the term's appropriateness at this late date.

Likewise, minimalism's simple-mindedness has been overstated by its opponents. Only a few of the earliest minimalist pieces can be considered simpler or lower in information than your average Haydn minuet.

By 1974, in works such as Reich's *Drumming* and Glass's *Music in 12 Parts,* the information level of minimalism was already such as to require— and, more so than most twelve-tone music had, to repay—fairly intense listening. In fact, thousands of people uninvolved in the quarrels of the professional music world have found in minimalist music a reason to start listening to new "classical" (or "post-classical," as it's being called on the internet) music again. Four of the five major composers discussed in this chapter—Riley, Reich, Glass, and Monk—are among the best-loved figures in American music.

One of the more controversial aspects of minimalism, however, is pretty easy to sort out: historical precedence. La Monte Young wrote the seminal works from which the aesthetics of minimalism began to grow in the late 1950s. Terry Riley has always graciously given Young credit for his precedence in the ideas that led to Riley's *In C* of 1964. Steve Reich was one of the performers in the premiere of *In C* and made his own first minimalist work, *It's Gonna Rain,* in 1965. And Philip Glass, in turn, played with Reich's earliest ensemble, taking a minimalist turn in his own music in 1967 with *Strung Out.* The seeds of minimalism were sown, then, between 1958 and 1968. The movement emerged as a mass audience phenomenon in 1974 with the release of Reich's Deutsche Grammophon recordings and in 1976 with the historic premiere of Glass's *Einstein on the Beach* at the Metropolitan Opera House. The death of minimalism, meanwhile, has been authoritatively announced every year from 1977 to the present.

La Monte Young

La Monte Young is the purist's minimalist, the originator, the visionary. For decades, his name was famous, his work unknown, and the situation has not completely changed even yet. Young enjoys a vague intellectual reputation in rock circles for his influence on the rock group The Velvet Underground, but for decades the stringent conditions he imposed on his performances made it impossible for all but a few to hear his music. Since 1960 he has performed most of his own music himself (sometimes with ensemble), and while he has toured Europe a few times, most of his concerts have taken place in his personal performance spaces in New York. Only in the late 1980s, after his funding from the Dia Art Foundation began to disppear, did he begin to put out recordings under commercial pressure. Yet if Cage gave American composers the permission they needed to ignore expectations nurtured by the European tradition, it was Young, perhaps more than any of Cage's other followers, who planted the seeds of a totally American aesthetic.

Born in a log cabin in a tiny Idaho town in 1935, Young loves to recount his earliest memories, of the wind blowing through a chink in the

Marian Zazeela and La Monte Young. *Photo by Sabine Matthes.*

cabin and the hum of a power line outside: two sounds that would help mold his conception of music. As a teenager he became a virtuoso jazz saxophonist, and, once at Los Angeles City College, beat the later-famed reed player Eric Dolphy for first chair in a band. In his early compositions, however, Young accepted the twelve-tone technique commonly taught at the time. In the mid fifties he visited the composers' seminar at Darmstadt, where he discovered the work of Cage and Stockhausen. Immediately, a change appeared in Young's musical thinking. His early twelve-tone pieces (such as *Five Small Pieces for String Quartet: On Remembering a Naiad,* 1956) had been aphoristically brief, in the manner of Anton Webern, who at that time dominated European musical thought. In Young's *Trio for Strings* of 1958, however, he took the unprecedented step of writing in notes that were to be held, motionless, for up to several minutes at a time.

Later, Young's long durations would blossom into a passion for tuning—getting chords and intervals perfectly in tune—but first he took a detour through conceptualism. Moving to New York in 1960, Young soon found (or made) himself the star of the scene that gelled into the Fluxus movement. Three of the conceptual works Young produced in this milieu could be called the first minimalist works as well. One is *Composition 1960 #9,* the score of which is simply a card with a straight, horizontal line on it. Another is *arabic numeral (any integer) for Henry Flynt* (1960), in which a sound is supposed to be repeated some number of times and the title of a performance is intended to be that number.

Traditionally, this piece has been played as a massive cluster on the piano or as the beating of a gong or cooking utensil. The most significant, though, in view of Young's later interest in tuning, is *Composition 1960 #7*, which notates two pitches, B and F♯, with the motto, "to be held for a long time."

Though Young provided the original impetus, early minimalism grew from the inspirations of several individuals, only two of whom—Young and Terry Riley—survived as major figures. Several didn't survive at all. The first person to follow Young into composition with long tones was Terry Jennings (1940–1981), a child prodigy on sax and clarinet. In 1960 Jennings wrote a *Piano Piece* of slow, soft, sustained tones similar to Morton Feldman's early music, and a String Quartet twenty-eight minutes long containing only forty-three notes. Jennings's development was squelched by a debilitating drug problem, and he was murdered at forty-one in California in a drug transaction turned sour.

Even more promising was Dennis Johnson, who in 1959 wrote a piece, *The Second Machine*, employing only four pitches drawn from Young's Trio. More significantly, in the same year Johnson produced a six-hour piano piece titled *November*—quiet, sustained, tonal, and delicately beautiful—that anticipated the length, tonality, and meditativeness (though neither the tuning nor complexity) of Young's later magnum opus, *The Well-Tuned Piano*. Despite his talent, Johnson had more brains for math than stomach for the music business, and he detoured into a career in computer science. The composer who introduced diatonic tonality and repetitive phrases into minimalism, though, was Young's friend from Berkeley Terry Riley. In 1960 Riley wrote a String Quartet similar to Young's Trio, but in pure, uninflected C major. The insistent phrase repetition that is minimalism's most recognizable trademark first appeared as tape-delay echoes in pieces Riley made in 1963, *Mescaline Mix* and a theater score called *The Gift*.

Listening to tones sustained for a minute or more, one begins to notice overtones, and eventually the subtle influences of tuning. It was Tony Conrad (b. 1940), a filmmaker trained in mathematics and also a violinist, who showed Young that perfect consonances were related as ratios of whole numbers in the overtone series. Young's first composition notated as harmonic numbers (instead of conventionally notated pitches) was a rule-based melodic improvisation later retroactively titled *The Pre-Tortoise Dream Music*, following a repetitive sequence of harmonics. Such pieces were performed by Young's group, The Theater of Eternal Music: Young and his wife Marian Zazeela on vocals, Conrad on violin, hand-drummer Angus MacLise, John Cale on viola, sometimes Jennings on sax, and Riley singing or playing violin.

The Theater of Eternal Music's performances would take place over a deafening drone audible outside the concert hall, with geometric lighting designed by Zazeela, a visual artist in her own right whose work with different colored lights parallels Young's work with sustained tunings. Listening to tapes of those performances, it is extraordinary how well one can hear the relationships between what look like a complex set of overtones: the 63rd harmonic as a whole step above the 7th (56th), the 42nd as a perfect fourth below the 56th, and so on.

Conrad, while still involved with Young and Zazeela, produced some minimalist music on his own, including *Outside the Dream Syndicate* and the several-hour-long *Four Violins* of 1964. After breaking with Young, he veered into the field of filmmaking and video, creating a film called *The Flicker* which remains a seminal work of the structuralist film movement. Later, in the 1980s, he returned to composition and attempted to recreate what he considered the essential aspects of the Theater of Eternal Music's work in *Early Minimalism* (a series of works made between 1985 and 1995) and *Slapping Pythagoras* (1995). Meanwhile Cale, while still working with Young, began a proto-punk rock group called The Velvet Underground and became part of rock history. In "The Black Angel's Death Song" from *The Velvet Underground and Nico*, the famous Verve disc with Andy Warhol's banana painting on the cover, the viola drone and static texture are legacies of Young's influence.

In June of 1964, Young tuned a piano to six pitches of *The Pre-Tortoise Dream Music*, tuning the six other pitches of the scale consonantly to fill out the octave. On this he performed a forty-five-minute improvisation on various chords separated by silences. This would grow into *The Well-Tuned Piano*, an improvisatory piano solo based on more than fifty complexly interrelated themes and chordal areas and lasting, in recent performances, over six hours. The piece (further discussed below) is probably the most innovative and influential American piano work since Ives's *Concord Sonata*.

Concurrent with the Theater of Eternal Music, Young and Zazeela began an ongoing project called Dream House, in which they played pure sine tones in perfectly-tuned ratios to observe the effect (if any) on the human nervous system and spirit. Through the seventies and most of the eighties, they were supported by the Dia Foundation, which allowed them to work full-time on installations and environments without the pressures to put music out commercially that most composers face. Young's early sine-tone assemblages, called *Drift Studies*, started out with relatively simple ratio patterns often including prime numbers Young was particularly interested in 31:32, or 63:64, or 7:16:18. Around 1980 Young obtained a super-accurate Rayna synthesizer, reliable to within one beat a year, and began moving into the higher reaches of the overtone series.

His most complex such sine-tone sculpture to date (1994) is titled *The Base 9:7:4 Symmetry in Prime Time When Centered Above and Below the Lowest Term Primes in the Range 288 to 224 with the Addition of 279 and 261 in Which the Half of The Symmetric Division Mapped Above and Including 288*

Frequency Ratio	Cents above Fundamental	Description
2224	143	(139×2^4) octave of twin prime
2096	40	(131×2^4) octave of prime
1096	118	(137×2^3) octave of twin prime
1072	79	(67×2^4) octave of prime
568	180	(71×2^3) octave of Young prime (P_{yII})
544	105	(17×2^5) octave of Young prime (P_{yII})
288	204	(9×2^5) octave of 9
283	174	twin and Young prime (P_{yI})
281	161	twin prime
279	149	(9×31)
277	136	prime
271	99	twin and Young prime (P_{yI})
269	86	twin prime
263	47	prime
261	33	(9×29)
257	7	prime
256	0	(2^8) octave of fundamental
254	1186	(127×2) octave of prime
252	1173	$(9 \times 7 \times 2^2)$ octave of 63
251	1166	Young prime (P_{yII})
241	1095	Young prime (P_{yII})
239	1081	prime
233	1037	prime
229	1007	twin prime
227	992	twin prime
224	969	(7×2^5) octave of 7
119	1074	(17×7)
113	984	prime
61	1117	twin and Young prime (P_{yI})
59	1059	twin prime
31	1145	twin and Young prime (P_{yI})
29	1030	twin prime
9	204	region boundary
7	969	region boundary
4	0	(2^2) octave of fundamental

EXAMPLE 8.1 La Monte Young, *The Base 9:7:4 Symmetry in Prime Time When Centered Above and Below the Lowest Term Primes in the Range 288 to 224 with Addition of 279 and 261 . . .*

Consists of the Powers of 2 Multiplied by the Primes Within the Ranges of 144 to 128, 72 to 64, and 36 to 32 Which Are Symmetrical to Those Primes in Lowest Terms in the Half of the Symmetric Division Mapped Below and Including 224 within the Ranges 126 to 112, 63 to 56, and 31.5 to 28 with the Addition of 119. This breathtaking title is a literal description of the entire piece, whose frequency ratios are given in example 8.1. I wrote, for the *Village Voice,* the following description of the piece while listening to it:

> Walk into The Base 9:7:4 Symmetry and you'll hear a whirlwind of pitches swirl around you. Stand still, and the tones suddenly freeze in place. Within the room, every pitch finds its own little niche where it resonates, and with all those close-but-no-cigar intervals competing in one space (not to mention their elegantly calculated sum- and difference-tones), you can alter the harmony you perceive simply by pulling on your earlobe. . . . Moving your head makes those tones leap from high to low and back, while that cluster in the seventh octave, with its wild prime ratios like 269:271, fizzes in and out. . . .[4]

Young's music offers images of infinity, its drones (either instrumental or electronic) sustained in a stasis that seems extracted from a potential eternity.

Listening Example: **The Well-Tuned Piano** *(1964–1973–1981–present)*

The Well-Tuned Piano is La Monte Young's masterpiece to date, an improvisatory but intricately structured piano solo whose most recent performances have exceeded six hours. The work uses one of the most unusual scales in the history of music, remarkable for the smallness of some of its pitch steps. The scale, in ratios and cents (rounded off to the nearest whole cent) measured from the fundamental E-flat, is as follows:

NOTES	RATIOS	CENTS ABOVE E♭
E♭	1:1	0
E	567:512	177
F	9:8	204
G♭	147:128	240
G	21:16	471
G♯	1323:1024	444
A	189:128	675
B♭	3:2	702
B	49:32	738
C	7:4	969
C♯	441:256	942
D	63:32	1173

Notice from the cents column that the scale does not uniformly ascend; G♯ is *lower* than G, and C♯ lower than C. This is to keep all perfect fifths (3:2 ratios) spelled as such on the keyboard. The tuning allows for great subtlety in adjacent pitches within certain melodies, while allowing a maximum of transposability to various keys.

There are two primary contrasting features to *The Well-Tuned Piano.* One is the themes that thread through the work in a glorious complexity of anticipations and reminiscences. These themes have fantastically imaginative names such as "The Goddess of the Caverns under the Pool," "The Theme of the Lyre of Orpheus," "Young's Brontosaurus Boogie in E♭," and—the most important theme—"The Theme of the Dawn of Eternal Time." (This last-named theme, which opens the work, is given in example 8.2.) The remainder of the piece consists of "clouds," indistinct chords of quickly repeated notes whose resonance in this pure tuning builds up tremendous continuums of tones, including sum- and difference-tones which are perceived without being played. The clouds are made up of notes from the various chords, including the Opening Chord (E-flat, B-flat, C, and F), the Magic Chord (E, F-sharp, A, and B in the left hand, D, E, G, and A in the right), the Romantic Chord, the Harmonic Rainforest Chord, and so on. Between them the Opening and Magic Chords divide up the ten pitches most used in the piece, which swings slowly back and forth between the two pitch areas.

Except for an additively built-up melody here and there, *The Well-Tuned Piano* really has little in common with most minimalist music. It uses plenty of dissonance, some of it quite sharp because of the tiny intervals involved, as well as pure consonance; there is rarely a steady beat for any length of time, nor any repetition to speak of; and the form is completely organic, ebbing and swelling under the force of spontaneous inspiration. Whether you listen to the clouds as a kind of ambient experience or follow the intricate network of themes, the work provides one of the most complex and well worked-out large-scale forms since Wagner's operas.

EXAMPLE 8.2 La Monte Young, *The Well-Tuned Piano*. Theme of the Dawn of Eternal Time. All the pitches in this example are exact overtones of E-flat. Thus the D-flat (actually played on C on Young's keyboard) is about 31 cents flatter than usual. The rhythmic notation here is Young's own, approximated from his improvisation.

Terry Riley

La Monte Young and Terry Riley have enjoyed one of the more remarkable friendships in the history of music, devoid of the jealous rivalry that
has marked so many pairs of originators. The relationship could have
been difficult, because for most of their careers Riley has enjoyed more
public success. This situation began in 1968, when Columbia Records
attempted to produce records by both Riley and Young. The Riley disc
was the premiere recording of his groundbreaking 1964 masterwork *In
C.* Young's recording was to have been of him and Zazeela singing in pure
tunings with the ocean in the background. Something went wrong with
the recording of the ocean, and Columbia wanted to rerecord the ocean
and overdub it with the voices. Young objected vehemently, feeling that
the singing was in response to the ocean and that an overdubbing would
amount to artistic dishonesty. On financial grounds, Columbia refused to
rerecord. Riley's disc appeared, Young's didn't, and Riley's reputation
soared. What keeps the peace is that Riley has always generously given
Young credit for the innovations that led to minimalism.

While Riley does not possess Young's adherence to generative theoretical principles, he has been equally original in less extreme ways.
Born in rural Colfax, California in 1935 (a few months before Young), he
was the son of a railroad man in the Sierra Nevada Mountains. Playing
violin, piano, and later saxophone, Riley became fascinated with bebop.
He attended San Francisco State University, where, studying with Robert
Erickson, he wrote in a rather neoclassic and always tonal style. In the
late fifties he supported his wife and child by playing ragtime piano in
San Francisco's racy Gold Street Saloon. In 1958, however, he began taking courses at Berkeley and fell under the sway of this ambitious Young
man who had scandalized the music department by writing a fifty-one-
minute String Trio with only eighty-three notes.

Young and Riley began giving concerts together in performances
which included playing catch, mowing the lawn, sleeping in sleeping
bags, and dragging trash cans around the perimeter of the concert hall.[5]
Where Young had found his aesthetic in sustained tones, Riley was fascinated by repetition and that same year wrote his first work using tape
loops, *Mescaline Mix,* for the dancer Anne Halprin. As he later noted,

> I think I was noticing that things didn't sound the same when you
> heard them more than once. And the more you heard them, the
> more different they did sound. . . . In those days the first psychedelic
> experiences were starting to happen in America, and that was chang-
> ing our concept of how time passes. . . .[6]

Restless, Riley headed for Europe with his family. In France, at a studio
of the French National Radio, he wrote his first piece using a technique
he would make famous, tape-delay. It was *Music for the Gift* (1963),

Terry Riley. *Photo by Sabine Matthes.*

accompaniment for a theater piece, and for the first time it used a tape playing in one tape player, being simultaneously recorded in another and then played back for an echo effect caused by the distance between the record and play heads on the second tape machine.

Returning to San Francisco in 1964, Riley gave a concert at the San Francisco Tape Center. The premiere on the program was modestly called *In C,* and the performers included, besides Riley, composers Steve Reich, Pauline Oliveros, Jon Gibson, Morton Subotnick, Phil Winsor, and Ramon Sender, to mention the more famous names. The score to *In C* (excerpts given in example 8.3) consists merely of fifty-three melodic fragments which each performer is to play in order, repeating each one

EXAMPLE 8.3 Terry Riley, *In C*, selected melodies.

any number of times and moving on to the next whenever he or she wishes. At rehearsals, it was difficult to keep the ensemble pulse together, so at Reich's suggestion, Riley added a relentless pulse on the top two Cs of the piano. The echoing of brief melodies from player to player provides a nonelectronic semblance of the tape-delay effect, while the swirling of motives around the pulse elicits a hypnotic, almost trance-like state from the listener. One of the most widely performed pieces of twentieth-century music (partly due to its unspecified instrumentation), *In C* has enjoyed unbroken popularity from the evening of its premiere to the present day.

Following *In C,* most of Riley's subsequent recordings, such as *Rainbow in Curved Air* (1968) and *Poppy Nogood and the Phantom Band* (1967), were solos either on the saxophone or the electric organ with tape delay, or on the piano. More than any other music of the sixties, his early music has the smooth, modal, groove-oriented feel associated with the psychedelic drug culture. In 1970, he and Young both began studying Indian raga singing with Pandit Pran Nath, and Riley dropped from public view for awhile. He reemerged with a disc of highly intricate counterpoint for just-intonation organ with tape delay, *Shri Camel* (1980), a series of tapestries over propulsive ostinatos. And when the Kronos String Quartet approached Riley for some chamber music in the early eighties, he responded with two beautiful multimovement cycles, *Cadenza on the Night Plain* (1984) and *Salomé Dances for Peace* (1985–1986).

Riley's most recent works are eclectic and resist characterization. He usually employs pure, just-intonation tunings, at least in his piano and string quartet music, though he does not adopt Young's extreme purist position or go to the extent of a special notation like Ben Johnston. He frequently makes use of rhythmically complex ostinatos that provide a Middle-Eastern flavor (the *Mythic Birds Waltz* for string quartet is an example). His *The Heaven Ladder* (1995) is a multimovement piece of ambitious, super-Beethovenian proportions full of ragtime fugues and lullabies, while other works, like *Chanting the Light of Foresight* (1987) for the Rova Saxophone Quartet, draw on the mythology of his Irish heritage. This tendency to never remain satisfied with a particular vein may have decreased the popularity his early reputation promised, but Riley is a superb and devout musician whose compositions are never superficial.

Steve Reich

For many fans, Steve Reich is the only minimalist who counts; Young's music is too inaccessible and austere, Riley's too inconsistent, and Glass's too repetitive and simplistic. Reich's music does have an elegant veneer of intricate surface detail that gives it a classical sense of polish, and its bouncy rhythms within a serene stasis of diatonic, white-note tonality enchant jazz and classical fans alike. Also, Reich quickly surpassed Young and Riley in visibility when his Deutsche Grammophon recording of *Drumming* appeared in 1974, and his earlier "process" works, *Come Out* and *Piano Phase,* have had tremendous impact on younger composers. As the minimalist who communicates to mainstream classical listeners, Reich is something of an Aaron Copland for the late twentieth century, a status confirmed in 1980 when he became the first composer in decades whose music attracted a sell-out crowd to Carnegie Hall.

The East Coast, urban upbringings of Reich and Philip Glass contrast markedly with Young's and Riley's rural, frontier origins. Born in

New York in 1936, Reich was the son of a lawyer and a lyricist-singer who divorced when he was a year old. Train trips between his parents in Los Angeles and New York, on which he was accompanied only by his governess, later influenced one of his most popular works, *Different Trains* for string quartet and recorded voice samples. At sixteen he entered Cornell to major in philosophy, eventually writing a thesis on Ludwig Wittgenstein. Like Young and Riley, he kept up a jazz band on the side, one that tried to sound, he says, somewhere "between George Shearing and Miles Davis."[7]

After graduation, Reich headed back into music, studying with William Bergsma and Vincent Persichetti at Juilliard, but cut his studies there short to head with the hippies to a hipper location, San Francisco. At Juilliard he had already written his first twelve-tone piece, and when he found that the celebrated Italian serialist Luciano Berio would be teaching at Mills College, he enrolled. Reich's approach to twelve-tone writing was unusual, however, and pointed to future tendencies: he used the row at the same pitch level over and over, without transposing. Finally, a frustrated Berio asked, "If you want to write tonal music, why don't you write tonal music?" Reich took the suggestion.

His first experiments in rebuilding tonality used tape loops, like Riley's. Having recorded a sermon by a San Francisco street preacher, he played two simultaneous loops of a shouted phrase, and found that fascinating aural phenomena resulted when the tape loops went slowly out of sync because of differences in tape player speed. The piece based on these loops became *It's Gonna Rain* (1965), and the next piece, produced back in New York, was *Come Out* (1966). *Come Out* was drawn from an interview with a victim of a police beating, who told Reich, "I had to, like, let some of the bruise blood come out to show them." (The victim couldn't be taken to the hospital unless he was bleeding.) In Reich's loop process, the phrase "Come out to show them" repeated increasingly out of phase with itself, begins to sound melodic once the verbal content is effaced by the blurring of nonsynchronous loops.

What Reich realized in listening to *It's Gonna Rain* and *Come Out* was that listening to a gradual musical process could be highly engaging, especially in contrast to the abstract music of Cage and the serialists, who hid their processes behind opaque walls of complexity. Audible process—"process music"—became Reich's touchstone for the next several years, up through *Drumming* of 1973. However, Reich was not satisfied to make music only to play on tapes, and he returned to live performance with *Piano Phase* (1967), in which he and another pianist performed the same phasing process heard in *Come Out* on two pianos with a simple twelve-note melody in B minor. (See example 8.4.)

When Reich gave a concert in 1967, Philip Glass, his old schoolmate at Juilliard, came up afterward to talk. Together with Jon Gibson on flute and saxophone and a few other musicians, they put together an

EXAMPLE 8.4 Steve Reich, *Piano Phase*. Reich's directions read: "The first pianist starts at 1 and the second joins him in unison at 2. The second pianist increases his tempo very slightly and begins to gradually move ahead of the first until, (say in 20–30 seconds) he is one sixteenth ahead, as shown at 3. The dotted lines indicate this gradual movement of the second pianist and the consequent shift of phase relation between himself and the first pianist.

ensemble to play their music, starting a downtown Manhattan tradition of composer-led ensembles. Forming one's own ensemble obviated the problem of working with orchestras and more conventional ensembles, whose habits and union rules prevented a composer from ever getting nearly the rehearsal time he or she needed for a sterling performance. Also, the attitude of orchestra players toward new music has been notoriously bad for decades, and with hand-picked players, one could count on sympathetic interpreters who would put their heart and soul into the music. The result was that, all through the seventies, the separate ensembles of Reich and Glass (who split up on acrimonious terms in 1971) gave the most exquisitely well-rehearsed new-music performances around.

In fact, no innovation by the minimalists has had more profound or lasting consequences than the Reich-Glass ensemble concept. Under serialist influence, classical chamber music had emphasized soloistic playing and individual virtuosity. Reich and Glass, writing music centered on simple processes and working with musicians who were not necessarily virtuosos, introduced ensemble playing in which players doubled each other's lines exactly, or at least in rhythmic unison. The result, amplified by the use of synthesizers and microphones (in Glass's music especially), wasn't chamber music in the conventional sense but a new kind of symphonic genre designed to focus the new materials to an audience in clear-cut lines. Just as Romantic orchestral music used entire brass or strings choirs playing the same melody, minimalist orchestration achieved similar effects with only five to eight players. This, as much as the tonal simplicity and rhythmic interest, was a key to minimalism's appeal.

As Young and Riley had found inspiration in Indian and Arabic music, Reich took a new impetus for his music from the study of African drumming. In the summer of 1970 he enrolled at the University of Ghana at Accra and spent five weeks (his stay curtailed by malaria) studying Ewe drumming. He found the phasing processes of Ewe rhythmic impulses akin to his own tape-loop processes, and upon his return worked at figuring out how to reconfigure African drumming techniques to fit into a Western performance tradition. The result was *Drumming* (1971), perhaps minimalism's first real public success. The seventy-odd-minute piece is divided, without pause, into four sections: the first for tuned bongos, the second for marimbas, the third for glockenspiels and piccolo, and the fourth for all those forces combined. Using only a few pitches in serene F♯ major modality, the piece uses beat-shifting and phase-shifting repetitions to create a shimmering surface of mellow mallet percussion.

With *Music for 18 Musicians* (1976), Reich began to move away from audible process, though this pulsing continuum, modulating as it does through one ambiguous key area after another, is nevertheless one of his most popular works. In the 1980s he began to receive orchestra commissions, which pulled him into a realm not entirely congenial to his musical personality; the results, such as *Desert Music* (1984) and *The Four Sections* (1987), blunt his music's delightful rhythmic edge. More fruitful are his continuing explorations of speech-melody, which took a new turn in *Different Trains* (1988) for string quartet and tape. In this, phrases spoken about train trips—both Reich's own as a child and the very different train trips that Jews in Europe were taking to the death camps—are spun into a synchronized counterpoint whose melodic contours are generated by the speech phrases. Similarly, the speech contours of Jews and Arabs discussing their common heritage are woven into *The Cave* (1993), a multimedia extravaganza made in collaboration with Reich's wife, the video artist Beryl Korot. *The Cave* is the largest and most exciting expression so far of Reich's renewed interest in his Jewish roots, which began in the late 1970s.

Listening Example: **Eight Lines *(1979)***

One of the audible processes that Reich grew enamored of early, and has remained faithful to, is the gradual elongation of a brief phrase. As precedent, Reich points to church organum of the twelfth century, in which composers like Perotin greatly lengthened notes of a chant to add more and more notes in the counterpoint above. Reich's version of this process first appears in his *Four Organs* (1970), which takes twenty minutes to turn a phrase of two staccato organ chords into a thick continuum. The process continued in *Music for Mallet Instruments, Voices, and Organ* (1973) and reached a kind of climax of elegance in his Octet (1979), also called *Eight Lines* when played with fuller and more practical instrumentation.

Throughout its eighteen-minute duration, *Eight Lines* rocks gently in a pleasantly asymmetric 5/4 meter. The instrumentation uses more than eight instruments, but never more than eight at a time: flute, piccolo, clarinet, bass clarinet, two pianos, two violins, viola, and cello (the string quartet can be doubled to relieve the difficulty of all the sustained tones). The piano parts are fiendishly difficult, a perpetual motion of parallel fifths leaping across the keyboard. When the texture is thickest, the pianos are echoing each other from one to four beats apart within the 5/4 rhythm; this intricate echoing against the meter accounts for much of the piece's aural liveliness. Each of the five continuous sections is diatonic, using a seven-note scale without accidentals. Overall, however, the key changes almost unnoticeably from a signature of five sharps to six sharps to five flats.

The piece's structure is defined by the repeating chord patterns in the strings, which are built up additively, phrase by phrase, in minimalist tradition. In the first section, the phrases are first two measures long, then expand to eight and then ten. The second section opens with a return to two-measure phrases, which are then expanded to four, and so on according to the following pattern:

Section	Phrase lengths in measures				Key signature
1	2	8	10		five sharps
2	2	4			six sharps
3	2	8	10		five flats
4	2	4			five flats
5	2	4	8	10	five flats

EXAMPLE 8.5 Steve Reich, *Eight Lines.*

(*Continued*)

EXAMPLE 8.5 *(continued)*

Each phrase pattern is repeated from two to twelve times (fully notated in the score, not left to the performer's discretion as in much minimalist music). Another method of sectional articulation is that the lower strings play chords with the violins in sections 2, 4, and 5, and in 1 and 3 play fast-note patterns similar to those of the pianos.

The flute melody that enters near the beginning of *Eight Lines* (seen in example 8.5) marks one of minimalism's first returns to a freely intuitive composing technique after years of strict objectivism. The tendency of the woodwinds in this piece to pick out patterns from the piano parts goes back to Reich's *Drumming*, in which the piccolo was asked to pick out and reinforce melodies resulting from the counterpoint of percussion lines. The physicality of *Eight Lines*'s swinging rhythm, plus the intricacy of its echoing patterns, demonstrate why Reich has become one of the best-loved of American composers.

Philip Glass

Philip Glass is the minimalist whose style is best known to the general public. This is partly due to the sheer bulk of his work—thirteen operas as of this writing—and his involvement with theater, a medium that never fails to generate more press than instrumental music. It is also due to the extreme clarity and recognizability of his style, occasionally amounting to a lamentable tendency toward self-repetition. His trademark, the repeating four- to six-note arpeggio used to articulate chromatically related triads, instantly identifies the music as his. Consequently, he has achieved a dubious reputation as the "lowbrow" minimalist, a reputation that does not do justice to the considerable tonal and rhythmic complexity of his best music. Glass did study at Juilliard and with the formidable Nadia Boulanger, and his easily caricatured idiom sometimes conceals structures of elegant sophistication.

Born in Baltimore in 1937, Glass took up violin, flute, and piano, and later studied at Juilliard, fascinated by the music of Webern. At the University of Chicago, he majored in philosophy (like Reich) and mathematics, then continued at Juilliard as a classmate of Reich's, likewise studying with Persichetti, Bergsma, and (at Aspen) Milhaud. Quite predictably given this training, Glass wrote many pieces in a Francophile, Coplandesque idiom. What's more intriguing is that more than twenty of these pieces were published. While Glass has disowned them, and they bear no relationship to his mature style, one can still find them floating around music libraries.

In 1964 Glass took the equally conventional career step of going to Paris to study with the seventy-seven-year-old Boulanger. Reduced to a childlike level of starting over by Boulanger's stern discipline, he nevertheless credited some part of his future success to the technique she instilled in him. The Paris music scene, however, was dominated (and would be for over another thirty years) by Pierre Boulez, who had turned it into (in Glass's words) "a wasteland, dominated by these maniacs, these creeps, who were trying to make everyone write this crazy, creepy music"[8]—i.e., serialist music. Despite Glass's early enthusiasm for Webern, he had long ago lost interest in strict atonality, considering it—as many composers did before European serialism renewed interest in it—an old-fashioned, prewar idiom.

Just as with Young, Riley, and Reich, Glass was turned in a new direction by exposure to non-Western music. In 1965, still in Paris, he was asked to transcribe some music by the Indian sitar player Ravi Shankar that was intended for use in a film. Working for months with Shankar and his tabla player, Glass learned the principles of Indian rhythmic structure, or tala, in which rhythmic cycles are built up by addition of different numbers of a small rhythmic unit. Under this influence, Glass began working in a new style using repetitions of tiny rhythmic patterns and very few pitches, a style that first appeared in his 1965 music for Samuel Beckett's *Play* (produced by the company that would later, in New York, become Mabou Mines). Perhaps the archetype of this phase of Glass's music is the simple piece *1+1* (1968), consisting merely of two rhythmic units—an eighth note, and two sixteenths followed by an eighth—tapped in any order and combination on any amplified surface.

Glass's ensemble, following the breakup with Reich, included Richard Landry, Jon Gibson, Richard Peck (all saxophonists, though

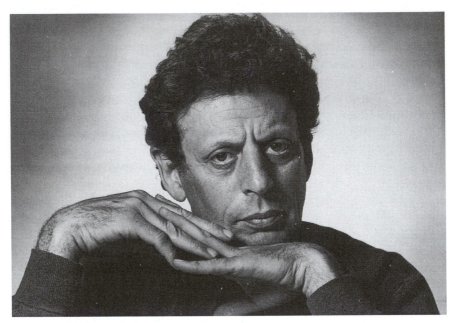

Philip Glass. *Photo © Jack Mitchell.*

Gibson often played flute), sound mixer Kurt Munkacsi, and at various times James Tenney, Frederic Rzewski, Joan LaBarbara, Barbara Benary, Richard Teitelbaum, and singers Iris Hiskey and Dora Ohrenstein. For this ensemble of lightning-quick reflexes Glass wrote a series of groundbreaking works: *Two Pages* (1969), *Music in Fifths* (1969), *Music in Contrary Motion* (1969), *Music in Similar Motion* (1969), *Music with Changing Parts* (1970), and finally, the magnum opus of his early years, the mammoth *Music in Twelve Parts* (1974). These mesmerizing monuments of melody, each less austere than its predecessor, were characterized by long but quick chant-like lines played in unison by the entire ensemble, or at least in rhythmic unison. Often the lines were built up by additive processes: 1, 1–2, 1–2–3, 1–2–3–4, and so on. Such processes often resulted in a bracing level of rhythmic complexity quite simply achieved, as repeated notes would build up complex accent patterns (see example 8.6 from *Music in Fifths*).

Glass's breakthrough to the public came in his opera *Einstein on the Beach,* which premiered November 21, 1976. The opera revolves around the figure of a madly sawing violinist dressed as Einstein, and the title refers vaguely to Einstein's responsibility for having paved the way for the production of the atomic bomb. *Einstein* was a collaboration with theater director Robert Wilson, already known by then for slow-moving theater works lasting many hours, in which visual logic and geometric

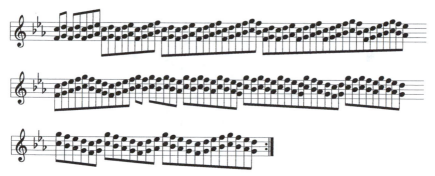

EXAMPLE 8.6 Philip Glass, excerpt from *Music in Fifths.*

patterns replaced narrative. At this point in his life, Glass was still driving
a cab; one story is that a couple of his passengers described having just
attended *Einstein on the Beach.* When Glass claimed to be the composer,
they didn't believe him.

Glass's music for his own electronic ensemble is quite different
from the music he has written for orchestras: his own exquisitely-
rehearsed ensemble achieves a sparkling precision no conventional
orchestra could match. In 1979, however, Glass was invited by the
Netherlands Opera to write his first more conventional opera: *Satya-
graha,* based on the life of Mahatma Ghandi. This was followed by a third
opera in a trilogy about famous men, this one on the Egyptian monothe-
istic ruler *Akhnaten* (1984). Example 8.7, from *Akhnaten*'s funeral scene,
shows how much more supple Glass's music became during the eighties.
He has nurtured a technique of gradually built-up polytonality, suggesting two or three keys at once but introducing each one so slowly that the
ear hardly notices the resulting dissonances. Here, over an invigorating
and never-quite-predictable drumbeat, a bascially A-major texture alternates over and over with a harmony on D♯. At first the D♯ enters only as
a neighbor note, but eventually it is introduced in the tubas, even against
the orchestra playing in A, until it begins to sound like a separate tonic.

By this writing Glass has over a dozen written operas. The ones after
Akhnaten include *The Juniper Tree* (1984), *The Making of the Representative for
Planet 8* (1986), *The Fall of the House of Usher* (1988), *The Voyage* (1992),
Orphée (1993), *La Belle et la Bête* (1994), *White Raven* (1995), and *Les
Enfants Terribles* (1996). Some of these are based in unusual formats.
Orphée, for example, is an operatic reworking of a film by Jean Cocteau,
and *La Belle et la Bête* is an accompaniment to another Cocteau film, to be
performed while showing the film. In addition, Glass has written a Violin
Concerto (1987), a *Low Symphony* (based on themes from the *Low* album
by Brian Eno and David Bowie), and several film scores including
Koyaanisqatsi (1982) and *Mishima* (1984).

EXAMPLE 8.7 Philip Glass: *Aknaten*, Funeral Scene.

Glass has often churned out pieces quickly, in an easily recognizable idiom of doodling arpeggios, and some of the operas and smaller orchestral pieces come close to self-parody. Consequently, much of Glass's best music has been underrated by disappointed former fans who have ceased to listen closely. In particular, *The Voyage, La Belle et la Bête,* and the *Low Symphony* contain some surprising polytonal complexities, long, subtle rhythmic cycles, and harmonic progressions that stick in the mind for positive reasons. Glass may well be the Rossini of his century, a composer whose works had an electric impact on the masses but only a portion of whose music seemed worthy of study by intellectuals.

Listening Example: **Einstein on the Beach,** *"Bed" and "Spaceship" scenes (1976)*

Einstein on the Beach has no real libretto, only chanted numbers and solfège syllables, a few repetitive spoken texts, and a visual unity created by the parallels and repetitions of Robert Wilson's staging. The work reveals both of Glass's most basic compositional strategies—additive rhythmic development and chromatically polytonal harmony—and shows him at the height of his inventiveness. In the "Bed" scene, the bed present in the preceding "Trial" scene now dominates the stage. Glass builds an ever-lengthening rhythmic structure around a progression of four chords: F minor, E-flat major, C major, and D major. It's easy to see

EXAMPLE 8.8 Philip Glass, "Bed" Scene from *Einstein on the Beach.*

in example 8.8 how with each new phrase the rhythm lengthens, from 7 + 4 to 9 + 4 to 9 + 7, until at last the wordless soprano is singing very long notes indeed. Glass makes the most of his chromaticism in the melody, drawing lovely connections between chords in this slowly rotating kaleidoscope.

The following "spaceship" scene is the opera's climax. The chord progression in example 8.9 spins by with lightning speed as the chorus chants numbers to keep the rhythm: "one–two–three–four one–two–three one–two–three–four one–two–three one–two–three–four." The rhythm of this progression goes through additive and subtractive processes similar to that of the "bed" scene. Meanwhile, the long, horizontal white bar that crept onstage earlier in the opera slowly rises over a six-minute period, finally lifting off into space. Partly because Glass and Wilson disdained operatic conventions, *Einstein on the Beach* was one of the twentieth century's most innovative and inspiring works, suggesting new directions for musical theater.

Example 8.9 Philip Glass, chord pattern from "Spaceship" scene, *Einstein on the Beach*.

Meredith Monk

Since the explosion in the number of women composers in the 1970s, a new genre of music has been added to the cultural scene. A handful or fewer of men work in this genre, but the practitioners are overwhelmingly women. Women composers are far more likely than men to use their own voices and bodies as material for their music; the singing of unusual and virtuosic vocal techniques, or the musical structuring of body movements, involves a vulnerability, a publicly emotive expressiveness, that men in our society are perhaps too inhibited to indulge. One can name a few men who make music from their own extended vocal techniques, notably Toby Twining and David Moss. There are dozens of such women: Diamanda Galàs, Laurie Anderson, Eve Beglarian, Elise Kermani, Joan LaBarbara, Shelley Hirsch, Pamela Z, Brenda Hutchinson, Maria de Alvear (Spanish), Bonnie Barnett, Christine Baczewska, Lynn Book, and on and on. To distinguish these composers from the usual kind who work in a more abstract way, writing notes or playing instruments, they are often called performance artists, but their role as composers of essentially musical structures should not thereby be diminished.

Oliveros might be considered the first example of this new, mostly female-identified genre, for she uses her voice in her sonic meditations. She is neither a trained vocalist nor a dancer, however, and the woman who has most epitomized the composer who employs her voice and body is Meredith Monk. Dancer, filmmaker, singer, and composer, Monk has been creative in so many media that she is as frequently (if not more often) written about by dance and theater critics as by music critics. And yet, she has said, "I call myself a composer. Even if I'm working with musical theater or with images, . . . I'm always thinking in musical terms. . . ."[9]

What she definitely does not consider herself is a minimalist. As she's put it:

> I come from a folk music tradition. I was a folk singer with a guitar. The repetition in my music I think of as being like folk music: you have your chorus and verse. I'm more interested in how the voice digs down into emotional reality. It's like the freedom of a jazz singer, it's not a patterning impulse. The minimalist thing is about reduction. Vocally, I always thought about magnification, expansion. The repetitions are just a layer for the voice to take off from and go somewhere, and also to land on again.[10]

All the same, Monk's music does concern itself with minimalist issues such as repetition and static tonality, and to call her a postminimalist would imply that she followed the minimalists in a subsequent generation, building on their work. In fact, she and Reich began their public careers at virtually the same time, for Monk's breakthrough piece, a film called *16-Millimeter Earrings,* appeared in 1966. Suffice it to say the Monk's music expresses an infectious emotionality that contrasts strongly with the clean, objective lines of Reich and Glass.

Monk was born in New York in 1942 and grew up in Queens. (She once told an interviewer she was born in Lima, Peru, a bit of false information that has spread into reference books.) The daughter of a professional singer who did radio commercials for CBS in the days before commercials were taped,[11] she studied theater, dance, and music in her teens, and attended Sarah Lawrence College. From the very beginning, she was accustomed to make no separation between the arts in her way of working.

Monk spent the sixties in New York in the invigorating atmosphere of the Tenney-Corner-Goldstein-Feldman crowd and around the happenings and performance art of the Judson Theater. In *16-Millimeter Earrings* (1966) she found a way to combine dance, theater, visual images, and music: she filmed herself dancing and made her own experimental soundtrack with three tape loops running at once. Her first large theater works, *Juice* (1969) and *Vessel: An Opera Epic* (1971, loosely based on Joan of Arc), each took place over three nonconsecutive nights in different spaces, in a bold attempt to break through concert conventions. In its first night, at the Guggenheim Museum, *Juice* used eighty-five singers with Jew's harps surrounding the audience for huge spatial effects.

In the early seventies, though, Monk withdrew into mostly solo work. Her training as a dancer made her realize that the voice could be approached with the same range and flexibility as the body, and she began building a repertoire of vocal sounds and techniques, many of which she later found out were akin to those used in Balkan singing, Tibetan chanting, and other non-Western vocal traditions. Monk's vocal techniques include glottal stops, warbly American-Indian-style vibrato, nasal singing, nonsense syllables, and many of the strange voice tones children use in games. Some pieces will contain only a word or two of text, such as "Oh, I'm scared" (*Scared Song*) or "Vacation" (*Double Fiesta*), spun out playfully over and over. Her *Lullaby #4* from *Songs from the Hill* (1976) took the sound "me-ow" as its complete phonic material, and Monk has said that the lullaby is one of her primary paradigms.

In 1978 Monk formed her own vocal ensemble and began to write for it, beginning with *Dolmen Music* (1979), a darkly mysterious theater piece of evocative chants. Many of her works have evoked themes of totalitarianism and holocaust. *Quarry: An Opera* (1976) contained a film shot in a rock quarry with singers dressed in white, and later bodies floating in black water. Centered on Monk as a little girl sick in bed, the piece depicted the rise of a malign dictatorship. Though Monk has called many of her works operas, her output climaxed in 1991 with her first work that looked like a conventional opera: *Atlas*.

Listening Example: Atlas *(1991)*

One of the most beautiful operas of the late twentieth century, *Atlas* is a nonnarrative opera whose three acts depict a spiritual as well as geographical journey. The work was inspired by the life of Alexandra David-Neel, a scientist and the first Western woman to travel in Tibet; however, she is renamed Alexandra Daniels in the opera, which does not portray her life literally.

Typical of Monk's music, several scenes from the opera are based on ostinatos, bass lines or chordal progressions that repeat over and over. Monk often trains her singers via vocal transmission and imitation rather than through notation, and sometimes the vocal lines over the ostinatos are worked out in rehearsal rather than composed in advance. Three of the operas' ostinatos are given in examples 8.10 through 8.12: the ones for Act I, scene 2 ("Travel Dream Song"), Act I, scene 5 ("Rite of Passage"), and Act II, scene 3 ("Agricultural Community"). These notations give little idea of the music's richness, for in *Travel Dream Song* singer Dina Emerson (as the young Alexandra) trills with Monk's

EXAMPLE 8.10 Meredith Monk, *Atlas* ostinato from "Travel Dream Song."

EXAMPLE 8.11 Meredith Monk, *Atlas* ostinato from "Rite of Passage."

EXAMPLE 8.12 Meredith Monk, *Atlas* ostinato for "Agricultural Community."

repeated-note techniques, and in "Agricultural Community" the singers sing a wild, wordless melody that accentuates the 5/4 meter like some whirling, Middle-Eastern dance.

The story of *Atlas* takes the heroine on a quest through an agricultural community, a rainforest, the Arctic, and the desert. "Choosing Companions" (Act I, scene 6) is delightful; Alexandra in effect selects her companions by having them sing the same athletically graceful melody she sings, and one of them fails with comic results. The "Ice Demons" scene of Act II is a trio of shrill sopranos singing high staccato notes and spine-tingling glissandos. The end of Act II contains perhaps the darkest music in Monk's output so far, full of nervous rhythms and unresolved dissonance. Act III, however, follows with an other-worldly calm. In "Other Worlds Revealed," Monk's ensemble uses a technique of each singer in a circle singing a note as soon as the previous person started it, for an amazing canonic effect of a slowly blurring, echoing melody (see example 8.13). These group vocal games have a calming, spiritual effect, and the opera ends with the elderly Alexandra alone, drinking coffee.

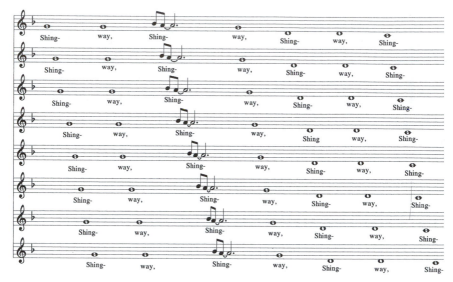

EXAMPLE 8.13 Meredith Monk, *Atlas* vocal canon from "Other Worlds Revealed."

Other Minimalists

Few minimalists have deserved the title more than Harold Budd did early in his career. One of his works, *The Candy-Apple Revision* of 1970, consists of only a D-flat major triad to be interpreted in any manner on any instruments. Budd, born 1936 in Los Angeles, exemplifies more than anyone else the mellow school of California minimalism (even Riley looks uptight by comparison), and he has also had a level of success in the pop-music world that other minimalists can only envy. Though he taught at California Institute of the Arts from 1970 to 1976, no other American figure seems so far from academia, so radically intuitive and uninterested in structures or explanations. His music feels like aural incense, almost ambient, characterized by silky, arpeggiated seventh chords played on electric pianos, harps, and vibraphones, modified by delays and harmonizers, in a lazy atmosphere. For example, "Rosetti Noise" from *Madrigals of the Rose Angel* (1972) consists of only fourteen leisurely chords arpeggiated beneath a soprano voice singing soft tones around which the chords pivot.

Around 1979 Budd began working with the British avant-garde–ambient rock star Brian Eno and learned from Eno how to use the recording studio as a medium. Such discs as *The Pearl* (with Eno, 1984), *Lovely Thunder* (1986), and *The White Arcades* (1988) are heavily processed in the studio, full of resonant atmosphere and often sensuously mournful. Budd's rock career hit a peak in 1986 when he released a disc (*The Moon and the Melodies*) with the post-punk group Cocteau Twins.

On the other hand, "an electronic swarm of bees" is how one musician aptly described his impression of Phill Niblock's music, the New York antipode to Budd's sweet consonance. A filmmaker with little musical training, Niblock has nevertheless been a strong influence on Manhattan's downtown scene. Niblock is the master and extreme example of the out-of-tune approach to tuning which seeks the complexity of sum and difference tones among pitches very close together. Most of his pieces consist of masses of closely tuned pitches; though rich in acoustic phenomena, his music is perhaps the most austere minimalism of all. His usual performance strategy is to prerecord most of the drones on the same or similar instruments on multitrack tape, with the performer tuning to a sine tone heard over headphones. For example, *A Trombone Piece* (1977; Niblock makes a fetish of flatly unimaginative titles) employs only the following frequencies, appearing in all combinations (cycles per second): 55, 57, 59, and 61 in one octave, 110, 113, 116, 119, and 121 in the next, and 220, 224, 228, and 232 in the highest octave. More developmental, *Five More String Quartets* (1992–1994), a work for string quartet overdubbed five times to create a moving drone of twenty pitches, begins with the following sets of frequencies:

STRING QUARTET NO.	FREQUENCY			
1	370	298	208	196
2	392	370	196	92
3	392	185	208	98
4	415	392	185	208
5	208	392	185	196

Over a period of twenty-five minutes, the music expands and contracts with imperceptible gradualness, finally resolving to octave Gs at 98, 196, and 392 cycles per second. In a typical live performance, as the tape plays at high volume, musicians move among the audience, playing the same pitches and traveling so slowly that the live and recorded sounds become confused in the ear. In addition, Niblock frequently superimposes his music over structureless silent films made on his Third-World travels, such as scenes of people involved in repetitive agricultural work.

In the late sixties, Charlemagne Palestine was considered as important a minimalist as La Monte Young. Born in New York in 1945, Palestine gave performances on the carillon and on the Bösendorfer grand piano that were astonishing in their relentless energy. In his mammoth *Strumming Music* (1970–1975) he employed a technique of strumming or drumming on the keys in such a way that overtones would build up and cause aural illusions. He blended sustained tones in electronic works such as *Two Fifths* (1973), and he gave three- to four-hour performances on church organs in a series called the *Spectral Continuum Drones;* he was searching, he said, for "the Golden Sonority,"[12] like an alchemist. A true downtown Manhattan eccentric, Palestine would dress flamboyantly for performances, crowd his piano with stuffed animals, and drink Napoleon Cognac as he played. By the mid-seventies, however, Palestine had turned to visual art, and he remains in the history of minimalism as a dim, not-very-well-documented legend.

Perhaps the only composer to frankly call himself a minimalist, Tom Johnson (b. 1939 in Denver, Colorado), has led a double career, as composer of operas and keyboard music and as critic from 1971 to 1982 for the *Village Voice* newspaper in New York (the only American periodical to run a regular column on experimental music). As a critic, he had a tremendous impact on how the music of the seventies was perceived and is remembered today. A student of Morton Feldman, he has lived in Paris since leaving the *Voice*. As a purveyor of both words and notes, Johnson is fascinated by musical logic and paradox and has developed a radically objectivist philosophy based on an attempt to *find* the music, not compose it.

Thus some of Johnson's compositions are strict workings out of logical sequences, such as *Nine Bells,* in which he paces around the room striking bells in a mathematically logical order—the visual results, however, remaining entertainingly theatrical. His *Chord Catalogue* is a succession of the 8,178 possible chords within one twelve-note octave, yet it achieves a meditative restfulness while testing the relativity of perception. Outside the avant-garde circuit, Johnson is best known for his chamber operas, which deconstruct the genre's conventions in clever ways. His famous *Four-Note Opera* (1972), using only the pitches D, E, A, and B, has a self-referential libretto, each singer announcing in each aria when a cadenza is coming, what scene we're in, where the highest note is, and so on. Even when more intuitively written, however, Johnson's pieces such as *An Hour for Piano* (1971) can be flat, repetitive, wandering, clocklike as a gamelan, but strikingly beautiful.

Daniel Goode has become one of the leading postminimalists, though by generation (he was born in New York in 1936) he is closer to the minimalists. He studied with Cowell and Luening at Columbia University and since 1971 has taught at Rutgers, though he is also known for his participation in Gamelan Son of Lion. His early works, such as *Circular Thoughts* (1974) and *Clarinet Songs* (1979, both for that instrument because he is a clarinetist), revel in strict, algorithmic processes, such as accenting every fourth note in a seven-note pattern. In later works, however, he uses minimalist patterns only as a background for other effects, sometimes with political intent as in his *Wind Symphony,* where the patterns are interrupted by musicians who come in from offstage holding cards which read "ALL," "IS," "NOT," and "WELL." Goode's best work is probably *Tunnel-Funnel* for chamber orchestra (1984), in which the quasi-minimalist patterns wind down an endless harmonic spiral, changing keys moodily and with compelling inevitability.

An associate of Goode's and an early minimalist composer of lovely, gentle works, Barbara Benary (born 1946 in Bay Shore, New York) has never received due acknowledgement partly because of her self-effacing personality. More consistently than Goode, she has always shown a fondness for geometric patterns and permutational processes within timbral fabrics of diatonic melody, beginning with her fifteen *System Pieces for a Droning Group* of 1971, a book of verbal instructions and diagrams. A violinist who learned South Indian violin technique in Madras, India, she also trained as an ethnomusicologist at Wesleyan and in 1974 helped found the ensemble Gamelan Son of Lion in New York; most of her works have been written for this Javanese-style gamelan orchestra. (The name Benary means Son of Lion in Hebrew.) Several of her gamelan works incorporate the patterns of English change-ringing, including *Sleeping Braid* (1979) and *Hot Rolled Steel* (1984–1985), this last a *perpetuum mobile* of interlocking contrapuntal ostinatos. Her most ambitious recent work has been *Karna* (1994), a shadow-puppet opera based on an elaborate Indian myth with comic overtones.

Jon Gibson (born 1940 in Los Angeles) holds the distinction of being the only person to have performed in the ensembles of all four leading minimalists: Young, Riley, Reich, and Glass. An early free improviser who graduated from San Francisco State University, he used change-ringing patterns in his early music, *Call* for alto flute, 1978, and *Melody IV* Part 1 for nine players, 1975, and he tends toward simple, linear structures. His solo pieces for flute or saxophone (such as *Untitled,* 1974) tend to grow from simple motives into longer melodic curves within closely circumscribed limits. However, he often employs improvisation or solo melody over thick, even lush, atmospheric backgrounds of electronic and environmental sounds or shimmering percussion, tending toward ambient, as in his *Extensions II* for saxophone and tape (1981 and 1992) and *Rainforest* (1982, part of a larger theater work about Darwin). Some of Gibson's works resort to extreme simplicity or repetition for the sake of either parody or Satie-esque naïveté.

One of the most talented minimalists was nearly lost to history, much like Johanna Beyer. Julius Eastman (1940–1990) was a phenomenal African-American presence on the New York Kitchen music scene in the 1970s who disappeared in the eighties and mysteriously died alone in 1990 in a hospital in Buffalo of causes that were never exactly determined. Born in New York, he graduated from the Curtis Institute in composition and was discovered by Lukas Foss, who conducted his music, including *Stay On It* (1973), one of the first works to introduce pop tonal progressions and free improvisation in an art context. Eastman was much in demand as a singer, with a sepulchral bass and an amazingly agile falsetto, both put to excellent use in *Eight Songs for a Mad King* by the British avant-gardist Peter Maxwell Davies. He was also a member of Meredith Monk's ensemble. Uneasy with success, however, he torpedoed his own career with his unreasonable demands and fell into heavy drug and alcohol use after 1983.

Applying minimalism's additive process to the building of sections, he developed a composing technique he called "organic music," a cumulatively overlapping process in which each section of a work contains, simultaneously, all the sections which preceded it. The pieces he wrote in this style often had intentionally provocative titles intended to reinterpret the minorities Eastman belonged to in a positive light: for example, *Evil Nigger, Crazy Nigger,* and *Gay Guerilla* (all circa 1980). These three pieces, all scored for multiple pianos, build up immense emotive power through the incessant repetition of rhythmic figures. Attempts being made to salvage Eastman's output for future performance face considerable challenges; at one point, his possessions, scores and recordings included, were thrown out on the streets of New York by the sheriff when Eastman was evicted from an apartment. For some time afterward he lived in Tompkins Square Park.

It's curious, the number of minimalists who made important contributions before disappearing without having fulfilled their potential. Like Charlemagne Palestine, Tony Conrad, Richard Maxfield, Dennis Johnson, and Terry Jennings, Eastman was an inventive minimalist whose untimely removal from the scene is all too regrettable.

Notes

1. Leonard Meyer, *Music, the Arts, and Ideas* (Chicago: University of Chicago Press, 1967), p. 118.
2. Ibid., pp. 118–19.
3. Kenneth Baker, *Minimalism* (New York: Abbeville Press, 1988), p. 9.
4. Kyle Gann, "The Tingle of $p \times m^n - 1$," *Village Voice*, October 4, 1994, vol. XXXIX No. 40, p. 84.
5. K. Robert Schwarz, *Minimalists* (London: Phaidon Press, 1996), p. 30.
6. Ibid., p. 35.
7. Quoted in ibid., p. 53.
8. Quoted in ibid., p. 114.

9. Quoted in William Duckworth, *Talking Music: Conversations with John Cage, Philip Glass, Laurie Anderson, and Five Generations of American Experimental Composers* (New York: Schirmer Books, 1995), p. 346.

10. Interview with the author, September 21, 1996.

11. William Duckworth, *Talking Music: Conversations with John Cage, Philip Glass, Laurie Anderson, and Five Generations of American Experimental Composers*, p. 347.

12. Quoted in Walter Zimmermann, *Desert Plants* (Vancouver: A.R.C. Publications, 1976), p. 265.

CHAPTER 9

New Tonality I—
The New Romanticism

The return to tonality that began with early minimalism held an enormous attraction even in musical circles that did not acknowledge minimalism as a valid style. It was as though serialist atonality were a huge balloon that grew and grew as it filled with water, until minimalism pricked a little hole, precipitating a trickle that turned into a torrent. The response within the classical-academic establishment, however, was not to turn toward simplicity, or process music, or unadorned diatonic consonance. The uptown Manhattan composers reacted as though music history were a single track that had reached a dead end with twelve-tone music, and if one could go no further, the only direction to go was— back. Composers who had surreptitiously written tonal compositions brought their sins out of the closet. Those who had been writing sterile twelve-tone essays with abstract titles returned to writing symphonies, concertos, sonatas, in styles that harked back to Bartók, Mahler (especially Mahler!), Brahms, even Beethoven and Handel. Culture had reached a *cul-de-sac*, and the future was a return to the past, specifically a European past: the New Romanticism.

The most dramatic turnaround was the apostasy of George Rochberg (born 1918 in Paterson, New Jersey), all the more striking because he had been one of the best twelve-tone composers to begin with. His *Serenata d'Estate* (1955), *Sonata-Fantasia* for piano (1956), and Symphony No. 2 (1955–1956) were among the best serialist offerings America had produced. A protégé of the Italian Luigi Dallapiccola, Rochberg had a less doctrinaire, more lyrical approach to twelve-tone writing than practically any American of his generation. In 1964, however, Rochberg's son Paul, a poet, died, and Rochberg underwent a very public change of mind. As he eloquently put it,

> With the loss of my son I was overwhelmed by the realization that
> death . . . could only be overcome by life itself; and to me this meant

through art, by practicing my art as a living thing (in my marrow bone), free of the posturing cant and foolishness abroad these days which want to seal art off from life.[1]

In 1965 Rochberg wrote a work bulging with quotations: *Music for the Magic Theater.* The work cross-cut Mozart's K. 287 Divertimento with blatant phrases from the *Adagio* of Mahler's Ninth Symphony, adding in snippets from Beethoven's Op. 130 Quartet, Webern's Concerto, Varèse's *Deserts,* and Miles Davis's "Stella by Starlight." (All the pieces quoted share a motive of descending half-steps.) The cat was out of the bag. Quotation mania spread throughout the classical music world. Lukas Foss based his *Baroque Variations* (1967) on works of Bach, Scarlatti, and Händel, Jacob Druckman his *Delizie contente che l'alme beate* (1973) on an aria by Cavalli, Joan Tower her *Petroushskates* (1980) on various works of Stravinsky. The fad peaked in 1968 in a masterful European extravaganza, Luciano Berio's *Sinfonia,* in one movement of which the Scherzo of Mahler's Second Symphony becomes a container for a breath-taking game of "name that tune."

Quotation allowed a return to tonality hidden beneath a veneer of irony; it offered a widened emotional palette without sullying the composer's fingers in the actual writing of tonal or pretty music. The next step was to retrace the mental path taken by the great European composers by writing in their styles. This Rochberg did not flinch from, and it earned him more opprobrium than the collages had. He frankly wrote his next body of work, particularly the String Quartets Nos. 3 through 6 (1972–1979; Nos. 4, 5, and 6 called the "Concord Quartets"), heterogeneously in the styles of earlier composers, most notably Beethoven, Händel, and Mahler, though broken up by passages of harsh atonality. (See example 9.1, a Mahler imitation from Rochberg's Quartet No. 3.)

Deserted and reviled by colleagues who accused him of "selling out," Rochberg became the most eloquent spokesman for the bankruptcy of the avant-garde, by which he meant both the twelve-tone serialist movement he had abandoned and the Cagean conceptualist movement

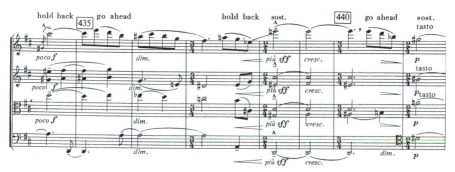

EXAMPLE 9.1 George Rochberg, String Quartet No. 3, fifth movement.

that offered its primary alternative. Composers, he charged, had fallen prey to worship of a superficial view of the scientist and had, unlike the scientists themselves, relinquished intuition and inspiration to chase after physical and quantifiable paradigms. In a simile that has not ceased to be relevant even yet, he compared many composers to the poet in Jorge Luis Borge's story "The Aleph":

> He read me many another stanza, each of which obtained his appro-
> bation and profuse commentary, too. There was nothing memorable
> in any of them. . . . I realized that the poet's labor lay not with the
> poetry, but with the invention of reasons to make the poetry
> admirable; naturally, this ulterior and subsequent labor modified the
> work for him, but not for others.[2]

In a self-searching essay, Rochberg asked,

> Why do you want to write music nobody can love? Do you hate your-
> self? Or do you hate them? . . .
> Why do you want to write music nobody can remember? Do you
> hate music?[3]

If not the first to notice, Rochberg was at least the most articulate at pinpointing the strict objectivist mindset that underlay both serialist music and Cagean chance procedures, the common inhibitions that made it taboo to rely, in either movement, on intuition and midcompositional impulse. (The same criticism applied to early minimalism as well, which was just getting under way as he was writing.) A little older than the first generation weaned on Webern, Rochberg argued passionately for a return to subjectivity. And gradually, by the time of his Oboe Concerto (1983) and his Symphony No. 5 (1984), he reintegrated the various threads in his music into a more homogenous, personal style, one that was, ironically, not too dissimilar from that of his early Symphony No. 2.

As Jacob Druckman later remarked, "not being a serialist on the East Coast of the United States in the sixties was like not being a Catholic in Rome in the thirteenth century."[4] Suddenly, however, composers devoutly reared in the religion of dissonant, complex, modernist, twelve-tone music abandoned dissonance, complexity, modernism, twelve-tone technique, or any combination thereof. Some disavowed serialism on grounds of personal expression, some on grounds of audience accessibility, others on more theoretical grounds; as example of the last, Fred Lerdahl wrote persuasive articles about "perceptual constraints," showing that the permutational note arrangements of serialism do not correlate to the way our brains process information.[5] The mass apostasy coincided with efforts to bring composers more into public view, such as Meet the Composer's orchestral residency program. When Druckman became composer-in-residence of the New York Philharmonic (1982–1986), curating the orchestra's "Horizons" series, the first season—containing works by Rochberg, Schwantner, Rzewski, Adams, Del Tredici, Harbison, Foss, Lerdahl, and others—was advertised with the question "Since 1968: A New Romanticism?" While one could quibble with the date, the new term had gone public in a major way.

An intriguing psychological peculiarity was the tremendous angst with which the classically oriented composers reapproached tonality. The minimalists stripped down to only a few pitches with apparent devil-may-care abandon, but in the academic and Euro-classical music worlds, renouncing the old ways meant overcoming peer pressure, facing the potential wrath of one's colleagues, and risking being regarded as—the worst possible insult—"not serious." There was (and still is) in the modernist mindset a kind of macho disdain for attractive music, a haughty contempt for the lay public, a feeling that one should stand tough against what David Schiff has nonsensically called "the tyranny of the audience."[6] (The pose would seem a little more heroic did not the poseurs so often speak from the comfort of a secure academic environment peopled with like-minded colleagues.) To fly in the face of this arrogance and imagined heroism seemed like admitting intellectual effeminacy, like having to tell your ex-marine father that you're gay. As David Del Tredici said,

> I certainly didn't sit down and decide to become a tonal composer. . . . I fought it all the way. I came of musical age in the 1960s when atonality, whether you happened to like it or not, was widely considered the only viable contemporary musical language. So I had a lot of conditioning to shed.[7]
>
> The situation gave me kind of a musical nervous breakdown. I thought, "My colleagues will think I'm nuts! I can't be so tonal in 1976. It's crazy. It's not legitimate." On the other hand, I had to look deeper into that part of my personality which had always done the composing, and it was as excited about the tonic and the dominant as it had always been about retrogrades and inversions. So I went with the excitement factor. I really had no choice.[8]

Making changes meant figuring out what was the baby and what the bathwater. Many decided that the problem all along had been an overinsistence on stylistic unity, and that a pluralistic society demanded pluralistic music not held hostage to a Germanic idea of organic form. This attitude, touted as "postmodernism," was summed up by John Corigliano, a composer of multistylistic concertos and coloristic orchestral works: "If I have my own style, I'm not aware of it. . . . I don't think of style as the basic unifying factor in music, as many composers do today[.] I feel very strongly that a composer has a right to do anything he feels is appropriate, and that stylistic consistency is not what makes a piece impressive."[9]

Returning to intuition and personal expression, however, was not easy after such whole-hearted reliance on systems and precompositional method. For Rochberg and many others, it first took the form of a slavish reliance on great works of the classical tradition. Most of the composers involved returned to classical genres such as concerto, song cycle, piano quintet, picking up the remnants of European history and resuming as though they had never been disturbed. William Bolcom took refuge in what earlier (and also younger) composers might have called a failure of imagination: "I find that ensembles call up their own histories, and that in writing a string quartet or music for small orchestra I cannot escape the memory of the great examples of the past."[10] Just as the art rockers and totalists would later incorporate the materials of rock in order to find a foothold in the American music business (see chapters 11 and 13), the New Romantics tried to find a ready-made niche by fitting in with the existing classical establishment.

The apex of nostalgia was reached in John Harbison's *November 19, 1828* (1988), titled for the death-date of Franz Schubert. Written for piano quartet, the piece includes a first movement in which Schubert crosses into the next world; a rondo in which a melodic fragment from an unfinished Schubert work recurs hypnotically; and a final fugue based on a theme from the name S–C–H–U–B–E–R–T (German spellings for E-flat, C, B, B-flat, E). Though this was an extreme example of channeling the spirit of dead great composers, it was hardly atypical. If Rosemary Brown, the Englishwoman who claimed she had channeled music by the spirits of Beethoven and Liszt, had had more political savvy, she could have led a flourishing career in the seventies as a New Romantic composer.

The composers in this chapter, then, are those who see the last hope of American music not so much in a linear continuation of the European tradition (as the serialists did) but in the continued patronage of a classical music establishment that had never warmed up to twelve-tone music anyway. These, consequently, are the composers whom the classical establishment rewards. Most of the winners of the Pulitzer Prizes of the last fifteen years—Christopher Rouse, Bolcom, Ellen Zwilich, Stephen Albert, Harbison, Schwantner—belong in this chapter. (The other winners have veered more toward twelve-tone music.) So do the American recipients of the Grawemeyer Awards (Joan Tower, John Adams) and orchestral residencies. The composers here are the ones who benefit most from the massive in-place resources of our orchestra halls and opera houses.

George Crumb

The return to Romanticism began almost contemporaneously with minimalism, in the dramatic innovations of George Crumb. Crumb is one of

George Crumb. *Courtesy New York Public Library.*

the most curious cases in American music, a comet whose parabolic career rose and fell with the swiftness and curvature of perhaps Edward MacDowell or, even better, Roy Harris. His music of the late 1960s was electrifying, almost as striking for the possibilities it opened up as the earlier work of John Cage. According to one survey, by the mid-1980s Crumb was the most widely performed composer in America. And yet by this same time his music had already sunk into disrepute among musicians in recognition of its patent self-repetition, its over-reliance on a small repertoire of melodramatic effects ad nauseum. It is clear that Crumb is a very talented musician. However, his success came suddenly and spectacularly, and few could have withstood the pressure to retain one's individuality under the career pressures Crumb faced.

A West Virginia native born in 1929, Crumb studied with Ross Lee Finney and Boris Blacher and taught at the University of Colorado and SUNY at Buffalo before settling in 1965 at the University of Pennsylvania. His early music was in an undistinctive, Bartókian idiom. A request from pianist David Burge led to the first work of Crumb's mature style: *5 Pieces for Piano* of 1962. The piece uses an exploded twelve-tone idiom of great sparseness, Webernesque, yet with already an original sense of gesture, the repeated-note motive being particularly prominent. Compared to music by other twelve-tone composers, the pitch structure is not sophisticated, and Crumb did not continue with dodecaphony for very long. What blew the lid off of the avant-garde piano repertoire, so to speak, was the extent to which Crumb asked Burge to play inside the piano, plucking strings, muting them with paper clips, and damping them with his fingers.

Crumb has shown a lifelong fascination with the poetry of the Spanish poet Frederico García Lorca; in the sixties he took Lorca's poetry as the basis for four books of madrigals (1965–1969), and of *Night Music I* (1963), *Songs, Drones, and Refrains of Death* (1968), *Night of the Four Moons* (1969), and *Ancient Voices of Children* (1970). These pieces, the madrigals especially, continue Crumb's exploration of timbral effects in a delicate style of mysteriously repeated motives and whispered phrases alluding to death. The work that caught the public imagination, though, was *Echoes of Time and the River* (1967) for orchestra, in which Crumb's expanded and theatrical use of instrumentalists was given free rein. The violinists additionally play antique cymbals, string players shout the nonsense syllables "Krek-tu-dai!", a hymn tune ("Were You There When They Crucified the Lord?") appears in harmonics, Crumb's rural background surfaces in the form of a prominent mandolin solo, and at one point the percussionists march across stage chanting the motto of the state of West Virginia: "Montani semper liberi" ("Mountaineers are always free").

In 1970 Crumb followed up with a work perhaps even more astounding: *Black Angels,* the first piece specified for electric (i.e., amplified) string quartet. The list of innovations in this piece staggers the imagination; hardly ever do the players use a conventional string technique. The performers play tremolos on long glissandos marked *pppp* and "gossamer." They chant nonsense syllables like "Ka-to-ko-to-ko" and numbers from one to seven in various languages. They apply great bow pressure to achieve "pedal tones" below the ranges of their instruments. They hit tam-tams. They bow their strings *above* their left hands, over the fingerboard, holding their violins like viols and fingering backwards. Most dramatically, they play, in movement 10, a chorale on bowed crystal glasses filled with water to create certain pitches. No mere string quartet, *Black Angels* is a theatrical extravaganza that inspired many imitations over the next two decades.

Another powerful aspect of Crumb's work was his inimitable style of notation. His father had worked as a professional copyist, and Crumb, drawing on inherited expertise, notated his scores in picturesque ways that directly reflected the music: combining four staves into one for a quartet playing in unison, placing staves in the shape of a cross, even (as in *Makrokosmos*, Vol. I, example 9.2) curving staves in a spiral to reflect

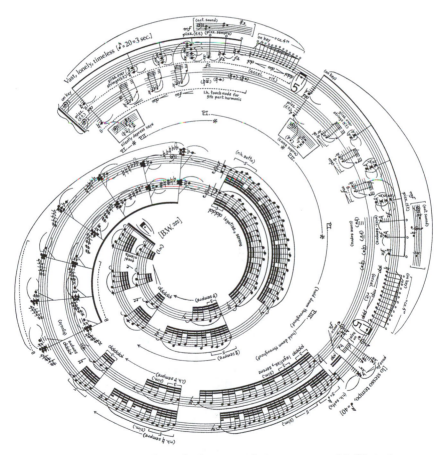

EXAMPLE 9.2 George Crumb, *Makrokosmos*, Vol. I, movement 12, "Spiral Galaxy."

the extramusical idea behind the music. Even if reading circularly printed music was inconvenient, Crumb made the world of notation seem suddenly wide open.

In his music from 1965 to 1970, from Madrigals, Book I to *Ancient Voices of Children,* Crumb had composed an undeniably evocative body of work. Even in these pieces, however, the drama was a little shallow; the succession of spooky motives led to a patchy continuity, the chanting of numbers and foreign words was meaninglessly portentous, and much of the interest relied on timbres whose novelty did not last long. The obsessions with death, "ancient voices," and a superficial numerology betrayed a sentimentality too thin to support an entire career. By the *Makrokosmos* piano cycles of 1972–1973, based on the zodiac, Crumb's overly idiosyncratic combination of nocturnal imagery, isolated motives floating in space, and bizarre sound effects (some of which required considerable time before and after for execution, breaking up the musical continuity) began to parody itself.

Nevertheless, Crumb's music of the late sixties had tremendous impact, opening composers up to the possibility of new instrumental techniques, the effectiveness of out-of-context quotation, the possibility of having instrumentalists speak and play subsidiary instruments. Even Stockhausen was reportedly influenced by Crumb's piano innovations, and Crumb's works of the late sixties remain crucial and engaging specimens from an exciting era.

Listening Example: **Black Angels *(1970)***

Crumb's large works tend to be fanatical in their symmetry and adherence to numerical patterns. *Black Angels* is a thirteen-movement arch form in which the first movement corresponds numerologically to the thirteenth, the second to the twelfth, the third to the eleventh, and so on, each pair of movements based on some deployment of the number 7, 13, or both. The movements can be characterized as follows:

1. "Threnody I: Night of the Electric Insects": the piece bursts out *fortississimo* with one of the ghastliest effects in music: a buzzy, glissandoing tremolo in all four amplified strings, in highest registers, all *sul ponticello* (bowed close to the bridge) for a thin, noisy tone. Sudden dynamic changes between *ffz* and *pp* come frequently, and a few languid glissandos provide the only melodic element.
2. "Sounds of Bones and Flutes": this brief movement summons up a primitive, spooky energy by having the cello and second violin play glissandos and double stops *col legno* (with the wood) and by having the players click their tongues and enunciate "ka-to-ko to-ko to-ko," and so on.

3. "Lost Bells": a duo for violin II and cello; it begins with a tone on a bowed tam-tam and continues with chords and a short melody in *pianissimo* harmonics.

4. "Devil-music": an athletic first-violin solo is interrupted by the other instruments playing the medieval death hymn "Dies Irae" in "pedal tones"—raspy undertones produced by pressing down hard on the strings.

5. "Danse Macabre": violin II and viola play a dance of demonic tritone double-stops augmented by rapping the instruments with knuckles or fingertips. Violin I and cello enter with the "Dies Irae" pizzicato, accompanied by maracas and ghostly whistling.

6. "Pavana Lachrymae": three of the strings play quotations from the second movement of Schubert's "Death and the Maiden" Quartet by holding the instruments upright on their knees, like viols, and bowing *above* the left hand. This gives a certain tentativeness to the tuning and timbre.

7. "Threnody II: Black Angels!": this climactic centerpiece is made up of demonic trills, glissandos, and tremolos, often with the players merging into unison. At various points the players shout the Japanese, Russian, and Swahili words for the number thirteen, and they end by counting to seven in German.

8. "Sarabanda de la Muerte Oscura": again holding the instruments like viols and bowing above the left hand, the players quote an old saraband.

9. "Lost Bells (Echo)": little more than a few pizzicato harmonics, the rattle of a maraca, and the numbers one through seven in French.

10. "God-music": The most famous (and indeed beautiful) section, this is where three of the players bow a kind of chorale on glasses filled with water and tuned to specific pitches. Violin I, with an ethereal, Messiaen-like melody, appears as the "Vox Dei," the voice of God. Note (in example 9.3) how the top melody of the chorale switches from instrument to instrument.

11. "Ancient Voices": each violinist gets eerie sounds by playing tremolos with a glass rod and metal plectrum (paper clip).

12. "Ancient Voices (Echo)": a few glissandos played with the instruments held mandolin-style.

13. "Threnody III: Night of the Electric Insects": at first this finale returns to textures of the first movement. It then restates the saraband of movement 8, but now in tremolos played with thimble-capped fingers.

In retrospect the content of *Black Angels* can seem a little thin, its insistence on weird timbres and on extremes of dissonance mannered. But in 1970, no one had ever heard anything like it, and it still retains some of the freshness of that feeling.

EXAMPLE 9.3 George Crumb, *Black Angels*, movement 10.

John Adams

John Adams made his early career as the "fifth minimalist" (after Young, Riley, Reich, and Glass), with works such as *Shaker Loops* and *Phrygian Gates*. In the eighties, however, he bounded away from minimalism in large leaps; traces of repetition remain in *Grand Pianola Music* and his bold first opera *Nixon in China,* but by his second opera *The Death of Klinghoffer* he found himself in a world that retained little in common with the music of Reich and Glass. Adams's philosophy, too, is more concerned with postmodernism and a new approach to history than with the hidden structure and smooth language of the postminimalists. "I embrace the whole musical past," he has said.[11] By existing, though, at the crossroads of two movements, combining minimalism's clarity with the New Romanticism's grand emotional expression, Adams has become one of the most popular of recent composers.

Adams was born in Worcester, Massachusetts, in 1947, and grew up in New Hampshire. Immersed in rock and jazz, he received a scholarship to Harvard but found the university stifling, as so many other young composers would over the coming decades:

> I was interested in jazz and rock, and then I would go into the music department, which was like a mausoleum where we would sit and count tone-rows in Webern. It was a dreadful time. But then we were all going back to our rooms and getting high and listening to Cecil Taylor and John Coltrane and the Rolling Stones. . . . Right from 1967 I knew I was leading a double life—and that it was dishonest.[12]

With perspicacity shown by few parents in the history of music, Adams's parents gave him a copy of John Cage's *Silence* for graduation; the book provided him with a new and much-needed perspective.

In the summer of 1971 Adams headed for the San Francisco area, where he has lived ever since, and got a job at the San Francisco Conservatory, where he taught until 1982. He had already heard the recording of *In C* at Harvard, and he converted to minimalism when Reich performed *Drumming* in San Francisco in 1974; the style, Adams said, was "a bucket of fresh spring water splashed on the grim and rigid visage of serious music."[13] With the appearance of Adams's first two major works, *Phrygian Gates* (1977–1978) for piano and *Shaker Loops* (1978) for string septet, the world seemed to have gained another minimalist: one interested in minimalism as textural springboard, not—as with Riley, Reich, and Glass—as audible process or linear progression. *Phrygian Gates* starts with a steady eighth-note momentum with lots of minimalist-type patterns, but the piece follows no strict process. It moves from texture to texture gradually, but with whimsical unpredictability.

Adams's next major work, *Harmonium* (1981), for chorus and orchestra, sets poems by John Donne and Emily Dickinson in a texture

John Adams. *Photo by Richard Morganstern.*

of minimalist repeated notes, but with grand brass flourishes reminiscent of nineteenth-century music. *Grand Pianola Music* (1981–1982), for two pianos and ensemble, uses repeated patterns to build up to a jocose theme of Beethovenian grandiosity. By *Harmonielehre* for orchestra (1985), named after a theory treatise by Schoenberg, the break with minimalism seems complete: the themes bounce with repeated notes, the textures swim in ostinatos, but otherwise the music's tempestuous emotional sweep seems more related to Mahler and Sibelius than Glass or Reich. For Adams after 1984, repeated scales and arpeggios are simply features of a basically neoromantic style.

In 1983 Adams was approached by opera director Peter Sellars, who had created scandals by his settings of Mozart operas in contemporary dress and atmospheres, about an opera about Nixon and Mao Tse-Tung. Adams resisted at first, but soon realized the mythic proportions of the story. Sellars chose his old Harvard classmate Alice Goodman as librettist, and she wrote the entire piece in a charming rush of rhyming couplets. The result, commissioned by the Houston opera, the Brooklyn Academy of Music, and the Kennedy Center, was the most widely-awaited opera in American history: *Nixon in China* (1987). With singers who eerily resembled Nixon and Kissinger, the visual aspect of the opera was well-nigh perfect, looking as much like actual film footage as an opera could.

Nixon in China opens with rising scales leading to a haunting peasant's chorus: "The people are the heroes now / Behemoth pulls the peasant's plow." A plane lands onstage, Nixon and his wife Pat emerge, and when Nixon in his excitement stutters, "News, news, news, news, news, news, news, has a, has a, has a, has a kind of mystery," the repeated notes Adams inherited from minimalism seem in tune with the emotions of the moment. The rest of the opera portrays a Nixon at first full of confidence, but in meeting with Mao and Chou En-Lai, finding himself immersed in cultural forces beyond his comprehension. In the closing scene, Nixon, Pat, Madame Mao, and Chou sit on beds and soliloquize about the paths that brought them to this meeting. Nixon reminisces about his World War II experiences, while Chou, more reflective, ends:

> How much of what we did was good?
> Everything seems to move beyond
> Our remedy. Come, heal this wound.
> At this hour nothing can be done.
>   . . . To work!
> Outside this room the chill of grace
> Lies heavy on the morning grass.

The moment is one of the finest in American opera.

Adams based his second opera on another contemporary event, the hijacking of the ship Achille Lauro by Arab terrorists and the killing of an elderly Jewish man named Klinghoffer in 1985. Somewhat unfortunately, its title *The Death of Klinghoffer* (1991) threw the opera's weight on a hapless, essentially anonymous victim, not a character capable of bearing the weight of grand opera. Adams has noted opposing veins in his work: "dark, intrsopective, 'serious'" works like *Harmonielehre* on one side, and on the other "the Trickster, the garish, ironic wild card."[14] The Trickster pieces, such as *Fearful Symmetry* (1988), retain the repeated motives of minimalism; some of these, such as *Short Ride in a Fast Machine* (1986) and *The Chairman Dances* (from *Nixon*) are quite jaunty and have become popular orchestral showpieces. The introspective works, like *The Wound-Dresser* (1988, based on Whitman), are in a thoroughly Romantic vein.

Listening Example: Grand Pianola Music *(1981)*

Grand Pianola Music is one of Adams's best Trickster pieces, a fascinating hybrid work that starts off from minimalist principles and moves into a grandly Romantic statement. The work is scored for peculiar forces: winds in pairs, three percussionists, three amplified women's voices, and two solo pianos. It takes its distinctive shimmering quality from a device that Adams transposed from the world of tape delays: the two pianos, and sometimes the pairs of winds as well, often play the same lines a sixteenth- or eighth-note apart, so that one is quickly echoing the other. (See example 9.4.) The work is in three movements, the first two joined to form Part I, the final one entitled "Part II: On the Dominant Divide."

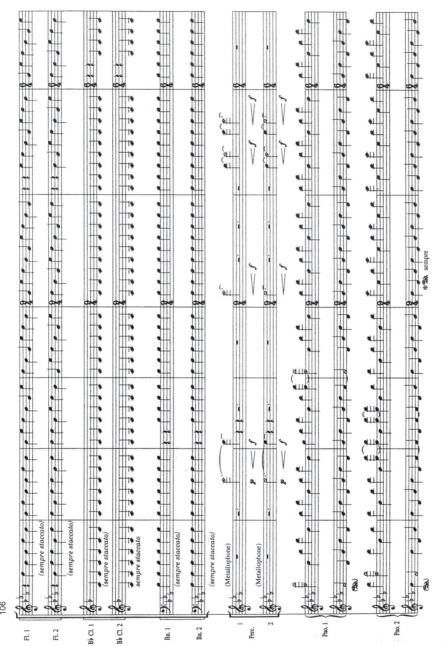

EXAMPLE 9.4 John Adams, *Grand Pianola Music*, mm. 106–112.

Grand Pianola Music opens sounding minimalist indeed: the winds and pianos play only quarter-notes on the pitches E-flat, F, A-flat, and B-flat. After about three minutes, the tonality begins quietly wandering as the woodwinds take over in long-ranged melodies. The three female voices enter singing triads in a lovely E-minor passage that eventually precipitates the end of the opening seven-minute crescendo, where the pianos suddenly plunge into heroic arpeggios on a B-flat-major triad. The following climax employs one of minimalism's favorite chord changes, ubiquitous in Glass's music: the chord shifts from B minor to B-flat major, the D held over as the third in both chords. (This same relationship, between E minor and E-flat major, returns at the final buildup of the third movement.) The remainder of the movement shifts subtly from key to key, and among winds, voices, and pianos, in quiet repeated notes.

After the repeated notes stop, the slow movement begins. In tonalities and melodic contours reminiscent of Copland's *Appalachian Spring*, an oboe solo leads us to a few loud, poignant chords. From here piano 2 begins a quiet melody—a single line at first, then in octaves, finally joined by piano 1 and a solo tuba in delicate counterpoint. The piano melody turns to sixteenth-note arpeggios up and down the keyboard, and here more than anywhere else is it audible that piano 2 is echoing piano 1's notes only a sixteenth-note later. The movement ends after a lovely decrescendo.

Intentionally or not, "On the Dominant Divide" suggests that we are about to leave minimalist principles behind and embark on a new Romantic course hinted at in the first movement's climax. Adams wrote this movement, he said, to see what would happen applying minimalist strategies to common tonic and dominant chords, a chord combination that minimalism had assiduously avoided. The movement begins with a long dominant preparation crescendoing and finally resolving to a grand A-flat major triad that turns out to be the subdominant of E-flat. At last the Beethovenian main theme (example 9.5) enters in piano 2, spreads to piano 1 and then the brass in a grand climax. The theme then dissipates, abstracted into only its harmonies, as the pianos and winds play minimalist arpeggios in C major. From here on out the work is a continuous crescendo, cadencing at last in triumphant A-flat major. The work is remarkable not only for its exquisite balance between minimalist logic and Romantic gesture, but for its masterful handling of large tonal areas.

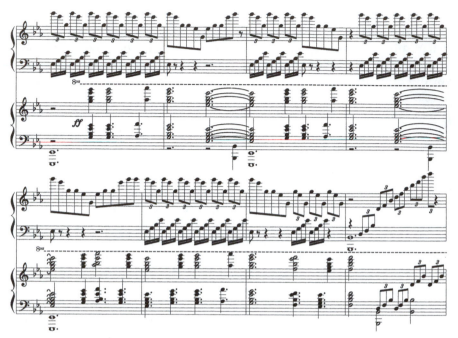

EXAMPLE 9.5 John Adams, *Grand Pianola Music,* main theme of Part II.

Frederick Rzewski

Frankly, Frederic Rzewski does not fit in this chapter, nor could a figure so Protean fit comfortably in any general classification. His first appearance on the public stage was as a card-carrying minimalist, yet one with a political bent, in the still-popular works *Attica, Coming Together,* and *Les Moutons de Panurge.* Only four years later, however, he wrote a massive set of piano variations, *The People United Will Never Be Defeated!,* whose rigor owed more to serialist thinking and a wealth of classical techniques than to minimalism. His inclusion here, then, should not be taken as associating him with the New Romantic movement, with which he has more differences than similarities. One could say, though, that as a phenomenal pianist-composer working in European-derived forms such as variations and with large orchestral and choral forces, that Rzewski (pronounced Zhev-ski) is the closest thing we currently have to a nineteenth-century Romantic-style figure. It is not so much his music that seems Romantic as the volcanic thrust of his career.

Born in 1938 in Massachusetts, Rzewski began composing at five. He studied at Harvard with Walter Piston and Randall Thompson (the latter, 1899–1984, a composer of lyrical choral works and symphonies) and at Princeton with Sessions and Babbitt. Two years in Italy on a

Fulbright fellowship (1960–1962) brought him into Luigi Dallapiccola's orbit, and he became well known in Europe as a masterful performer of works by Boulez, Stockhausen, Cage, Kagel, Feldman, and others. Rzewski's playing is extraordinary for its violent energy and absolute command of the keyboard. In Rome in 1966 he founded a pioneering live electronics improvisational ensemble, Musica Elettronica Viva, with Alvin Curran and Richard Teitelbaum. MEV (as it is often called) was most active from 1967 to 1970, but the group still reunites for special performances.

Rzewski first came to major attention as a composer with three works securely in the minimalist tradition, all based on additive processes. The first, *Les Moutons de Panurge* (1968) is a sixty-five-note melody to be played in (attempted) unison by any ensemble. Each person is supposed to play the first note, then the first two, then the first three, and so on, until the entire melody is played, after which notes are subtracted from the beginning. Mistakes are inevitable, and once the players have gotten off, they are to remain off, as the different lines echo each other at gradually increasing distances. The other two works, often paired in performance, mark the beginning of Rzewski's involvement with political music: *Coming Together* and *Attica* (both 1972). Both of these are diatonically tonal, one angry and in a minor key, the other tranquil and major, and each uses a spoken text by a political prisoner involved in the uprising at Attica prison.

Rzewski's flirtation with minimalism, however, was short-lived. His more loyal ties were to a growing group of political composers that included Christian Wolff on the East Coast, Cornelius Cardew and the Scratch Orchestra in England, and Frank Abbinanti in Chicago. The minimalist idiom raised for Rzewski questions about musical language, and as he put it, "It seemed to me there was no reason why the most difficult and complex formal structures could not be expressed in a form which could be understood by a wide variety of listeners."[15] He attempted to prove this assertion in his next work and still his best known: *The People United Will Never Be Defeated!* (1975), a mammoth set of variations on a Chilean revolutionary song by Sergio Ortega. In thirty-six variations exploring a dazzling universe of different pianistic techniques, the piece holds a deserved place next to Beethoven's *Diabelli Variations* or Brahms's *Händel Variations*. Whether it achieves its ostensive extramusical aim—to make a political point in favor of Chile's revolutionary movement—has often been the subject of heated debate.

The idiom Rzewski created in *The People United* is one he calls "humanist realism," defining it as

> A conscious employment of techniques which are designed to establish communication, rather than to alienate an audience. That does not necessarily mean an exclusion of what's called avant-garde style,

by any means. [But] . . . if one is seriously interested in communication, then I suppose that a rigorous, say, formalistic style such as the style of the formalist composers and so on would be at a serious disadvantage.[16]

In 1977 Rzewski was invited by the French composer Henri Pousseur to join the faculty of the Conservatory of Liege. Graced with a new level of financial security, he began writing larger works, such as *A Long Time Man,* for piano and orchestra (1979), and *The Silence of Infinite Spaces* (1980). The latter is a cosmological meditation on a text by Pascal, for singers with orchestra divided into seven parts to portray the seven planets known at the time. However, it remains for his piano music that Rzewski is best known, partly because his interpretive skills are so compelling. After *The People United* he wrote *Four North American Ballads* (1978–1979) based on political folk songs, each mercurial and whimsical in inspiration, ranging from minimalist simplicity to thundering contrapuntal complexity.

Rzewski's most compelling recent work is probably his *De Profundis* (1991) for pianist, a moving and highly emotional setting of excerpts from the long letter Oscar Wilde wrote while incarcerated in Reading Jail. The text itself is stunning in its fearless examination of the human soul:

> People point to Reading Gaol, and say, "That is where the artistic life leads a man." Well, it might lead to worse places. Mechanical people to whom life is a shrewd speculation depending on calculation always know where they are going, and go there. They start with the ideal desire of being the parish beadle, and they succeed in being the parish beadle and no more. A man whose desire is to be something separate from himself succeeds in being what he wants to be. That is his punishment. Those who want a mask have to wear it. But . . . [p]eople who desire self-realization never know where they are going. They can't know. To recognize that the soul of a man is unknowable, is the ultimate achievement of wisdom. The final mystery is oneself.[17]

The setting requires the pianist, while playing and speaking the text, to make vocal noises, whistle, hit the outside of the piano, honk a bicycle horn, and slap his face and body. Such actions serve a profound dramatic purpose in context. Rzewski is one of the most relentlessly honest and musically sophisticated composers America has produced, regardless of category.

Listening Example: The People United Will Never Be Defeated! *(1975)*

Rzewski's *The People United* is one of the great works of the American piano literature, and probably the most popular piano work the 1970s produced, with competition only from John Adams's *Phrygian Gates*. This is despite, if not because of, a complexly intellectual structure and a range of styles that encompasses jazz, modal quasi-improvisation, serialist fragmentation, minimalist patterns, Romantic climaxes, and Ivesian texture-layering. If this gives the impression that Rzewski is a postmodernist working in a collage idiom, the piece itself does not strike the listener that way. It does, however, express a stream-of-consciousness freedom that transcends its intricate formal plan.

There are thirty-six measures in the theme of *The People United,* and Rzewski writes thirty-six variations. These are divided in six sets of six variations each. Within each set, the sixth sums up the previous five in four-measure groupings. That is, within variation 6, the first four measures refer to variation 1, the next four to variation 2, the next four to variation 3, the next four to variation 4, and the next four to variation 5; the last four present new material. This pattern is repeated for variations 7 through 12, 13 through 18, 19 through 24, and 25 through 30. The final set, variations 31 through 36, is an even more remarkable tour de force: variation 31 sums up the first variations of each earlier set (nos. 1, 7, 13, 19, and 25), variation 32 sums up the second of each set (nos. 2, 8, 14, 20, and 26), and so on. This daunting plan is carried out with tremendous freedom and imagination and virtually no literal quotation. A few landmarks to the hour-long structure are given here:

- The theme (example 9.6) states the folk song in spare octaves, then relaxes into a dark, almost bluesy setting.

- Variation 1 breaks the theme into single notes, dispersed throughout the range of the keyboard in a quasi-serialist manner.

- Variation 5, marked "Dreamlike, frozen," takes its impulse from staccato chords to be played in "a swift, sudden grabbing motion . . . like picking berries, or fruit." The sustain pedal is pressed *after* each chord to capture some resonance.

- Variation 10 features wild glissandos up and down the keyboard.

- Variation 11, breaking down the theme into an isolated beat here and there, asks for optional sound effects such as slamming the piano lid, a short vocal cry, and whistling; this is a common feature of Rzewski's piano writing that he shares with John Cage and Christian Wolff.

- Variation 13 returns simply to the theme with a jazz feel, quick flurries of notes in the right hand over walking chords in the left. At the end, the music pauses for a *pianississimo* quotation in the treble of the Italian socialist song "Bandiera Rossa."

EXAMPLE 9.6 Frederic Rzewski, *The People United*, theme.

- Variation 20 states the theme over a virtuosically repeated D.

- Variation 24, recapitulating nos. 19 through 23, climaxes on a both-hands tremolo on a high B, lasting fifteen to twenty seconds.

- Variation 27 departs from the overall scheme, starting with a free modal melody in the right hand over a drone on E and B. The long digression that follows is the most minimalist-sounding part of the piece, with modal melodies articulating charmingly irregular rhythmic patterns of alternating 5/8, 9/8, and 8/8 meter. A final section in 22/8 meter (6+5+6+5) over running eighth-notes in the bass suggests process pieces like Philip Glass's *Music in Fifths*.

- Variation 28 returns us to reality with a march-like momentum but subsides into a gentle rippling between the two hands.

- Variation 36, just before the restatement of the theme, pauses after a series of *pianissimo* perfect-fourth intervals for an optional improvisation which the pianist may extend for up to five minutes.

Like Beethoven's "Hammerklavier" and Op. 111 Sonatas, *The People United* has become one of the piano works pianists venture as a way of proving their mastery in the most technically and emotionally challenging large forms. In it, Rzewski proved that music could be complex in structure and still win over enthusiastic audiences time and again.

Jacob Druckman

Despite his public connection to the New Romanticism, Jacob Druckman retained the closest ties to serialism of any composer in this chapter. Though he renounced the twelve-tone row, he never renounced modernism. His music rarely refers to conventions of earlier European music except through quotation. More essentially, Druckman has a reputation as an extremely fluid orchestral colorist. Many others have tended in the same direction, but no other American's music is so abstract, yet so light and incorporeal, so delicate and evanescent in its interplay of vanishing timbres. One of his favorites among his own works, *Aureole,* he likened to a Fourth of July sparkler shooting off sparks as it is swung through the air;[18] the simile is relevant to much of his music. Druckman (along with Gunther Schuller, Joseph Schwantner, Mario Davidovsky, and others) was also one of new music's most visible power brokers, an enormously influential presence on grant and award panels.

Druckman was born in 1928 in Philadelphia and grew up as a violinist and jazz trumpeter. He studied with Copland at Tanglewood and with Persichetti and Mennin at Juilliard, where he would later teach from 1957 on. Consequently, he started out as something of a neoclassicist. In *Dark Upon the Harp* (1962), for mezzosoprano, brass, and percussion, Druckman began breaking out of the neoclassic mold, moving toward serialism and using elements of big-band jazz in the final movement. A brief involvement with serialism peaked in his Second String Quartet of 1966.

Druckman was drawn away from the common serialist wisdom of his day by his experiences in 1965–1968 at the Columbia-Princeton Electronic Music Center. He later said,

> Electronic music is a great debunker of the vanities that composers hold. Intellectual ideas crumble in the face of listening to the actualities of electronic music. . . . [I]f you listen very honestly to what comes out of the machines, you'll find that very often it has very little to do with what you thought you were putting into it.[19]

At the same time, since Druckman was repelled by the idea of listening to loudspeakers (his only pure electronic work is *Synapse* of 1971), his electronic works moved into the direction of theater. His *Animus* series for instruments or voice and tape accentuates the theatrical relationship of performers to instruments and their surrounding sound environment.

The electronic, experimental phase of Druckman's career diminished in importance through the seventies. His mature style set in with *Windows* (1971) for orchestra, which experimented with proportional notation (he called it analogue notation), leaving the timing of certain entrances to be left to the conductor or individual player. From this point on, the aesthetic of Druckman's orchestral works—*Chiaroscuro* (1977), *Prism* (1980), *Nor Spell Nor Charm* (1990)—remains consistent: atmospheric, coloristic, highly detailed in orchestration, with wispy effects such as glissandos, tremolos, harmonics, and percussion gestures that decrescendo rapidly.

Druckman's early use of musical quotation is slight and subtle. *Incenters* (1968) draws its material from two seventh chords from Mussorgsky's *Boris Gudonov,* which are softly quoted at one point near the end. *Windows* alludes texturally to Debussy's *Jeux,* and *Mirage* (1976) contains three quotations from Debussy's *Sirenes.* In *Prism,* Druckman's most extensive quotation piece, there is no attempt to imitate the style of his archaic sources; earlier music appears in the background, interrupted by Druckman's fragmented textures. All three movements are based on music from earlier operas about the Medea myth, by Charpentier, Cavalli, and Cherubini. Medea was also the subject of Druckman's 1974 *Lamia* for soprano and orchestra, and of the opera he wrote for the Metropolitan. In 1986, however, this last work was canceled because Druckman was far behind schedule, and has never been performed. He died in 1996.

Listening Example: Druckman, **Aureole** *(1979)*

Aureole, a fine example of Druckman's orchestral technique, was an attempt to write an orchestra work that consisted of basically a single line; there are often only one or two notes heard at a time, and yet every page of the score uses instruments from every section of the orchestra,

EXAMPLE 9.7 Jacob Druckman, *Aureole.*

and that single line changes color continually. The idea of the aureole is heard in textures that surround the primary pitch with a halo of subsidiary notes. More personally, the piece is dedicated to Leonard Bernstein and develops its pitch line from the Kaddish theme of Bernstein's *Kaddish Symphony.* The most important motif is a dotted-eighth- and sixteenth-note rhythm that appears especially in the ubiquitous unpitched percussion; this rhythm is the rhythm of the *Kaddish* text. The textures are mercurial and evanescent except for two passages, one of them in the final pages, in which the divisi strings pick up a regular momentum of galloping repeated notes. Example 9.7 shows the end of the first such passage, along with the subsequent return to the orchestrated single line and its aureole.

Nancy Van de Vate

One of the finest New Romantic composers has remained little known in America, first because in the years she was active here there was little attention paid to women composers, and second because she has been an expatriate since 1982. Nancy Van de Vate is a superb orchestral colorist, and a composer of atmospheric, melancholy, and memorable works. Like Roy Harris and William Schuman, she has a tendency to limn her orchestral sonorities with dashes of percussion, especially vibraphone, xylophone, piano, and celeste. More pervasively, though, her music shows a kinship to the East European school of Penderecki and Lutoslawski, with thick, sustained string textures (sometimes tone clusters) and ultrachromatic melodic motives.

Born in 1930 in Plainfield, New Jersey, Van de Vate lived in the rural South for twenty years as she taught at a variety of schools. In 1968, she had her Piano Concerto performed under the name N. Van de Vate; upon introducing herself to the conductor, he asked why her husband wasn't present, assuming that *he* had been the composer. Subsequent to that experience, Van de Vate has become an active organizer for women composers, forming the International League of Women Composers in 1975 and serving as its chairperson for seven years. Eventually her academic career took her to the University of Hawaii in Honolulu, where she gained close-up experience of Asian music. Her first response upon discovering Indonesian gamelan was to write *Music for Viola, Percussion, and Piano* (1976)—a charming, energetic work whose ethnic influences bring it closer in sound to Bartók, however, than to anything Asian. In 1982 she moved to Jakarta, Indonesia, and she relocated in 1985 to Vienna, which has been her home base ever since. Her music's peculiarly colorful sadness stems from a smooth fusion of these disparate influences, postwar Polish avant-garde techniques with Balinese gamelan.

Consequently her best works evince an atmosphere of distance, such as *Journeys* (1981–1984), begun and finished in Jakarta and composed partly in Czechoslovakia. In *Journeys,* a warlike, four-note brass motif over a muted march rhythm gradually gives way to an extravaganza of percussion; and when the march motive reappears, it is now in percussion, with a calmer, more Asian feel. Much of Van de Vate's music deliberately evokes the spirit of wartime Eastern Europe, a Mahleresque blend of militarism and mourning heard in her *Katyn* (1989), *Chernobyl* (1987, commemorating the nuclear power plant accident), and *Krakow Concerto* (1988) for six percussionists and orchestra. The last-named work takes its impetus from an melody played by an offstage trumpet that is brutally interrupted by percussion, in reference to a story about a thirteenth-century bugler who was shot in the neck as he attempted to warn the people of Krakow about an approaching attack.

Van de Vate's music is more frankly tonal than Druckman's or Rochberg's, though it is never without an underpinning of dissonance. More saliently, her music has a long, slow emotional curve with much reliance on linear melody. As she explains, talking of the Asian influence on her music,

> Americans tend to be very fast-moving, to want to get to the bottom line. This does affect their music. Whereas in somewhat older cultures, the sense of speed is not so immanent. A piece can unfold very slowly. It can sit on just one note for 20 or 30 or 40 seconds, and people can enjoy just listening to the sound of the instrument.[20]

Van de Vate gives the appearance of coming by her Romanticism naturally, rather than in conscious imitation of any previous style. Because of this, and because her music is less abstract than that of most of the neoromantics, it is more memorable as well.

Postmodernists

The New Romantics can be divided into the postmodernists—who sought stylistic pluralism in a collage aesthetic (middle-period Rochberg, Bolcom, Foss, Del Tredici)—and those who resynthesized a smooth, consistent language analogous to nineteenth-century Romanticism or mild-mannered early modernism (Van de Vate, Singleton, Harbison, Tower, Bresnick). As a collective movement, collage was a short-lived aesthetic of the late sixties and seventies. However, several composers have sustained the assertion that stylistic unity is a dead issue and that the past is ours to imitate and plunder.

Chief and most talented among these is William Bolcom, the leading "Uptown" proponent of the attempt to break down barriers between classical and vernacular music. Bolcom seems to have been impelled toward postmodernism by a congenital inability to devote himself either to "high" or "low" musical genres to the exclusion of the other. He has led an active performing career as a leading pianist in the ragtime revival of the sixties and as a performer of American theater music with his singer-wife Joan Morris. These connections inform Bolcom's music as well, which is thoroughly and deliberately polystylistic. His stated desire is to "treat the musical language more like spoken language: as a constantly evolving creature always taking on new flesh and bone, yet retaining its most ancient elements."[21]

Born in Seattle in 1938, he studied with Milhaud and Messiaen in Paris and has taught at the University of Michigan since 1973. He entered the postmodern fray early; by 1971 he had written a pastiche for orchestra, *Commedia,* made up of phrases that could have come from Berlioz or Mozart or Donizetti, covered over at times by quasi-serialist gestures and Ivesian tone-clouds. Bolcom's *Open House* (1975), a setting of seven Theodore Roethke poems, is frankly heterogeneous; the first two movements are atonally expressionistic, the third a late-Mahler adagio, the fourth a light-hearted waltz, the fifth in a jazzy theater style, the seventh modeled after Bach. The aims of *Open House* were extended in what is considered Bolcom's masterpiece, *Songs of Innocence and Experience,* an evening-length cycle of songs based on William Blake. This massive work, which Bolcom labored on from 1956 to 1981 and which received its premiere in 1984, ranged in style from high Romanticism to atonality to jazz to rock. In general his style of the late eighties is more homogeneous, though the funny "Scherzo Mortale" of his Fifth Symphony (1990) takes the wedding march from *Lohengrin* as counterpoint to "Abide with Me," then rushes into a foxtrot version of the love-death music from *Tristan.*

Lukas Foss could be placed in almost any chapter because his career went through so many phases. Born in Berlin in 1922, he moved to the U.S. in 1937, studying with Randall Thompson and Hindemith. He began, in his 1944 cantata *The Prairie,* as a neoclassicist with strong Romantic leanings. His interests changed when, teaching at UCLA, he tried out twelve-tone techniques, controlled improvisation, proportional notation, limited chance processes, theater pieces, game pieces, and finally quotation and collage in experimental works such as *Echoi* (1963) and *Paradigm* (1968). His most widely known work used to be *Time Cycle* of 1959–1960, a setting for soprano and chamber orchestra (with a version for large orchestra) of texts by Auden, Housman, Kafka, and Nietzsche that all have to do with time. Though it is a nicely crafted response to the then-prevalent Webern worship, with its textually motivated evocation of ticking clocks, in hindsight its idiom of rampant major-seventh and minor-ninth intervals seem thin and undistinctive.

Foss's most successful work after *Time Cycle* was *Baroque Variations* (1967), a three-movement work based on pieces by Bach, Händel, and

Scarlatti. The work contains such techniques as the orchestra playing Händel with many of the notes silent, so that only a chord here and there is actually heard; and string clusters and glissandos obscuring a Scarlatti sonata played on a harpsichord, whose phrases are echoed out-of-tempo in the brass and winds. The surreal result is a stream of musical conventions dimly remembered, distantly heard, and distorted. The unsentimental reworking of earlier music played an increasing role in Foss's work, one of his prettiest and least satirical homages being his *Renaissance Concerto* for flute (1986). It is difficult to deny that Foss was something of a style-chaser, though his solid Germanic musical training brought polish to his every phase. He has been a lively figure in American music, less as a composer than as conductor of the Brooklyn Philharmonic from 1971 to 1991.

David Del Tredici has led a career remarkably associated with a single literary work: Lewis Carroll's *Alice in Wonderland*. Born in California in 1937, he studied with Seymour Shifrin, Roger Sessions, and Andrew Imbrie before coming to public attention with a thorny twelve-tone setting of two James Joyce poems called *Syzygy* (1966; the title means the strong union of opposites or unrelated elements). Starting in 1968 with *Pop-Pourri*, however, he mined the vein of Carroll's *Alice* books, which led to a new aesthetic of quotation and satirical Romanticism. His early *Alice* works, such as *The Lobster Quadrille* (1969, later part of *An Alice Symphony*) were dissonant and angular and yet playful, with ironic quotations. By *Final Alice* (1976) for orchestra with saxophones, mandolin, banjo, accordion, and narrator, he had evolved a style steeped in Romanticism but often skewed, with huge Mahlerian climaxes blurred by instruments playing out of sync. Del Tredici's list of *Alice*-inspired works—including *Vintage Alice* (1972), *Child Alice* (1977–1981, over two hours long), and *Haddocks' Eyes* (1986)—suggests monomania, but a charming one.

It is surprising, given the inherent dramatic tensions of their music, that the postmodernists have not included a generation of born opera composers as the Americana movement did. Several of the New Romantics tried their hands at an opera or two: Rochberg's *The Confidence Man* (1982), Bolcom's *McTeague*, Alvin Singleton's *Dream Sequence '76* (1976), Harbison's *The Winter's Tale* (1974). Aside from Adams's two efforts, however, the movement's most successful opera was John Corigliano's *The Ghosts of Versailles*, premiered by the Metropolitan in 1992, a climax of postmodern pastiche. So focused was Corigliano (born 1938, son of the concertmaster of the New York Philharmonic) on the classical tradition that he and his librettist William M. Hoffman took as their starting point the third play of Beaumarchais's *Figaro* trilogy, of which the first two had served for Mozart's *The Marriage of Figaro* and Rossini's *The Barber of Seville*.

The Ghosts of Versailles is an opera-within-an-opera, the outer structure involving a supposed romance between Marie Antoinette and

Beaumarchais. The playwright stages an opera to entertain Marie's court of ghosts and also to change history by depicting her being rescued from prison and whisked off to America. The action revolves around the long-time operatic hero Figaro, who steals a diamond necklace to buy the queen's ransom. Just as the plot is about to succeed, however, Marie Antoinette realizes that the judgment of history was correct; by accepting her own death, she is freed. Corigliano's music ranges freely among eighteenth-, nineteenth-, and twentieth-century styles, using Mozartean recitative for the internal opera (including quotations from Mozart and Rossini), ambiguous chromaticism for the ghost scenes, and passionate Romanticism for the love scenes and emotional climaxes. Despite the seriousness of the plot, the opera contains a strong element of self-conscious caricature; at the first act's chaotic climax, a soprano in Wagnerian valkyrie garb enters to wail, "This is not opera!" She is wrong, however; this is an opera in love with the European history of opera.

Other New Romanticists and Unreconstructed Classicists

More numerous are the composers who developed their own homogenous languages drawn from the materials of late romanticism and early modernism. Typically, these composers shy away from well-worn tonal materials such as triads and seventh chords, preserving tonal ambiguity while allowing a general feeling of tonality. As a result (and Van de Vate is a strong example), their musics tend to have some affinity with that of East European composers who embraced modernism without renouncing tonality: Bartók, Lutoslawski, Martinů, even late Scriabin and Stravinsky's milder neoclassic style.

One of the best of these composers is Alvin Singleton. Like Van de Vate, he spent much of his career as an expatriate; born in New York in 1940, he lived in Vienna and Graz for fourteen years in the seventies and early eighties. From 1985 to 1988, however, he was composer-in-residence for the Atlanta Symphony, and he remains there. As a rare African-American working in a European-derived symphonic medium, he offers an unusual sensibility: "My musical ideal," he has said, "would be to combine the spirit of James Brown with the organizational skill of Lutoslawski."[22] Despite that aim, the elements of his work are well integrated, and in his orchestral works such as *Shadows* (1987) and *A Yellow Rose Petal* (1982), the Lutoslawski connection is more evident. Particularly effective and akin to Van de Vate's music, *Shadows* is a long orchestral crescendo over a drone on E, a passacaglia whose competing melodies in quietly conflicting tonalities suggest "shadows" of various jazz and classical styles.

Joseph Schwantner's musical language has much in common with Crumb's, in terms of writing atmospheric works dotted with odd instrumental effects; he, too, has used crystal glasses rubbed with wetted fingertips, bowed cymbals, whistling instrumentalists, and gongs lowered into water after being struck. Schwantner was born in Chicago in 1943 and has taught at Eastman since 1970. His early works were twelve-tone, but from the early seventies on extremely coloristic, and since 1975 his music has veered toward a bittersweet tonality. A basic Schwantner rhetorical archetype—an angular solo melody over a shimmering, indistinct background—appears as early as the twelve-tone *Diaphonia Intervallum* (1965). *Modus caelestis* (1972) is noteworthy for its tinkly backgrounds of mallet percussion and cloudy sonorities of twelve flutes. *Aftertones of Infinity* (1978), an orchestral work, relies on recurring gestures within a mysterious stasis of ringing sonorities. Some of Schwantner's most effective textures (for instance in *Distant Runes and Incantations* of 1987) stem from the ostinato-like repetition of complex figures. While Schwantner's music doesn't have the immediately recognizable aura of Crumb's, it is meatier in musical content, and he may be a better colorist than Druckman.

John Harbison, Joan Tower, and Martin Bresnick can all be characterized as having neither returned to Romanticism nor quoted earlier musics, but having instead settled into accessible yet somewhat thorny idioms that wed clear motivic processes to a constant level of tonal ambiguity. Harbison, the most prolific of the three, was born in New Jersey in 1938, and studied with Piston, Sessions, and Earl Kim. He has been composer in residence with both the Pittsburgh and Los Angeles symphony orchestras.

Harbison's music is translucently clear in its motivic development, Romantic in its fluid continuity, neoclassic in its forms, and never without a dash of polytonal dissonance. The edge in his music is sometimes achieved by applying twelve-tone devices (such as inversion of sonorities) within basically tonal contexts. His 1981 Piano Quintet is a particularly accessible example of his chamber music. Harbison sets the English language with pragmatic effectiveness; he is known for song cycles that set off the poetry well, such as *Words from Paterson* (1989) for voice and ensemble, based on William Carlos Williams. He has written an effective chamber opera after Yates, *Full Moon in March* (1977), notable for its ensemble use of a prepared piano, and his Christmas cantata *The Flight into Egypt* (1986) is stately in its Stravinskian archaic grandeur. At its best Harbison's music memorably recreates the motivically generated climaxes of his classical predecessors; at his worst, the music is overly facile and a little generic.

Joan Tower, born 1938 in New Rochelle, New York, writes music of tremendous energy and clarity in a style that is neither dissonant nor quite tonal. Her music is supremely organic, growing from a central principle. Her orchestral piece *Sequoia* (1979–1981), for example, is structured like a redwood tree, starting with a central drone on G from which symmetrical harmonies grow, branches developing smaller branches. Often some type of transformation occurs, as in *Black Topaz* (1976), for piano and six instruments, in which the music's unusual, piano-studded textures move from harsh dissonance to gently shimmering consonance. Tower dedicated her *Celebration* to First Lady Hillary Rodham Clinton and conducted it at the White House in 1993. A curious problem developed when she won the Grawemeyer Award in 1990 for her orchestral work *Silver Ladders*; the papers announced that she was the first native American to win the award (meaning the first winner born in America), but it came out as Native American, and she was deluged with questions as to what tribe she came from. Her forebears, nevertheless, came over from Europe.

Martin Bresnick has not become nearly as well-known as the quality of his music deserves; no other recent uptown composer possess a style so elegantly smooth or can say so much with so few notes. Born in New York in 1946, he studied in Europe with Ligeti and Gottfried von Einem and at Stanford with John Chowning. Bresnick's works are marked by economy of materials and lyrical intensity. For example, his superb Piano Trio of 1987–1988 opens with a slow, downward arpeggio of four sustained notes: D, F♯, B, D♯. From this point, the movement hardly changes texture as it moves with inexorable logic from one tonal area to another. The secret of Bresnick's language is that he has developed an intervallic way of working with tonality that allows for a smooth continuum between tonality and atonality. His busily buzzing *B's Garland* (1973), scored for eight cellos, ranges fluidly from busily buzzing cluster effects to sweet romanticism without sounding like pastiche. Recently, Bresnick has become best known as an influential teacher at Yale for several of his students—Michael Gordon, Julia Wolfe, David Lang, and Evan Ziporyn (all discussed in chapter 13)—are among the best composers of the new generation.

Christopher Rouse's Symphony No. 1 (1988) seems to pick up the symphonic tradition where Sessions and Mennin had left it; its final moments even culminate in a quotation from the *Adagio* of the Bruckner Seventh. However, quotation is incidental to Rouse's aesthetic; he is so much an adherent of the Great Romantic tradition that he might rather be called simply neoromantic than New Romantic. Born 1949 in Baltimore, he studied at Oberlin with Randolph Coleman (a fine Midwestern conceptualist whose reputation remains primarily local), with Karel Husa at Cornell, and privately with Crumb. His works such as *Phantasmata* (1985), with its perpetual-motion middle movement *The Infernal Machine*, are characterized by extremes of speed and slowness, soaring violin lines in the highest register, extreme dissonance within basically tonal contexts, and climaxes punctuated by heavy percussion.

Ezra Sims is one of those unclassifiable figures whose relation to any movement can only be tangential. Born in 1928 in Birmingham, Alabama, he studied with Quincy Porter, Milhaud, and Kirchner. His music has a streak of postromanticism, but he is distinguished from the other composers in this chapter by being a microtonalist. He divides the octave into seventy-two steps—a versatile division that allows for quarter-tones, sixth-tones, and good approximations of the seventh and eleventh harmonics. His Sextet (1981) makes mellow chamber music from Louis Armstrong's rendition of "St. James Infirmary," accurately matching the great trumpeter's inflections. Like his fellow Southerners Johnston and Duckworth, Sims evinces an affection for the Southern hymnody of his youth; for example, *All Done from Memory* (1980) is a violin variation on "Lily of the Valley." As a microtonalist he has had neither the academic security nor the commissions of most composers discussed in this chapter, and he has worked as a steel worker, mail clerk, and music librarian at Harvard. He has written mostly chamber music, including four string quartets, and his music is as deeply felt as it is intonationally peculiar.

Much better known, Ellen Taaffe Zwilich has been celebrated as the first woman to receive the Pulitzer Prize for music (in 1983 for her First Symphony). As the first woman marked with the official imprimatur of the classical establishment (unlike Oliveros, Lockwood, Monk, Anderson, and Van de Vate, who have all remained outsiders), she has received a continuing abundance of commissions; also, one suspects, because of her mild, conservative, middle-of-the-road style. Born in 1939 in Miami, she studied with Carter and Sessions, and her works (Concerto Grosso of 1985, Double Quartet of 1984) tend to be abstract, in traditional multimovement forms. Like many oft-commissioned composers, she tends toward concertos, and she has written one each for trumpet (1984), flute (1990), trombone (1988), oboe (1991), and piano (1986). A violinist herself, she writes music of great polish, but her style is not distinctive, and seems to belong to an earlier era.

The New Romantics: Younger Generation

There are many, many younger composers still working within basically classical idioms, most of them students of either the composers discussed in this chapter or of the twelve-tone composers. A few of the best of them will be mentioned here. Most began working, under the influence of their academic training, in a complex, virtuosic idiom, then at some point rebelled and moved in the direction of clearer forms and tonalities evocative of past music.

For example, like George Rochberg, George Tsontakis (born 1951 in New York) broke with modernism between his Second (1984) and Third (1986) String Quartets. As a student of Sessions and Stockhausen, he wrote his early music in a Bergian, chromatic vein, but in the Third Quartet discovered a thoughtful, introverted idiom capable of mediating among several tonal and atonal styles. His *Four Symphonic Quartets* (1996), for orchestra without voices yet based on the *Four Quartets* of T. S. Eliot, are characterized by a French-style orchestration, with passages akin to Debussy and Brahms.[23] Tsontakis's music possesses a sense of grand, almost Beethovenian gesture.

Peter Lieberson (b. 1946) burst upon the scene in 1983 with a Piano Concerto whose tonality, cadences, and airy orchestration owe much to neoclassic Stravinsky but whose mercurial continuity is more reminiscent of his twelve-tone teachers Babbitt and Donald Martino. Born in 1946, the son of the composer and Columbia Records executive Goddard Lieberson (1911–1977), he became involved in Tibetan Vajrayana Buddhism, which he studied with Chogyam Trungpa. The interest has found expression in several of Lieberson's works based on Tibetan sources, such as the *Drala Symphony* (1986), *Gesar Legend* (1988) for orchestra, and the chamber opera *King Gesar* (1991), the latter two based on the life of a Tibetan warrior king. Lieberson lives in Halifax, Nova Scotia, where he teaches Buddhism as director of Shambhala Training.

Robert Carl (b. 1954) was a student of Rochberg, among others, and inherited something of his lyrical and quotation-oriented sensibility. Yet Carl also did his doctoral dissertation on Carl Ruggles's *Sun-Treader,* and the great angular leaps of Ruggles's music pervade Carl's as well, if in less strident tones. Carl's music often plays with ghostlike anticipations and reminiscences; for example, one of his most characteristic essays, *Time/Memory/Shadow* (1988), is written for two trios, of which one comments ethereally on materials played by the other, all leading up to a nostalgic quotation of a neoclassic march Carl wrote in youth. Perhaps his germinal work, a piano sonata called *Spiral Dances* (1984), likewise gradually wrings a waltz in F minor from the crashing jaws of atonality. In recent chamber works such as *Pensées Nocturnes* (1994), Carl has settled into a more serene, meditative idiom, but still with a dissonant edge. Since 1984 he has taught at the Hartt School of Music.

Scott Wheeler is a rare Virgil Thomson protégé, and he also studied at Brandeis with Arthur Berger and Harold Shapero and privately with Peter Maxwell Davies. His music, which started in a rather complex, twelve-tone-derived idiom, has gone in "the direction of Irving Fine neoclassicism. . . . It has a sense of reserve that I like, expressive on a modest scale, never in an overblown romantic style."[24] This is certainly true of works like *Four Corners* (1990, a memorial for Thomson), a quiet, tonal, almost impressionist tone poem for small orchestra with touches reminiscent of Copland and Thomson. However, Wheeler's more overriding aim has been to achieve an operatic idiom that learns from Broadway's clear sense of theater. So far this aim has found its largest expression in his large lyric cantata, *The Construction of Boston* (1988), a neoclassic work complete with harpsichord and banjo. Born in Washington, D.C., in 1952, Wheeler was a cofounder of Boston's Dinosaur Annex ensemble and has directed it since 1982.

Daniel Asia (born 1953 in Seattle) writes symphonies in a solidly tonal, somewhat impressionistic style drawn from brief, diatonic melodic motives. The reliance on these motives gives the music a slight postminimal flavor, and the combination of that flavor with a sense of grand orchestral gesture gives Asia's music an aura not too dissimilar from some of John Adams's post–*Grand Pianola* music. He studied with Druckman and Krzystzof Penderecki at Yale, founded the New York ensemble Musical Elements in 1977, and in 1988 joined the faculty of the University of Arizona at Tucson. His symphonies, four so far, include No. 2, the *Celebration Symphony* (1988–1990), written in memoriam Leonard Bernstein, and infused with the mood of Jewish liturgy. These composers have found viable career paths in the classical music world, and as long as that world exists, there will probably always be a New Romanticism.

Notes

1. Quoted in liner notes to *Contra Mortem et Tempus,* Composers Recordings Incorporated 231, New York.
2. George Rochberg, "No Center," in *The Aesthetics of Survival* (Ann Arbor: University of Michigan Press, 1984), p. 234.
3. Ibid., pp. 158–59.
4. Quoted in Cole Gagne and Tracy Caras, *Soundpieces: Interviews with American Composers* (Metuchen, N.J.: The Scarecrow Press, Inc., 1982), p. 156.
5. For instance, "Cognitive constraints on compositional systems," in John A. Sloboda, ed., *Generative Processes in Music* (Oxford: Clarendon Press, 1988), pp. 231–59.
6. David Schiff, *The Music of Elliott Carter* (London: Eulenberg Books, 1983), p. 132.
7. Quoted in liner notes to *Steps and Haddocks' Eyes,* New World Records NWR 80390-2.
8. Quoted in Richard Dufallo, *Trackings: Composers Speak with Richard Dufallo* (New York: Oxford University Press, 1989), p. 163.
9. Quoted in liner notes, *John Coligliano: Concerto for Clarinet and Orchestra,* New World NW 309, 1981.
10. William Bolcom, liner notes to *Open House and Commedia,* Nonesuch H-71324, 1976.
11. Quoted in K. Robert Schwarz, *Minimalists* (London: Phaidon Press, Ltd.), p. 179.
12. Ibid., pp. 174–75.
13. Ibid., p. 179.
14. Quoted in liner notes, *The Wound-Dresser and Fearful Symmetries,* Nonesuch CD 9 79218-2, 1989.

15. Liner notes, *The People United Will Never Be Defeated!*, hat ART CD 6066.
16. Ibid.
17. Quoted in liner notes, *De Profundis*, hat ART CD 6134, 1993 (slightly condensed from Wilde's original text).
18. Quoted in Richard Dufallo, *Trackings: Composers Speak with Richard Dufallo*, pp. 247–48.
19. Quoted in Cole Gagne and Tracy Caras, *Soundpieces: Interviews with American Composers*, p. 155.
20. "The Music of Nancy Van De Vate," *American Public Radio Program*, Ev Grimes, producer.
21. William Bolcom, liner notes, *Open House and Commedia*.
22. Quoted in liner notes, *Shadows, After Fallen Crumbs, and A Yellow Rose Petal*, Nonesuch 9 79231-2, 1989.
23. Interview with the author, December 26, 1996.
24. Interview with the author, December 15, 1996.

CHAPTER 10

Electronic Music

Electronic music, like opera, refuses to behave like regular music. Its history intersects with the more general history of music at many points but is conditioned by so many other factors that it begs for independent discussion. Within the tale of electronic music, technological advances have more impact than do beautiful works or widely publicized performances. One could conceivably write a history of electronic music without reference to individual pieces of music; to do so without discussing hardware and software, however, would be impossible. This is also the area most difficult to discuss without bringing European (and Japanese) music into play, since the invention and refinement of electronic devices and techniques has involved much international give-and-take.

To discuss American composers who use electronics in their music would, by the end of the century, include almost everyone. Rare is the 1990s composer who has never used synthesizer, tape, or computer. The term "electronic composer" had fairly specific connotations in the fifties and sixties, because the field was only open to specialists; by the eighties, it had become almost meaningless, except perhaps when applied to those few who never use acoustic instruments. Almost everyone is now an electronic composer. Nor, as electronic composers frequently point out with pride, does the use of electronic technology imply any stylistic preconceptions. The electronic medium embraces minimalists (such as Carl Stone), strict atonalists (Mario Davidovsky), Cagean appreciators of ambient sound (Charles Amirkhanian), improvisers (Richard Teitelbaum), conceptualists (Salvatore Martirano), and composers of every stripe except the most Eurocentrically traditional.

At the same time, however, what electronic music teaches more forcefully than any other genre is that, as Marshall McLuhan said, the medium is the message. Tape-splicing encourages the musical fragmentation of either pointillism or collage. Tape loops lead to repetition and minimalism. Computer algorithms suggest a language-based approach to music. Samplers suggest an imagistic approach grounded in the concrete sound-complex. Voltage control and frequency modulation make certain operations easier and more gratifying to work with than others. It is probably moot to ask in each case whether the composer chose the medium because it did what he or she wanted done, or whether the medium sent the composer spinning off in the direction it facilitated. To some extent electronic music has been the voice of the machine, and many pieces have been made more to demonstrate the machinery or software than to express the composer's imagination. This is not to imply a value judgment; if meaningful music may spew forth from a set of *I Ching* operations or a minimalist process, why not from a computer algorithm or piece of circuitry as well? Electronic music took off as it did not only because the gadgets were there but because its potential suited mid-century aesthetics.

Many of the composers who have advanced the field of electronic music are discussed in this book under other auspices: Gordon Mumma and David Behrman under the Sonic Arts Union, Pauline Oliveros and Sal Martirano with the conceptualists, David Tudor with the Cage group, Larry Polansky with the totalists, and so on. This chapter will be devoted to those whose reputation is arguably more related to the development of electronic music itself than to any other movement or scene. I will not defend or even define my criteria for placing a composer here rather than in some other chapter: they are based on the most subjective impressions, such as whether, when a composer comes to my mind, the word "electronic" does as well.

The history of electronic music goes back further than the century. In 1877 Thomas Edison recorded and reproduced, on a tin-foil cylinder, his own voice reciting "Mary Had a Little Lamb." German-born Émile Berliner improved upon Edison by inventing a gramophone with a flat vinyl disc and began marketing the contraption in 1894; the grooved disc was fated to last a little less than a century. Tape was to come along much later. Recording via magnetized particles proved impracticable until 1927, when J. A. O'Neill patented the first magnetic tape. Frequency response was still limited, though, and it took World War II— in which the combatants found tape recording a helpful medium for both espionage and propaganda dispersal—to develop the tape recorder to a level sufficiently sophisticated for musical purposes. The first commercial tape appeared in 1947, and two years later the first stereo tape machine, as well as a little item once ubiquitous in music studios, now obsolete: the splicing block, used to cut and join pieces of tape.

Meanwhile, the search for electronic sound-production instruments kept apace. The first was Thaddeus Cahill's Telharmonium, patented in 1897 and unveiled to the public in New York in 1906; it was a kind of Muzak machine, intended to pipe electronic versions of the classical literature into restaurants. More successful, and far more lasting in its influence, was the Theremin, first demonstrated in Moscow in 1920, on which one controlled pitch and volume by moving one's arms in space, determining distances from a pair of metal rods. Leon Theremin (1896–1992) interested Lenin in the instrument, toured Russia with it, and then swept across Germany, France, and the U.S. In 1930, ten of his Theremins played at Carnegie Hall, where two years later he returned with an orchestra of fingerboard and keyboard Theremins. In 1938, however, Theremin was abducted by Soviet agents and required to do war work for the KGB. When the fall of Communism in 1989 left him free to travel, he returned to the U.S. for the first time in 1991 for a flurry of homages and emotional reunions. The Theremin remains a popular instrument in downtown music and performance art.

In subsequent years, several electronic instruments were invented, mostly in Europe; the only one to secure a place in musical practice (mostly in French works) was the Ondes Martenot, invented in 1928 by Maurice Martenot, who played it by pulling a ribbon with one hand to vary the pitch and affecting the timbre and loudness with the other. In 1935 the first commercial electronic instrument, the Hammond organ, was manufactured and made its way into the entertainment world. The Canadian electronics pioneer Hugh LeCaine completed, in 1948, an Electronic Sackbut, which allowed the performance of scales and arpeggios as one controlled pitch with one hand and timbre with the other; with it, LeCaine could imitate a cello, a bluesy saxophone, or the clarinet at the beginning of *Rhapsody in Blue* with startling realism.

Since most early electronic instruments were employed to play not new music but electronic renditions of the classics, the real history of electronic music begins in 1942 when Pierre Schaeffer, living in German-occupied Paris, founded the *Studio d'Essai*. He produced his first tape piece, *Etude aux Chemins de Fer* (made from recorded sounds of trains), in 1948, and in 1950 he and Pierre Henry presented the first live concert of what Schaeffer had termed *musique concrète*, music consisting of acoustic sounds recorded on tape and manipulated. The Americans were only a little behind. On May 9, 1952, Vladimir Ussachevsky presented five electronic studies at a Composers' Forum concert at Columbia University. This led to collaborations with Otto Luening and to a more public concert of their tape works in October of that year.

In the next few years electronic music studios sprang up all over the world: the WDR Studio in Cologne (1952), Nippon House Kyokai in Tokyo (1954), Studio di Fonologia Musicale in Milan (1955). Karlheinz Stockhausen's early works at the Cologne studio—*Studie I* (1953), *Studie II* (1954), and especially *Gesang der Jünglinge* (1956)—garnered worldwide attention. The Midwest charged onto the scene in 1953 with a concert at the University of Illinois that included John Cage's tape-splicing extravaganza *Williams Mix* along with works by Stockhausen, Boulez,

Luening, and Ussachevsky. In 1957 RCA introduced the Mark II Electronic Music Synthesizer, and Milton Babbitt, Ussachevsky, and Luening obtained a Rockefeller grant for Princeton to buy one. Thus one of the two most important American electronic music centers of the sixties was born in 1959. The other, the San Francisco Tape Music Center, opened in 1962. Between them, these two studios defined opposite ends of the American electronic music spectrum.

Luening, Ussachevsky, and the Columbia-Princeton Studio

American electronic music could hardly have picked two more unlikely pioneers than Otto Luening and Vladimir Ussachevsky. Both had claims to being almost as much European composers as American. Luening (1900–1996) had been born to first-generation Americans who returned to Germany in his youth; Ussachevsky (1911–1990) was born in Manchuria to Russian parents. Both, in the first halves of their long lives, had written conservative music of European polish and influences. Luening's style owed much to his teacher Ferruccio Busoni, while Ussachevsky continued the tradition of Tchaikovsky and Rachmaninoff. And both of them, relatively late in life (ages 52 and 41) suddenly found themselves impelled into the most rarefied reaches of the avant-garde by the modest fact that, in 1951, Columbia University acquired its first tape recorder and assigned Ussachevsky, as the junior faculty member, to take care of it.[1]

Both were also from old-world musical families. Luening's was involved in the Milwaukee beer business, but his father had been educated at the Leipzig Conservatory and sang in a performance of Beethoven's Ninth Symphony under the baton of Richard Wagner; thus the Luening family leap-frogged from Wagner to electronic music in one generation. When Luening was twelve his father took the family from Milwaukee to Munich, where Otto was educated as a flutist and composer. After America entered the First World War, he continued study at the Zürich Conservatory. He took private lessons with Busoni, whose groundbreaking *Sketch of a New Aesthetic of Music,* written in 1907, mentioned Thaddeus Cahill's Telharmonium (called at that point a Dynamophone) as a new electronic instrument that would make exploration of microtonal pitch systems possible.

Luening returned to Chicago in the middle of that city's gangster era and played in theater orchestras, obtaining in 1924 a post as director of the opera department at the Eastman School of Music. This was followed by a series of academic positions, the final one beginning in 1949 at Columbia University.

Vladimir Ussachevsky and Otto Luening in the Columbia-Princeton Electronic Music Studio. *Courtesy BMI Archives.*

Meanwhile, Ussachevsky had moved to the U.S. in 1930, studied at Pomona College, and studied in graduate school at Eastman with Howard Hanson and Bernard Rogers. Though he was drafted in 1942, his knowledge of languages, especially Russian and Chinese, won him a position (like Milton Babbitt) in the Intelligence Division. After the war ended, he went to Columbia for postdoctoral work, where he studied with Luening and joined the faculty in 1947. He would remain at Columbia for thirty-three years.

Ussachevsky had been entrusted with not only the Ampex tape recorder but also with a Magnechord tape recorder, a microphone, and a primitive reverb box. With these he began working and, on May 9, 1952, presented five electronic studies at a Composers' Forum concert at Columbia. Henry Cowell reviewed the presentation in *The Musical Quarterly.* Ussachevsky described to the audience his attempts to achieve sounds above and below the ranges of conventional instruments, and Cowell was especially impressed (as he would be, given his overtone-based theories) by the timbre of overtones made by a piano tone transposed downward below the threshold of human hearing. Luening, who was directing a composers' program at Bennington at the time, convinced his colleague to bring the equipment to Bennington, where they started a primitive studio.[2]

Luening was a flutist, Ussachevsky a pianist, and so they used their own instruments as source material. As Luening later explained:

> We soon saw that the possibilities were endless, and we felt the need to limit ourselves to specific objectives. We had a choice of working with natural and "nonmusical" sounds [as the French musique concrète composers had done] like subway noise and sneezes and coughs, or widening the sound spectrum of existing instruments and bringing out new resonances from the existing world of instruments and voices. We chose the latter. . . .
>
> We used two basic manipulations. Simple as feedback and speed variation in a two-to-one ratio may seem now, their use for artistic purposes was at that time a revelation for both of us.[3]

(By feedback, Luening means here what would later be called tape delay: feeding the output of the tape recorder's playback head back into the record head to get a rapidly deteriorating repetition of the original sound.) The pair were soon invited to present their works at one of Leopold Stokowski's concerts at the Museum of Modern Art. Though skeptical of so much attention so soon, they relocated their studio to Henry Cowell's cottage at Shady Point and went to work. Here they produced four pieces, one by Ussachevsky and three by Luening, that were presented on October 28, 1952, at the Museum of Modern Art along with more conventional works. It was the first true concert of electronic music in America.

Despite the alien nature of the medium, the pieces were "designed to communicate with audiences conditioned to impressionistic, virtuoso, and tonal music in its broadest sense."[4] Ussachevsky's work, *Sonic Contours,* is a mélange of piano tones, metamorphosed into bell-like and harplike tones through artificial cutoff of decays and attacks, speed alteration, and tape echoes. Luening made his *Fantasy in Space* by a technique that would become ubiquitous in popular music: overdubbing. He recorded four flute lines, each time listening to previous lines over headphones. The piece is mellow and atmospheric, ending, for a familiar touch, in a folk-song-like melody. *Low Speed,* as its title suggests, is made up of pulsating flute tones slowed down well below the range of the instrument. *Invention in Twelve Tones* is a set of spare variations on a twelve-tone row, developing into a virtuosic triple canon.

The concert made Luening and Ussachevsky famous. It was broadcast over many radio stations, and soon the pair appeared on a television talk show demonstrating their equipment. By spring of 1953, their music was presented in Paris. Next came a commission from the Louisville Orchestra for the first-ever work for orchestra and tape. The result,

Rhapsodic Variations (1954) was the first of an unusual series of collaborations between Luening and Ussachevsky, followed by *A Poem in Cycles and Bells* (1954) and *Concerted Piece for Tape Recorder and Orchestra* (1960). The unprecedented team became the darlings of all who wanted "weird, spacey" music for their plays and television productions. Meanwhile, their work had sparked Edgard Varèse's long-denied interest in electronic sound, and he came through with his own orchestra-and-tape work—*Deserts*—soon after *Rhapsodic Variations*, followed soon after by the tape work *Poème Electronique*.

Soon Luening and Ussachevsky were able to demand space at Columbia. The next phase was to obtain a synthesizer. Milton Babbitt at Princeton was also interested, so the two schools joined forces on a grant application and in 1959 received funds for the new RCA Mark II Electronic Music Synthesizer. The Columbia-Princeton Electronic Music Center was born. In 1959 the Turkish composer Bulent Arel (born in Istanbul in 1919), who had been making *musique concrète* at Ankara, came to the studio, followed the next year by Argentinean Mario Davidovsky. Pril Smiley (b. 1943) and Alice Shields (also b. 1943) came soon afterwards to complete the Center's staff.

The legendary Mark II filled most of a room and contained 750 vacuum tubes driven by two paper drives and encoded by a series of four-bit binary switches. Its four identical synthesizer units were capable of producing sawtooth waveforms and noise and of controlling the pitch, envelope, volume, and spectrum of the waves produced, as well as possessing controls for tremolo and portamento. Two paper drives—primitive sequencing devices—allowed for a polyphony of four simultaneous voices. "The machine was extremely difficult to operate," Babbitt remembers.

> First of all, it had a paper drive, and getting the paper through the machine and punching the holes was difficult. We were punching in binary. The machine was totally zero, nothing predetermined, and any number we punched could refer to any dimension of the machine. There was an immense number of analog oscillators but the analog sound equipment was constantly causing problems. . . . It was basically just a complex switching device to an enormous and complicated analogue studio hooked to a tape machine. And yet for me it was so wonderful because I could specify something and hear it instantly.[5]

Babbitt created what remain probably the most enduring works from the Columbia-Princeton Center: *Composition for Synthesizer* (1961), *Ensembles* (1964), and especially *Vision and Prayer* (1961, based on a Dylan Thomas poem) and *Philomel* (1984), both of the latter for soprano and tape. On May 9 and 10, 1961, the Center presented its first public concerts, featuring the *Composition for Synthesizer*, Ussachevsky's *Creation-*

Prologue, Luening's *Gargoyles for Violin Solo and Synthesized Sound,* Davidovsky's *Electronic Study #1,* and other works.

Luening and Ussachevsky were born early enough that their aesthetics were not strongly affected by the mandates of the twelve-tone style. Luening, in particular, produced a lifelong body of chamber music marked by dissonant Romanticism and old-world polish; Ussachevsky has been less well known for his nonelectronic works. In the hands of Babbitt and Davidovsky, however, as in those of Europeans like Stockhausen and Nono as well, the new tape-and-synthesizer medium fused with twelve-tone aesthetics. Tape-splicing (although Babbitt avoided it) was conducive to the pointillism this generation had inherited from Webern, as were the idiomatic noises of the Mark II, as Davidovsky explains:

> I found that it was almost impossible with that technology to produce long sounds that were beautiful—they would tend to become dull. But I found that sounds of short duration and percussive-like sounds were accessible.[6]

Twelve-tone composers saw tape music as the perfect post-Webern medium, allowing total control over musical elements that had been serialized down to the finest detail.

Although he did not employ strict twelve-tone method in his music, Mario Davidovsky, originally from Argentina (born 1934 in Buenos Aires) epitomizes the detailed pointillistic approach to electronics. He is a purist when it comes to electronic sound, disdaining short cuts and building each sound up oscillator-by-oscillator for maximum subtlety. Though trained in Buenos Aires, he studied with Babbitt at Tanglewood and worked at the Columbia-Princeton studio from 1960 to 1964. He thereafter taught at the Manhattan School, Yale, and others before returning to Columbia in 1981 and then moving to Harvard in 1994. Not prolific, Davidovsky is best known for his eight *Synchronisms,* pieces for various solo instruments or ensembles and tape. His chief and oft-noted achievement in these pieces is that the live and taped sounds are so expertly blended that the ear is unable to tell when a tone passes from the instrument to the tape and vice versa. *Synchronisms* No. 1 (1963) is for flute; No. 2 (1964) for flute, clarinet, violin, and cello; No.3 (1965) for cello; No. 4 (1967) for male voices or mixed chorus; No. 5 (1969) for percussion ensemble; No. 6 (1970) for piano; No. 7 (1973) for orchestra; and No. 8 (1974) for woodwind quintet.

Although considerably younger than their male colleagues at the Center, Pril Smiley and Alice Shields maintained independent approaches to electronic composition from the start. Smiley's best-known work, *Kolyosa* (1970—the title means "wheels" in Russian), whirls burbling and rattle sounds through space from speaker to speaker with a pleasure in sustaining sensuous noises more akin to David Tudor than to Babbitt. Shields is something of a mystic performance artist who uses her voice and texts from Eastern religions in most of her works. Her *The Transformation of Ani* (1970) takes its material almost entirely from her own voice, reading and singing a passage from the *Egyptian Book of the Dead* in both English and Egyptian. Not only has Shields departed from her colleagues in producing long theatrical works—nine operas and music dramas, including electronic operas like *Shaman* (1987), *Mass for the Dead* (1992), and *Apocalypse* (1990–1993, a work based in Indian dance-drama with a libretto in English, classical Greek, Gaelic, and Sanskrit)—she is herself a professional opera singer who has played the role of one of the Valkyries in Wagner's *Ring* at the Kennedy Center.

In the first ten years of its existence the Columbia-Princeton Center produced 225 works by more than sixty composers from eleven countries.[7] In 1976, though, thieves broke into the Center, stole as much as they could, and destroyed the Mark II's wiring. It has never been used since. By the time this vandalism occurred, however, electronic music had already discovered other, more sophisticated methods.

Listening Example: Vladimir Ussachevsky, **Sonic Contours** *(1952)*
Of the works on the first American electronic music concert, Ussachevsky's *Sonic Contours* is the most complex and also the first to fuse "musical" (piano) with "nonmusical" (spoken conversation) sounds, while its impressionistic atmosphere of repeated notes and melodies anticipated by eight years Terry Riley's work with tape delay. The seven-minute piece begins with the low booming of slowed-down piano notes. After twenty seconds, piano chords enter, sometimes cut off abruptly by tape-splicing. Trickles of notes enter canonically, echoing each other, and at 1:45 (one minute, 45 seconds) a piano chord appears backward. From here on the texture becomes increasingly thick with echoes of tape delay, not only chords and individual notes, but brief motives that turn into ostinatos. At 4:04, a sped-up conversation with "feedback" (tape delay) is heard between Ussachevsky, his wife, Betty, and technician Paul Mauzey. From this humble beginning, the new technology already suggests its own methods of continuity.

Morton Subotnick and Synthesizers

Without doubt, two signal events of the 1960s jolted public consciousness that electronic music had arrived and was here to stay. One was the 1968 release of a recording called *Switched-On Bach,* a group of compositions by J. S. Bach played on synthesizer. The recording was made by Walter Carlos (born in Pawtucket, R.I., 1939), who had studied music and physics at Brown University before going on to study at Columbia with Luening and Ussachevsky. The record was a tremendous popular success, and Carlos followed it up with groundbreaking electronic film scores for *A Clockwork Orange* and *The Shining*. In the seventies, he became the first musical celebrity to undergo a sex-change operation, changing his/her name to Wendy Carlos in 1979. As Wendy, Carlos has remained an important theorist for computerized microtonal tunings.

The other event was also a recording: *Silver Apples of the Moon* (1967), the first synthesizer piece written specifically for recording rather than performance, by Morton Subotnick. In fact, Subotnick has rarely done anything in which he wasn't the first: the first "ghost electronics," the first cross-continental MIDI performances, the first live-conducted computer, the first totally composed CD-ROM. Born in Los Angeles in 1933, Subotnick studied at Mills College and studied with Kirchner and Milhaud. In the late fifties he made his first pieces of *musique concrète* by taping the sounds of an electric piano and junkyard percussion and occasionally running the tape backwards.

San Francisco was an exciting center in the early sixties. Pauline Oliveros and Ramon Sender (born in Spain in 1934, a student of Cowell and Elliott Carter) had gotten together some old equipment and given a concert at the San Francisco Conservatory on December 18, 1961, with fellow composers Terry Riley and Phil Winsor. In their next efforts, Subotnick joined them. The concerts were relentlessly experimental; in Sender's *Tropical Fish Opera* (1962), for example, fish in a tank swam in front of a conceptual score from which the group performed the fish as notes or dynamic indications. The piece that induced the Conservatory to throw the group out was *Smell Opera with Found Tape*, in which dancers went around spraying the audience with perfume as a found tape was played of a woman talking to her minister about her out-of-wedlock baby. Forced to relocate, the composers found an old house scheduled for demolition and turned it into the San Francisco Tape Music Center.

The Center became a hothouse for all kinds of new music, including the latest European electronic music, improvisation, theater pieces, free-for-all happenings, and even minimalism: this is where Riley's *In C* was premiered in 1964. The Center particularly nurtured an approach to homemade circuitry associated with composers that this book has already discussed elsewhere: David Tudor, David Behrman, Gordon Mumma. After a few years, however, the SFTMC ceased to be a breeding ground for experimentalism, and in 1966, Subotnick headed for New York to teach at New York University.

Meanwhile, in 1949 a fifteen-year-old Robert Moog had read an article on how to build Theremins and began building them. Within five years he and his father had formed the R. A. Moog Co., and Robert had to interrupt his studies to keep up with the growing demand. Moog began researching voltage-controlled oscillators and amplifiers, and by 1965 began selling his modules; in 1967 he began advertising them as "synthesizers" (a word that, before this point, had only been applied specifically to the RCA Mark II). A huge, imposing black box dotted with knobs and holes for cables, the Moog Synthesizer was the beginning of an apparently endless series of electronic sound-generation machines.

Improvements followed quickly. In 1963 Donald Buchla (born 1937) began working at the San Francisco Tape Music Center on an oscillator controller of his own, adding a pressure-sensitive keyboard and a built-in sequencer—an automation device with which a composer could store a sequence of notes or pieces of information. The latter device freed composers from having to splice a new piece of tape for every note and allowed them to work in larger musical units. The "Buchla Box" premiered in 1966. By the late sixties, rock groups had begun to see synthesizers as a glamorous addition to their acts. Keith Emerson bought a Moog to use with Emerson, Lake, and Palmer, Pink Floyd incorporated one in their album *Dark Side of the Moon,* and a sudden commercial market led to a series of analog synthesizers: the Minimoog, ARP, Oberheim, Prophet-5.

In 1966, Nonesuch Records offered Subotnick a $1000 advance on an electronic piece for a recording. The result was a series of works made on the Buchla synthesizer, starting with *Silver Apples of the Moon.* The piece's burbles, glissandos, and rhythmicized hisses, and its wild dance of looping ostinatos on side two, sounded like moon-music indeed, much more detached from conventional musical possibilities than the *musique concrète* produced by the earlier Luening-Ussachevsky experiments. As the then-mind-blowing liner notes about the Buchla Synthesizer read,

> It is possible to produce a specific predetermined sound event . . .
> and it is also possible to produce sound events that are predeter-
> mined only in generalities . . . this means that one can "tell" the
> machine what kind of event you want without deciding on the spe-
> cific details of the event. . . . This gives the flexibility to score sections
> of the piece in the traditional sense . . . and to mold other sections
> (from graphic and verbal notes) like a piece of sculpture.[8]

The sense of sculpture was reinforced by a diagram for the gentle bird-like tweeps that ended Part II, "A single silver child-angel in a glittering garden of silver star-fruit" (example 10.1).

Like his fellow Californian Henry Cowell before him, Subotnick felt that records demanded a new repertoire and that there was something dishonest about putting on discs experiences that were meant to be heard live; his intimate electronic works intended for records were "a kind of chamber music 20th-century style." He followed up *Silver Apples* with *The Wild Bull* (1968), *Touch* (1969), *Sidewinder* (1971), *Four Butterflies* (1973), *Until Spring* (1975), and *A Sky of Cloudless Sulphur* (1978). *Sidewinder* grew from a crescendoing, rattly click that sounded like a rattlesnake; *Four Butterflies* structured quiet pings in energy-envelopes that reflected the tripartite structure of both the butterfly's life and its body.

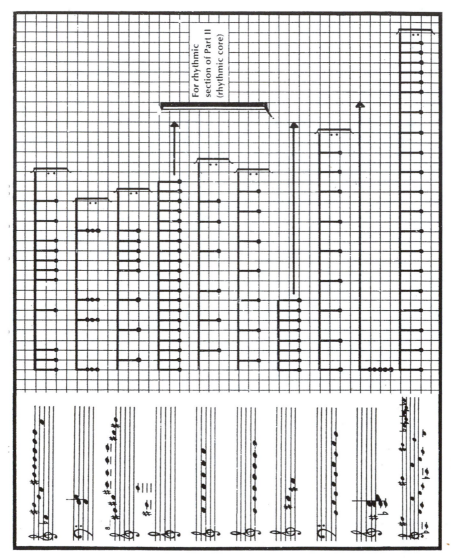

For rhythmic
section of Part II
(rhythmic core)

EXAMPLE 10.1 Morton Subotnick, *Silver Apples of the Moon.*

In 1969 Subotnick left New York to teach at the California Institute for the Arts, and in 1979 he married the singer-composer Joan LaBarbara.

By 1977, starting with *Liquid Strata* for piano, Subotnick had returned to live instruments, now modified to the point of unrecognizability by what he calls "ghost electronics." In these, sounds played by the musicians are picked up by microphones, modified by the composer, and then redirected through loudspeakers scattered around the hall. Next, he began working with computer systems capable of following the performer's tempo, so that predetermined computer sounds and ensembles could coexist in flexible give-and-take. The most engaging result of this research is *The Key to Songs* (1992) for two pianos, three mallet instruments, viola, cello, and computer, which spins the mournful melody of Schubert's song *Erlkönig* over a riveting pulse of repeated drone notes. With its virtuoso hairpin turns, *The Key to Songs* is possibly Subotnick's most unforgettable work.

The list of Subotnick's innovations continues. His *Return* (1986), intended as background for a planetarium exhibit, documented the cyclic reappearance of Halley's Comet through a series of computer-modulated quotations of plainchant, Scarlatti, Mozart, Liszt, and so on. In his *Angel Concerto* (1994), he depicted angels by having a MIDI piano played by computer, the piano's keys depressed by an invisible hand; at one Electronic Café performance at the Kitchen in New York, he played the piano long-distance from Santa Monica, California, over the phone lines. And, just as Subotnick had made the first composition specifically for record, he also produced, in 1993, the first composition specifically for CD-ROM, *All My Hummingbirds Have Alibis*. Some of Subotnick's compositions have seemed profoundly attuned to our times, others seemed merely to push the technology ahead for the sake of doing so. But he has always been out in front.

The Origins of Computer Music

Computer music was arguably the first musical technology ever in which the Americans led the rest of the world. An interest in computer-generated sound began at Bell Telephone Laboratories in Murray Hill, New Jersey, in the late 1950s. The electrical engineer Max V. Mathews (born 1926 in Columbus, Nebraska) joined the acoustic research department of Bell Labs in 1955, hired to help develop computer equipment to study ways to improve telephone sound. In the course of his work, he invented a converter that could refigure sound as digital information for computer use and then refigure it back. He quickly realized that his converter made it possible to generate music on the computer. Mathews interested John Pierce (coiner of the word "transistor") and Newman Guttman in the project, and together they created the first computer-generated sounds in 1957. Mathews wrote a sound-generating program called Music I, a program he later described as "terrible—it had only one voice, one waveform, a triangular wave, no attack, no decay, and the only expressive parameters you could control were pitch, loudness, and duration."[9]

Equally terrible, and produced via Music I, was the first piece of computer music, credited to Guttman, a linguist and acoustician: *In the Silver Scale* (first heard May 17, 1957), a nineteen-second melody leaping through diminished-seventh chords before a quick tonal cadence. The first dozen computer works were by computer technicians and have mainly historical interest. From the beginning, though, Mathews experimented with the computer's ability to effortlessly transform one sound into another via algorithms. His *Numerology* (1960) features the gradual change of a timbre from piano to bowed string, and a finale in which the notes accelerate, Nancarrow-like, to the point of unintelligibility. Mathews also computer-synthesized a version of the old song "Bicycle Built for Two" in which the computer sings over a honky-tonk accompaniment; the piece was later used in Stanley Kubrick's 1968 film *2001, A Space Odyssey.*

The first works to possess an interest more musical than technical were by David Lewin, Ercolino Ferretti, James Tenney (whose tenure at Bell Labs from 1961 to 1964 has been discussed in chapter 7), and James K. Randall. Tenney was perhaps the first composer to use the computer *idiomatically,* to let it make compositional choices and employ logics unknown in previous music. In Tenney's Bell Labs pieces, such as *Analog #1: Noise Study* (1961), *Dialogue* (1963), and *Ergodos I* (also 1963), he programmed the computer to deploy the sounds in a statistical manner within given guidelines. Since Tenney came armed with notions of timbre and structure from Varèse and Cage, his computer pieces are much more accepting of noise and surface complexity than those by the technicians, who had tried to mimic conventional musical results.

From these early days to the late 1970s, computer music was made by punching Hollerith computer cards in stacks of maybe 3,000 for a few seconds' worth of music, sending those cards out to a mainframe computer for processing, then having the resulting number-coded tape run through a digital-to-analogue converter to get actual sound. This generally meant punching your cards and waiting two weeks for them to come back—often only to find that some number error or miscalculation had torpedoed the desired results. Along with Godfrey Winham and Hubert Howe, Mathews worked on successive generations of Music I which became quicker, more subtle, and more user-friendly.

Princeton University was the first institution to create computer music outside Bell Labs. On the faculty there since 1958 had been James K. Randall, born 1929 in Cleveland, a product of Columbia, Harvard, and Princeton who had studied composition with Sessions and Babbitt. One of the most effective early computer works was his *Mudgett: mono-*

logues by a mass murderer (1965) for soprano and computer tape, in which the soprano delivers, in singing and *Sprechstimme* (speech-song) a collage of texts narrating the life of a nineteenth-century murderer. Randall's *Lyric Variations for Violin and Computer* (1965–1968) is in twenty variations; the violin plays the first five solo, the next five are for computer, and the last ten are for computer and violin together. The work has a slow, thoughtful, sad quality to it, as the computerized sounds rumble and swell in the background. Just as tape splicing was conducive to pointillism and collage, the computer encouraged gradual or linear sound transformations, and so from the very beginning computer synthesis led generally to a slower, smoother aesthetic than did tape or synthesizer music.

The same can be said for much of John M. Chowning's music. Though few people know of him as a composer, everyone involved with synthesizers is at least vaguely aware of him, for Chowning invented an innovation that had an enormous impact even in pop music: FM synthesis, or frequency-modulation synthesis. Born in Salem, New Jersey, in 1934, he studied for three years with Nadia Boulanger in Paris, got inspired by Mathews's 1963 article "The Computer as a Musical Instrument," and in 1964 found himself at Bell Labs. Experimenting with extreme vibrato, Chowning used one pitch signal to modify another and found that by so doing, he could achieve changes of not only pitch but timbre, far more quickly and with less calculation than by the methods of previous synthesis. Yamaha licensed the technique in 1974, and the Yamaha DX synthesizers became ubiquitous in the 1980s. Chowning's *Sabelithe* (1966–1971) is the first work to use FM synthesis, and *Turenas* (1972) the first to create the impression of a continuous 360-degree soundspace with just four loudspeakers.

Perhaps the most durable body of early computer music work is that of Charles Dodge, for he keeps his musical premises simple enough that the technology doesn't overwhelm the musical message. Born in 1942 in Ames, Iowa, Dodge has taught at Columbia, Princeton, Brooklyn College, and Dartmouth. Synthesizing computer-generated speech had been a major goal since Mathews's early experiments, and Dodge made a breakthrough. In 1972 he recorded his voice into a computer via microphone and had the computer analyze the pattern and replicate it. The eventual result, primitive-sounding now but widely celebrated then, was *Speech Songs*, a group of poetic fragments read by computer.

The achievement of speech synthesis opened the way to a number of speech compositions, including *In Celebration* (1975) and a computerized version of Samuel Beckett's radio play *Cascando* (1977) with robotic speech and raspily hesitant background noises that capture the existential mood of Beckett's atmosphere of futility. One of Dodge's tours-de-force is *Any Resemblance Is Purely Coincidental* (1978), in which he took recordings of the great opera singer Enrico Caruso from which all the scratchiness of the original records had been removed—along with the piano accompaniments as well. Dodge resupplied a new accompaniment and bent Caruso's voice to his will, doubling it, transposing it, distorting it into his own melodies.

While Tenney, Subotnick, and others have allowed computers and synthesizers to make compositional decisions according to logical structures, few composers have used technology to write music for live performers to play. The composer best known for computerized composition was the Greek avant-gardist Iannis Xenakis, but he was anticipated by one of the most unusual computer achievements ever: the computer-composition of the *Illiac Suite* for string quartet by Lejaren Hiller and Leonard Isaacson. The pair composed the work via the Illinois Accumulator computer (thus the title *Illiac*) at the University of Illinois in 1957 in order to demonstrate the computer's ability to follow compositional logics such as the rules of counterpoint. In four movements, the *Illiac Suite* explores strict counterpoint, randomness, twelve-tone writing, and statistical probability. The piece has a charmingly unpretentious American flavor reminiscent of Cage's 1950 String Quartet.

Born in New York in 1924, Hiller began his career as a chemist, working for DuPont for ten years. He later received a master's in music from the University of Illinois in 1958 and taught there until 1968, when he relocated to SUNY at Buffalo. Aside from his computer activities, he was a fairly conventional composer of seven string quartets, two symphonies, and six piano sonatas. His early music, as evident in his Sonata No. 4 (1950) and *Fantasy for Three Pianos* (1951), wavers between grand Romanticism and a wryly humorous neoclassicism. In his computer work, however, he remained for many years the leading pioneer of computer-composed music. After the *Illiac Suite,* Hiller's best-known work was probably his theater piece from 1968, *Avalanche,* for "pitchman, prima donna, player piano, percussionist, and pre-recorded playback," featuring a player-piano roll containing a random array of ninety themes from the symphonic literature that grow thicker and thicker in an avalanche of words and sounds.

Hiller's greatest public exposure came in 1969, when he collaborated with Cage on a spectacular sound environment called *HPSCHD*—the computer handle for harpsichord. Using a computerized *I Ching* to make the thousands of chance decisions required, the two assembled quotations of music by Mozart, Beethoven, Chopin, Schumann, Gottschalk, Busoni, and Schoenberg to be played on harpsichords by seven soloists, accompanied by tapes from fifty-six tape recorders. The event attracted 6,000 spectators to the University of Illinois' Assembly Hall, presaging and dwarfing ambient music-and-video environments of the 1990s.

Listening Example: Charles Dodge, Viola Elegy *(1987)*
Though not connected to his better-known speech synthesis, Dodge's *Viola Elegy,* written upon Morton Feldman's death as a memorial, is typ-

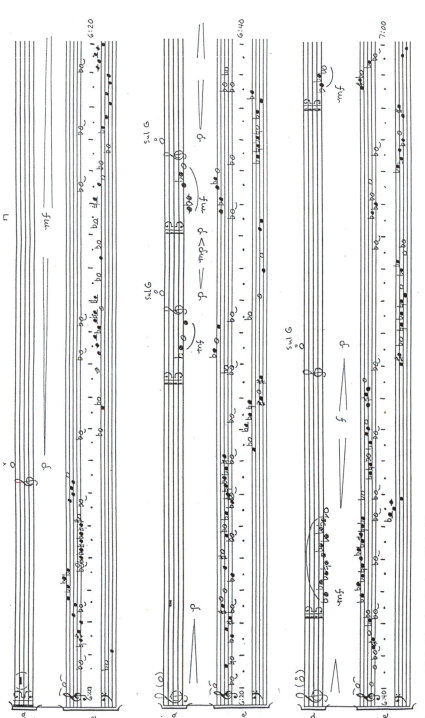

EXAMPLE 10.2 Charles Dodge, *Viola Elegy*.

ical of the lyricism and linear simplicity he brings to the computer medium. In the score the electronic tones are marked "Elusive, with no obvious onset," and the computerized tones move by in a gentle blur in which individual pitches are difficult to distinguish. The live viola part emerges almost mystically from the computer tones, and in fact always doubles something in the computer part at the unison or octave. Dodge wrote the computer part algorithmically, then wrote the viola part by choosing from the notes of the computer, so that the computer surrounds the viola like a halo. The viola choices emphasize certain pitches over and over as boundaries—much as Feldman sometimes did in his own music—including, in example 10.2, a high G and a low E-flat, the latter of which increasingly appears pizzicato as the piece continues. As the work progresses the viola becomes more active, until at last the tape ends and the viola has a long soliloquy grounded in that pizzicato E-flat. The work proves that the computer can be a source of sonic poetry.

The Personal Computer Revolution

In the early 1980s, the whole nature of the game changed, cleaving the history of electronic music neatly down the middle. From 1952 to 1980, electronic music was pretty much a studio activity. The computers involved were huge, mainframe machines obtainable only by large institutions such as universities. The necessary synthesizers and tape recorders took up a lot of space, and it was more efficient to have them at a central location where everyone could work. Except for a few wealthy rock-star hobbyists, electronic music was essentially a collective activity. The advent of personal computers, in conjunction with an explosion of digital technology, changed that forever.

First came the development of a revolutionary new type of instrument that would eventually transform the face of music: the sampler, which could record any sound through a microphone and play it back at any pitch level, usually by keyboard. The sampler also allowed composers to turn sounds backwards, loop them, and gradually transform one sound into another. Perhaps more exciting, one could record a cicada, a train whistle, a car crash, and play cicada melodies, train whistle melodies, car crash melodies. With the sampler, the old promise of electronic music—that any noise could become available for musical use—has become virtually a reality, if not a virtual reality.

For the first few years, samplers were prohibitively expensive. The first was the Fairlight CMI (Computer Music Instrument), introduced in 1980 at $25,000.[10] The Synclavier II followed, and then the Emulator I, at $10,000. By 1984, Ensoniq had developed a sampler called the Mirage for an affordable $1,295. By the mid-1980s, any working stiff could have sound-producing and -manipulating power in his basement that put the great electronic studios of the 1970s to shame.

At the same time, the entire music field was revolutionized, for better or worse, by the organized move toward a universal standard for computer music controls. In 1981 technicians from three companies—Roland, Oberheim, and Sequential Circuits—met to begin designing a universal interface for electronic instruments, so that equipment from different manufacturers would be compatible within one system. By 1983 several Japanese companies had come up with MIDI: Musical Instrument Digital Interface. Through MIDI, all electronic keyboards (and eventually electronic wind instruments, guitars, and drum machines as well) could hook up to computers for interactive sequencing, sound manipulation, playback, and so on. MIDI was not everyone's cup of tea. It had a strong orientation toward keyboard performance, tied into the concept of the individual note, that old-time analogue synthesizer users felt imposed a conceptual grid on the compositional possibilities. Nevertheless, MIDI broke through so many communications barriers that it quickly took over both the commercial and the academic markets.

Armed with sequencing and sound-manipulation software, a small home computer, and a few thousand dollars worth of synthesizers and samplers all MIDI-cabled into a central keyboard, the isolated recluse could now produce electronic results every bit as sophisticated as any mogul of a world-famous computer music center. If the downtown conceptualist scene of the seventies had seen the rise of the solo composer-performer, the digital revolution made that route not only viable but attractive. Since the early eighties, the American composer has had the option of becoming self-sufficient and independent from all institutions and organizations, without having to make the heavy sacrifices that characterized the careers of Ives, Partch, and Nancarrow.

Laurie Spiegel

Laurie Spiegel started out as a folk musician, playing lute, mandolin, banjo, and guitar, and these origins have profoundly influenced her conception of computer music. She sees the computer itself as a kind of folk instrument, and as a grassroots phenomenon; as she says,

> I don't think it's a coincidence that there seems to be a high percentage of women, and other composers who the musical mainstream might discriminate against, working in electronic media. You gain a lot by being able to go all the way from idea to playing the piece for people without having to get support from established organizations.[11]

The most extreme expression of Spiegel's folk-music philosophy has been a software program called Music Mouse (example 10.3), which con-

EXAMPLE 10.3 Laurie Spiegel's Music Mouse.

tains complex networks of musical logic that can be altered to create musical languages that sound more like conventional tonality, or more like Bartók, or Ligeti, and so on. In Music Mouse, even small movements of the mouse can bring down cascades of notes in complex harmonic progressions of changing timbre. Many rock musicians have employed Music Mouse in their recordings, and the software is so conditioned by Speigel's own algorithmic sense of composition that the use raises troubling and perhaps unanswerable questions about copyright and intellectual property. Spiegel's own music sometimes uses Music Mouse and sometimes not; when it does, however, her synthesizer setup is so complex that the music is generally more conditioned by the setup than by the slight mouse movements used to trigger events.

Spiegel was born in Chicago in 1945 and studied classical guitar at Oxford. Upon her return to the U.S. she enrolled at Juilliard as an early-music player on Baroque and Renaissance lutes. She also studied composition with Jacob Druckman and computer composition with Emmanuel Ghent. At the same time, she began working at Bell Labs (1973–1979), where Max Mathews gave her access to a computer system called GROOVE (Generating Realtime Operations On Voltage-controlled Equipment), on which she composed her first computer works: *Appalachian Grove* (1974), *Patchwork* (1974–1976), *Old Wave* (1975), *Pentachrome* (1974), and *The Expanding Universe* (1975). GROOVE allowed her to create and manipulate patterns of change over a period of time, parameter by parameter instead of note by note. In deliberate reaction against what she called "an overdose of heavy, sad, introspective contemporary music," specifically the twelve-tone variety, she made computer music in a sprightly minimalist style reminiscent of rural banjo-picking.

In the early eighties Spiegel lived as an independent composer, writing film scores and works for piano or classical guitar. By 1985, however, she had developed Music Mouse, an "intelligent musical instrument" capable of extending simple mouse movements into a complex system of decisions. In Music Mouse, the performer selects in advance whether to use chordal harmony, melodic ornamentation, contrapuntal lines, and so on, and then guides a cursor through an on-screen grid (example 10.3). "In coding Music Mouse," Spiegel explains,

> I tried to minimize violations of musicality while allowing maximal variety of output. I used constraints, logical tests, filtration, transformation, a loosely enforced bias toward continuity in all dimensions, and very careful specification of non-user-settable constants for harmonic progression and modulation. . . . For me, the most interesting material tends to happen when Music Mouse is played with only minimal mouse movement but with lots of use of the qwerty keyboard to change the compositional, orchestrational, and other interpretive variables. . . . [A]ll sound is in direct response to player action. Nothing is random. The player is in control.[12]

The phrase "a loosely enforced bias toward continuity in all dimensions" is a key to the aesthetics of Spiegel's music, for her works have a remarkable tendency to transform complex textures with extreme gradualness, with a large-scale rhythm reminiscent of natural processes: the resonant boom of ice cracking on a lake, the slow crescendo of a rainstorm. In works like *Sound Zones* and *Riding the Storm* (both 1990), she performs, using Music Mouse, on a Macintosh computer MIDI-controlling a synthesizer and two signal processors, recording each piece directly. The resulting textures are orchestral in scope, with shimmering bells, energetic drums and rattles, waves of sound that crest with glacial inevitability.

Paul Lansky

If there is anyone whose computer music is even more accessible than Spiegel's, it is Paul Lansky. Though he began in twelve-tone work, he declared his apostasy in the late sixties and became devoted to the idea of using computer music to reflect one's daily life. In *Table's Clear* (1990), for example, he used the noises of his children banging away on tableware, and in *Quakerbridge* (also 1990) the sounds of people shopping. Yet the resulting pieces are highly structured, the sounds abstracted and listened to for their richness of texture rather than for superficial associative value. The stripped-down pitch language of his music was partly inspired by minimalism, partly the result of working with speech synthesis; his return to tonality, he says, came as a result of "simplifying the pitch landscape to allow you to pay attention to something else."[13]

Born 1944 in New York, Lansky studied at Queens College and Princeton with Perle and Babbitt, becoming involved in Perle's theory of twelve-tone tonality. At first he began using the computer to program all of the complicated, serialized rhythms and pitch relationships that live performers couldn't handle. In 1975, though, through Godfrey Winham and Charles Dodge, he became interested in speech synthesis, and realized that "real world sounds were a lot more interesting than anything I could invent on the machine."[14] His first important speech synthesis work was *Six Fantasies on a Poem by Thomas Campion* (1978–1979), which used the voice as a trigger for resonance frequencies. Remarking on resonant pitches one can find while singing in the shower, Lansky sets up, In works like *Smalltalk* (1988) and *Word Color* (1992), what he calls "dozens and dozens of tiny little shower stalls" within the computer software, whose frequencies are triggered as the voice sweeps past them. The result is a halo of sound that can either draw attention to selected qualities of the vocal sound or flow through various harmonies as the piece progresses.

A breakthrough came for Lansky one day as he heard a group of inner city youths hassling a cop in rap. Attempting to elicit similar qualities from rhythmic speech, he recorded Hannah MacKay's voice, and—taking a cue from the phase music of Steve Reich—layered it in loops of different lengths. The result, *Idle Chatter* (1985), suggests a kind of complexly textured minimalism, a babble of almost-comprehensible voices that gives the ear, as he likes to say, "room to dance in." Two later companion pieces, *just_more_idle_chatter* (1987) and *Notjustmoreidlechatter* (1988), moved in the direction of greater harmonic and contrapuntal complexity. Infectious despite their surface complexity, these pieces have won Lansky, as the "computer postminimalist," a following beyond the specialist audiences of electronic-music mavens.

The Sampler: Stone, Amirkhanian, Gwiazda, Rolnick, Creshevsky

The sampler's greatest contribution to music is a philosophic one and is only beginning to be felt: it makes the new unit of musical thought not the individual note but the sound complex. The sampler works against the musical atomism of which serialism was the most extreme expression, an atomism that tape splicing and early analogue synthesizers encouraged. Composers who use sampling begin not at the level of the individual note, as composers have done since the development of notation, but at the level of the found sound object, a complex to be deconstructed. The composer can either reveal the inner nature of the sound complex, transform it globally, let it be itself, or combine it with yet other sound complexes. The sampler frees composers from the habits inculcated by Western notation.

With that philosophic shift come more practical, even legal, considerations, for to sample is also to steal. Rap musicians, who were quicker than composers to take advantage of the sampler, have often run into copyright difficulties, and several lawsuits have resulted from a rap artist stealing, say, a drum sound from a James Brown disc. What does it mean, in terms of intellectual property and artistic morality, that one person can produce a sound and another incorporate it into his or her own work?

One Canadian composer, John Oswald, confronted the issue directly: in 1989 he released a disc called *Plunderphonics* made entirely from samples stolen from other recordings and twisted, slowed down, looped, and so on. He used soundbites from the Beatles, Michael Jackson, Beethoven's Seventh, *Le Sacre du Printemps,* Dolly Parton, Metallica, often in humorous juxtapositions. He covered himself, too: he sent copies of the disc out for free, and never received a penny, stating in the liner notes that no copies could be bought or sold. Nevertheless, the Canadian Recording Industry Association threatened a lawsuit (largely because, to illustrate the gender-changing quality of his speed transformations, Oswald had printed a cover with Michael Jackson's face pasted above a naked woman's body), and ordered him to destroy the remaining copies. Oswald has since released other, more legal Plunderphonics discs, but the experience made him a martyr and inspiring symbol to dozens of American sampler composers.

Perhaps the best known American sampler composer, Carl Stone seems like the quintessential composer-performer of personal-computer technology. He performs his work by sitting at a table, typing keys on his laptop computer. As he taps the occasional key, orchestras burst forth, sound environments emerge, loops lengthen or shorten, and prerecorded music articulates harmonies and rhythms that the original musicians had never dreamed of playing. Born 1953 in Los Angeles, Stone studied composition at CalArts with Subotnick and Tenney. He served as Music Director at KPFK, one of the country's leading radio advocates for new music, from 1978 to 1981.

In *Shing Kee* (see the listening example below), he looped a segment of a Schubert lied, changing the length and speed of the sample as it looped. In *Hop Ken* he played with and sped up samples from *Pictures at an Exhibition,* finally using its chords to beat out a propulsive rock rhythm that would have surprised Mussorgsky. In *Mom's* (1990, named for a barbecue joint) he shattered samples of Asian music into fragments of a few milliseconds each, then used permutational techniques to switch them around into different groupings, with a jerky but infectious rhythmic momentum. More recently Stone has turned to longer works such as *Kamiya Bar* (1992), a sensuous, seven-movement tapestry of the environmental sounds of Tokyo. Famously, all of Stone's works are named after restaurants, usually those that serve Asian cuisine. (It was I who took him to the rural Pennsylvania diner named in his 1996 piece *The Wagon Wheel*.)

Another lover of environmental sounds, Charles Amirkhanian creates a kind of extended, pictorial *musique concrète* with some of the longest samples in the business. Born in 1945 in Fresno, California, he was influenced on one hand by Steve Reich's *Come Out* and on the other by Gertrude Stein and the sound-text poet Clark Coolidge; the combination made him something of a half-poet–half-composer, using tape loops, delay, and multitracking to base text-sound works on the more playful aspects of words. Performing over taped accompaniment, he would turn phrases like "rainbow chug bandit" (*Seatbelt Seatbelt,* 1973) or "dichotomy bongo" (*Dot Bunch,* 1980) into an engaging rhythmic interplay. Such pieces relied on Amirkhanian's radio-announcer's ability to articulate phrases like "rubber baby buggy bumper" in fast, precise rhythms, for from 1969 to 1992, he was Music Director at San Francisco's KPFA public radio station. The first radio personality to champion minimalist music and Nancarrow, he exercised profound influence on the exposure of American composers.

In 1984, however, he discovered the Synclavier II synthesizer, which he valued for its ability to record and play back samples of three minutes or more. Using it, Amirkhanian has produced a series of natural-sound tone poems, often made as tributes to composer friends or historical figures: *Metropolis San Francisco* (1985–1986), *Walking Tune* (1986–1987, an homage to Percy Grainger), *His Anxious Hours* (based on a Brahms Intermezzo), *Pas de voix* (1987, a Samuel Beckett tribute), and *Politics as Usual* (1989). "One of the things that's interested me about environmental sounds," Amirkhanian explains,

> is that, if you hear footsteps, you visualize something. If you hear a violin, you just hear a violin. The sounds have a different kind of affect and are pictorial in nature. That has an interesting effect on the listener, because at the same time you're listening in the Cagean manner (all sound is music) but you're also getting a mental picture.[15]

Amirkhanian's *Walking Tune (A Room-Music for Percy Grainger),* for example, overlays reverbed lines for solo violin with the humming of hummingbirds, the squeaking of rusty gates, and footsteps crunching on a gravel path. *Pas de voix* took its title from the fact that Beckett refused to allow anyone to record his voice. Amirkhanian went to Beckett's Paris apartment building and recorded the ambient noise of construction workers, football fans, and a metro station. He layered these sounds with the voices of French children, fart sounds ("orally synthesized," he assures us), and the flushing of a toilet magnified by being played on

Henry Gwiazda. *Photo by Jaime Penuel.*

sampler as a forearm tone cluster—all in keeping with Beckett's insistence on including the less savory details of daily life in his plays.

Meanwhile, Henry Gwiazda has combined the sampler with a technology of which he is the chief pioneer: virtual audio. Born in 1952 in New Britain, Connecticut, Gwiazda played in garage bands as a teenager and has taught at Moorhead State University since 1981. In 1986, he discovered the Ensoniq Mirage sampler and made it his primary instrument. In collage works like *whErEyoulivE* (1989) and *wM* (1992—running words together and eccentric capitalization are Gwiazda idiosyncrasies), he performs by playing guitar and sampler keyboard at once. Gwiazda makes extensive use of sound effects libraries and, rather than manipulate the sounds, places them next to each other to create tone pictures drawn from daily life. In *MANEATINGCHIPSLISTEN-INGTOAVIOLIN* (1990), a lithe violin phrase recurs over and over in conjunction with the crunch of potato chips, as cows moo and dogs bark.

Gwiazda's virtual audio works allow him to choreograph sounds and control their perceived location in space above and outside the placement of the actual loudspeakers. His first—*buzzingreynold'sdreamland* (1994)—must be listened to with loudspeakers at chest level, fourteen feet apart, with the listener seated about ten feet away from them. If you position yourself correctly, you hear a seagull circle lazily through the air, a person work in a virtual kitchen before walking around to your right, and at one point a basketball bouncing toward you. Another virtual audio work, *thefLuteinthewor Ldthef Luteis thewor Ld* (1995), must be heard on headphones for proper effect. A door opens behind you, a person walks up and begins to cut your hair, and then sneezes over your right shoulder with frightful auditory realism.

One of the most active East Coast electronic musicians is Neil Rolnick (born 1947 in Dallas, Texas), who specializes as a live computer performer using sampled material. His samples reflect his travels and passions: an extended stay in Yugoslavia just before that country broke apart resulted in his use of recorded Balkan music in *Balkanization* (1988) and *Requiem Songs—for the victims of nationalism* (1993), the latter a lament in which the computer is joined by violin and two sopranos in simple, folk-like melodies. Rolnick often employs video or film. His *Sanctus* (1990), for example, takes samples of masses from Machaut to Verdi to beautifully accompany a film of moving X-rayed skeletons. A smooth showman, he employs striking performance techniques, as in *Macedonian Air Drumming* (1990), where he triggers samples already stored in the computer by gesturing with velocity-sensitive, computer-wired wands. Rolnick directs the iEAR Studio at Rensselaer Polytechnic. His works vary tremendously in style and materials but are always whimsical and human.

Noah Creshevsky (born 1945 in Rochester, New York) is a reclusive composer of trenchant electronic collages. He worked with Virgil Thomson at SUNY at Buffalo and Nadia Boulanger in Paris, later studying at Juilliard with Berio, and now teaches at Brooklyn College. Like a latter-day Ussachevsky, Creshevsky revels in using digital sampler and computer to extend the possibilities of conventional acoustic instruments, in effect to create a music of impossible ensembles in which organs play devilishly fast rhythms and voices stray outside the range of the human throat. His *Variations* (1987) sounds like a thick ensemble of strings, voices, harps, and electronic instruments, often alternating notes in quick succession, and his *Talea* (1991) uses a fourteenth-century isorhythmic principle as a hidden structure for notes produced by a variety of voices, winds, keyboards, and so on. Creshevsky's music is witty and sometimes political; his *Strategic Defense Initiative* (1986), a collage of interruptions within a militaristic beat, was a response to one of President Reagan's more whimsical foreign policies.

Listening Example: Carl Stone, **Shing Kee** *(1986)*

Stone's *Shing Kee* is a classic of sampler technology, a supple minimalist work that makes the potential of the medium immediately apparent. Stone's complete source material is a recording of a Schubert lied—"Der Lindenbaum" from *Die Winterreise*—sung by a Japanese pop star, Akiko

Yano. As the piece opens, we hear a piano chord reverberating in suspended animation. As Stone lengthens the repeating loop, Yano's voice enters, first as merely a breathing sound, only later perceived as a sung tone. The German phrase grows longer and longer, finally breaking (at 8:30) into a later phrase from the song. As this latter phrase repeats, Stone gradually slows down the sample until it blurs into a wavery melody. The result overall is sensuous and restful, as hypnotic as any minimalist music. And Yano's pop inflection, Japanese accent, and German text create a sharp ambiguity as to the nature of the source; in Stone's hands, the sampler shows how drastically a few milliseconds can alter our recognition of familiar sounds.

Interactive Computer Systems: Chadabe, Teitelbaum, Lewis, Rosenboom, The Hub

In the hands of interactive-software composers, the computer has become a jazz partner to jam with. New software enables a computer to receive and quantify sounds from an instrument (or, alternately, supplied by the computer operator) and then transform them to send out, usually via MIDI, to synthesizers and other sound generators for replication. "Transform" in this case may mean something as simple as transpose or slow down, or something as complex as the mapping of quantities onto other parameters so that a pitch contour becomes a metaphor for timbral change or vice versa. The computer's echoes can be obvious, but more often it is used to create an entire language from the input it receives, and the sonic results often remain mysterious to the listener. Interactive computer music hasn't solved its aesthetic challenges yet, but no one has had to delve more deeply into the archetypes of musical language than those composers who program computers to do their musical thinking.

The first composer to entice interactive performance from electronic systems was Joel Chadabe. Born 1938 in New York, he studied with Elliott Carter at Yale and has taught at SUNY at Albany since 1965. Just out of graduate school, Chadabe was asked by SUNY to set up an electronic studio, something he knew nothing about at the time. Gathering together "the world's largest concentration of Moog sequencers under a single roof,"[16] he programmed random processes in complex enough arrays so that the sonic results would be surprising. The first result was *Drift* (1970), in which melodies swooped through musical space beyond his control. In *Ideas of Movement at Bolton Landing* (1971), Chadabe shared control with the sequencers. In 1987 Chadabe completed a software program called M, which has since been used by many live-computer performers. An example of M's potential is Chadabe's charming *After Some Songs* (1987–1995), a group of pieces based obliquely on jazz standards. In these works, percussionist Jan Williams improvises along with what he hears from the computer, while Chadabe modifies the computer output to fit with what Williams is playing.

Richard Teitelbaum's music has also centered around automata, in his case the gradual bringing to life of a musical machine. Born in New York in 1939, Teitelbaum graduated from Yale studied in Italy with Luigi Nono and Goffredo Petrassi. Returning to New York in 1966, he bought a Moog, and when he returned to Rome to join Rzewski and Alvin Curran in the group that would become Music Elettronica Viva, he took with him the first Moog synthesizer that Europe had seen. Teitelbaum's first work to receive much attention was a set of Nancarrow-inspired pieces called "Digital Piano Music," in which he interfaced three pianos with a computer via the Marantz Pianocorder system, a large black box placed over the piano keys to play them with rubber-tipped rods. In *In the Accumulate Mode* (1982), for example, the computer would store all information Teitelbaum would play on one piano and then recirculate it to the other pianos. With an expansion in computer memory came more complex works like his *Concerto Grosso* (1985), which he wrote for himself, trombonist George Lewis, and reed player Anthony Braxton as soloists and for four synthesizers and two digitally-controlled pianos as accompanying orchestra. In this work, anything that happens in the orchestra is only a response to the soloists; the computer stores up information, and makes changes in delay, transposition, and so on, as triggered by the soloists' input. As Teitelbaum explains,

> To me improvising has a lot to do with the unconscious. My system reflects these actions back to me like a mirror. If it's complex enough that I don't quite know what I'm doing, it simulates the unconscious in a way. You don't know exactly what consequences your actions are going to have. It's like a shrink, a self-reflexive loop with your unconscious mind.[17]

With Teitelbaum's passion for musical automatons, it was natural that he gravitated toward the Jewish Golem myth of Rabbi Lowe, who in 1580 supposedly created a Frankenstein-type man intended to save the Jewish people, but which had to be destroyed because it ran amok. Similarly, Teitelbaum's *Golem* series, computerized improvisation-and-response systems are pushed gradually to a point of complexity at which the relationship between input and results is no longer audible and the system overloads. The series climaxes with Teitelbaum's opera *Golem* (1989), based on kabbalistic chant and number gematria formulas (Hebrew numerology) with video projectors, slide projectors, and two vocalists; at the chaotic climax, the computer goes out of control. Like Stone, Teitelbaum has frequently visited Japan, and in 1988 he was the only non-Asian composer commissioned to write a piece for twenty Buddhist monks: *Iro Wa Nioedo* (Colors Will Fade), in twelfth-century Japanese notation.

Teitelbaum's associate George Lewis is an unusual figure, his life a synthesis of two worlds: computer-interactive software and the free improvisation associated with the Association for the Advancement of Creative Musicians (AACM, for whom see chapter 11). Born in Chicago in 1952, Lewis studied with Muhal Richard Abrams before getting a degree at Yale, and he often plays trombone with Roscoe Mitchell and other AACM figures. He might have had the life of an improvising trombonist had he not visited Mills College in 1976, where David Behrman introduced him to the KIM-1 computer; his first piece for computer was *The KIM and I* (1979), for microcomputer, synthesizer, and improvising musician. Subsequently Lewis began to incorporate electronics into his AACM-style group improv situations, as in *Chicago Slow Dance* (1977). In his more frequent solo works for soloist and "interactive computer music composer-listener," as he calls the system, such as *Rainbow Family* (1984) and *Voyager* (1987), Lewis uses his digital partner as a fellow improviser.

Perhaps no composer has used more complex logical processes than David Rosenboom, a brilliant and multi-talented musician who also performs virtuosically on both piano and violin. If Chadabe's electronic systems remain cool and consistent and Teitelbaum's go out of control and self-destruct, Rosenboom's grow organically according to some seeded plan. His primary interest is in models of evolution, often starting with the paradigm of the primeval drone from which everything emerges—evident in one of his largest and most compelling works, *Systems of Judgment* (1987), which opens with a resonant, pulsating drone like distant thunder. Born in Iowa in 1947, Rosenboom studed at the University of Illinois with Martirano and others. Living in New York in the sixties, he worked with La Monte Young, Terry Riley, and Morton Subotnick. Rosenboom's *How Much Better If Plymouth Rock Had Landed on the Pilgrims* (1968), a lively perpetuum mobile of diatonic patterns, is reminiscent of Riley and the psychedelic sixties.

In 1968 Rosenboom became interested, like Lucier, in biofeedback, leading to several brain-wave works, the most important titled *On Being Invisible* (1977). Rosenboom would perform with small instruments and computer; the computer would begin producing music algorithmically, change some parameter, then check through sensors to see whether Rosenboom had registered the change, in a mental feedback loop. Rosenboom moved in 1979 to Mills College, and in 1990 to Cal Arts. By 1981 he had developed—with Larry Polansky (for whom see chapter 13) and later Phil Burke—an object-oriented programming language called HMSL, or Hierarchical Music Specification Language, which he first used in an evening-length work for percussion and computer called *Zones of Influence* (1986). Much of Rosenboom's music has been collaborative; he wrote the computer environment *Layagnanam* (1990) for the South Indian *mrdangam* player Trichy Sankaran to improvise in, and *Two Lines* (1989) for Anthony Braxton. If Rosenboom's concepts are among the most abstract in the business, his sonic results are often sensuous and arrestingly meaningful.

Interactive computers have generally encouraged group creativity. The most important interactive collective so far has been the Hub, a group of six San Francisco-area computer composers: Mark Trayle, Tim Perkis, Phil Stone, Scot Gresham-Lancaster, John Bischoff, and Chris Brown. When the group first formed around 1985 (they were born in the mid-fifties), they would perform all hooked into a central computer. The advent of MIDI freed them to decentralize, though they use MIDI, they say, "as it was never intended to be used: as a medium of communication between players."[18] Each of their works is "composed" by one of the members, who specifies what kind of data will be exchanged and what the rules will be. (They have been known to perform together located at different spaces, connected via telephone wires.) Despite the abstractness of the venture, the Hub's music has a warm, tactile quality of irreverent sonic gestures.

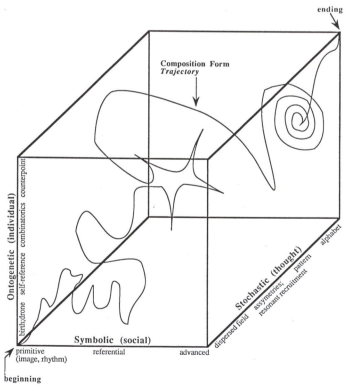

EXAMPLE 10.4 Concept space for Top-level Organization of David Rosenboom's *Systems of Judgment.*

Listening Example: David Rosenboom, **Systems of Judgment** *(1987)*

Systems of Judgment is one of the most remarkable and listenable works made so far with interactive computer software. The concept of the piece is that Rosenboom moves through a three-dimensional framework charted by three models of evolution, any one of which may exert more influence than the others at a given moment. The first model is that of a drone whose microscopic fluctuations, greatly magnified, eventually give rise to other tones. The second, complementarily, is that of random white noise, within which aberrations inevitably begin to suggest a specific direction. The third is an anthropological model of how we make distinctions between "primitive" and "more advanced" symbolic systems. Within these three possibilities, Rosenboom (playing piano and violin as well as guiding the electronics) follows the path graphed in example 10.4.

The piece begins with a prologue in which a low, pulsating drone blends into samples of thunder and a sampled mountain stream. The next section (out of seven), introduces the "Theme of Wonderment" (example 10.5), which recurs throughout the work in various forms. Part

EXAMPLE 10.5 David Rosenboom, *Systems of Judgment,* "Theme of Wonderment."

three is the "Central Section," the work's core and longest movement, which opens with "Rhythms of Self-Reference," i.e., rhythms which become more complex by replicating themselves at various levels. Sections 4 and 6 are interruptions; in the fifth section, "The Macro-organism begins to reveal itself to the separate entities; the paths of counterpoint continuously approach and veer away from one central attractor." The final movement is a microcosm recapitulating all that has gone before, ending with the chugging of sampled trains as metaphors for white noise. Interestingly, *Systems of Judgment* follows a curve from primeval unity to differentiated civilization similar to that of La Monte Young's *The Well-Tuned Piano*, and Rosenboom's "Theme of Wonderment" is reminiscent, at least conceptually, of Young's "Theme of the Dawn of Eternal Time." There the resemblence ends, but few computer-driven works remain as fascinating on repeated hearings as *Systems of Judgment*.

Sound Installations and Other Electronic Strategies

In freeing composers from the live performer, electronic machines have opened up a new social situation to the composer: the sound installation. Since they need never go the bathroom or pop out for a sandwich, computers and synthesizers—if programmed to run themselves—can sit in a gallery, building lobby, or outdoor space playing their digital hearts out for sixteen, even twenty-four hours a day. As a result, many electronic composers work in situations more reminiscent of sculptors and other visual artists than of the traditional musician, setting up works for audiences to come in and observe for any length of time.

One of the best installation artists, and a true American original, is Maryanne Amacher (born 1946 in Kane, Pennsylvania); unique and also mysterious, because the physical requirements of her works make her performances and installations rare, though more common in Europe than in America. As a child she was obsessed with acoustics: "I didn't play the piano too well," she remembers, "because I was listening to the overtones."[19] She attended the Philadelphia Conservatory of Music and the University of Pennsylvania, where she started working with computers and met her most important teacher, Karlheinz Stockhausen. An early series of installations called *City Links* (1967–) wired environmental sounds—from steel mills, airports, rivers, utility companies, open fields—to distant locations.

Perhaps Amacher's best-known works are her *Music for Sound Joined Rooms* (1980–1995) and *Mini-Sound Series* (1985–   ), in which she customizes sound environments to fit the architectural features of a building, including transmitting sounds so deep and loud that they resonate through the building's structure: as she puts it, "The rooms themselves become loudspeakers."[20] Because she requires so much time to prepare the building, Amacher can hardly be prolific, yet she has implemented installations in Vienna, Basel, Lugano, Rome, Berlin, Minneapolis, San Francisco, and Tokushima, Japan. Heard in their intended acoustic environments, her thick drones and huge, booming sounds—just as likely to come from a trash can as a violin or synthesizer—beggar description. As Ron Kuivila has said of her, "She's the only person I've ever seen get away with a half-hour fadeout."[21]

Kuivila is a composer whose output consists of sound installations and performances with no clear-cut distinction. Born in 1955 in Boston, he studied at Wesleyan and Mills with Lucier, Ashley, and Behrman and joined the Wesleyan faculty in 1983. His work has stemmed from several ideas used in combination. One is an interest in motion sensing, for which he originally used ultrasound and later video motion sensors. He has played with sounds that integrate themselves into their environments; in *Musical Chameleon* he used ultrasound to track movement as people searched for noises that would disappear if you got too close. From 1987 to 1990 he explored an interest in algorithmic composition, typified by *Loose Canons* (1987), a computer-composed Nancarrovian tempo structure. Noting that a spark is the visual analogue of a sound, Kuivila has made *Spark Harmonicas* and *Spark Harps* (with wires and pipes through which 12,000 volts of electricity shoot periodically) as sound sources to create a soft *ts-ts-ts-ts* of sparks. In *Civil Defenses* (1994), Kuivila performed at a keyboard as his movements, registered by video camera, triggered sounds via motion-sensitive points on a screen. If Kuivila's work sounds abstract, it is conceptually, but his pieces are often bracingly visceral.

Nic Collins (born in New York in 1954) attended Wesleyan at the same time as Kuivila and also studied with Lucier. A residency by David Behrman stirred his interest in homemade electronics, and for several years he worked in David Tudor's group, Composers Inside Electronics. Collins' primary instrument is a computerized trombone through which he can play sampled sounds that loop at the touch of a button, and send them to various speakers around the room. A landmark in his output was *Devil's Music* (1985), made by scanning, sampling, and looping the radio airwaves, making a thick collage of bits of pop songs. In *It Was a Dark and Stormy Night* (1990), an actor tells a story-within-a-story-within-a-story, each new phase beginning with the piece's title, as the words increasingly trigger voice-activated percussion and drones from the mixed ensemble. Collins also made a rather humorous CD quintet called *Broken Light* (1991) for hot-wired CD player and string quartet, with movements named for the composers violated: Corelli, Locatelli, and Torelli.

Given Collins's aptitude for musical ventriloquism, it was fitting that his primary attempt at theater so far is a musical séance. *Truth in Clouds* (first performed in progress in 1992) represents a séance held to contact two nineteenth-century figures, the pre-Raphaelite painter and spiritualist Anna Mary Howitt, and Elizabeth Siddal, wife of the poet Dante Gabriel Rossetti. The singers contact spirits via what must certainly be the first "Ouija-board-to-MIDI converter," which sends voices to loudspeakers placed all around the hall.

No computer composer of the younger generation has received more exposure than Tod Machover. Born in New York in 1953, Machover studied at Juilliard with Carter and Sessions, and from 1978 to 1985 he was Director of Musical Research at Pierre Boulez's prestigious IRCAM Institute in Paris. Since then he has taught at the MIT Media Lab. In 1994 he composed an opera, *Media/Medium,* for the magic duo Penn and Teller, and in 1996 his *Brain Opera* ran as an interactive installation at Lincoln Center in New York, afterward touring Europe. Inspired by the writings of the artificial intelligence expert Marvin Minsky and couched inside the ricercar from Bach's *Musical Offering, Brain Opera* allowed audience members to play rhythms and record remarks that would be incorporated into later performances of the opera; internet audience members could even contribute, although with so many individuals involved the chance of hearing one's own changes coming into play was like relocating a sesame seed dropped into the ocean.

Machover's more significant role has been as the developer of hyperinstruments, instruments augmented by computer-wired gloves that will transmit a tremendous range of information that can be used to elicit a halo of sounds from MIDI synthesizers. In his *Begin Again Again...* (1993) for hypercello, an FM radio transmitter in the bow, electronic sensors along the fingerboard, and a pressure-sensitive glove send information to three computers that let the cellist's melodies trigger other sounds, sending the accompaniment sweeping around the hall. Perhaps Machover's major work so far, though, is his electronic science-fiction opera *Valis* (1987), based on a novel by the popular writer Philip K. Dick. Scored for six singers, a massive video array, and only two musicians, the work was a landmark in the transformation of opera via computer into a medium that could achieve tremendous complexity with only a few performers; a landmark also in the assimilation of rock idioms into computer music.

Jon Appleton has had a career associated with a single instrument: the Synclavier, which he helped develop in the late seventies. Born in 1939 in Los Angeles, he worked in 1965 at the Columbia-Princeton Studio, joining the faculty at Dartmouth two years later and founding the Bregman Electronic Studio. Appleton's early music was in the nature of tape collage, often commenting on culture, as in the irreverent *Chef d'Oeuvre* (1967), based on a TV spaghetti commercial, *Apolliana* (1969), using recorded voices of astronauts, and *C.C.C.P.* (also 1969), which layered the voice of Tolstoy with Russian music gradually sped up and slowed down. Although he was one of the inventors of the Synclavier, he has primarily used it as a sound-generating performance instrument instead of a sampler, in tonal works full of almost minimalist patterns, such as *Degitaru Ongaku* (1983) and *Brush Canyon* (1986), the latter a delightful evocation of Old-West musical archetypes.

Tom Hamilton is New York's leading improviser on analog synthesizers, instruments like the Serge Modular, the ARP 2500, and the Oberheim Matrix 12, whose replacement by digital MIDI machines has given them the character of museum pieces. Born in 1946 in Wisconsin, he is known for works that act either as sound installations or as backgrounds for improvisation. His first installation, *Morelos Sin Termino* (1979), attempted to evoke memories of Mexico in an audio form that gallery visitors could observe the way they look at paintings. In *Ejector Room* (1991), he videotaped four soloists, who then played live along with their juxtaposed tapes. Several of his pieces have been inspired by mass-transit systems, including *Third Rail Jumper* (1989), in which soloists drifted in and out of the space on schedule, and *Off-Hour Wait State* (1995), an installation for Oberheim sounds on a pair of randomly accessed compact discs, the structure of whose drones, whirrs, and noises were determined by taking timings from the station stops of the E-train in Manhattan.

Trimpin

One of the most phenomenal computer composers has never used an electronic sound in his music. Trimpin, the German-American composer, engineer, and inventor, has created an incredible world of computer-operated instruments that produce acoustic sounds via MIDI. Trimpin's stringed instruments use levers to bow cellos and pegs to finger the fingerboard. His MIDI-triggered clarinets use pumps to force air through reeds. His MIDI xylophones tap away upon digital commands. But conventional instruments are only part of Trimpin's story: upon MIDI directives, water drips from buckets in complex polyrhythms, duck calls spin a ripple of squawks around the room, xylophone notes zip up and down staircases with lightning speed. Trimpin has brought a new acoustic soundworld to life, and while for economic reasons they have not yet had widespread effect, they are bound to revolutionize music in the foreseeable future.

Trimpin (the name is his last name, and he no longer uses his first) was born in 1951 in the town of Istein, Germany, near the French and

Swiss borders. His father was a brass player, and as a child Trimpin had access to old instruments he could cut up and exchange the parts of. At twelve he would go to the junkyard and stack up old short-wave radios, risking his life by hooking them up to electricity and antennas.[22] Declared incapable of learning by his early teachers because his mind ran in such strange channels, he studied metal work and electronics. In his music therapy class, he invented a light-sensitive keyboard that handicapped patients could play by moving a light pencil with their mouths. A brass player, he had to give it up when he developed a skin sensitivity to the mouthpiece. His musical interests turned to other channels.

In 1980, Trimpin came to America because it was too difficult to find surplus material and used or obsolete high-tech equipment in Europe; America has far superior junkyards. He settled in Seattle in a studio bulging with ribbon cable, computer parts, and old instruments. One of his installations of the early eighties was a microtonal xylophone six stories high running through the center of a spiral staircase in an Amsterdam theater, with computer-driven melodies ripping up and down it. Another piece was an installation of water fountains dripping into glass receptacles, the drips digitally timed in complex rhythmic fugues. Commissioned for a dance piece, Trimpin designed dancers' shoes with small bellows that played duck calls. He has sent bass drums, beaten by mechanical mallets, traveling across the room suspended from tracks on the ceiling.

Another project is a gamelan with iron bells suspended in air by electronic magnets; when they rise to a certain point, the circuit is broken by a photo sensor, keeping the bell in an oscillating stasis in which, since they don't touch anything, they will ring with a phenomenally long decay. Trimpin's *Extended Woodwinds* was a quartet of extra-long bass clarinets with extra keys spiraled around the instrument for a scale of tiny microtones. Since humans only have ten fingers, the keys are played by computer, and all the humans do is blow. In 1987 Trimpin met Nancarrow, a mechanically-minded kindred spirit, at the Holland Festival. Having built a machine to convert player-piano rolls into MIDI information, Trimpin convinced the initially skeptical Nancarrow to allow him to save his complete works as computer files. Subsequently, Trimpin has arranged performances of Nancarrow's music for instruments other than player piano. Nancarrow's final work, Contraption No. 1, was written for Trimpin's IPP 71512, an "Instant Prepared Piano" played by mechanical bows and hammers.

As much as the sheer novelty of these Dr. Seussian inventions would suffice for historical interest, Trimpin's own music does not merely demonstrate them, but elicits engaging music from them. He creates spatial melodies that run around the room, tempo canons, and quick echoes that make pitches appear to dash through space. He doesn't object to amplification on principle, but he does object to loudspeaker design, the one element of sound reproduction that hasn't changed in almost hundred years:

> this big magnet with a magnetic coil and a physical membrane—it's laughable. Digitally, every detail gets recorded, but the output lacks the resonance of the instrument. The future of loudspeakers is a different design that resembles more the acoustic resonance of instruments.[23]

Because Trimpin's music requires the transportation of so much equipment and so large a space to be heard in its spatial entirety, performances of his work have been rare, especially in penny-pinching America. There is little doubt, however, that someday composers will hear their music played by acoustic instruments, via computer, without a single human performer involved, without a single mistake, without any need to worry about whether enough ticket buyers will show up to pay for the concert, in perfect acoustic fidelity, with the sounds coming from a 360-degree radius. When that day comes, we may well look back to the genius-inventor Trimpin as the first musician of the new age.

Notes

1. Alice Shields, liner notes to *Pioneers of Electronic Music*, CRI CD 611, 1991.
2. Otto Luening, *The Odyssey of an American Composer* (New York: Charles Scribner's Sons, 1980), p. 512.
3. Ibid., pp. 512–513.
4. Ibid., p. 514.
5. Quoted in Joel Chadabe, *Electric Sound: The Past and Promise of Electronic Music* (Upper Saddle River, N.J.: Prentice Hall, 1997), pp. 16–17.
6. Ibid., p. 47.
7. Liner notes, *Columbia-Princeton Electronic Music Center Tenth Anniversary Celebration*, CRI SD 268.
8. Liner notes, *Silver Apples of the Moon*, Nonesuch 71174, 1967.
9. Quoted in Joel Chadabe, *Electric Sound: The Past and Promise of Electronic Music*, p. 109.
10. This and other prices and dates are from Joel Chadabe, op. cit.
11. Liner notes to *The Expanding Universe*, Philo 9003, 1980.
12. Quoted in Joel Chadabe, *Electric Sound: The Past and Promise of Electronic Music*, pp. 335–336.
13. Interview with the author, January 29, 1997.
14. Interview with the author, January 29, 1997.
15. Interview with the author, January 30, 1997.
16. Chadabe, op. cit., p. 286.
17. Interview with the author, February 7, 1997.
18. Tim Perkis, liner notes to *The Hub: Wreckin' Ball*, Artifact ART 1008, 1994.

19. Conversation with the author, January 30, 1997.
20. Personal communication to the author.
21. Conversation with the author, February 3, 1997.
22. This and following information from Kyle Gann, "Trimpin's Machine Age" in *The Village Voice*, April 20, 1993, pp. 84 and 87.
23. Ibid.

CHAPTER 11

Interfaces with Rock and Jazz

As late as 1975, jazz was jazz, rock was rock, and classical music was classical music. Even the minimalists and conceptualists, independent of Europe as they were, knew which side their music stood on. The general public had no problem with that. But with each passing generation musicians were becoming increasingly unhappy as more and more grew up trained in parallel traditions and were impatient with having to compartmentalize their abilities. Jazz and classical music had carried on a mutual flirtation since the 1920s or earlier, but rock was a newcomer and ostentatious about its vernacular, "low art" status. To cross that line from classical music into rock—if line there was, or perhaps only a magic fire like the illusion with which Wotan surrounded Brünnhilde—was a daunting taboo. Future generations will probably have difficulty understanding that it occasioned more anxiety than even the New Romantics' return to tonality.

Rock went through its most fertile, aggressive, electrifying period in exactly the years in which classical music was most caught up in dry, cerebral complexity; almost as though the two streams had polarized in some chemical reaction by which all the physical and emotional energy rushed to one side, all the analytical energy to the other. The years that forged rock-and-roll in the crucible of black popular music by performers such as Billy Ward and the Dominoes, Joe Turner, Big Mama Thornton, and Chuck Berry—1951 to 1955—were the very years in which Cage turned to chance processes and Babbitt and others to serialism.

Rock and roll emerged as a social force in 1955, the summer when "Rock Around the Clock" by Bill Haley and the Comets became the most popular recording in America. Elvis Presley made his first recording in 1954 and dominated the pop charts of the late fifties. Then, in the sixties rock-and-roll became simply rock, developing lyrics of greater political significance and making more of electronic amplification and distortion. Almost exclusively the domain of the young, the new style came to symbolize the social and political upheavals of the sixties, especially after the creative energy had flowed into English bands. Most notably, the Beatles appeared on the Ed Sullivan show in 1964, capturing the heart of America's youth. Continued by artists such as Janis Joplin, Jimi Hendrix, Bob Dylan, the Rolling Stones, the Doors, the Beach Boys, and the Grateful Dead among many, many others, rock became *the* music of hip, liberal, young America.

Given all this, it is amazing in retrospect how separate the avant-garde classical musicians kept themselves from rock as late as 1978. In the musics of Robert Ashley, Steve Reich, and Philip Glass, one can sense the desire to tap into the physical energy that rock thrived on, but the materials and formulas of rock were off-limits, not to be considered. To the dismay of the purveyors of serialist complexity, certain artists like Leonard Bernstein defected to the pop world, finding there a healthier and more confident energy. In 1966, Bernstein wrote:

> as of this writing, God forgive me, I have far more pleasure in following the musical adventures of Simon and Garfunkel or of The Association singing "Along Comes Mary" than I have in most of what is being written now by the whole community of "avant-garde" composers. . . . Pop music seems to be the only area where there is to be found unabashed vitality, the fun of invention, the feeling of fresh air. Everything else suddenly seems old-fashioned: electronic music, serialism, chance music—they have already acquired the musty odor of academicism.[1]

Bernstein was hardly alone. As much as serialism and conceptualism represented diametrically opposed poles of the classical spectrum, one seeking after consummate control and the other a complete abnegation of control, both were marked by a cerebral quality almost totally devoid of physicality. Milton Babbitt's serialized time-point rhythms and La Monte Young's "This piece is little whirlpools out in the middle of the ocean" had in common that you couldn't tap your foot to either of them.

The classical prejudices against rock were deeply based in training and musical values, and not entirely without basis. One prejudice was against rock's extreme harmonic simplicity, stemming as it did from a musical practice in which the harmonies I, IV, and V sufficed for most musical structures. To classical composers trained to value pitch structures above rhythmic energy or timbral sophistication, such voluntary abnegation of subtlety seemed suicidal. An even more serious problem was notation, for the drumbeats and guitar riffs of rock had nuances that notation could not capture nor classically trained ears always register. For hundreds of years the classical composer had lived by writing down his melodies and rhythms for someone else to read; rock musicians worked more along the lines of Indian or Arabic music, working musical materials out in rehearsal, memorizing them, and improvising around basic structures. These two vastly different models could not simply be reconciled by an act of will.

Furthermore, the popular appeal of rock was grounded in a sexually exciting, highly physical performance style that few conservatory-trained composers were temperamentally prepared to imitate. The truth is, despite rock's harmonic simple-mindedness, it had evolved its own highly inflected idioms that classically trained composers could not simply pick up with any authenticity. One could no more step into that tradition without the proper background than one could suddenly pick up a sitar and sing Indian ragas. Attempts to notate rock rhythms or to have classically trained percussionists try to drum rock-style have invited justified ridicule. As Rhys Chatham admitted after his experience with rock,

> I, too, had a fairly arrogant attitude as I first approached the study of rock. I had very few insecurities as a classical musician, so I thought, "I've been a musician all my life, I've played Pierre Boulez's *Sonatine for Flute and Piano,* and I know how to count to four, so this ought to be easy.". . . [B]ut my playing was stiff, very stiff. I was counting the rhythms in my head rather than really feeling them.[2]

Furthermore, the tremendous commercial success of rock musicians incited composers to envy and self-righteous resentment; in the seventies the poverty of avant-garde musicians became a badge of integrity.

However, with minimalism came developments that eventually paved the way to at least a partial rapprochement. First of all, in *In C* and other works, Terry Riley reintroduced a steady beat. Reich proved in *Four Organs* that not only could three chords provide sufficient harmonic interest for an extended work: one would do just fine. (To this day, however, even the most laid-back postminimalists avoid the well-worn I–IV–V progression.) Glass's electronic keyboards and amplified winds and strings edged closer to the timbral and dynamic aspects of rock. Perhaps most importantly, by working closely with their own ensembles, Young, Glass, Reich, and the downtown Manhattan composers who followed them initiated a new performance practice that was not entirely dependent on notation; inflections could evolve within the rehearsal process, and composers could impart their ideas to the performers directly without the filter of the printed page. The new-music band of the sixties and seventies, largely because of economic pressures, began to resemble the rock group, structurally and socially.

Conciliatory moves were coming from the other direction as well. The British rockers David Bowie and Brian Eno heard Philip Glass's *Music with Changing Parts* when his ensemble performed it in England in 1971, and soon after began incorporating drones and repetition of motives in their rock albums. Passages of composed, sometimes quasi-minimalist patterns began appearing in the early seventies music of groups like Yes,

Genesis, and Pink Floyd. Protean rocker Frank Zappa incorporated wild improvisation and dissonant gestures into his music and wrote liner notes that sparked rockers' interest in Varèse, Webern, and Feldman. Even the Beatles got into the act: their public enthusiasm (and that of The Who as well) for Stockhausen caused a temporary run on that composer's recordings, and in 1968 they appropriated tape-splicing and loop techniques for the tape collage *Revolution No. 9* on their "White Album."

Further outside the mainstream, underground bands like Henry Cow used unusual meters and sharply turning stream-of-consciousness forms that, to the embarrassment of many composers, were more adventurous and challenging than most of what passed for excitement in the academy. Starting with his *Music for Airports* (1978), and partly under Cage's influence, Eno revived Erik Satie's ninety-year-old dream of "Furniture Music," reborn as ambient: a music specifically made to be used as neutral background. (It would be another fifteen years, though, before ambient music would make effective inroads into the new-music world, having made a detour through hip hop first.) Having cornered the market on physicality, late seventies rock made an aggressive bid for serious intellectual respect as well.

Under these pressures it was inevitable that definitions would blur into invisibility, at least temporarily. Starting in 1977 Rhys Chatham caused a furor by inviting experimental rock bands to play at the Kitchen, mecca of conceptualist and minimalist music. About the same time Robert Ashley began collaborating with rock artists such as Peter Gordon from the new-wave group Love of Live Orchestra and the songstress Jill Kroesen. Laurie Anderson, performance artist, surprised herself by becoming a rock star. Glenn Branca switched from punk songs to symphonies. Peter Gordon wrote operas. As it became impossible to tell which context some performers were meant to be heard in, Robert Ashley, realizing that long pieces required more structural support than short ones, ventured a distinction: "If it's under five minutes it's rock, over five minutes it's classical."[3] No one came up with a better definition.

Except for Diamanda Galàs—always a special case no matter what the topic—the composers covered below are those who fused some aspect of minimalism with a rock beat. Tensions between rock and the avant-garde didn't resolve in the eighties but only sharpened, and most of the composers who more selectively worked rock materials into their musical language will appear in chapter 13, in the totalist generation.

Laurie Anderson

"Ha—ha—ha—ha—ha—ha—ha—ha. . . ." This lightly intoned mantra suddenly zoomed out of the art-world avant-garde into mass conscious-

Laurie Anderson. *Photo by Jeffrey Mayer.*

ness in 1981 as Laurie Anderson's disarmingly innovative song "O Superman" hit no. 2 on England's pop charts. Actress, singer, violinist, composer, dancer, designer, standup comedienne, Anderson practically invented a new type of theater so striking and unclassifiable that the term "performance art" was coined to refer to it. Probably no other per· son in this book has achieved such popularity as a performer.

Laurie Anderson was born in 1947 and grew up near Chicago. As a teenager she avidly studied violin and spent her summers at Interlochen Music Camp in Michigan. At sixteen, however, she decided that being a virtuoso took more time than she wanted to commit to any one thing. After taking art classes at the School of the Art Institute, she studied with Carl André and Sol LeWitt at the School of Visual Arts and then attended Columbia as a sculpting major, where, as she put it, "the esthetic was that sculpture should be a) heavy and b) made of steel. I didn't fit into this esthetic very well."[4] (Her sculptures were made of newspaper or fiberglass.)

In 1973 Anderson met Philip Glass and began hanging around with other artists at his mesmerizing rehearsals. Though a sculptor, she started making pieces that involved sound and performance, starting that year with *Automotive,* a concert for automobiles. She tried her hand at small films, and since she never finished the soundtracks in time for showings, she would stand in front and perform the stories and music live: thus "performance art" was born. Her first real performance art piece was *As If* (1974), in which she told stories and played the violin while wearing ice skates whose blades had been frozen into blocks of ice, as she waited for the ice to melt. Violins became her favorite props: she sanded one, burned one, mounted a loudspeaker inside one, filled one with water, popped popcorn inside a tin one, and, in one of her most famous routines, played a violin—whose bridge had been replaced with a tape recorder head—with a bow whose hairs had been replaced with audiotape with words recorded on it. The latter trick gave her an interest in backwards speech, such as "god" being "dog" in reverse.

The turning point came in 1981. Helped by a $500 NEA grant, a small New York label had pressed 1,000 copies of a single album she made with two songs, "O Superman" on one side and "Walk the Dog" on the other. Unexpectedly, "O Superman" climbed to number two on the pop charts in England. In order to deal with the sudden demand for copies, she signed a deal with Warner Brothers Records. "I quickly found out," she wrote later,

> that in my world (the New York avant-garde) this was considered "selling out. . . ." The avant-garde in the late '70s was extremely protective of its own ideas, territory, and privilege. I myself had benefited from this attitude. I had been supported and protected by this network. It had always been a safe place to work, until I signed a contract with a "commercial" company. A couple of years later, this process was known as "crossing over" and was looked on more favorably by the avant-garde.[5]

"O Superman" was from a four-hour multimedia work that Anderson premiered in 1980, *United States I-IV.* The song was soon more permanently recorded on a full-length LP, *Big Science* (1982). Subsequent albums confirmed Anderson's status as a rock star from the avant-garde: *Mister Heartbreak* (1984), *Home of the Brave* (1986), *Strange Angels* (1989), and *Bright Red* (1994).

It would be impossible in a quick survey to even list all of the technological tricks in Anderson's performances. She sings in total darkness with a lit light bulb in her mouth so that all you can see are the shapes of her words. She projects words in light and makes them visible by swinging her bow in front of the light fast enough for the words to be seen. She dances in a body suit fitted with electronic drum-machine components, so that every time she hits her wrists or elbows against another part of her body, booms emerge. She wires her violin to a Synclavier synthesizer so that she can play birdcalls, buzzers, voices. In many performances she alternates between microphones, one of which feeds into a harmonizer that turns her voice into a deep male voice that she calls "The Voice of Authority."

During the late eighties, she began to use less music in her performances and concentrate more on political commentary. With a major work, *Stories from the Nerve Bible,* though, she returned to postminimalist songs and technical effects, including a "video clone": an altered video version of herself, with mustache, to serve as her diminutive male alter ego. Meanwhile, her fame and irrepressible adventurousness have brought her dozens of unusual experiences. She experimentally went through the winter of 1972 without wearing a coat, and, in the summer of 1973, tried to hitchhike to the North Pole via mail planes; she got within 200 miles. She has had a press conference with Bishop Tutu, met the Prince of Ubud in Bali, and in 1993 she trekked the Tibetan Himalayas with twenty-seven yaks, eight sherpas, and ten hikers. No one else in American music has had a life like Laurie Anderson's.

Listening Example: "O Superman" (1980)

In 1978 Anderson was deeply affected by a recital she heard by the Black vocalist Charles Holland, whose career had been squelched for decades by racism in the classical music world. Holland sang, in the aria "O Souverain" from Massenet's *Le Cid,* "O souverain, ô juge, ô père": "O Sovereign, O Judge, O Father." Anderson decided, in homage, to write her own version of the song, kind of a "cover," with her own translation of the words. The song begins with her voice looped on a repeating "Ha—ha—ha—ha—ha—ha." The pitch is E, and the entire song rocks back and forth between two chords: C major and E minor. The text is riddled with clichés from American life:

> O Superman. O Judge. O Mom and Dad.
> O Superman. O Judge. O Mom and Dad.
>
> Hi. I'm not home right now.
> But if you want to leave a message,
> just start talking at the sound of the tone.
>
> Hello? This is your mother. Are you there?
> Are you coming home? Hello? Is anybody home?
>
> Well you don't know me but I know you.
> And I've got a message to give to you.
> Here come the planes.
> So you better get ready, ready to go.
> You can come as you are, but pay as you go.
> Pay as you go.
>
> And I said: OK! Who is this really?
> And the voice said:

> This is the hand, the hand that takes.
> This is the hand. The hand that takes.
> Here come the planes.
> They're American planes, made in America.
> Smoking or nonsmoking? . . .
>
> 'Cause when love is gone, there's always justice,
> and when justice is gone,
> there's always force,
> and when force is gone, there's always Mom. Hi Mom!

The music slowly dies away again with bird songs and ostinatos, finally leaving only that repeating "ha," which abruptly stops. A hybrid of minimalism, rock, and performance art, "O Superman" is one of the most memorable productions of the New York avant-garde.

Rhys Chatham

More than anyone else it was Rhys Chatham who opened the floodgates that allowed rock aesthetics and practices to flow into the "classical" new-music world. The impact of his music has been exceeded in this respect by his impact as the first musical director of the Kitchen in New York; from 1971 to 1973 and again from 1977 to 1980 he was in charge of the music programming at New York's most groundbreaking space for new music. Here he scandalized the classical new-music world by programming experimental rock, and then further by appropriating the sounds of rock and writing music for electric guitars himself. Most notable are Chatham's works written for massive ensembles of 100 electric guitars: *An Angel Moves Too Fast to See* (1989), *Warehouse of Saints, Songs for Spies* (1991), and *Music for Tauromaquia* (1992–1993).

Chatham was born in Manhattan in 1952. At New York University he studied with Morton Subotnick and worked at the NYU Studio with Maryanne Amacher, Serge Tcherepnin, Charlemagne Palestine, and Ingram Marshall. Through this crowd Chatham developed an interest in minimalism, specifically a music of long durations, and he studied with La Monte Young, whose piano he tuned in return for lessons. Chatham's first works in New York were extremely quiet, mostly drone pieces for Buchla synthesizers whose overtones were subtly manipulated. In 1976, however, his dynamic level skyrocketed as he became interested in working in a hard rock format. "Essentially," he wrote later,

> my idea has always been to draw upon the vocabulary of the classical avant-garde to form a music with a rock-like veneer behind which lies a more universal, hence Western set of concerns. Even though

the music I make without a question comes out of the classical avant-garde, I felt the time dictated playing the work in a rock context.[6]

He switched to writing for ensembles of electric guitars.

The history of art-rock from 1977 to 1982 has been a controversial subject, mired in sibling rivalry. In the mid-seventies, it became an art-world fad for visual artists to start their own rock bands; musical ability wasn't much of a requisite for rock, and the effect sought after was a rough, noisy quality anyway. This was one of the original meanings of art-rock—rock made by (visual) artists. When neo-abstract expressionism took hold around 1982, the art world lost interest and moved on. Meanwhile, however, a renegade theater performer named Glenn Branca and his guitarist friend Jeffrey Lohn had formed a band called Theoretical Girls that had picked up quite a following in New York. Branca asked Chatham to play bass with Theoretical Girls, in hopes that Chatham would book the group at the Kitchen. It worked. Chatham, meanwhile, had formed his own group.

Chatham had written a *Guitar Trio* (1977), which played with overtones of a single pitch. Chatham would later claim that Branca stole the idea and got credit for it because, more connected to the rock world, he was able to get recordings out more easily. In any case, both emerged writing extended works for massed electric guitars using overtones and pure tunings, and both claiming precedence.

Guitar Trio is minimalism with a rock beat: as the drummer plays a hard-rock 4/4, the three guitarists strum the same syncopated rhythm over and over, gradually bringing out different overtones of the drone note. *Drastic Classicism* (1981) is a faster, noisier work for four guitars and drums along the same lines, but with the guitars tuned at half-step intervals for maximum dissonance. The D guitar is tuned D, A, D, D♯, E, D, and the others are similarly based on C♯, D♯, and E. Tuning of each guitar is according to the twelfth, sixteenth, seventeenth, and eighteenth harmonics of the fundamental—the same tuning as Young's *Second Dream of the High-Tension Line Stepdown Transformer. Drastic* alternates between a dense chord of shimmering overtones and textures of rhythmic riffs and single-string overtones.

After exploring electric guitar ensembles for five years (and losing much of his hearing in the process), Chatham became interested in brass instruments. He learned to play trumpet from Ben Neill (for whom see chapter 13) and wrote pieces like *Waterloo No. 2* (1986) for brass ensemble, keyboard, and percussion. The work runs traditional military drum patterns such as double paradiddles and eleven-strike rolls through minimalist additive processes, while the brass melodies refer to the history of marching bands with relentless 4/4 cadential patterns, ending with a quotation of Terry Riley's *A Rainbow in Curved Air.* In *Manifeste* (1987), Chatham used solo trumpet with computerized live electronics to explore the same qualities of the overtone series that he had started with in *Guitar Trio*.

In 1987 Chatham moved to Paris. His most outrageous gesture came afterward, in *An Angel Moves Too Fast to See,* scored for 100 guitars. Because it would be quixotic to try to find 100 guitarists who all read music, the work's ensemble is divided into two tiers, one larger group who need not read music extensively, the other a smaller, virtuoso group who perform the more complex rhythms. Since guitarists who can't read music can at least count, he set up structures in which a group of guitars would repeat the same chord or pattern after so many beats. In example 11.1 from the fifth movement, for example, one group of guitarists strums a B and E every seven beats, another group E and G♯ every eight beats, and so on. The collective melody that results is given in example 11.2. The work has been performed to great excitement in fourteen cities so far since its 1989 premiere in Lille, France.

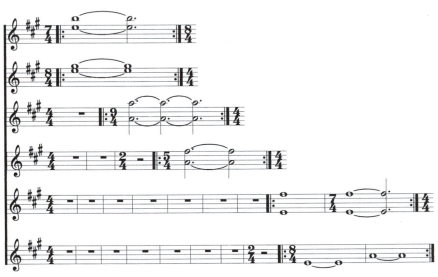

EXAMPLE 11.1 Rhys Chatham, *An Angel Moves Too Fast to See* (1989), fifth movement.

EXAMPLE 11.2 Rhys Chatham, *An Angel Moves Too Fast to See,* composite melody, fifth movement.

Glenn Branca

Like La Monte Young, Branca is spoken of with reverence in rock circles, not only for his own ambitious works, but for having influenced the popular rock group Sonic Youth as Young did the Velvet Underground. Not only did one of the trio's guitarists—Lee Ranaldo—start out in Branca's guitar ensemble, but Branca produced the group's records in the early years before their new, minimalist-influenced idiom caught on. Most of all, though, heavy metal fans and classical aficionados alike have found something like religious ecstasy basking in the massive volume and glacial harmonic movement of Branca's symphonies, eight out of ten of them (so far) scored for multiple electric guitars.

Like Laurie Anderson, Branca didn't come from the music world. Born in Harrisburg, Pennsylvania, in 1949, he nourished an enthusiasm for Broadway musicals, especially those of Steven Sondheim, and ignored rock until attracted to the repetitiveness of certain songs by the Kinks and Paul Revere and the Raiders. He claims to have taught himself composition by listening to guitar feedback at point-blank range for forty-five minutes at a time. Seeing himself, however, as a theater person, he moved to Boston and founded the Bastard Theater. His plays were plotless and abstract, and he provided his own music with pots, pans, and broken-down musical instruments.

Moving to New York in 1976, he and a composer-theater friend, Jeffrey Lohn (born 1947 in Chicago), formed a rock band, Theoretical Girls, which lasted from 1977 to 1979.

> Jeff and I got into an incredible competition as to who could make the most outrageous, completely ridiculous piece. I plugged a recording of white noise into the p.a.—a *wall* of white noise. Then we played a jagged version of "You Really Got Me" by the Kinks underneath it. In one piece I wrote, each musician played at a different tempo. I played a fast Chuck Berry thing. The bass player did a sort of reggae pattern, at not only a different tempo, but a different feel entirely. The drummer was instructed to play something completely off with everything he heard. It sounded fabulous.[7]

In the anti-art atmosphere punk had pioneered, such emblems of chaos became hip, and the age of the "art-band" began.

Branca's epiphany came in 1979, when he brought together six guitarists to play a work he called simply *Instrumental*. At the time, Branca's favorite composer had become Krzysztof Penderecki, the Polish composer (b. 1933) whose most characteristic device was strings building up huge cluster chords note by note. Branca tried imitating such effects. The deafening din of six guitars playing cluster chords was more complex than he had imagined, and he became fascinated by the resulting sum and difference tones and clashing harmonics.

Glenn Branca. *Photo by James Welling.*

In early multiple-guitar pieces such as *Dissonance* and *The Spectacular Commodity* (both 1979), Branca would simply mis-tune the instruments randomly. To understand the mathematical relations between frequencies needed to reinforce the effects he wanted, however, he began studying acoustics, becoming interested in the mystical philosophy of Dane Rudhyar and the diagrams of Hans Kayser (1891–1964), an obscure German theoretician who devoted his life to exploring properties of the whole number series and its ramifications for acoustics. As the pieces grew longer, Branca began calling them symphonies and numbering them—a controversially pretentious move, many thought, but justifiable insofar as a symphony is basically a large-scale harmonic movement from one place to another. (Branca's four-fold repetitions, articulating a harmonic progression, invite comparison with Bruckner.)

All of Branca's symphonies to date are scored for multiple electric guitars with drum set except for Nos. 7 and 9, which are for orchestra;

in addition, No. 1 also incorporates trumpets, saxophone, and French horn. With Symphony No. 3, "Gloria" (1983), Branca ventured into just intonation, employing all 127 harmonics of the first seven octaves of the overtone series. After Symphonies No. 4 (1983) and 5 (1984), he abandoned pure tuning as too difficult to work with for conventional instruments, although Nos. 6, "Devil Choirs at the Gates of Heaven" (1987–1988) and 7 (1989) do approximate overtones with pitch-bending. In Symphony No. 9 (1993), "L'eve Future" for conventional orchestra with voices, Branca achieved a long-sought-after goal of creating a seamless musical surface in which the texture slowly modulates from within according to mathematical algorithms.

Because of the expense of producing his increasingly ambitious schemes, Branca nearly disappeared from the American scene during the eighties, producing his commissioned symphonies in Graz, Linz, Seville, and other European cities. Branca's influence, though, has created a tradition of electric guitar ensembles in New York, some of them headed by guitarists from his group, including John Myers's Blastula, the Wharton Tiers Ensemble, and Phil Kline's Orchestra of the Lower East Side.

Listening Example: Symphony No. 10, 2nd movement, *"The Horror" (1994)*

The first movement of Branca's Symphony No. 10 is called "The Final Problem," the second "The Horror." The sonic material is unusual even by Branca's standards. Each guitarist tunes all six strings of his or her guitar to almost the same pitch and its octave, though within each trio of strings, one is tuned 120 cents below the main pitch, another 20 cents below. Each melodic line is to be played on a trio of three strings all at once.

"The Horror" opens, like so many Branca movements, with a loud unison, spreading out quickly into dissonance. After a dramatic fermata, the piece gets going rhythmically with the passage in example 11.3 (at 2:10 on the Atavistic recording—the drums are not notated), at a stately tempo of about quarter-note = 72. With the score reduced here to combine three guitars on each stave, it is easy to see that basically the same phrase is played in all three staves, but guitars 7, 8, and 9 play it in 14 beats, guitars 4, 5, and 6 in 16, and guitars 1, 2, and 3 in 24 beats. The result is a quasi-tempo canon at ratios of 7:8:12, although unlike Nancarrow, Branca employs durations that only approximate the tempo relationships.

After 14 measures this canon gives way to a polyrhythmic section in which guitars 7 through 9 play quarter-notes and half-notes in a 3/4 pattern, guitars 1 through 3 play a 5/8 pattern divided 2+3, and the middle guitars play an irregular pattern. Similar textures continue throughout the movement, interspersed with passages of cluster chords moving in parallel, crescendoing (if possible) to a triumphant cadence that dies away in a long, feedback-laced decay. Branca can be said to be

EXAMPLE 11.3 Glenn Branca, Symphony No. 10, second movement quasi-tempo canon, mm. 34–57.

the only symphonist whose music does not come in any way from European tradition.

Diamanda Galàs

No other presence in new music is so dramatic, so frightening, so controversial as Diamanda Galàs. Her voice is the most phenomenal in new music: she has a range of three and a half octaves, tremendous vocal power, and consummate control. She could have easily had a career singing Mozart or Wagner. Instead, covered with bizarre makeup, she performs her own intense, harrowing works on themes of death, torture, schizophrenia, powerlessness, and the AIDS epidemic. She is perhaps the only new-music composer with a subversive enough impact to have been targeted by the Christian Right; Reel to Real Ministries has condemned her *Litanies of Satan* for its sacrilegious text:

> To thee o Satan, glory be, and praise.
> Grant that my soul, one day, beneath the Tree
> Of Knowledge may rest near thee.

That text is not her own, however, but was written by Charles Baudelaire (1821–1867). As much as Galàs's works fly in the face of accepted conventions, they always operate in the service of a compassion for those whom society has cast aside.

Outwardly, Galàs's origins give little hint of her subsequent life's work. Born in 1955 in San Diego, she was a concert pianist who performed a Mozart concerto with the local orchestra at fifteen, and she studied biochemistry and psychology as well as music at UC San Diego. Experiments as a medical student involved investigation of bizarre mind-altered states; these led to an understanding of psychopathology and schizophrenia that have contributed to major themes in her music. She started her performing career using her amazing voice control in works of the European avant-garde, singing Globokar's *Un Jour Comme une Autre* and Xenakis's *N'Shima* in the early eighties. Quickly, however, she turned to using her own voice as an instrument for her own amazing works for voice and electronics, including *Wild Women with Steak Knives* (1981–1983) and *Litanies of Satan* (1982).

Galàs's works explore a dialectic of power and powerlessness, the psychology of the torture victim and his omnipotent tormentor. To an extent her vocal techniques in *Tragouthia apo to Aima Exoun Fonos* ("Song from the Blood of Those Murdered," 1981) and *Panoptikon* (1982–1983) stem from the European avant-garde vocal tradition of Berio, Xenakis, and Dieter Schnebel. She babbles, screeches, wails, shouts, while the electronics (provided by Richard Zvonar) allow her to overdub her voice, layering it over a background of slowly transforming noises. In *Panoptikon*, she uses two microphones, one of which lowers her voice à la Laurie Anderson, but with more sinister effect: the two Diamandas become interrogator and prisoner.

In 1984 Galàs began a trilogy based on Edgar Allen Poe's "Masque of the Red Death," intending it as an allegory about AIDS. Soon it became clear that mere allegory was too indirect for the crisis at hand; she would provide her own text dotted with passages from the Bible and religious liturgy, and make the work a direct assault on bigotry, a counterattack against religion for its condemnation of homosexual AIDS victims. The 1986 death from AIDS of Galàs's brother Philip, a playwright and performance artist, added fuel to the fire. Galàs's *The Masque of the Red Death* (dates given: from 1984 to "the end of the epidemic") is one of the most powerful music theater pieces of the 1980s. It is divided in three parts—*The Divine Punishment, Saint of the Pit,* and *You Must Be Certain of the Devil*—and portions are rearranged for a related work, *Plague Mass.*

The Divine Punishment is mostly based on Biblical passages from the books of *Leviticus, Psalms,* and *Lamentations.* In the opening number, "This is the law of the Plague," Galàs croaks laws from *Leviticus* over a darkly repetitive background of groans and slow drumbeats:

> And if any man's seed of copulation go out from him,
> he is unclean.
> Every garment, every skin whereon is the seed, is unclean.
> And the woman with whom this man shall lie will be unclean.
> And whosoever toucheth her will be unclean.
> This is the law of the plague:
> To teach when it is clean and when it is unclean.

In the last number, "Sono l"Antichristo," she wails her own text in Italian:

> I am the scourge.
> I am the Holy Fool.
> I am the shit of God.
> I am the sign.
> I am the plague.
> I am the Antichrist.

In an interview Galàs explained the significance of her identification with the Antichrist as an acceptance of that which society has cast out and demonized:

> When a witch is about to be burned on a ladder in flames, who can
> she call upon! I call that person "Satan. . . ." It's that subversive
> voice that can keep you alive in the face of adversity. I have this
> text, "You call me the shit of God? I am the shit of God! You call
> me the Antichrist? I am the Antichrist!" So you say, "Yes, I am the
> Antichrist. I am all these things you are afraid of."[8]

The Masque of the Red Death climaxes in *You Must Be Certain of the Devil,* more heavily based in musical vernacular than the other sections, and scathingly satirical. She begins with a version of "Swing Low, Sweet Chariot" so tortuously stretched out in time and pitch-space as to be almost unrecognizable. The second number, "Double-Barrel Prayer," weaves her angry poetry around a blankly chanted text from the Catholic mass: "Glory to God in the highest and on earth peace to men of good will. We praise thee; we bless thee; we adore thee; we glorify thee. . . ." Galàs plays the piano and sings parodies of country, blues, and pop idioms, that, savage as they are, do not obscure the sincerity of her poetry:

> In Kentucky Harry buys a round of beer
> to celebrate the death of Billy Smith, the queer,
> whose mother still must hide her face in fear.
>
> Let's not chat about despair.

The Masque of the Red Death remains Galàs's major work to date. More recent pieces have retreated somewhat from the direct expression of her protest in words. In *Insekta* (1993), she enacted the part of a mental patient trapped in a large cage suspended over the stage. In *Schrei X* (1996) she fell back on solo voice, unaccompanied by electronics, in an almost wordless tone poem of fear and despair. Despite the opacity of these performed enigmas, their psychological impact cannot be denied. Galàs's themes of death, sickness, and satanism have much in common with heavy metal, and her social protest, directed against religious self-righteousness and bigotry, has gained her something of the status of a rock star. She is Meredith Monk's evil twin, an operatic Queen of the Nightmare.

Jazz Meets Classical

The relationship between classical music and jazz has always been complex; indeed, the two have never really been independent of each other since jazz was born. Charles Ives worked ragtime into his piano music in the 1890s; Scott Joplin wrote an opera, *Treemonisha*, in 1911. But for all those decades that Copland and Milhaud were sneaking jazz phraseology into their orchestral music, and "Duke" Ellington was keeping a close ear on Debussy's and Ravel's orchestration, there was never any confusion about what the differences were: jazz was improvised along the lines of certain types of rhythmic and harmonic backgrounds, classical music was notated, not subject to an ongoing rhythmic groove, and free from harmonic constraints. In classical music the performer's relationship to the music is assumed to be transparent; his presumed purpose is to get to the essence of, say, Bach, to recreate an idealized perfect performance, not to draw attention to his own aberrations of tone color and phrasing. Jazz, on the other hand, never seems discussible without reference to the personal style of the performers, and the concept of "the work" cannot be cleanly abstracted from the specific performance.

Jazz itself, however, paved the way to an intersection. First, in the 1940s and 1950s, Black musicians grew dissatisfied with the big-band jazz of the Swing era; led by Charlie Parker and Dizzy Gillespie, they introduced a higher level of harmonic and rhythmic complexity into jazz, creating the style known as bop or bebop. This process was accelerated by the pianist-composer Thelonious Monk, who—with his metric freedoms and sometimes virtually atonal chord structures that never forfeited a sense of intuitive rightness—has probably had more influence on classically identified composers than any other single jazz figure. The use of modal harmonies and melodies by Miles Davis and John Coltrane brought jazz a step closer to—and in some cases inspired—the directions the early minimalists were moving in. It is impossible to imagine the early sax playing of Young and Riley without Coltrane's example.

The crucial challenge to jazz's identity, though, came with the next generation, spearheaded by Cecil Taylor and Ornette Coleman. By the late fifties Taylor—trained as a classical pianist—was introducing dissonances, ambiguous harmonies, and a percussive piano style that earned comparisons with Bartók and Stravinsky as often as with any earlier jazz. Coleman, meanwhile, overthrew almost all the features with which jazz had been popularly identified: harmonic framework, periodic phrasing, even the basic relationship between soloists and rhythm section. In his 1960 album *Free Jazz*, he produced a forty-minute barrage of hectic, free-for-all playing within a spare, tenuous structure that was higher energy and more avant-garde (if avant-garde means harder to sit still during and absorb) than anything any classical composer had ever perpetrated, even John Cage.

From this moment on, it became harder and harder to give jazz a definition that would stick, and if you can't define jazz, how can you prove it is different from classical music? In the late fifties and sixties, a movement was formed to fuse the two. In 1957 Gunther Schuller (born 1925 in New York) coined the term "Third Stream" to connote an in-between music, either classically notated with room left open for harmonic improvisation or approached from a jazz perspective with certain sections carefully worked out in advance. One of the clearest expressions of the Third Stream idea was his *Transformation,* which starts out pointillistically twelve-tone and gradually transforms itself into chamber jazz; Schuller also used jazz moments in his most popular orchestral work *Seven Studies on Themes of Paul Klee* (1959). Despite the contributions of both black and white musicians—William Russo, George Russell, John Lewis—Third Stream never grew to be much more than an obvious hybrid, and Schuller, in his later years, became something of a New Romantic. The impulse, however, would return with reinforcements.

More significant was the school of black composers that grew from Chicago's Association for the Advancement of Creative Musicians, or AACM. Founded in 1965 in Chicago by Muhal Richard Abrams, the

AACM is a loosely organized school devoted to what it terms Great Black Music. Early figures in the AACM include Anthony Braxton, Leroy Jenkins, Roscoe Mitchell, Lester Bowie, and Leo Smith, and in 1969 the organization began a school, with the older AACM musicians teaching up to fifty mostly inner-city students. Most importantly, the AACM has been associated with a free-jazz-based movement that leaves behind such traditional elements of jazz (some of them European derived) as the harmonic framework and melody-accompaniment texture. AACM groups— the Art Ensemble of Chicago foremost among them—have also introduced more Afrocentric percussion into their music, such as rainsticks, bells, gourds, mbiras, and wind chimes, and have often painted their bodies and worn African costumes to perform.

At the same time, paradoxically enough, many of the AACM musicians have turned to fully notated composition, writing string quartets and concertos usually in an atonal and complex, though rarely harshly dissonant, modernist idiom. Such works usually leave some room for individual improvisation. More often, the style of the music requires a loose, swinging style of performance that goes beyond what can be adequately captured in the notation. Much AACM music cannot be called jazz (even the free variety) without stretching the term to the point of meaninglessness, and several of the composers involved vehemently reject being called jazz musicians. The instrumental style has the growling intensity of jazz, the cultural references include African music, but the composed forms achieve a level of European abstractness. Nevertheless, most of the figures who follow here have played at least as large a role in jazz history as in new music, and at this stage of criticism are more often written about by jazz critics than classical ones. The emphasis below will be on their identifiably nonjazz contributions.

Muhal Richard Abrams

Though less visible than some of his AACM colleagues, Muhal Richard Abrams deserves the title of father of creative black music. It was his dissatisfaction with bop that began the impulse for the AACM's music, and his charismatic nature that drew dozens of young musicians into its sphere. His stress on spirituality communicated itself both ethically and musically. A primary aim of the AACM, he proclaimed, was "to set an example of high moral standards for musicians";[9] as a result, AACM musicians tended toward moral behavior and abstinence, reversing the trend toward alcoholism and heroin addiction that had cut short so many bop careers. At the same time, Abrams stressed original work as opposed to recreating jazz standards. "We could play a tune like *Body and Soul* forever," he said, "and not express what *we* feel—only variations of what the original composer felt."[10] Accordingly, Abrams evolved a theory of spirituality in music, tied to melody and rhythm rather than harmony, that set the pattern for the AACM's atonal, multilinear idioms.

Born in Chicago in 1930, Abrams studied at Chicago Musical College and started out as a hard bop pianist. He delved into the historical sources of jazz piano for inspiration: Scott Joplin, Art Tatum, James P. Johnson, Earl "Fatha" Hines. Increasingly dissatisfied with the limitations of bop, however, he began, in 1962, rehearsing with friends every week at a tavern on Chicago's South Side, and issued an open invitation to any musician adventurous enough to join. The group who responded—Roscoe Mitchell, Jack DeJohnette, and Joseph Jarman among them—became informally known as the Experimental Band.

Soon South Side jazz musicians began meeting to consider forming an organization that would provide gigs and a helpful network, and Abrams and Phil Cohran (trumpeter for cosmically eccentric bandleader Sun Ra) led the discussions. Out of these came a not-for-profit co-op that was chartered in 1965 as the AACM. By the mid-sixties the AACM ensembles had attracted a public following. Through the seventies, Abrams led a sextet and conducted weekly concerts with the AACM big band, as well as continuing his solo piano concerts. In 1977, though, discouraged like so many musicians at the difficulties of making an artistic living in Chicago, he moved to New York, ending by his departure an era in Chicago music.

Abrams divided existence into two aspects, the concrete and the abstract. Harmony he connected with emotion and therefore with the concrete; melody and rhythm were aspects of the abstract and were therefore spiritual. Besides, harmony had its sources in Europe, not Africa, and Abrams had come to see bop's obsession with harmonic changes as an aesthetic barrier with European roots. Multimelodic improvisation became his favored terrain. "You don't need much to get off the ground," he said in 1967,

> when your musicians are spontaneous enough—just rehearse and let things happen. [Multi-instrumental jazz player] Donald Garrett used to tell me that someday there wouldn't have to be written compositions—he saw it before I did. I had to write quite a bit until I had musicians who could create a part, and then I wrote less and less. Now I can take eight measures and play a concert.[11]

From the beginning, Abrams's recorded music doesn't sound like jazz, but neither does it sound in any way classical. The title cut from his early album *Levels and Degrees of Light* (1967) is particularly striking; Penelope Taylor sings a slow but burning modal melody, followed by Abrams's own high-register clarinet musings, over a luminous background of vague cymbal shimmerings and vibraphone arpeggios in rhythmless ecstasy. Even more "outside" is *Spihumonesty* (1980), which features Yousef Yancey's eerily singing Theremin over changing quiet drones, veering closer to meditational minimalism à la Oliveros than to free jazz. More typical, though, is the freely contrapuntal texture of *Ancient and Future Reflections* (recorded 1981). At first the wind players squawk with raucous individuality, but they soon settle into a polyphonic texture that returns over and over to certain pitch areas and motives rather than a central tonality or harmonic framework.

While in the late sixties and seventies the AACM had had to compete with the tremendous upsurge in the popularity of rock, they next had to compete with their own history, for the eighties (a conservative decade in so many ways) introduced an "authentic practice" approach to "classic jazz." Trumpeter Wynton Marsalis, the curator of the Lincoln Center Jazz Festival with a smooth, scholarly approach to jazz history, was sanding off the sharp edges of thorny mavericks like Monk, and the brittle modernism of the AACM went out of fashion. As a result, several AACM composers turned more toward notated composition, finding that new-music performers such as Ursula Oppens and the Kronos Quartet were more receptive to them than the jazz spaces were. Abrams in particular has written many notated compositions for classical performers, including his Variations for Solo Saxophone, Flute, and Chamber Orchestra for New Music America '82 and *Folk Tales 88* (1988) for the Brooklyn Philharmonic. He still works with improvising big bands as well, and remains a primary inspiration for younger generations.

Anthony Braxton

No one holds a more ambiguous position vis-à-vis the jazz and classical worlds than Anthony Braxton. Jazzers consider him a brilliant saxophonist extending the tradition of Coltrane and Coleman, yet Braxton's own descriptions of his development refer more often to Ives, Webern, Xenakis, and especially Cage and Stockhausen than to jazz figures, and his music rarely sounds remotely like jazz. In fact, Braxton can be characterized as a kind of American Stockhausen: the same type of all-encompassing philosophical imagination, the same ability to turn out reams and reams of music from his personal systems, the same private symbolic universe not always transparent to public scrutiny. Shaman or charlatan, conceptualist genius or pseudo-intellectual, Braxton astonishes listeners with the limitlessness of his invention and confuses them with the quirky geometrical diagrams that serve as both subtitles and structural guides for his compositions. Though he first gained fame as a soloist and quartet leader, in recent years Braxton has headed in the direction of theater and opera, attempting to express his metaphysical speculations in a toweringly ambitious array of *Gesämtkunstwerk*.

Born in 1945 in Chicago, Braxton grew up listening to rock, and when he started paying attention to jazz in 1959, his father bought him

Anthony Braxton at The Kitchen, 1976. *Courtesy New York Public Library.*

an alto saxophone. In 1963 he met Roscoe Mitchell (see below), who steered his enthusiasms for Dave Brubeck toward more adventurous black performers like Coltrane, Coleman, and Cecil Taylor. Playing in the Army Band between 1963 and 1966, Braxton developed his sax style and discovered Schoenberg's Op. 11 Piano Pieces, the first work that made him feel that classical music wasn't only for whites. Returning to Chicago, he found the AACM in full swing, joined in, and formed a first trio with the violinist Leroy Jenkins and the trumpeter Leo Smith. In 1968 he recorded the sax solos that would make up the disc *For Alto*. The first improv recording ever made for an unaccompanied solo instrument other than piano, it had an enormous impact on both black and white improvisers across the country.

In 1969 Braxton went to Paris with his trio and spent much of the next few years in Europe. He was enticed by Rzewski to tour with Musica Elettronica Viva; ever since, Braxton has been as likely to duet with composers from the classical avant-garde (especially electronics mavens like Teitelbaum and Rosenboom) as with free jazz figures. A return to bop in the seventies seduced jazz critics into thinking Braxton had reentered the mainstream. However, as Radano describes his unyielding ambivalence,

> Celebrated as a jazz star, Braxton retorted, "Jazz is only a very small part of what I do"; compared to Bach and Webern, Braxton insisted on the preeminence of the black aesthetic; compared to his Chicago cohorts, he branded the Art Ensemble's "Great Black Music" logo as "racist."[12]

In the eighties Braxton toured Europe with one of his most important groups, the Anthony Braxton Quartet—Marilyn Crispell on piano, Mark Dresser on bass, and Gerry Hemingway on drums; their talents graced some of his most imaginative compositions. The following years brought academic stability and honors: Braxton taught at Mills College from 1985 to 1990 and at Wesleyan University since then, and in 1994 he was given the MacArthur "Genius" Award.

Braxton is at least as much conceptualist as improviser. "I tend to put models together," he has said, "stick models together, and build greater and greater models."[13] Braxton calls his system of thought TRIAXIUM— a combination of "tri-," or three, plus "axiom" in one of Braxton's frequent deliberate misspellings. As explained in his dauntingly jargon-glutted *Tri-Axium Writings*, every aspect of his "Tri-Centric" philosophy breaks into three aspects: individual, group, synthesis; mutable, stable, and summation logics; architecture, philosophy, and ritual-ceremonial. The bulk of his works, even dramatic ones with texts, are titled simply Composition with a number, and at least as early as Composition No. 5 (1968) his titles are accompanied by diagrams with letters, lines, triangles, circles, and so on which are alleged to reveal the structure of the piece (a few are given in example 11.4). Leo Smith tells us that "any advanced student of mysti-

Composition 161

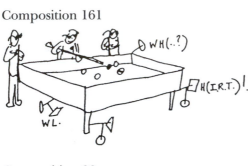

Composition 105

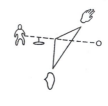

Composition 98

Composition 82

for four orchestras (1978)

Composition 40K

Composition 5

for piano (1968)

EXAMPLE 11.4

cism or metaphysical science can readily read the code and symbolism embedded in his titles."[14] Perhaps so.

Braxton's early piano works from 1968 on pick up where the early *Klavierstücke* of Stockhausen leave off: they are filled with extreme leaps of register, extreme contrasts of dynamics, and a constant denial of linear continuity. With his trios and quartets Braxton explored "multiple logic musics" (in which, say, two performers might be reacting to each other as a duo while a third plays a solo), "collage improvisations," and "opposition improvisations." In the eighties, like Cage before him, Braxton worked with "collage form structures" which allowed for different works to be played simultaneously. His compositions range from simple, lyrical saxophone lines like Composition No. 138A (1988) to Composition No. 82, *For Four Orchestras* (1978), whose sonorities bounce among 160 musicians for two hours.

Likewise, his scores range from verbal instructions to picturesque graphics, to Earle Brown-ish open forms, to pages of modular notation in which phrases float in no particular order, to strict conventional notation, and even to bizarre attempts to suggest three-dimensionality on the page as in Composition No. 76 for trio (1977, example 11.5). Starting with Composition No. 105A (1983), Braxton began including little human figures in his title diagrams, and later landscapes, trees, and even pool tables. Composition 105A was also the first of Braxton's "pulse track structures," works integrating his pitch fields into the framework of a steady pulse in one or more instruments.

Despite the "maximalist" density of most of his music, Braxton has taken an interest in minimalism (his *104° Kelvin* series of works for solo sax build up phrases via additive process, and the first one, from 1971, is dedicated to Philip Glass), and his late music often shares with minimalism an intensity of focus, a determination to derive half-hours of music from narrowly limited materials. By 1996 the pulse track structures had led to what Braxton calls his Ghost Trance Musics, in which he uses unchanging long-term strategies to achieve a kind of trance state. In Composition No. 185 (1996) for sextet, for example, streams of mostly staccato notes, often running up and down scales, march by for twenty-seven minutes before suddenly dissolving into a mellow cacophony of seemingly unrelated solos.

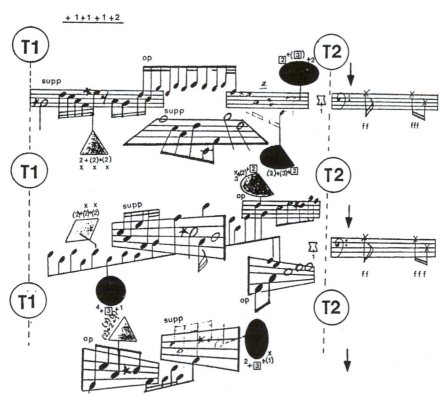

EXAMPLE 11.5 Anthony Braxton, Composition No. 76 (excerpt).

Braxton's systematic thinking modes render even his programmatic and textual works abstract, sometimes to a deliberately comic extent. The program notes to Composition No. 165, a work for eighteen musicians whose sonorities float and collide like clouds, describe two teenagers who get lost in the woods and find their way back by studying the sound map and reading the code of the music. Composition 173 (1994) is a play with music about four people united for some indeterminate business who plan sonic strategies in lines like, "What about a NNNEEEETTTT-TWWWWWCZZZZZX kind of sound that sinks in under the fireplace light—boy, I bet you two to one odds that you people would see a new attitude emerge." As abstract as Braxton's methods are, his central aim is spiritual, and that new attitude is just what he's after.

Listening Example: Composition No. 95, **For Two Pianos** *(1980)*

Composition No. 95, recorded by Ursula Oppens and Frederic Rzewski under the title *For Two Pianos*, is a turning point in Braxton's output, and the first of his "Ritual and Ceremonial" compositions. The abstraction and pointillism of much of the piano writing harks back to the keyboard works of the late sixties and seventies. The costumes worn by the two performers, though—monkish robes with hoods that obscure their personal, racial, and sexual characteristics—point to Braxton's upcoming theatrical phase, while the occasional passages of steady notes and ostinatos suggest a foreshadowing of his "pulse track structures" as well. Written at the dawn of Reagan's conservative eighties, Composition No. 95 was written, Braxton wrote, as

> a vehicle for understanding that the *vibrational and physical universe particulars of a given focus are changing and as such, the spirit should be made aware and prepared.* . . . This work is designed to be performed for any context that involves vibrational and/or physical universe change, as that change concerns spiritual matters—for instance, DOCUMENTATION (i.e., the rise and fall of a given culture), WARNING (of an impending change), CELEBRATION (of a given focus or postulation), ACKNOWLEDGEMENT (i.e., of the change of the season, etc.). My original intention when composing this work was that I sensed and felt that the next immediate cycle in social

EXAMPLE 11.6 Anthony Braxton, Composition No. 95, ostinatos.

reality promises to be extremely difficult—*and there is danger in the air* for all people and forces concerned about humanity and positive participation.[15]

In addition, the cone symbol in the title diagram refers to nuclear power.

The pianists enter from opposite sides of the stage, playing interlocking ostinatos on melodicas (small keyboard instruments like ocarinas). These ostinatos gradually move to the pianos, and the abstract passages that follow give examples of Braxton's "multiple" and "oppositional" logics. That is, a frequent strategy is for one pianist to play in a soloistic manner which the other plays against him or her. After about ten minutes come the strings of interlocking eighth-note patterns. Throughout the work the melodicas reappear playing arabesques that interact with the opposing piano, and at times the pianists also softly twang away on zithers. The variety of timbres in this two-piano work are reminiscent of the multi-instrumentalism of so much AACM music, but also of Stockhausen's *Mantra* for two pianos with antique cymbals and electronics. By fusing together the traditions of jazz improvisation and American experimentalism, Braxton achieved what some regard as the ultimate goal of American music.

Roscoe Mitchell, Leroy Jenkins, and Other Post-Free-Jazz Figures

If Braxton is free jazz's Stockhausen, its Cage must be Roscoe Mitchell, for, like Cage but from a very different direction, Mitchell stripped away music's conventions and rediscovered sound in a field of silence. Mitchell was born in Chicago in 1940, and, in 1961, answered Abrams's call to play with the Experimental Band, and put out the first recording of AACM music in 1966, appropriately titled *Sound,* with a sextet that included Malachi Favors on bass and Lester Bowie on trumpet. Tellingly, the disc displays no conventional instrumental sounds: only harmonics, squeaks, honks, notes in-between-the-pitches. By 1969 Mitchell's fluid sextet eventually solidified into a quartet—Mitchell and Jarman on reeds, Bowie on trumpet, Favors on bass—famous ever since as the Art Ensemble of Chicago. That year the quartet left for Europe (followed soon by Braxton's trio) and in France added to the group the percussionist Don Moye.

The Art Ensemble's performances tend towards theater and even slapstick comedy. At one concert, a player in a Lyndon Johnson mask got smacked in the face with a custard pie; at others, one member would dance with a Raggedy Ann doll, or they would dress as the Spirit of '76 with fife, drum, and bandages. In the seventies Mitchell embarked on a series of "Nonaah" pieces, Nonaah being a fictional character he created to provide a personal atmosphere within which to improvise. Many of the "Nonaah"s are alto sax improvs, though he has written them for string quartet, orchestra, and sax quartet. In one 1976 concert in Switzerland, he began a *Nonaah* by playing the same phrase over and over sixty-six times for seven minutes to an increasingly unruly audience, gradually smearing the notes in a free-jazz kind of minimalist process. Mitchell is an expert at circular breathing and can keep one lightning-fast line of elegant arabesques in constant motion for ten minutes without a break in sound.

Mitchell's most experimental side can be heard in *L-R-G* (1978, named for Leo-Roscoe-George), written for himself, Leo Smith on trumpets, and George Lewis on tuba and trombones. To write it Mitchell made a collection of favorite or most characteristic sounds of the three performers and put the sounds together like pasting photographs in a collage. To a large extent the result is parallel to Cage's works of the late fifties and early sixties such as *Atlas Eclipticalis,* with their pointillist, random-seeming textures made up of blurps of sound; riffs and flurries of activity, however, give evidence of individual personalities. By 1986, though, Mitchell wrote a completely-notated *Nonaah* for flute, bassoon, and piano: a thoughtful, totally contrapuntal work of mercurial textures closer to Wolpe than to Coltrane.

Leroy Jenkins, an important sideman for Braxton, Abrams, Carman Moore, and others, is one of the most classically trained members of the AACM. As such, he has had more success in notated music than virtually anyone except Braxton, having been commissioned by the Munich Biennale for an opera—*The Mother of Three Sons*—as well as turning out a cantata, several string quartets, and numerous other chamber works. In both jazz and classical worlds he is known as a violinist with a distinctively rough-hewn tone and agile technique. Born in 1932 in Chicago, Jenkins toured with the AACM in its heyday, working with Braxton, Abrams, Roscoe Mitchell, and Leo Smith, settling in New York in 1970. By 1980 Jenkins was close enough to the new-music crowd to play on New Music America, and soon afterward wrote his first completely notated work, a string quartet for the Kronos Quartet.

Choreographer Bill T. Jones brought Jenkins to the attention of the German composer and entrepreneur Hans Werner Henze, who arranged a commission for an opera combining Jones's choreography, a libretto by Ann T. Greene, and Jenkins's music. *The Mother of Three Sons* (1991) is drawn from an archetypal Yoruban myth about a woman who demands three sons and becomes enraged when each one is born with some crippling flaw. Vibrant and dance-driven, the work succeeded in expressing an African ethos within a European format. Jenkins is good at injecting a strong blues element into the rather Schoenbergian-Bartókian idiom so many AACM composers favor in their notated music;

a delightful example is his string quartet, *Themes & Improvisations on the Blues* (1986). In recent years his music has become overtly political, starting with an energetic cantata based in gospel traditions, *The Negros Burial Ground* (1996), about the history of a slave burial ground accidentally uncovered in Wall Street in 1991.

If there is a figure whose presence in two worlds is nearly as schizophrenic as Braxton's, it is Anthony Davis, jazz pianist and ensemble leader and composer of operas and concertos. Born in 1951 in Paterson, New Jersey, he studied at Yale and worked afterward with several of the leading AACM musicians, including George Lewis, Leo Smith, and Leroy Jenkins. Much in demand in the nineties, Davis has taught at Yale and Harvard. As a member of a younger generation, he writes less thorny, smoother music than the older AACM masters, reliant on ostinatos in irregular meters and full of harmonies that are tonally ambiguous, but never harsh. Much of Davis's most sensitive music, such as his poignantly coloristic tone poem *Undine* (1987), results from his work with his ensemble Episteme. Presumably the high point of his career to date, however, is the most celebrated opera yet to emerge from the black improvisation tradition: *X: The Life and Times of Malcolm X* (1985).

The opera presents vignettes from Malcolm X's life, including a hectic scene in which he learns his father has been killed by white men; an effective jazz scene in which Malcolm is introduced to city life; a calm prison scene over drones and ostinatos in which Malcolm reads the *Koran*, converts, and meets Elijah; a crowd scene with Malcolm preaching the Muslim faith on the street; reporters questioning Malcolm about Kennedy's assassination and his famous reply that "the chickens have come home to roost"; Malcolm's rebuke by Elijah; Malcolm's pilgrimage to Mecca, sung with deep spirituality over a drone; reporters blaming Malcolm's "hate speech" for Harlem riots of the sixties; and the opera's abrupt end when Malcolm is shot at a meeting of the Organization of Afro-American Unity. Scenes are often separated by interludes that allow for improvisation by leading free-jazz instrumentalists such as the pianist Marilyn Crispell, the clarinetist J. D. Parran, or the saxophonist Marty Erlicht; there are as many "characters" in the orchestra as onstage. Davis has followed *X* with three more operas: *Under the Double Moon* (1989), *Tania* (1992), and *Amistad*.

Carman Moore has developed his own elegant jazz-classical interface outside the angst-ridden, modernist idioms of the AACM; he often manages to weave jazz conventions and mellow notated music together with no impression of heterogeneity. Moore was born in 1936 in Lorain, Ohio, and studied at Juilliard, where he worked with Berio, Persichetti, and Wolpe. In 1985 he renamed his ensemble Skymusic, making with it soothing yet sophisticated works tinged with various African and Middle Eastern musics, such as *Righteous Heroes: Sacred Spaces* (1987). His larger works are motivated by a deep humanitarianism, notably his mammoth

Mass for the 21st Century (1994), scored for soprano, children's and adult choruses, twenty-five dancers, and his Skymusic ensemble. This twenty-one-movement oratorio runs a range of styles from its opening fugue to gospel to Gregorian chant to hip hop, though Moore's technique is fluid enough to avoid an effect of pastiche. He puts his diagnosis of mankind's ills (his own words) in the mouths of children:

> Till everything is possible and everything is mine,
> And everything is multiplied many, many times . . .
> Till everyone is specialized and knows just what to do,
> And every law is averaged and all the people too . . .
> Progress. Progress. This is Manchild's dream.

Standing outside the usual new-music circles, Moore has garnered an enthusiastic local following in New York.

Several of the other AACM musicians have composed works that remain less well known than their jazz improvisations: Joseph Jarman, Henry Threadgill, Julius Hemphill, Oliver Lake, Douglas Ewart, all saxophonists who double on other instruments as well. Also deserving of mention in this respect is the ROVA Saxophone Quartet. Although its original members are white—Jon Raskin, Larry Ochs, Andrew Voight, Bruce Ackley—they have been strongly influenced by the AACM tradition and have turned out remarkably well-sculpted group-composed works in a style partly reminiscent of both Bartók and Thelonious Monk, and partly quite original.

John Zorn and the Free Improvisation Scene

Following the AACM's creative music movement came a far-flung, mostly white free improvisation movement, often called "New York Noise," that dominated music in New York and other large cities from about 1983 to 1990 and is still highly active. Just as the AACM's music opened up a space for the modernist impulse in Black music, the Downtown improv scene of the eighties was an aggressive resurgence of modernist complexity and noise, and a reaction against the audience-friendliness of minimalism. Echoing the earlier twelve-tone composers, the improvisers prided themselves on the difficulty and acerbity of their music. Since improvised music could often be thrown together without rehearsal, the movement was reinforced by the economics of the eighties, which had put both rehearsal space and time at a high premium.

The undisputed king of the improv scene, and its least typical member, was and is John Zorn. Zorn is the downtown postmodernist, a collage artist with a self-described short attention span, whose music cuts from one style to another, omnivorously quoting European avant-garde music, bluegrass, bebop, Beethoven, heavy metal, TV commercials, Indian ragas, thrash. He was born in New York in 1953 and studied briefly at Webster College in St. Louis, where, after exposure to musicians from the AACM, he started playing alto saxophone. Moving to New York in 1974, he assembed like-minded musicians and wrote game pieces partly inspired by the aleatory techniques of Earle Brown and Christian Wolff. The earliest of these, such as *Pool* and *Archery* (both 1979), tended to sound, with their statically noisy textures, like European post-serialist music, though with a theatrical element that had to do with the players cueing each other. The climactic work in the series was *Cobra* (1984), an aleatory structure open enough to act as an improvised collage, with turn-on-a-dime group changes achieved by players signaling each other like traffic cops. The work has become a permanent icon of downtown improvisation.

In 1986, Zorn's breakthrough to the public came in a recording called *The Big Gundown*, a series of arrangements of film music by Ennio Morricone. Morricone's gun-slinging stylizations, heard through the haze of Zorn's crazy intercutting and raucous Downtown side effects, caught the public imagination, and Zorn was suddenly a star. Suddenly it became hip to make "high art" music with vernacular or "low art" materials. The game pieces gave way to a technique Zorn called file-card composition, in which ideas for moments would be written on file cards, such as: "Pianist, do Renaissance kind of shape for ten seconds," and "Flute player, play as fast as you can."[16] A major influence on this kind of composing was Carl Stalling, the composer for the Warner Brothers "Bugs Bunny" cartoons, whose music juxtaposed everything from Wagner to pop songs to sound effects in split-second juxtapositions.

In this manner Zorn produced his next recorded work, *Spillane* (1986), a tribute to the detective novel: a woman screams, a jazz quartet plays, a trombone moans over recorded voices, slow atmospheric music comes in, each change as abrupt as switching radio stations. Even Zorn's notated works for classical performers are written in the file-card style. *Cat o' Nine Tails* (1988, subtitled *Tex Avery Directs the Marquis de Sade*) for string quartet consists of sixty moments, including quotations from other string quartets, improvisatory flareups, cartoon elements, tangos, waltzes, classical cadences, and noise. Zorn's primary significance for downtown music, aside from his incorporation of diverse vernaculars, was that he recognized many of the pitfalls of free improvisation—formal amorphousness, inability to make sudden changes in ensemble texture, self-indulgence—and figured out strategies for overcoming them.

The number two most visible group leader on the downtown scene in the eighties was Elliott Sharp, famed for the density and volume of his noise barrages and for his use of fractals and the Fibonacci series in the structuring of his works. Born in 1951 in Cleveland, Sharp graduated from Bard College, where he studied with Benjamin Boretz, and worked with Lejaren Hiller at SUNY at Buffalo. He moved to New York in 1975 and formed his most important ensemble, Carbon, in 1980. A self-described "science nerd," he refers often to scientific and mathematical concepts in his music, as evident in titles such as *Iso-* (1984), *Singularity* (1986), *Sili/Contemp/Tation* (1986), *Self-Squared Dragon* (1986), and *Hammer Anvil Stirrup* (1988, for string quartet). *Larynx* (1987), Sharp's major work of the late eighties, is based on the idea of a chaotic ensemble of reeds, amplified string quartet, and percussion as a gigantic throat, with reference to the throat singing of Mongolia and Inuit Canada. The use of Fibonacci numbers in this work and others determines both structural proportions and string tunings (1:1, 3:2, 8:5, and 5:3 yielding C, G, A-flat, and A). With his propulsive drumbeats and relatively steady-state noise textures, Sharp's music may be closer to rock than jazz, but he improvises on guitar and sax in a variety of contexts.

The third in the downtown improv triumvirate is Anthony Coleman: an improviser who studied classical twelve-tone technique with Druckman and Donald Martino. Born 1955 in New York, he went to New England Conservatory and Yale before ending up back on the New York scene in 1979. As devoted to Thelonious Monk and Charles Mingus as to Webern and Feldman, Coleman derives material for his works through improvisation and uses improvisers for his performances, but he composes his intervallic structures and extremes of register with great specificity. The difference, he says, is that of

> a frame of reference. Classical improvisers look for a way of honoring the intentions of the composer. My improvisers look for a link to the other kinds of improvisation they do. Nothing in the structure of my music sounds like jazz, but the way they play it sounds like jazz.[17]

The result, in chamber ensemble pieces like *The King of Kabay* (1988) and *by the book* (1991), is a music of strikingly original textures, often marked by slowly lumbering contrapuntal lines played with a jaunty roughness. In *the hidden agenda* (1989) for piano, Coleman intercut among four different types of music with postmodern collage effect, but derived all four from exactly the same interval structure. His *Latvian Counter-Gambit* (1995) for orchestra is a textural homage, sans quotations, to Thelonious Monk, with a good dash of Varèse audible in its growling sonorities.

By the time all these people joined the New York scene, Shelley Hirsch had been performing there for years. Born in East New York in Brooklyn in 1952, she grew up fascinated by ethnic vocal traditions, and, at eighteen, went to California to study Japanese Kabuki—only to learn that women weren't allowed to perform it. She returned to New York in 1972 and started performing with Kirk Nurock (a brilliant jazz pianist who also does workshops with experimental vocal techniques) and Jeffrey Lohn. Her seminal early work was *The Beach is Her Home* (1983), an opera with percussion and electronics about a woman who lived on the beach. From the beginning Hirsch told stories in her music, often collecting them from crazy, repetitive street people. Her vocal pieces started out somewhat minimalist as a result, but evolved into a complex, improvisatory idiom of shrieks, burbles, faked foreign languages, Tibetan-style overtone singing, and other virtuoso effects. Sort of the Meredith Monk of New York Noise, she has done some of her best pieces with the electronics artist David Weinstein, including *Haiku Lingo* (1988), in which she and the taped electronics would switch styles exactly in sync in a zig-zagging roller coaster of sound.

David Weinstein, meanwhile, has become leader of one of New York's strangest ensembles: Impossible Music, a chamber orchestra of CD players. Born in Chicago in 1954, he studied with Johnston and Martirano and founded, with the improvising trombonist Jim Staley, a performance series in Chicago and later New York called Roulette, one of the country's most important spaces for new music. Weinstein spent the early eighties working on *Illuminated Man* (1981), a beautifully elaborate graphic environment—a painted floor, actually—structured according to nestings of the Fibonacci series, which were used as paradigms for rule-based improvisation. In 1990, he and Tim Spelios began exploring the possibilities of making music with CD players, cutting and looping among different tracks. The resulting music combined repetitive bits of sound effect discs, world music recordings, classical CDs, and other paraphernalia in a music whose ecumenicism fulfilled Henry Cowell's dream of a music without cultural boundaries. One of Impossible Music's signal achievements, in 1992, was the first live performance of the Beatles' tape collage from their "White Album," *Revolution No. 9.*

The fusion and confusion of rock, jazz, and new music didn't last— or at least, in the nineties the separate genres momentarily retired to their respective corners for a breather. Many of the most talented musicians on the improv scene—including the drummer Robert Previte, the pianists Marilyn Crispell and Myra Melford, the pianist-vocalist Robin Holcomb, the guitarist Wayne Horvitz, and several of the AACM composers—settled into a more definable jazz idiom after the eighties ended. Others, such as the trombonist Jim Staley, the cellist Tom Cora, the harpist Zeena Parkins, the turntable-spinner Christian Marclay, the percussionist Michael Zerang, and the trombonist and computer-improviser Don Malone (these last two in Chicago), have persisted in free improvisation. Part of the difficulty of bringing the genres together is that rock and jazz led new music in opposite directions: rock toward the narrow focus of an intensified minimalism, jazz back to modernist complexity, dissonance, and fragmentation. The dream of a "one-world music" still persists, though, and attempts to merge will undoubtedly recur in the twenty-first century until a new, more inclusive musical practice results.

Notes

1. Leonard Bernstein, *The Infinite Variety of Music.*
2. Rhys Chatham, *Composer's Notebook 1990: Toward a Musical Agenda for the Nineties,* via the Internet, http://sun.goddard.edu/students/wgdr/kalvos/chatess1.html, 1990.
3. Conversation with the author, 1981.
4. Laurie Anderson, *Stories from the Nerve Bible: A Retrospective* (New York: Harper Perennial, 1994), p. 13.
5. Ibid., p. 155.
6. Liner notes, *Die Donnergötter,* Dossier Records DCD 9002, 1988.
7. Quoted in Kyle Gann, "Harps from Heaven," *Village Voice,* November 22, 1994, vol. XXXIX, No. 47, p. 49.
8. Re\Search Publications #13: Angry Women.
9. "Jazz Musicians Group in Chicago Growing," *Down Beat* (July 28, 1966), p. 11; quoted in Ronald M. Radano, *New Musical Figurations: Anthony Braxton's Cultural Critique* (Chicago: University of Chicago Press, 1993), p. 266.
10. Ibid.
11. Quoted in John Litweiler, "Richard Abrams, a Man with an Idea," *Down Beat* (October 5, 1967).
12. Ronald M. Radano, *New Musical Figurations: Anthony Braxton's Cultural Critique* (Chicago: University of Chicago Press, 1993), p. 266.
13. Quoted in Graham Lock's liner notes to *Anthony Braxton, Quartet* (London) 1985, Leo Records.
14. Leo Smith, liner notes to *The Complete Braxton 1971,* Arista/Freedom 1902.
15. Anthony Braxton, *Composition Notes E* (Hanover, N.H.: Tree Frog Music, 1988), 1–24.
16. William Duckworth, *Talking Music* (New York: Schirmer Books, 1995), p. 454.
17. Interview with the author, January 8, 1997.

CHAPTER 12

New Tonality II—Postminimalism

It used to be, if you asked composers what one piece made them decide they wanted to become a composer, dozens of them, as diverse as Conlon Nancarrow and William Schuman, would reply: *"The Rite of Spring."* Today, ask the same question to composers born after 1940, and you'll often get one or both of two answers: Terry Riley's *In C* and Steve Reich's *Come Out.* The music of the forties and fifties, often characterized by rampant complexity and daunting analytical pretensions, was not very inspiring for the young. Suddenly, *In C* and *Come Out* seemed to cut through the Gordian knot of contemporary compositional problems and offer music a chance to be fun again. Between them, *In C*'s idea of repeating modules and *Come Out*'s arithmetic of phase-shifting provided both the melodic and structural starting points for a new musical language. That language has grown into a lingua franca across the country. We still have no better name for it than postminimalism.

Clearly, the term says more about where the music came from than about what it is like. Postminimalism can be characterized as an idiom of mostly diatonic tonality, usually with a steady and sometimes motoric beat. Often the music is written according to strict contrapuntal or rhythmic procedures, with an underlying numerical structure. Postminimal composers are fond of taking minimalism's out-of-phase loops or additive forms (A, AB, ABC, ABCD) as a structural background, which they then disguise with a wealth of surface contrapuntal activity. The music is not necessarily static, but neither is it volatile, and a movement of postminimal music will generally, like a Baroque work, have the same texture and possibly dynamics from beginning to end. Emotional expression in postminimal music tends to lie in qualities of the entire piece, not in moment-to-moment swings of mood. It is this inability or unwillingness to shift moods within a passage, occasionally felt as a limitation, that makes postminimalism seem like possibly an early classic phase of a new musico-historical era. But postminimalism is also, in this respect, a continuing reaction against the ugly discontinuity and fragmentation of academic music of the twelve-tone school.

Criteria distinguishing postminimalism from minimalism are bound to be subjective. One problem dogging postminimal composers is that newspaper critics tend to keep calling them minimalists, incorrectly writing them off as Johnnie-come-latelies of an earlier style. Following a cue from Tom Johnson, the postminimalist composer Paul Epstein claims that the correct distinction is simply "the amount of intervention the composer makes in the process";[1] in effect, he says, music of strict, "discovered" processes is minimalist, whereas music in which the composer has altered the results of a process to suit his or her taste and expression is postminimal. By that stringent rule, Riley's *In C* would have to be considered postminimal, since its process is neither linear nor predictable.

The criterion I apply, however, is that minimalist music is synonymous with audible structure; a listener can tell from listening how a minimalist piece is put together. Works like William Duckworth's *Time Curve Preludes* and Janice Giteck's *Om Shanti* share minimalism's diatonic modality and additive processes, but aurally they are more mysterious, and some examination of the score is usually necessary to figure out what the music's processes are. Repetition in postminimal music is rarely completely absent, but it is also rarely immediate, and is often elaborately disguised. Minimalist composers, Reich and Glass in particular, were interested in creating processes to listen to. Postminimalist composers may often use strict processes, but rarely at an audible level; the listening focus lies elsewhere.

By this criterion, postminimalism began clearly, I think, as a change in emphasis within the new tonality around 1980, starting with Duckworth's *Time Curve Preludes* (1978–1979), Giteck's *Breathing Songs from a Turning Sky* (1980), Peter Gena's *Beethoven in Soho* (1980), and the works of Daniel Lentz's Los Angeles period (such as *The Dream King*, 1983). Suddenly, music one would once have called minimalist was no longer so predictable or easy to follow; though still melodically lucid, it had acquired a kind of mystically impenetrable surface, and a tendency to take surprising turns. Equally suddenly, composers who had earlier found minimalism too simplistic now abandoned conceptualism (as Duckworth and Giteck both did) or twelve-tone music (as Jonathan Kramer did) to plunge into the new, stripped-down but now contrapuntally subtle diatonic tonality.

Postminimalism and the New Romanticism have not been carefully distinguished by critics, but the two represent extremely different phenomena and attitudes. The New Romanticists explicitly return to a preserialist past: "This is a very exciting transition moment in music—the looking backward" (Druckman); "I embrace the whole musical past" (Adams). Postminimalism has nothing to do with the past, least of all with

European Romanticism; it builds on minimalism and looks forward. The New Romanticists work within the convenient categories of mainstream classical music, writing concertos and pieces for conventional orchestra; following the minimalists, the postminimalists build up their own ensemble concept often involving electronic keyboards. The New Romanticists have returned to a nineteenth-century manner of volatile emotional expression, based on climaxes and a wide and ever-changing dynamic range. Postminimalism is a cooler, more objectivist style, capable of great nuance of feeling, but subtle.

Like the serialists, the postminimalists have striven to create a consistent and coherent musical language, though this language is usually as smooth and linear as the serialist language is abrupt and fragmented. Although postminimalism has drawn inspiration from African music, Japanese koto, Balinese gamelan, medieval European motets, and even bluegrass, it integrates such inspirations into a self-contained musical language in an organic, seamless way that rarely (aside from dramatic exceptions such as Lentz's *wolfMASS*) suggests pastiche or even eclecticism. Some of the postminimalists offer the impression that music began with a clean slate in 1964 with *In C,* as though the world of new composition had been leveled by a nuclear apocalypse.

While most of the postminimal composers are older than those of the preceding chapter, their music emerged later as a public phenomenon. One could take the second performance of Duckworth's *Time Curve Preludes* at New Music America in 1980 as the onset of public recognition, but it wasn't until the late eighties that it became obvious that a new style had emerged with distinct and generalizable characteristics. This is partly because, unlike minimalism and conceptualism, postminimalism does not have a "scene," with composers performing together and borrowing each other's ideas; it consists of a set of individual, usually isolated responses to the new opportunities minimalism offered. Given that, it is astonishing how similar many of the responses are among composers who are totally unaware of their postminimal colleagues.

Within postminimalism's clearly definable characteristics, however, the style leaves tremendous room for differentiated personal expression, as much so as minimalism and more. Another interesting aspect of postminimalism is its geographic diversity, involving composers from Alaska to Florida and Hawaii to Maine, with special emphasis on the West Coast; the one place the style *hasn't* flourished is New York, which nurtures more aggressive sonic archetypes.

William Duckworth

No composer offers the qualities of postminimalism in purer concentration than William Duckworth, whose *Time Curve Preludes* (1978–1979)

William Duckworth. *Photo by Terry Wild.*

might be said to be the movement's first classic, if not indeed its starting point. Smooth and cool with an understated rhythmic liveliness, Duckworth's music always achieves a convincing musical logic, often through the use of numerical rhythmic structures whose closure is instinctively felt rather than consciously understood. In fact, beneath Duckworth's limpid textures runs an undercurrent of mysticism akin to that of medieval music, one of his early interests. Yet Duckworth was also exposed to bluegrass music as a child, and all his music has a lightly sprung syncopated feel distilled from American vernacular traditions.

This trademark syncopation, along with a bluesy and ambiguous alternation of the major and minor thirds of the scale, make Duckworth's style recognizable at first hearing.

Born in North Carolina in 1943, Duckworth came from blue-collar surroundings; his father played bluegrass guitar. He entered East Carolina University intending to become a band director and absorbed there a Howard Hanson-ish Americana tradition from Martin Mailman (b. 1932, well known in the band-music world). This background later fused with a Cagean influence at the University of Illinois, where Duckworth studied with fellow Southerner Ben Johnston between 1965 and 1972. Between Mailman and Johnston, Duckworth never formed any attraction to the European serialist music so much in the air at the time. In fact, an early conceptual piece of Duckworth's called *Pitch City* (1969) pokes fun at serialism, requiring players to wend their way slowly through sustained pitches in a twelve-tone row matrix.

Duckworth's early style involved graphic notation, often filled in with pitches to be used. *Gymel* of 1973, for example, for four mallet percussionists or keyboards, contains pitch patterns connected by lines in a web, through which the performers can move at will in a minimalistically tonal and pulsating texture. Its method of performance, of course, shows the influence of Riley's *In C*; however, while attracted to minimalism, Duckworth had no wish to copy what seemed like Glass's and Reich's easily identifiable styles. Instead, he turned to the French composer Olivier Messiaen, borrowing what Messiaen called "non-retrogradable rhythms," that is, rhythms that are the same forwards as backwards. Duckworth had also been interested in the numerical rhythmic structures of medieval music, ever since organizing a college early music performance group in the sixties. In 1976, with the chamber piece *A Book of Hours* and *The Last Nocturn* for piano, he began writing in a new, simpler style, marked by hidden rhythmic structures and quotations of Gregorian chant.

By now, all the elements were in place for Duckworth's early magnum opus, his major piano cycle *The Time Curve Preludes*: a piece that summed up all his ideas about rhythmic structure, additive structures, reductive structures, and rhythmic cycles. The *Preludes* are a cycle of twenty-four piano pieces, each pursuing a melodic, rhythmic, or textural idea through a brief form that usually curves in on itself through some accelerative or reductive process. Except for No. 6, the only movement which contains repeat signs, Duckworth repudiated the repetition of Reich and Glass and moved away from minimalism's externalized structure toward a mysterious background logic.

Duckworth followed *The Time Curve Preludes* with a similarly ambitious vocal cycle. At Illinois, his friend Neely Bruce (a composer and pianist who premiered the *Preludes*) had reintroduced Duckworth to shaped-note singing, the rural tradition that East European immigrants had nurtured in Appalachia, a tradition of rough-hewn but vigorous hymns notated with different-shaped notes for didactic purposes. (Many of the best shaped-note hymns were written by William Billings.) For months Duckworth locked himself up with the old American hymn collection *Southern Harmony,* and he selected twenty of the hymns to de- and reconstruct. He abstracted phrases, repeated melodies, built hymns up through additive processes, changed meters according to numerical systems, and colored vocal lines with his trademark major-minor ambiguity. The result, *Southern Harmony* (1980–1981) is a massive and beautiful choral cycle unlike anything else produced out of the minimalist tradition; in fact, its only predecessor in downtown music is an early choral piece by Philip Glass, *Another Look at Harmony.*

Over the next decade, Duckworth consolidated his achievement in *Time Curve* and *Southern Harmony* by extending his mature style in several directions, yet all recognizably in his personal style. *Simple Songs About Sex and War* (1983–1984), on poems of Hayden Carruth, was a smooth attempt to write postminimal "pop songs." *Imaginary Dances* (1985/1988) was a follow-up to the *Preludes,* seven piano dances graced by a mild pop influence, engaging in their intricate rhythms and bittersweet tonalities. Duckworth's tendency toward cycles of brief movements in all these works gives him something of the image of a modern Robert Schumann, his *Imaginary Dances* being analogous in genre and weight to Schumann's *Carnaval* or *Davidsbündler Tanze.*

Duckworth's early music had been inspired by Cage via Johnston; in 1976 Duckworth met Cage, and he studied chess with him as Cage had with Duchamp. Cage's influence survives in Duckworth's late music in an intriguing way, for he still uses the *I Ching* to make certain kinds of decisions. In late works such as *Their Song* for voice and piano (1991), *Gathering Together/Revolution* for percussion ensemble (1992–1993), and *Mysterious Numbers* for mixed chamber group (1996), he has used the *I Ching* to chance-determine scales, time lengths, the order of precomposed passages, and even texts. What makes his use of chance so unusual is its integration into a technique so smooth that nothing in the result sounds random.

Duckworth's magnum opus of the 1990s is an ongoing multimedia piece created for the internet which opened June 10, 1997, and is planned to run through 2001. Called *Cathedral,* the piece is based on texts surrounding five seminal moments in human history: the building of the Great Pyramid, the groundbreaking for Chartres Cathedral, the founding of the Native American Ghost Dance religion, the detonation of the first atomic bomb, and the creation of the World Wide Web. The work contains an interactive component as well as sections that will be coordinated with live performances, and the project promises to be a grand culmination of Duckworth's smoothly contoured mysticism.

Listening Example: **The Time Curve Preludes** *(1977–78)*

It is quintessential to the postminimal aesthetic that, although several strands of musical reference are woven into *The Time Curve Preludes*—quotations from Erik Satie's *Vexations,* the medieval *Dies irae* chant, bluegrass plucking patterns, Indian ragas, Fibonacci rhythmic patterns, occasional minimalist repetitions—they are so closely interwoven that the twenty-four preludes seem almost variations on a theme, delicate, bristling, sad, and reassuring by turns. The Fibonacci series is the series of numbers of which each is the previous two added together: 1, 1, 2, 3, 5, 8, 13, 21, 34, 55 and so on. The series occurs commonly in nature, as in the arrangement of seeds in certain flowers, and, before Duckworth, was used by Béla Bartók as a rhythmic structuring device.

The pianist in *Time Curve Preludes* precedes each prelude by pressing down silent drone notes to be held with weights; after each prelude, the pianist pauses to allow the sympathetic vibration of lower strings to be heard. In Prelude I one can hear the influence of bluegrass guitar playing, in the frequent alternation of notes back and forth between hands. Prelude IX is based on the bass line from Satie's *Vexations*: an enigmatic piece that Satie marked with the instruction that it should be played 840 times. (Something of a modern-music icon, *Vexations* has been played many times in eighteen- to twenty-four-hour marathon concerts, the first organized by Cage in 1962.) After an introduction with both hands in unison, the bass line appears in the left hand in an accelerating pattern: first in half-notes, then double-dotted quarters, then dotted quarters, and so on, subtracting a sixteenth-note duration per note until the hands are swept back into a unison conclusion.

Prelude XIII (example 12.1) gives an idea both of Duckworth's trademark alternation of the major and minor third (A in the scale on F is flatted at about every other appearance) and his use of the Fibonacci series as a structural device. The piece is divided in phrases of 8, 13, 21, 13, 8, 13, 21, and 34 beats. On a more detailed level, the melody sometimes uses Fibonacci numbers of eighth-notes separated by pairs of sixteenths; two eighths, then three, then five, then three, as shown in the diagram. Prelude XV (example 12.2) evinces Duckworth's modality and

EXAMPLE 12.1 William Duckworth, *The Time Curve Preludes*, No. XIII.

EXAMPLE 12.2 William Duckworth, *The Time Curve Preludes*, No. XV.

his fluidly unpredictable sense of almost-repetition. In a scale of two flats dotted with frequent F-sharps, the melody runs up and down with very much the feel of an Indian raga. It also creates medieval-sounding cadences with the left hand drone, which shifts between E-flat and D, making the scale sound either Phrygian or Lydian by turns. Such irregularities should give the prelude a nervous feel, but it seems calm and centered, smoothed by Duckworth's streamlined sense of composition.

Janice Giteck

Only sometimes a postminimalist, Janice Giteck is difficult to pigeonhole. Theatrically, however, she's quite consistent: her music has a basic concern with ritual. She has written that the three basic components of ritual, regardless of culture, are "people coming together (gathering), the intended activity (performing), and the going away (leaving/dispersing)." "This format may be completely obvious," she continues, "but . . . the ritual frame has not lost its charge. . . . It is, quite innocently, a function of our being human, something we *need* to do."[2] Consequently, she brings into her music anything that will reinforce a ritual atmosphere and offer the possibility of collective transformation: American Indian chanting, East European folk melodies, Balinese melodic patterns, performance art, pantomime, earthy comedy, colored lighting, even periods of silence. Hers is also a postminimalism heavily informed by more different world musics, perhaps, than that of any other composer of her generation.

Giteck (born 1946) grew up in New York near Coney Island, exposed on a daily basis to Orthodox Jews chanting their daily prayers on the boardwalk and Hasidic cantorial chant at her parents' synagogue. She composed at eight, and when she was twelve she discovered the indigenous music of Indian America—primarily Pima, Papago, and Yaqui—when her family relocated to Tucson, Arizona. At a high school program at the University of Arizona, she studied with composer Barney Childs (b. 1926), then teaching in the English department. Childs had been a creator of contrapuntally modernist symphonies, but by 1961 when Giteck met him, he had come under Cage's influence and had begun writing freely notated chance scores. While he offered a freeing influence, from the beginning Giteck gravitated toward modal composition, with little interest in atonality or even modulation.

Giteck's next important teacher was the French composer Darius Milhaud, whom she met at Aspen and went to study with at Mills College. Here, between 1964 and 1969, she attended Morton Subotnick's theory classes and was exposed to Oliveros, Luciano Berio, Robert Ashley, Terry Riley, and most of all Cage. After she graduated, Milhaud convinced her to study in France, where attended Messiaen's classes at the Paris Conservatoire. Studies with Milhaud, Messiaen, and Xenakis (who frequented Messiaen's class) did not efface Giteck's eclectic Americanness, but they did lend her a European polish and fluidity of technique that few minimalist-influenced Americans can boast.

Back in America in 1971, Giteck immersed herself in theater and native American materials with *Magic Words* (1972), songs on native American texts for mezzo-soprano, baritone, piano hand percussion, and flute. Her theater pieces of the seventies, such as *Thunder, Like a White Bear Dancing* (1977) and *"Callin' Home Coyote"* (1978), are eclectic, integrating repetitive textual elements of American Indian ritual into frameworks partly operatic, partly reminiscent of Javanese gamelan and the ritual theater of Harry Partch. In 1979 Giteck took a job at the Cornish Institute in Seattle, and her first Seattle piece, *Breathing Songs from a Turning Sky* (1980), is a classic postminimal statement based on the Hebrew Kabala and alluding to Javanese music through its motoric textures. The piece comprises ten meditations on different states of enlightenment, and the seventh—"Majesty"—consists of silence: like *4'33"* only with attention to inwardness instead of ambient sounds.

In the mid-eighties Giteck went through a creative crisis during which she didn't compose for three years. She took a Master's degree in psychology and began working at the Seattle Mental Health Institute dealing with AIDS patients, schizophrenics, and geriatric cases. She considered the five-and-a-half-year experience a hands-on laboratory for her interest in music as ritual healing. With schizophrenics she practiced nonverbal communication, trying to prove that music is more primal than language. She enticed the aged to tell her the stories of their lives, and what the wish of their lives had been. "I was trying," she has said of the period, "to strip music down to as primitive an experience as I could. I wanted to ask where does music come from? What's the common denominator for being a human and being a musician?"[3]

Out of this experience came *Om Shanti* (1986), one of her most deeply moving works, which she wrote in a two-month burst of inspiration that broke her several-year silence. This became the first in a series of "healing ritual" pieces which now includes *Home* (1989), for male chorus, gamelan, cello, and synthesizer, in which the chorus sings a chant on the word "home" (which, significantly, includes "Om"); *The Screamer* (1993), for soprano and six instruments; and *Sleepless in the Shadow* (1994), for mixed ensemble, a theater piece based on East European folk music. All of these pieces step outside the framework of conventional musical performance to confront the audience, for, unlike the other postminimalists especially, Giteck has no interest in formalist musical patterns for their own sake. "I'm still trying," she has often said, "to reach people's hearts."

Listening Example: Om Shanti *(1986)*

Dedicated to people living with AIDS, *Om Shanti* is the first work in Giteck's "music and healing series." *Om* is the primordial human tone used in yogic meditation; *shanti* means "peace" in Sanskrit. Scored for soprano, flute, clarinet, violin, cello, percussion, and piano, the work is typical for Giteck in the way it fuses elements of Javanese, Hasidic, and Buddhist musical traditions into a joyous unity. In the first moment, the soprano sings a Sanskrit text by the poet Shankaracharya:

> I am without thought, without form. I am all pervasive,
> I am everywhere, yet I am beyond all senses.
> I am neither detachment nor salvation
> nor anything that could be measured.
> I am consciousness and bliss. I am Shiva! I am Shiva!

The soprano's ethereally floating line repeats certain modal formulas over and over in the pitches G, E, and A, though without strict repetition. Meanwhile, the other instruments softly enter over a drone on D, with melodic arabesques from the D mixolydian scale.

The second and fourth movements borrow heavily from Javanese gamelan, particularly the thumping eighth-note beat in the synthesizer and piano and the half-step alternation in the clarinet and synthesizer (example 12.3). The third movement, the work's emotional center, is a rhythmically free duo for violin and cello in a mode of two sharps, reminiscent of Hasidic cantillation. The two lines intertwine the first time through, but when the violin repeats the opening of the movement, the cello merely drones on a low B, its lower string tuned down a half-step. The cello's absence in melody (though it is still present in spirit through the drone) creates a poignant sense of loss.

Movement four bears the inscription "Sound floats in space, in some way perhaps we draw comfort in acknowledging our own death while we are still alive." The piano opens with a rhapsodic line patterned after the flute improvisation with which Javanese ensemble works begin.

EXAMPLE 12.3 Janice Giteck, *Om Shanti*, third movement.

This is the most gamelan-inspired movement, with rapturous melodies doubled among the different instruments over a modal ostinato (example 12.4). The sounds "floating in space" presumably include the pairs of octaves on F doubled in the piano and antique cymbals. After such joyous energy, the final movement is stunning in its sad, motionless ecstasy. As the instruments drone on E and B, the soprano sings "Om Shanti" over and over in nonrepeating chants using only the pitches C, B, E, and G, with "shanti" repeated over and over on either B or G. *Om Shanti* is a beautiful example of postminimalism's ability to mediate between forward motion and stillness.

EXAMPLE 12.4 Janice Giteck, *Om Shanti*, fifth movement.

Daniel Lentz

When Daniel Lentz began writing, in 1970, what he aptly calls his "pretty pieces"—only fellow West Coaster Harold Budd can match Lentz for sheer voluptuousness—he had not yet heard of minimalism. Among those who have used minimalist processes, Lentz is unusual for his straightforward return to conventional tonality. His music pulses with energy through simple chord progressions, depending for its considerable originality on bright electronic timbres, vibrantly nervous textures of repeated notes reverberating via digital delay, and a strong element of rhythmic surprise. No other postminimalist seems so forthright and unselfconscious.

Lentz (born 1942) grew up in rural western Pennsylvania. Interestingly, his most formative influence was Rembert Weakland, his professor at St. Vincent College, later the liberal Archbishop of Milwaukee and also the world's leading expert on Ambrosian chant; this helps account for the frequent appearance of chant and Renaissance counterpoint in Lentz's works and also for his composition of two masses. Later teachers at Ohio University, Tanglewood, and Brandeis wielded less influence: Sessions, Berger, and Harold Shapero. As Lentz explains it, his mother had always told him, "Whatever the teacher's point of view is, take the opposite—at least you'll be noticed."[4] Following this advice, Lentz gravitated toward conceptual and theatrical works.

Lentz's early music, some of it published in *Source,* aimed at outrageousness, giving a negative view of ecclesiastical and political authority. His *Anti-Bass Music* includes graphic notations with pictures of guns, tanks, and explosions, and concludes with a reading of a list of American composers not killed in Vietnam (which includes virtually all of them, so far as is known). In a statement published at the time, Lentz made his connection between musical and military authoritarianism clearer:

> I too am sad. In fact, I am very sad. Men are still fighting wars and playing music. Some are guerrilla wars, and some are guerrilla compositions. But they are, nevertheless, war and music. They are fought with weapons and instruments. There is so little difference. One type is used for the defense of an army or nation; the other, for the defense of a vestigial culture. Do we need the protection of generals and composers?[5]

Gospel Music (1965) features a cigar-smoking preacher who glares at audience members as electronic tapes play and ushers take up a collection by passing tambourines through the audience. Other pieces are only thoughtful, or humorous. In *Hydro-Geneva: Emergency Piece #3,* the performer pours drops of hydrogen peroxide in the audience members' ears, asking them to listen to the melting of their own ear wax.

In 1970, however, Lentz abandoned conceptualism and began writing "pretty pieces." Calling himself "very space-conscious," he has changed his musical style each time he's changed geographic locations. The pieces of his Santa Barbara, California, period (1968–1982) are mellow, tinkly, almost too pretty in their dreamy melodies over major-seventh chords. The magnum opus of this period is *Missa Umbrarum* (1973), one of the few avant-garde masses suitable for liturgical use. The *Missa Umbrarum*—"Mass of Shadows"—requires the singers to strike wine glasses with mallets and rub the rims with wetted fingers to create ethereal drones, changing pitch occasionally by sipping the wine. The singers deconstruct the mass text phoneme by phoneme, echoing each one from one singer to another. The result is slightly similar to vocal pieces made in Europe at the time by people like Penderecki and Dieter Schnebel, but far more lovely and meditative.

Structurally, *Missa Umbrarum* also presents one of Lentz's primary compositional archetypes: as each phrase or cycle of the piece is sung, the previous cycle is played back on tape, so that each cycle is an accumulation of previous cycles. (Julius Eastman played with a similar structure.) Other Santa Barbara pieces include *Okewa* (1974) and *Lullaby* (1977); the latter is composed of plinked major triads on harp and synthesizers, with notes sustained by voices. In 1982 Lentz moved to Los Angeles and formed his own ensemble. The major work of this period is *The Crack in the Bell* (1986), an engaging rhythmic essay for small orchestra on a poem by e. e. cummings, still centered, however, on Lentz's electric keyboards and digital delay. Lentz's second mass, *wolfMASS* (1986–1987) is an extravagant collage, weaving together wolf howls, a rondeau ("Ma fin est mon commencement") by the fourteenth-century composer Guillaume de Machaut, "When Johnny Comes Marching Home Again," "Yankee Doodle," and that Renaissance favorite "L'homme armé" into a free-association free-for-all. Though hardly typical, *wolfMASS* makes more explicit than Lentz's other works the stream of consciousness that underlies his compositional thinking.

In 1991, Lentz left Los Angeles to take a teaching job at Arizona State University at Phoenix, and so changed style once again. His most recent large work, *Apologetica* (1992–1995), exemplifies his Arizona style: mournful, slow, darker than the Los Angeles period, almost impressionist in its lush tonality, yet enlivened by cross-rhythms and slow glissandos within the harmonies. Scored for choir, vocal soloists, strings, MIDI keyboards, and percussion, the piece is an hour-long lament in fifteen movements for the native peoples killed by the Spanish explorers under Cortez, with a text from a Mayan book of prophecies.

Listening Example: **The Crack in the Bell** *(1986)*

The Crack in the Bell is one of Lentz's most popular works, and a classic of postminimalism. Scored for his ensemble with augmented instrumentation—female voice and electric keyboards plus flute, brass quartet, percussion, piano, and string quartet—the piece is based on a mock-patriotic poem by e. e. cummings, *next to of course god*. The most unusual effect is a digital delay applied to the voice, so that the singer's lines often combine with themselves in canonic counterpoint. In addition, the singer sings through a vocoder which splits her voice into three-note chords, whose pitches she controls by playing a synthesizer. (It frequently sounds as though there are three sopranos, but there is only one.)

The work's pretty three-minute introduction is set in triadic arpeggios in the three electric keyboards, piano and percussion, often with the same pitches at different speeds in each instrument for an indistinct, feathery effect. Where cummings quotes American songs and clichés, Lentz provides the appropriate musical quotations as well (example 12.5; some instruments are omitted):

> next to of course god america i
> love you land of the pilgrims' and so forth oh
> say can you see by the dawn's early my
> country 'tis of centuries come and go
> and are no more . . .

(Coincidentally, in the same year Duckworth used the same poem, with the same melodic quotations, in his *Music in the Combat Zone*.)

Next a rousing, steady eighth-note pulse begins in the keyboards and continues until the end. Throughout the work the meter changes fluidly among 3/4, 4/4, and 5/4 in a smooth and natural way, yet so irregularly that the rhythmic continuity still sounds lively after many hearings. Especially effective is the tendency of Lentz's melodies to return at different speeds, say, in half notes in 4/4 and then in dotted halves in 3/4.

(*Continued*)

EXAMPLE 12.5 Daniel Lentz, *The Crack in the Bell*, mm. 16–22.

EXAMPLE 12.5 *(continued)*

Over repetitiously hammered triads, the singer sings the follow lines, achieving chords by singing through the vocoder:

> . . . what of it we should worry
> in every language even deaf and dumb
> thy sons acclaim your glorious name . . .

Finally we reach the work's central political gist when, over speciously happy major triads, the singer tunes cummings's ironic lines, reminiscent of the old saying, "dulce et decorum est pro patria mori":

> why talk of beauty what could be more beautiful than these
> heroic happy
>   dead
> who rushed like lions to the roaring slaughter
> they did not stop to think they died instead

From here Lentz recycles earlier phrases to rework them in different meters and tempos. At a mention of "beauty," passages of Renaissance-style canonic counterpoint appear in the brass (example 12.6; the keyboard notation is simplified) granting the words a kind of mock solemnity. The climax brings two-octave glissandos in the voice part. Suddenly the rapidly pulsing chords stop, and the singer performs one more delay effect. Once the phrase "america is just" slowly becomes audible, she adds the closing words: "another country"—a line not in

EXAMPLE 12.6 Daniel Lentz, *The Crack in the Bell,* Renaissance-style canonic counterpoint.

the original poem, but added by the composer. Despite Lentz's limiting himself to triadic harmonies and a consistent pulse, *The Crack in the Bell* possesses a wild, whimsically wandering beauty and kaleidoscopic rhythmic variety.

Elodie Lauten

If Pauline Oliveros and Janice Giteck devote their music to the greater benefit of humanity, Elodie Lauten seems to bypass humanity to direct her work to the cosmos itself. Her music has a vague, introvertedly musing quality to it, as though we are overhearing music meant for other ears. Since the early seventies she has composed within what she calls "universal correspondence systems," in which correlations are drawn among Indian Vedic cosmologies, hexagrams of the Chinese *I Ching,* astrological signs, scales, keys, and rhythmic patterns. Her pieces tend to maintain the same scale, texture, and mood throughout a movement in a kind of antigravity stasis, though the materials involved may be considerably complex, even polytonal. She often claims that the goal of her music is to achieve the "soundless sound" of Buddhist meditation. Her music has never quite seeped into public attention, partly because after each major work she retires from view to incubate the next one.

Lauten was born in Paris, France, in 1950, the daughter of the jazz pianist and drummer Errol Parker; however, while much of her music is improvisatory, it shows little resulting jazz influence. After playing in art-rock bands in Paris, she came to New York in 1972, where she quickly became part of the fashionable underground drug culture of seventies Manhattan, singing female lead for a band called Flaming Youth, shaving her head before it was fashionable, and performing with the cult poet Allen Ginsberg. Meanwhile, she studied with La Monte Young and the mystic musician Shri Chinmoy, and she began to produce recordings of her own music.

Lauten's early works were minimalist piano pieces in a Terry Riley-ish vein, mostly improvisatory and based on scale and ostinatos; sometimes she would notate them after recording them. *Cat Counterpoint* and *Imaginary Husband* (1983), for example, feature repetitive piano patterns played over electronic backgrounds. Some of her nonelectronic pieces, like *Adamantine Sonata* (1983) and *Sonate Ordinaire* (1986), have a neo-classic flavor, squeezing traditional melody-and-accompaniment textures into a meditative mode. One of Lauten's most lovely works is her *Concerto for Piano and Orchestral Memory* (1984), a rambling, eight-movement form in which the piano takes the lead by playing patterns over an electronic tape with a burbling beat. The "memory" consists of a group of instrumentalists whose reminiscences of the piano's material surround the piano's melodyless musings with a halo of sustained tones.

Lauten's first major work to receive much attention was an opera, *The Death of Don Juan* (1987). Hardly operatic in any conventional sense, the piece features static textures with soft, rhythmically free chants by multiple voices, as Don Juan, back turned to the audience, watches video images of his life in which Death comes to him in the form of a woman:

> I am your Death
> Death am I I
> Your Death am I
> Your faithful Death. . . .
> The human in me says
> You are forgiven
> Death in me says
> You will suffer
> The Supreme in me says
> You will forget your past

In the end, Don Juan dies from a mental and spiritual breakdown. An even more abstract later opera, *Existence* (1990), attempted to sum up all of reality, with a vocal quartet singing texts from Pythagoras, Pascal, and the Indian *Dhammapada* as Lauten played piano patterns, ending with the vapid sitcom pattern of a tiny TV as electronic drones died slowly away.

Example 12.7 gives a chart of part of Lauten's universal correspondence systems, called "The Gaia Cycle Matrix." The keys go around the circle from no sharps or flats to six flats, then back; twelve hexagrams from the *I Ching* go from all straight lines to all unbroken lines and back; and these are correlated with the astrological signs from Aries to Pisces. These correlations partly explain the choices of key and mode in Lauten's *Tronik Involutions* (1993), a cycle of twelve electronic pieces improvised in eight tracks on the Proteus synthesizer. In the mid-nineties, Lauten began a large, operatic opus that sums up decades of her work, called *Deus ex Machina* and scored for a quasi-Baroque ensemble of two sopranos, baroque flute, cello, and harpsichord, augmented by synthesized and computer-sequenced electronics. Fusing her mystic and neoclassic tendencies with universal texts about the mystery of existence, *Deus ex Machina* may be Lauten's most profound work yet.

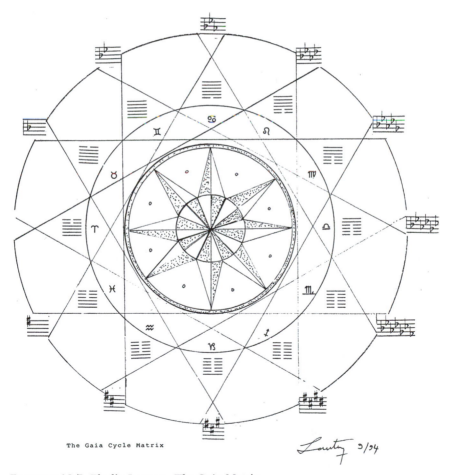

The Gaia Cycle Matrix

EXAMPLE 12.7 Elodie Lauten, *The Gaia Matrix*.

Paul Dresher

Paul Dresher is kind of a Philip Glass for the younger generation: i.e., a good musical businessman (by his own admission) and a prolific writer of theater music. He first became known for three theater works he wrote with the theater director George Coates: *The Way of How* (1981), *Are Are* (1983), and *See Hear* (1984). Further collaborations with the extraordinary singer, actor, and writer Rinde Eckert—*Slow Fire* (1985–1988), *Power Failure* (1989), *Pioneer* (1990), and *Awed Behavior* (1993)—confirmed his reputation as perhaps the premiere theater and dance composer of his generation. In recent years, though, the Paul Dresher Ensemble has concentrated more on concert music, both Dresher's own and that of other composers. Meanwhile, Dresher's music has moved from strictly permutational, almost minimalist simplicity to a more polytonal and world-music-influenced complexity.

Born in Los Angeles in 1951, Dresher played guitar from the age of eleven and spent his teenage years playing rhythm and blues and writing his own songs. He dropped out of the University of California at Berkeley for five years to do studio work, play in Steve Reich's ensemble for a few months in 1974, sit in on Terry Riley's composition seminar at Mills, and study with a sitar virtuoso, Mikhil Banerjee. He returned to Berkeley to gain experience in African drumming and in Berkeley's Balinese gamelan. Upon graduating, he moved to the University of California at San Diego to study with Reynolds, Oliveros, Bernard Rands, and, most importantly, Robert Erickson. In 1979–1980 he spent time in India and Indonesia, taping environmental sounds that he eventually processed through delays and harmonizers to create the ambient-sounding tape work *Other Fire* (1984).

Dresher's theory teacher at Berkeley had been Janice Giteck, during her brief teaching stint there; and it was through her husband, the singer John Duykers, that he began working with Coates. "When I write for theater," Dresher has said, "I'll often make more explicit appropriative use of recognizable styles that the audience will have some connection with. When I write chamber music, I try to make it more abstract, and use more consistent strategies."[6] Dresher's early chamber works, most characteristically *Channels Passing* for seven instruments (1981–1982) and *Casa Vecchia* for double string quartet (1982), are indeed fairly abstract; one step removed from minimalism, they churn with repetitive diatonic patterns run through strict procedures, slowly changing and playing with aural tricks such as (in *Channels*) a melodic line being passed quickly from instrument to instrument. Starting with *See Hear* in 1984, he abandoned rigorous procedures for a more intuitive approach, though as he says, "Every piece requires a backbone of formal rigor in at least one parameter."[7]

Double Ikat for violin, piano, and percussion (1988–1990) is a strong example of Dresher's recent style: propulsive, heavily indebted to game-lan for its rhythmic style but mercurial in its formal twists and turns. Instead of existing within a diatonic stasis like his earlier music, the piece weaves several pentatonic scales sometimes in polytonal combination; *Blue Diamonds* for piano (1995) moves even further in this direction, virtuosic and at times atonal. Interestingly, given his guitar background, Dresher's only piece to use rock idioms is *Den of Iniquity* (1994), for the Dresher Ensemble, for good reasons: "I found rock more useful in theater," he explains, "and most chamber musicians can't play rock and roll."[8]

Other Postminimalists

Postminimalism has so far received so little recognition as an important stylistic current that many postminimal composers, several well into mid-career, have not yet received due attention. One of the most unjustly neglected is Peter Gena, Chicago's premier exponent of the style. Born in 1947 in Buffalo, New York, Gena studied at SUNY at Buffalo with Lejaren Hiller and Morton Feldman. Soon after minimalism appeared, Gena became fascinated by drones, partly because Hiller had gotten him involved in computer music and drones were something early comput-ers could do easily. Gena's *Egerya* (1972), for computer tape, was a turn-ing point, soft, postminimal, and based detail for detail on a Scandinavian rya rug. From here he moved to Feldman-influenced works like *Stabiles* (1976), for piano with long-sustained sonorities, some-times timing sonorities according to the number of beats among over-tones of a sustained chord.

Gena's early postminimal works have political overtones. Particularly dashing is *McKinley* (1983), for violin, piano, and drums, a rousing process piece based on three folk songs about the assassination of President McKinley. In 1980, Gena wrote *Beethoven in Soho* to express his conviction that, "were Beethoven alive today, he would be playing in the lofts of Downtown Manhattan rather than at Lincoln Center." For two pianos and electric bass, the piece runs the Allegretto from old Ludwig's Op. 54 Sonata, through lightning-quick minimalist-style processes. In the nineties, with the assistance of the geneticist Charles Strom, Gena began drawing computer music from digitally synthesized DNA sequences, the first example being *Beta Globin* (1994). The point of such music is not sim-ply to generate melodies according to biological algorithms, but to trans-late biological behavior into musical behavior in meaningful ways. *Red Blood Cells* (1995), for example, mimics the tendency of bone marrow to randomly create antibodies until one matches an invading virus. Gena's current project is to map the entire immune system in music.

One of the most popular postminimalists is Ingram Marshall, whose dark, moody music is the closest American analogue to the East European mystic composers such as Arvo Pärt and Henryk Gorecki. While minimalistically tonal, Marshall's music rarely contains driving momentum or a steady beat; its delicate textures blur into one another like a slow cinematic fade. He has often been associated with John Adams, with whom he shared a house from 1976 to 1980 in San Francisco; during the early years of Adams's *Shaker Loops* and Marshall's *The Fragility Cycles* (1976) some mutual influence was apparent. But Marshall's music, set in motion by tape delays and often pervaded by recordings or samples of natural sounds, is Romantic only in mood, not structure, and his flat, meditative, nonclimaxing forms are far from any European aesthetic, despite his frequently-noted quotations of Sibelius.

Born in Mount Vernon, New York, in 1942, Marshall studied electronic techniques at Columbia with Ussachevsky and Davidovsky, but he found more congenial the New York scene around Palestine, Chatham, and Maryanne Amacher. In 1970 he went to CalArts, where he became Morton Subotnick's teaching assistant and studied gamelan. He spent time in Bali and in Sweden; his music seems like a fusion of these two influences, static Indonesian patterns plus Nordic gloom. His first piece to gain popularity was *Fog Tropes* (1979/1982) for prerecorded foghorns, ambient sounds, and brass sextet run through a delay system. Tape delay reappeared, along with background recordings of Corsican singing, in *Gradual Requiem* (1979–1981), for mandolin, piano, synthesizer, and gambuh (Balinese flute), and of ambient sounds in *Alcatraz* (1984), which incorporates boomy recordings of the slamming of great prison doors among minimalist-type arpeggios. Because of the filmy indistinctness of his gestures, Marshall's use of tape delay doesn't create melodic repetitions like Terry Riley's, but rather melancholy, atmospheric textures.

One of the finest postminimal composers is Philadelphia's Paul Epstein, who was born in Boston in 1938—putting him virtually in the same generation with the original minimalists—and who teaches at Temple University. Like Lentz, Epstein studied at Brandeis with Shapero and Fine, but in graduate school at Berkeley he fell under more freeing influences as a costudent with La Monte Young and Terry Riley. Through the seventies he worked much with theater music; his postminimal period took off upon first working with Philadelphia's Relache ensemble in 1981. Epstein is fascinated by the algorithmic aspects of minimalist processes, and with keeping those processes hidden behind a smooth musical surface. He employs formal devices such as palindromes—audible in his *Palindromic Variations* for trio (1995)—and intricate canons, such as those in his *Solstice Canons* (1995). Borrowing from Tom Johnson, Epstein has developed the idea of self-replicating melody, that is, a melody in which the pattern of notes is duplicated by taking every other note, or every third note, and so on. "I like to set up procedures," he has said, "that will give me a level of unpredictability."[9] Some of Epstein's best music has used texts by poet Toby Olsen, including his chamber opera *Dorit* (1994) and his song cycle *Chamber Music: Three Songs from Home* (1986): a vocal setting for winds and keyboards of great contrapuntal beauty.

Mary Jane Leach (born 1949 in Vermont) started out as a minimalist, a composer of austere, unchanging textures. Her first characteristic pieces, starting with *Note Passing Note* for vocalist and two taped vocalists (1981), were scored for multiples of the same instrument (or voice), usually performed by a soloist who had recorded the other lines on multitrack tape. These pieces, including *4B.C.* (1984) for four bass clarinets (three on tape) and *Feu de Joie* for eight bassoons (1992), take advantage of carefully calculated psychoacoustic phenomena of beats, difference tones, and combination tones, employing pitches not exactly in tune. Beginning in 1985 with *Green Mountain Madrigal*, however, Leach has increasingly composed for choir, usually of female voices only. Once she started down the choral trail, her aesthetic broadened to include quotation and reworking of earlier music, especially that of Claudio Monteverdi (1567–1643), though she also used a chord progression from Anton Bruckner's Eighth Symphony in *Brückstuck* (1989). Such virtuosic choral pieces as *Mountain Echoes* (1987) are remarkable for their permutational echoes among pairs of voices situated in opposite corners of the performing space.

Like Conlon Nancarrow, Stephen Scott (born 1944 in Corvallis, Oregon) has based most of his output on an eccentric medium, the bowed piano. He began as a jazz-influenced neoclassicist, but his allegiance switched to minimalism after he went to Ghana to study African music in 1970 and met Steve Reich the first day there. Around 1977 Scott heard a work called *Ordres* by Curtis Curtis-Smith (born 1941), who had invented a technique of playing the piano by pulling nylon threads threaded through the strings. The technique clicked with Scott's desire to find an ensemble style based on hocketing, and he wrote *Music One for Bowed Strings* in 1977.

Scott has taught since 1969 at Colorado College, where his student ensemble learns to play his music by pulling nylon threads across and underneath the piano strings—a labor-intensive performance medium since, as with handbells, each player can be responsible for only a few pitches. In some of Scott's pieces the bowed-string effect is slow and droning, but he also uses rhythmically active hocketing effects with a vivaciousness that made his *Rainbows* (1981) one of the most popular new-music works of the early eighties. The unconventionality of sound in Scott's droning, rasping, almost attackless music is compensated for by his formal lucidity. Pieces like *Minerva's Web* (1985) and *The Tears of Niobe* (1986) fan outward from simple motives slowly developed, and each piece achieves as much contrapuntal complexity by the end as it can, given the medium's severe limitations. In *Vikings of the Sunrise* (1995), Scott expanded his repertoire of effects, adding muted keyboard playing, strings struck with piano hammers by hand, and drumming on the outside of the piano.

Mary Ellen Childs is young enough (born 1957 in West Lafayette, Indiana) to be included with the totalists in Chapter 13, but she is one of the few of her generation uninfluenced by rock, and her music is classically postminimalist. Growing up as a dancer had a strong effect on her sense of composition, for several of her works have a choreographic element, notably *Click* (1988), for three claves players whose rhythms flow from the intricate permutational tappings of each other's claves, and *Crash* (1994–1995), scored for six crash-cymbal players riding on roller blades and handcarts.

More characteristically, though, her works move through a somewhat repetitive or permutational diatonic pitch language changing so gradually that you don't notice the changes until after they've happened. That's not to say that there aren't dramatic gestures, such as the exciting point in *Parterre* (1988) at which the soprano and drums suddenly enter over a texture of winds and accordion. But Childs uses such stark contrasts sparingly. In *Carte Blanche* (1991), she begins with a spare, soft, repetitive texture—in this case small, high chromatic clusters with sighing glissandos in the flute and viola—as introduction to an irregularly repetitive syncopated bass. Her note-to-note procedures are often strict, but her overall strategy, if smooth, is unpredictable.

The music of David Borden (b. 1938 in Boston) tends to rely on relentless streams of steady beats and reiterated patterns and has mostly been written for the Mother Mallard Ensemble, a synthesizer group that he founded in 1969 and ran until 1991. Borden's magnum opus is his monumental three-hour work in twelve sections, *The Continuing Story of Counterpoint* (1976–1987). Each section of *Continuing Story* spins out of a characteristic rhythm; for example, part 4 begins with a lovely 7+7+6+5 metrical pattern, part 6 with a five-beat pattern variously divided 4+1, 3+2, and 2+3. Part 9 contains a canon between soprano and basset horn, and Borden's obsession with counterpoint even extends to the texts of the vocal movements, which repeat names and phrases from the history of counterpoint like "Gradus ad Parnassum," "hocket," and "Orlando di Lasso." Borden tends toward long series of pieces, the most recent example being *Notes from Vienna*, a group of chamber concertos for guitar, cello, and so on, in which the soloists quote classical works by Haydn, Beethoven, and Schubert.

Jonathan Kramer (born 1942 in Hartford) is an interesting case; he began as a postminimalist but in recent years has spun off in a very different direction. Kramer has written some important books, among them *The Time of Music* (New York: Schirmer Books, 1988), an investigation of linear time versus timelessness in music; and his own music has often fused a linear time sense with a non-Western sense of timelessness, usually by having a variety of rhythmic activity take place within static harmonic fields that use only five, six, or seven pitches. Kramer's seminal work, *Moving Music*, for twelve clarinets and solo clarinet (1975–1976), is drawn from a melody using only the pitches F, G, A-flat, C, and D, and has a drone on F running throughout the piece. Above this drone all sorts of textures ebb and flow: pointillistic notes, repeated-note melodies, dense contrapuntal textures, virtuoso solos of agile leaps. Likewise, Kramer's *Music for Piano Number 5* (1979–1980) is a Terry Riley-ish romp in 11/16 meter within a six-pitch mode, and *Moments in and Out of Time* (1981–1983), a big, growling orchestra piece that might sound like Mahler were it not for its stubborn adherence to the unadorned E minor scale.

By the time he wrote *Atlanta Licks* (1984), however, Kramer was using the six-pitch conceit as a way of unifying a wide variety of musics in one piece. From here it was a short step to the style clashes of post-modernism, which he explored in *Notta Sonata* (1992–1993) for two pianos and percussion, an intended companion piece to Bartók's Sonata for the same instruments. *Notta Sonata* intercuts sharply among imaginary styles, sometimes abruptly returning to where the piece had left off long ago. Passages of the work sound like Baroque counterpoint on mallet instruments, tonalized fragments of Boulezian serialism, piano horn calls from a Weber opera reworked by Stockhausen with raucously ringing glockenspiels. The combinations of idioms that never really existed before give the piece the remarkable feel, not of a collage, but of disconcerting fractures within a single musical subjectivity.

If the accordion has played a disproportionate role in postminimalist timbre (in works by Duckworth, Childs, Epstein, and others), the reason is primarily Guy Klucevsek, an accordionist who has worked with many of these composers and whose own music has a whimsical logic. Klucevsek (born 1947) grew up in the outskirts of Pittsburgh, where playing accordion was part of the local Polish culture. Impresssed by *Come Out* and *In C*, from 1972 to 1985 he wrote what he called "take-no-prisoners minimalism," until working with John Zorn showed him how he could incorporate the vernacular styles he grew up with. As a result, Klucevsek writes works for solo accordion and for ensemble, usually postminimalist and based on vernacular sources. His *Stolen Memories* and *Tesknota* (both 1993) are based on simple but not obvious quasi-minimalist processes, and many of his works play off of ethnically derived metrical irregularities; *Viavy Rose Variations* (1989), based on melodies from Madagascar, is a charming example. He has also written pieces in popular and East-European folk idioms with crazy titles like *Transylvanian Software* and *Flying Vegetables of the Apocalypse*. All of Klucevsek's music is unpretentious, audience-pleasing, and superbly musical.

Neely Bruce (born in 1944 in Memphis) is a prolific composer and one difficult to classify, except that the majority of his works are vocal. In works such as *Eight Ghosts* (1989), he has been one of the few postminimalists to create a viably madrigalistic choral style. Based on texts of concrete poetry, *Eight Ghosts* includes electronic vocal processing and references to rock and jazz. A larger theater work, *The Plague* (1983–1984), eclectically mixes Renaissance polyphony, unusual vocal techniques, and a rock idiom to create an apocalyptic metaphor for our time. Teaching at Wesleyan University in Connecticut, Bruce has been one of the premier pianists and conductors for American music, both recent and historical.

One of New York's most popular composers is Rafael Mostel, director of and composer for the Tibetan Singing Bowl Ensemble—not really a postminimalist, but influenced by minimalism and not really fitting any category at all. Born in Passaic, New Jersey, in 1948 (the nephew of the great comedian Zero Mostel), Mostel grew up with an intense musical background of Eastern European synagogue chants and Broadway showtunes. At Brown University, he, Stephen Scott, and others gave the New England premiere of *In C* in 1968. In 1973 Mostel studied briefly with Nadia Boulanger in Paris, though she was by then too old to be of much help. Then, back in New York in 1983, Mostel walked one day into a handicraft shop, saw a Tibetan bowl, thumped it with his finger, and heard an entire career in its rich, enduring ring.

Mostel gave the first concert of his Tibetan Singing Bowl Ensemble in Central Park in 1984 in the middle of the night. His works, often evening-length, tend to be ritualistic and meditative yet rough in timbre, with drones emanating from the rubbing of the Tibetan bowls. *Nightsong* (1989) is a motionless meditation for the bowls with a soft solo on the lyzarden, an obsolete wind instrument. Other works, like *Swiftly, How Swiftly . . .* (1987) are noisier yet as calm as a night in the jungle, with the mournful wails of Tibetan thighbone trumpets, the rattle of rainsticks, and slow drumbeats reminiscent of Japanese *gagaku*. Performed in such grand spaces as the Cathedral of St. John the Divine, his larger works like *Ceremonial for the Equinox* (1985) conjure up an archetypal sonic power.

There are many other postminimalists whose music, though powerful, has achieved only regional significance so far. Of these one might mention Phil Winsor (born 1938 in Illinois) at North Texas State University, whose music has included acoustic works written via computer algorithms; Joseph Koykkar (born 1951 in Milwaukee) at the University of Wisconsin, whose postminimal chamber works have a propulsive drive; Thomas Albert (born 1948 in Lebanon, Pennsylvania), whose *A Maze (With Grace)* (1975) turns the song "Amazing Grace" into a beautifully meditative process piece; Wes York (born 1949 in Portland, Maine), a Feldman-influenced postminimalist of delicate structures; and Sasha Matson (born 1954 in Seattle), a student of John Adams, whose *Steel*

Chords, a triple concerto for pedal steel guitar, violins, and strings introduces into new music a timbre usually associated with country and western music. Such a legion of highly individual composers is indicative of a fertile style that deserves more public recognition than it has received.

Notes

1. Interview with the author, October 23, 1996.
2. Janice Giteck, "Beyond Performance: The Ritual Frame," unpublished paper to be published in *Contemporary Music Review.*
3. Ibid.
4. Interview with the author, July 23, 1996.
5. Quoted in David Cope, *New Directions in Music* (Dubuque, Iowa: Wm. C. Brown Company Publishers, 1971), p. 102.
6. Interview with the author, October 27, 1996.
7. Ibid.
8. Ibid.
9. Interview with the author, October 1996.

CHAPTER 13

Totalism and the 1990s

Any characterization of music in the 1990s must deal first and foremost with the overwhelming fact that there are far more active composers today than at any previous time in history. For one thing, the American birth rate rose dramatically during the period of post–World War II expansion and euphoria, resulting in the "baby boom" which began around 1946 and peaked in 1955. Released from economic worry by their parents' newfound prosperity and at the same time reacting against the bland conformity of their Eisenhower-era upbringings, people born in this era entered the arts in unprecedented numbers. Cage, at the end of his life, wrote about the problem in a mesostic (a poem in which a key-word is spelled in capital letters down the middle) on the words "over-population and art":

abOut 1948 or 50 the number of people
liVing
all at oncE
equaled the numbeR who had ever lived at any time all added together
the Present as far as numbers
gO
became equal to the Past
we are now in the fUture
it is something eLse
hAs
iT doubled
has It quadrupled
all we nOw
kNow for sure is
the deAd
are iN the minority
they are outnumbereD by us who're living

whAt does this do to

    ouR

way of communicaTing

    mail's rarely frOm people we know . . .

everything's as muLtiplied

        As we are

     each momenT

        Is magic

   we have nO idea

   what's beiNg seen

    or heArd

    the quaNtity

   is beyonD count

    the quAlity is

       Readymade

     arT[1]

Laurie Anderson wrote a song, "Daddy, Daddy, it was just like you said / Now that the living outnumber the dead." And, asked for a statement on the current scene, Robert Ashley once wrote: "I have tried to forget what certain composers are up to, because that doesn't seem as important as that there are so many of us."[2]

More than ever, the music of the 1990s cannot be generally characterized in terms of styles, for the era is too chaotically diverse. There is, however, a deep unity running through the music in terms of the social conditions influencing its production. Composers born in the 1950s all face certain challenges and all benefit from the explosion of media, both cursed and favored by the rapid shrinking of Planet Earth. Along with the tremendous increase in the number of artists, which exerts a huge effect on public perception of individual artists as well as on how careers are made, composers who find themselves in their forties as the millennium ends have had the following experiences in common:

- The generation born in the 1950s is the first to benefit from greatly increased exposure to non-Western musics in college. In the past, such an advantage came primarily as an accident of geography: West Coast composers like Cowell and Partch grew up with musics other than European as their major musical environment. Today, however, it is common for all students to encounter African, Indonesian, Japanese, Indian, and other musical traditions presented side-by-side with the European tradition—not to mention the increased teaching of jazz and the vastly greater availability of European medieval and

Renaissance music on recordings. Whether a composer takes advantage of this exposure or not, he or she is far more likely to learn at a formative age that European music of the common-practice period is just one music among many, with no privileged position. In fact, with greatly decreased classical concert attendance, the prestige of European music assumed by earlier generations has been fading rapidly.

- In a contrary tendency, music education has been phased out of many school districts, decreasing even further students' early exposure to music and the establishment of any common musical culture beyond what is heard on radio.

- Since the mid-1980s, sequencing software has become such a common mode of music-making that notation has been fading in importance as a compositional intermediary. Much music today is made, even by amateurs, directly on the computer screen. Even where notation remains central, the process of composing increasingly takes place without a paper trail of revisions. No matter how traditional a composer's training has been, the process of working on a lit screen rather than on paper has a powerful, if often unconscious, effect on assumptions about how to structure music, just as writing poetry on a word processor effects how poems are formed differently from a typewriter.

- Accompanying the deemphasis on notation is the fact that music publishers have quit publishing all but a tiny amount of the most conservative new music. It is nearly impossible for a composer to get his or her scores distributed through commercial channels in the 1990s. On the other hand, compact discs have become relatively cheap to produce, and distribution channels have multiplied. Therefore, whereas the mid-twentieth-century composer distributed his music through scores and had a difficult time getting recorded, those possibilities are reversed for today's young composer. To at least some extent this reversal has been healthy, for midcentury composers showed a tendency to consider the score the actual music, with a corresponding loss of concern for how the music sounded; today, more and more music can be judged only for how it sounds, for the score may either not exist or be practically unavailable.

- The ubiquity of samplers has effected a drastic physical change in the materials of music. The musical atom is increasingly no longer the note, but the sample, a sonic entity that can just as easily be a sound complex or quotation as a single tone from a musical instrument.

- Growing up in an environment pervaded with rock music has become an almost universal experience. It is increasingly rare, then, for composers to write without taking the rhythms, instrumentation, or performance conventions of rock into account. For many, rock has become the vernacular bedrock from which music must grow in order to gain any currency with a large audience.

- In addition, the overpopulation of artists in all fields has led to a drastic splintering of audiences and a daunting multiplicity of subcultures. The number of routes toward a successful career has increased proportionately with the impossibility of getting a significant hearing outside one's subculture. The orchestral circuit, the opera circuit, the improvisation scene, the new-music community, the theater music world, the academic music world—as each of these milieus grows, they all become more cut off from each other, and moving among them becomes difficult with so many dozens of composers jostling each other for commissions, performances, and reputations in each one.

Out of all these forces, a characterizable style did arise in the 1990s, however, one which came to be called *totalism*. In the rawest meaning of the word, totalism suggests having your cake and eating it too: in this case, writing music that appeals to audiences on a sensuous and visceral level, and yet which still contains enough complexity and intricate musical devices to attract the more sophisticated aficionado. It also implies using all of the musical resources available, so that Indian raga-like melodies may fit together with jazz harmonies within classical structuring devices. Totalist composers are those who admired minimalism's ability to communicate to large audiences, yet also admired serialism's ability to yield more and more information on further hearings, and who also appreciated the inherent complexity, especially rhythmic complexity, of non-Western musics.

As a result, totalist music can generally be characterized as having a steady, articulated beat, often flavored by rock or world music. That beat becomes a background grid for polyrhythms of great complexity. Elliott Carter and Milton Babbitt employ complex rhythms too, but without a grid to hear them against; for totalist composers, being able to hear and calculate the complexity is essential. Totalist harmony can be either consonant, dissonant, or both—the distinction having ceased to be very important—but it is usually fairly static, concentrating on harmonic or melodic images that are easily memorable even when quite complex. Especially in the music of Mikel Rouse, Michael Gordon, David First, Ben Neill, John Luther Adams, Diana Meckley, Larry Polansky, and several others, there is often some kind of implied correspondence between the ratios of simultaneous or successive tempos or pulses and the frequencies of the harmonic series, a theoretical tendency going back to

Cowell. The similar structuring of pitch and rhythm in a kind of musical "unified field theory" is another nuance of the word *totalism*.

A few composers follow totalist criteria rather strictly, many more compose in a populist-yet-intellectual spirit akin to totalism, and still others have taken a different route altogether. Obviously, no guarantee can be offered concerning the relative future importance of the composers described below. Careers move at different rates, people drop out, others bloom late, and if a list made in 2050 of important composers of the 1990s overlaps to any extent with the selections below, it will be through pure serendipity. All that can be guaranteed is that these composers exemplify the forces that have been at work on those who came of age artistically after 1985, and so far, some of the most inventive solutions.

Mikel Rouse

No other artist better expresses the intent of totalism, or more delicately straddles the line between pop accessibility and intricate classical structures, than Mikel Rouse. His music for his rock quartet Broken Consort—synthesizer, sax, bass, and drum set—explores rhythms drawn from the Schillinger system, with underlying patterns such as 3 against 5 against 8 spreading out in hypnotically geometric patterns. Yet, far from abstract, the music is memorably melodic, with a foot-tappable beat. In Rouse's songs he innovated a technique he calls "counterpoetry" by analogy to counterpoint, in which he overdubs rhythmically different versions of the same text for a complex rhythmic interplay, yet still closely orbits pop genres. And in his operas *Failing Kansas* and *Dennis Cleveland,* Rouse has achieved a daring synthesis of rock and electronic theater that makes him a natural successor in the genre to Robert Ashley.

The son of a state trooper, Rouse was born in 1957 and grew up in the rural Missouri "boot-heel" region near Arkansas. In third grade he permanently changed the spelling, though not the pronunciation, of his name Michael to its present form. Equally talented at music and art, he studied both at the University of Missouri and the Kansas City Art Institute respectively, which were across the street from each other. He formed a rock band, Tirez Tirez (French for "pull pull," stencilled on double doors in Paris), which was the only local band progressive enough to open for Talking Heads when they played in Kansas City. In 1979 the band relocated to New York. Rouse studied African rhythms in A. M. Jones's *Studies in African Music,* and also chanced upon one of the few teachers in New York qualified to teach the Schillinger method. "Schillinger was never a system like 12-tone music," Rouse notes. "It was a set of vocabularies . . . I was drawn to it because it was so naturally the way I thought."[3]

Mikel Rouse in his opera *Dennis Cleveland*.

Rouse's early magnum opus, the source work for his later rhythmic style, is *Quorum* (1984), for intricately sequenced Linn drum machine. From *Quorum*, a totally rhythmic exercise, Rouse expanded his language in Broken Consort pieces such as *Quick Thrust* (1984), a twelve-tone rock piece that varies its row only rhythmically, and *Leading the Machine* (1990). *Quick Thrust* (see example 13.1) is a concise example of what Rouse gained from Schillinger technique: every rhythm in the piece is derived from rhythms of 2-against-3-against-5-against-8, defined either as durations in eighth-notes or as divisions of a cycle of thirty eighth-notes. The saxophone line has a new attack every third eighth-note, every fifth eighth-note, and every eighth eighth-note, (some of the attacks coinciding, of course). Likewise, thirty eighth-notes in the bass line are divided in half by one note, in thirds by two others, and in fifths by four others. The result is that three forms of the same twelve-tone row pass by each other at different rates.

Rouse unveiled his counterpoetry in a compact disc called *Living Inside Design* whose lyrics, poking deadpan fun at American pop culture, attested to his talent with words as well as with notes and colors (from "Thinking About Myself"):

> He warms the streets deserted palms
> Erasing where he wept
> His favorite pastime?
> Barking up the wrong tree where he slept
>
> The envelope and history
> Of two wrongs make a right
> Sits well upon the bottoms
> Of America 2-Night

EXAMPLE 13.1 Mikel Rouse, *Quick Thrust* (1984), twelve-tone row at different rates.

Counterpoetry led to Rouse's one-man "opera" *Failing Kansas* (1995). Rouse had been fascinated by the novel *In Cold Blood* by Truman Capote; the author had grown up in circumstances similar to Rouse's, and the murders it describes happened in Kansas, also country Rouse knew well. For his libretto Rouse fanatically scoured through the same newspaper and court documents Capote had relied on and used words spoken by the actual murderers, Dick Hickock and Perry Smith. Rouse performs the opera by speaking in rhythm over a rich taped accompaniment.

Rouse followed *Failing Kansas* with an even more innovative opera, *Dennis Cleveland* (1996), in which he played the title role: a talk show host. As Dennis, a cool postmodern guru, speaks his Buddhist-flavored commentary on modern society, the opera's other characters rise to speak from the audience as their host walks around with a microphone. Many theater directors have broken down "the fourth wall" in this fashion, but no composer had ever before synchronized such acting feats with a computer-sequenced tape. Complex canons arise from the chorus of talk-show "guests" onstage, and passages of music return superimposed on each other for polytonal effects that are as musically challenging as they are emotionally thrilling. Several recent composers have equalled the rhythmic intricacy of Rouse's music but none have combined it with such an insightful attunement to mass culture.

Listening Example: **Failing Kansas *(1995)***

Those familiar with Capote's superbly crafted novel *In Cold Blood* will catch references to the story in *Failing Kansas,* but Rouse's treatment of the text is abstracted, fragmented, into what he's called a "75-minute pop song." In nine movements, the opera is structured with four primary sections separated and surrounded by a prelude (in which Rouse plays harmonica), three interludes (in which the counterpoetry technique is less dense), and a closing song. The rhythmic devices that liven the first major section, "The Last to See Them Alive," are typical. The section is in a rock 4/4 beat, and yet Rouse speaks the Protestant hymn that Perry Smith sings, "In the Garden," in 12/8 meter, so that his measure, stretched across $1\frac{1}{2}$ measures of the rock beat, creates a continual polyrhythmic tension.

The middle of the movement (example 13.2) provides a simple, transparent, and delightful example of totalist rhythm. Notice that the guitar ostinato outlines an eight-beat pattern, while the bass and harmonica change pitch every five beats. The bass's rhythm—$3 + 3 + 1 + 3$ in eighth-notes—is a recurring motif through several movements of the opera, as is the bass's pitch line. Meanwhile, Rouse's voice, intoning a ballad Perry Smith composed, plays around the 4/4 downbeat, sometimes starting on it, sometimes shifting away from it, with an off-balancing feel typical of Rouse's text setting. No other work has demonstrated the apt-

EXAMPLE 13.2 Mikel Rouse, *Failing Kansas* (1995), from "The Last to See Them Alive."

ness of totalist rhythmic structure for dramatic form as eloquently as *Failing Kansas,* the first viable music-theater work of the new generation.

Michael Gordon

The contrast between Rouse and Michael Gordon is symptomatic of the 1990s. Where Rouse's music represents the application of classical structures and strategies to rock materials, Gordon's music is the opposite: an infusion of rock energy into classical materials. Rouse uses a trap set and a rock beat to achieve cool, objectivist, arithmetically patterned textures. Gordon uses mostly classical instruments—violins, bass clarinets, a percussionist rather than a drummer—to create a pulsing, irregular energy reminiscent of rock groups such as Led Zeppelin. Rouse's rock is clean and elegant, Gordon's chamber music is raw and crude. Yet just as Rouse played for years with Tirez Tirez, Gordon played keyboard for a New York band called Peter and the Girlfriends. Similar experiences, similar desires and misgivings, very different results.

Gordon was born in Miami to Polish parents in 1956 and lived until the age of eight in Managua, Nicaragua. He began composing as a child as a strategy to distract his piano teacher from the fact that he hadn't practiced, and, back in Miami Beach as a teenager, played in rock bands. His checkered college career included graduation from New York University and afterward, at Yale, study with Martin Bresnick. Even while at Yale Gordon lived largely in New York, playing with Peter and the Girlfriends from 1979 to 1983. When that band disbanded, he formed—after the tradition of Steve Reich and Musicians and the Philip Glass Ensemble—the Michael Gordon Philharmonic, which lasted from 1983 to 1996.

The Philharmonic's first concert in December of 1983, in a small Manhattan art gallery, featured a work already in classic Gordon idiom: *Thou Shalt!/Thou Shalt Not!* (1983). The title refers a the clash of wills represented in the piece as a clash of tempos, for the violin, viola, electric organ, and electric guitar, playing reiterative patterns in 9/8 and 6/8 meter, are periodically interrupted in angry terms by the marimba and drums who impose their own time-frame of four or five quarter notes.

In particular, a bumpy gear-shifting effect of suddenly changing tempos is characteristic of Gordon's music. The Michael Gordon Philharmonic became expert at keeping two beats in their collective head at once, so that one half the ensemble was playing off subdivisions of a triplet quarter-note beat, the other half off of a dotted eighth-note beat. This technique climaxed in *Four Kings Fight Five* (1988), in which nine instruments gradually build up a Nancarrovian array of simultaneous tempos, in ratios such as 8:12:18:24:27. A later work, *Yo Shakespeare* of 1993, treats triplet quarter-notes as independent units, so that a measure might contain triplets in groupings not divisible by three (see example 13.3). Another common Gordon device was the use of repetitive patterns of different lengths, which would loop and recombine differently with each repetition. All of these rhythms are couched in memorable but deliberately inelegant lines, as crudely pounding as the bass line of a rock guitarist.

In 1984 Gordon married another composer, Julia Wolfe (for whom, see more below). In 1986, the pair founded, with third composer David Lang, the Bang on a Can festival, which since 1987 has been New York's annual outlet for totalist, postminimal, and experimentalist music. All three composers had studied with Bresnick and inherited his open-minded, nondogmatic appreciation of various contemporary styles. Remarkably successful, Bang on a Can began at the fairly raw R.A.P.P. Arts Center in New York and graduated to prestigious Lincoln Center in 1994.

EXAMPLE 13.3 Michael Gordon, *Yo Shakespeare*, opening cross-rhythms.

One of Gordon's largest works was his *Van Gogh Video Opera* (1991), made in collaboration with the video artist Elliot Kaplan and based on Van Gogh's letters to his brother Theo. Even more ambitious is *Trance* (1995), written for Holland's Icebreaker ensemble: amplified, continuous, and fifty-two minutes long, hammering home Gordon's trademark rhythms, and containing sampled religious vocal sounds such as the chanting of Buddhist monks and muezzins singing the *Ku'ran*.

Listening Example:* Four Kings Fight Five *(1988).

Like *Thou Shalt!/Thou Shalt Not!*, the title of *Four Kings Fight Five* speaks of conflict, and an unequal one at that. The title is a Biblical reference to an incident in the book of Genesis; here the reference is to nine players: oboe, clarinet, bass clarinet, electric keyboard, percussion, violin, viola, cello, and electric guitar. The opening melody, descending and climbing somewhat atonally over a drone on E, goes back and forth between quarter-notes and dotted quarters, laying out the basic rhythmic conflict at once. The work is dedicated to Glenn Branca, and the strumming of

EXAMPLE 13.4 Michael Gordon, *Four Kings Fight Five.*

open E strings and quadruple stops on the electric guitar does seem reminiscent of the energy of Branca's symphonies.

After three minutes the piece builds to a climax followed by a brief pause. At this point, a slow textural crescendo begins: first with six quarters to a measure against four dotted quarters, then with a tempo 3/4 as slow as the dotted quarters, triplet quarter notes, and so on, finally suggesting no fewer than eleven different tempos, at ratios of 8:9:12:16:18:24:27:36:48:54:60 (see example 13.4). As the rhythmic complexities increase, however, the harmony grows more and more static, as though so much complexity can only lose its melodic clarity in a textural blur. At last, after some nineteen minutes, the viola enters with a long, lonely soliloquy played out over the motivic repetitions of the other instruments. Few totalist works have surpassed *Four Kings* in either complexity or clarity.

Lois V Vierk

Although many, many Americans born after 1935 have taken inspiration from the musics of non-Western cultures, Lois V Vierk is a rare example of an ethnomusicologist who turned to composing. Her best-known and most characteristic works have been scored for multiples of the same instrument, a common medium among postminimal composers. Where others came to this concept through minimalism, however, Vierk reached it via the ancient Japanese court music *gagaku*, which contains passages of identical wind instruments playing a melody at slightly different rates. Through her study in Japan, Vierk has become the American composer most expert in *gagaku* and became, in 1996, the first American to ever be commissioned to write for a *gagaku* ensemble.

Born in 1951, Vierk grew up just south of Chicago. When the family moved to Philadelphia in 1966, she discovered a passion for Beethoven (via a new piano teacher) and a fascination with the ethnic diversity of her new community. Her interest in ethnomusicology, still an exotic subject at the time, eventually brought her to UCLA, which offered courses in Chinese music and dance, Balinese gamelan, Ghanaian drumming, and Yugoslavian dance, as well as concerts of rare Asian art forms. Studying *bugaku* dance, she encountered *gagaku*, the music that accompanies it, and fell in love with it. Until 1982, throughout her time in Los Angeles, Vierk performed in UCLA's *gagaku* ensemble.

Though she had composed since high school, Vierk didn't look to composition seriously until after graduation in 1974. She sought out Leonard Stein, Schoenberg's assistant, and advised her to go to CalArts. There she studied with Mel Powell and Morton Subotnick. Meanwhile, Vierk supported herself accompanying dance classes and working as assistant music director under Carl Stone at KPFK radio. In 1980

UCLA's *gagaku* orchestra was invited to play in Japan, where Vierk took lessons with Sukeyasu Shiba, an expert *ryuteki* player who could trace his family back through thirty-two generations of members of the royal *gagaku* ensemble.

Vierk's earliest mature works, from 1977 to 1978, were scored for homogenous groups such as three clarinets, eighteen trombones, or six male voices. She brought with her an interest in minimalism from her CalArts days, but as with many in the current New York scene, the minimalist who most influenced her was Phill Niblock, with his austere clusters of densely-packed, sustained tones. In all of Vierk's work, one can hear the expressive glissandos of *gagaku*, the effect of different lines played by multiples of one timbre, and the sustained linearity of not only Niblock, but Lucier's *Music on a Long Thin Wire*, another important piece in her development. The basic formal idea she has reworked again and again, however, comes from no minimalist or Asian sources at all: the idea of a gradual, almost imperceptible transformation from a still, quiescent texture to a rousingly active one, often in a kind of exponential curve.

Vierk studied in Japan again from 1982 to 1984. Her return to America was not to the West Coast but to New York. The first piece with which she went public was *Go Guitars* (1981), the first word of which, "go," is Japanese for five: thus, five guitars, or more often in performance, four taped guitars and one live one. The piece begins with a steadily plucked, Glenn Branca-ish energy, enlivened by microtonal pitch waverings. Gradually long glissandos are mixed into the texture, until by the end it is a pulsating mass of up and down glissandos. *Go Guitars* represents a straightforward and fairly linear pattern (though there are more textural details than mentioned here) that Vierk would refine and develop in subsequent works, including *Cirrus* (1988) for six trumpets and *Simoom* (1986) for eight cellos. The slight pitch-bendings which inflect Vierk's music give it an Asian flavor, but her development of an initial meditativeness into textures of great complexity is a Western tendency she attributes to her love for Beethoven. The combination makes for a distinct and recognizable personal flavor.

Listening Example: **Timberline** *(1991)*

Scored for flute, clarinet, bassoon, viola, double bass (alternating with electric bass), synthesizer, and percussion—the instrumentation of the Relache Ensemble from Philadelphia, which commissioned it— *Timberline* was Vierk's first major work to explore her sense of large-scale textural crescendo in an ensemble of diverse timbres. The opening pentatonic scales and small glissandos between scale notes in the viola give the piece a mildly Japanese flavor. Soon, one of the piece's most beautiful features begins: melodies of little thirty-second-note arabesques in the piano. As always with Vierk, the texture and plot thicken in tandem, leading to an ornate texture of rising pentatonic scales.

This time, however, the energy level drops down after climax to a slowly moving bass line providing a foundation for glissandoing melodies. The crescendo back to maximum energy is complex, running through mysterious trills and abrupt key changes to a lively texture with repeating chords hammered in the piano (see example 13.5). *Timberline* is a remarkable example of the extreme and eclectic originality of texture brought by young composers of the nineties to a classical chamber medium.

EXAMPLE 13.5 Lois V. Vierk, *Timberline*, mm. 281–284.

Eve Beglarian

Eve Beglarian (born 1958 in Ann Arbor and raised in Los Angeles) is typical of her generation in the eclecticism of her sources, exceptional in the audience appeal of her music, and quite unusual in her development. Interestingly, she is the daughter of a composer: her father, Grant Beglarian (b. 1927) is a Russian-born composer of chamber music in a style grounded in Bartók and Stravinsky. Beglarian began her career as an "Uptown" composer, trained at Princeton and Columbia. During the early eighties, however, her music gravitated toward postminimalism and vernacular sources, and she soon found her work unwelcome in the academic circles where she worked as administrator of the International Society for Contemporary Music. Finally, around 1991 she was discovered by Mary Jane Leach, the composer-singer Kitty Brazelton, and David First, who programmed her music in downtown Manhattan circles, where it became an instant sensation.

Beglarian has written contrapuntal variations on medieval songs, computer-altered disco collages, postminimal and numerically structured synthesizer pieces, songs of nonsense syllables, and wild theater pieces. Her largest theater piece to date is *TypOpera* (1993–1994) written for the California E.A.R. Unit, based on the *Ur Sonata*—an abstract vocal sonata of nonsense syllables from the 1920s—by the German painter Kurt Schwitters. Part of her transition from uptown to downtown, though, was that she went from writing music for ensembles to primarily performing her own music. Often speaking texts over electronic backgrounds, she is almost as much performance artist as composer, and she concertizes with pianist Kathleen Supové in a duo named Twisted Tutu. *No Man's Land* (1995) is characteristic; over an intentionally ugly background of industrial noises, she intones a text describing the provisional and mutually unrelated character of the businesses surrounding the corner of Church Street and White Street in New York. The piece wittily conjures up an atmosphere as dirty as the neighborhood it depicts.

Beglarian has often based her works on earlier music. Especially notable in this regard is her *Machaut in the Machine Age* series, which transforms various vocal pieces by the fourteenth-century master Guillaume de Machaut. In the most daring of these, *Machaut a GoGo* (1991), the medieval French love poetry

> Moult sui de bonne heure née,
> Quant je sui si bien amee
> De mon doulz ami . . .

is translated literally into supremely modern lyrics over a Gogo beat (a type of jazzy rap music popular in Washington, D.C.):

> How very much was I under lucky stars conceived,
> When so much good, good love do I happily receive,
> From my amazing lover, who ignores every other
> And his heart completely leaves for the love of me.

(The translation is by Kitty Brazelton.) Sung to a cool beat in which the words feel right at home, the piece eloquently makes the point that, while musical styles have changed considerably in 600 years, the basic impulse of erotic poetry is unaltered.

Beglarian makes her living as a sound producer, and as a result possesses a high-tech sophistication that she applies to simple sonic materials. Her *FlamingO* (1995) broke new ground in combining chamber orchestra and samplers in such a way that the samplers dominated, the orchestra emerging from an engulfing whirr of electronic noise that came from a sampled bull-roarer or thunderstick, a flat piece of whale baleen swung on a string. In her *Wonder-Counselor* (1996) for organ and tape, flurries of melody on the organ are laid over an ecstatically ebbing and flowing harmonic series, with the occasional accompaniment of natural sounds: the ocean, bird songs, a couple having orgasms. One of new music's most uninhibited spirits, Beglarian is not afraid to tackle subjects of sex and religion in her music, sometimes both at once, and her music has a rare joyous and uplifting quality.

Peter Garland

Peter Garland has been better known as a scholar than as a composer; specifically, from 1971 through 1991 he edited the journal *Soundings*, which for years was the only published source for music and writings by and about many of the most original American experimentalist composers: Nancarrow, Lou Harrison, Tenney, Lentz, Harold Budd, Rudhyar, and many others. But though this activity has overshadowed Garland's own music, he is an heir to the musical traditions of Cowell and Harrison. His musical style is based in a modal idiom with frequent but irregular repetition of rhythms and motives. "I feel influenced," he has said, "by American modernism from the '20s, not the '50s and '60s. My take on modernism goes back to Cowell and Rudhyar."[4]

Born in Maine in 1952, Garland attended Ussachevsky's electronic music class at Columbia, dropped out after one semester, and headed west. He became part of CalArts' signal founding class in 1970, studying (like John Luther Adams and Guy Klucevsek) with Tenney and Budd and befriending Harrison, Rudhyar, and the irascible Harry Partch. Garland starting *Soundings* through a publishing workshop with Fluxus composer Dick Higgins. The journal ran erratically for twenty years, publishing some of America's most significant music in an era in which no conventional publisher would pay any attention (not to imply that this era is over). Meanwhile, Garland lived in Oaxaca, Mexico in 1975–1976 and again in 1977–1979, eventually settling in Santa Fe in the early eighties. In his travels he has become a leading authority on the musics of several Native Mexican tribes, as well as of American Indian culture in general.

The postminimal orientation of Garland's music obscures the fact that his style comes not from minimalism per se, but from a combination of older influences. The repetitions of simple motives in *A Song* for piano (1971) owe more to Erik Satie than to Reich or Glass. Some of Garland's early music—notably *The Three Strange Angels* and *Three Songs of Mad Coyote* (both 1973) for piano, bass drum, bull roarers, and other percussion—roars with the booming of forearm piano clusters and the wail of sirens, minimalist in its limitation of materials but inspired by the raucous soundworld of Varèse. In later works, his modal sense of melody can be traced to Lou Harrison and the late work of Cowell. Going straight to the sources of American music, American Indians included, Garland has fashioned a repetitive, modal idiom that is only coincidentally postminimalist.

Garland's largest theater work has been *The Conquest of Mexico* (1978), written for the Peter Garland Ensemble, couched in an ensemble timbre modeled after "colonial Mexican Indian baroque," with harpsichord, harp, and recorder playing alongside Aztec percussion. Two of his most beautiful essays are piano cycles, *Jornada del Muerto* (1987) and *Walk in Beauty* (1989). The "Turquoise Trail" movement of the latter piece is interrupted by a tune in 6/8 meter that represents the ghost of Satie, and in another movement—"A Pitch-Pine Basket"—the pianist builds an intimate melody by pressing tone clusters and releasing certain notes to leave ringing triads. Example 13.6 from *Walk in Beauty* demonstrates Garland's tendency to form gentle contrapuntal lines from only a few repeated notes.

EXAMPLE 13.6 Peter Garland, *Walk in Beauty.*

The Roque Dalton Songs (1988), based on poems of an assassinated Salvadoran poet, are grounded in percussion with triads in the harp and piano, with long rhythmic patterns repeated over and over. This and other works like his String Quartet No. 1, "In Praise of Poor Scholars" (1986), give an impression of only a few notes used over and over in recurring rhythms, but with nothing ever happening the same way twice. No other young American composer writes music of such heartfelt simplicity, a delicate music of the desert that seems too quiet for the hectic 1990s.

John Luther Adams

In 1976, John Adams met John Adams. The former didn't give the coincidence much thought until the latter's *Nixon in China* appeared in 1987, making him something of a household name (by contemporary opera standards, anyway). At that point the John Adams who *didn't* write *Nixon* had to do something to distinguish himself from his older and better-known colleague, so he began using his middle name professionally. John Luther Adams, however, has his own distinctive features, notable among them that he is the only well-known composer associated with Alaska and that he has been as active as an environmentalist as a composer, a fact that has had an impact on his music as well. The evocative power of his musical landscapes has become so attractive to audiences that, for many fans of American music, he has become the more important Adams to keep an ear on.

J. L. Adams was born in 1953 in Mississippi but grew up in many locations. His early passion for rock was given expression by the formation of a garage band, which he led from the drum set. His hero was the eccentric rocker Frank Zappa (1940–1994), whom Adams calls "a major influence in my musical education, not so much for his own music as for the music he directed us kids to."[5] Reading the back of Zappa's records, Adams became curious about Varèse, Webern, and Feldman, and when he heard Feldman's *Piece for Four Pianos* on an early recording, he says, "I thought I had died and gone to heaven. That piece changed my life."[6] Under this new influence the fascination with rock dissolved, and Adams headed for brand-new, freewheeling CalArts.

Here he received a Germanic style of rigor from Leonard Stein and a more persuasive American rigor from James Tenney. His hatred of Los Angeles, though, turned him into an environmentalist (he spent his free time outside the city searching for condors), and he moved to Alaska in 1975, playing timpani with the Fairbanks Symphony from 1982 to 1992. All this time he lived as rugged an outdoor life as he could manage; not until 1989 did he have running water. That was also the year he became successful enough with commissions to quit his jobs and become a full-time composer.

Adams's music can be superficially described as the intersection of two diverse influences: Feldman and Cowell. He discovered *New Musical Resources* in 1970, and his scores bear the ubiquitous marks of Cowell's multitempoed rhythmic structures, with each measure divided into three, four, five, seven beats at once. The Feldman influence manifests as a delight in delicately balanced sonorities used as recurring images, although Adams's sonorities are generally more diatonic, or "tonal," than Feldman's. From his earliest mature composition—*Songbirdsongs* (1974)—Adams's music has consciously evoked nature and particularly the wintry landscapes of his adopted state, with sparse textures, colorful timbres, and feelings of stillness or at least rough-hewn naturalness. In early works like *Night Peace* (1977) this evocation mimics Feldman's quietness without matching his mystery or subtlety. From the late eighties on, however, Adams's style has deepened into a beautiful language of bittersweet chords and cyclic rhythms, complemented by joyously totalist tempo superimpositions in his percussion music.

Adams's largest works to date are an opera, *Earth and the Great Weather* (1993), and a huge, seventy-five-minute orchestra piece on which he worked from 1990 to 1995, *Clouds of Forgetting, Clouds of Unknowing*. The former isn't an opera in the sense of having a plot; it is rather a celebration of Alaskan geography, complete with recorded environmental sounds and recitation of Eskimo place names. The ocean roars and delicate harmonics are interrupted by ferocious and rhythmically complex drum quartets that themselves sound like thunderous natural phenomena.

Listening Example: Dream in White on White (1992)

The title of *Dream in White on White* is in one sense quite literal: the score, for string quartet, harp, and string orchestra, is entirely in what would be "white" notes on the piano, for there are neither accidentals nor a key signature. At first the string orchestra plays widespread sustained chords (called "clouds," La Monte Young-style) over which the harp plucks poignantly rising four-note motifs. After awhile the string quartet breaks into the "Lost Chorales," simple chord progressions based on a phasing process of, for example, five repeating beats in the violins against four in the viola and cello (example 13.7). After these have been heard unaccompanied, the orchestral chords return in quietest harmonics, and the

EXAMPLE 13.7 Caption?

harp and quartet pluck patterns of rising or falling fourths and fifths, the harp at a tempo 5/4 as fast as the quartet.

The penultimate texture is a lush polyrhythm, with the orchestra playing a slow three beats to the measure, the harp five, and the quartet four. Finally, the opening texture returns with the harp's lovely four-note motifs. The variety of dreamy textures Adams achieves with a few simple materials is lovely.

David First

Among the totalists, David First is the composer most analogous to Alvin Lucier or La Monte Young in an earlier generation, in that he works most directly with unpredictable sonic phenomena. His music is microtonal, but rather than work with precise tunings, he works with the beats caused by notes slightly out of tune, especially the accelerating and decelerating beats that come from imperceptibly slow glissandos. Difficult to fully capture on recording, his music is more focused on acoustic phenomena than Glenn Branca's, more dynamically active than La Monte Young's, much louder than Alvin Lucier's, and powerful in the way its acoustic patterns viscerally absorb the listener.

First (born in 1953) grew up in Philadelphia as an aspiring rock guitarist with little formal training, though he learned about oscillators, sum and difference tones, and acoustical phenomena from his father, an electrical engineer. Involved early in free jazz, he started his professional career playing in Cecil Taylor's band at Carnegie Hall in 1974. Soon afterward he formed an instrumental trio called the Note Killers, which he describes as "free jazz meets Steve Reich meets Jimi Hendrix"; in the group's 1980 New York premiere they shared a bill with Glenn Branca. Torn like so many New York musicians of his generation between notated and improvised music, First embodies that dichotomy with particular clarity. As he puts it,

> It has always been a standing offer on my part to give up improvising on the day someone plays for me a piece of composed music that has the energy, passion, and rhythmic/melodic subtlety and complexity represented in the best improvised musics. Conversely, one could play spontaneously with others from now till the end of time and never create the powerfully magical effects available through a simple set of agreements that are possible through the language of notation. It is at the intersection of each axis, for me, that the most profound results exist.[7]

Few composer-improvisers have reached such delicately balanced solutions.

Moving to New York in 1984, First began a series of groups that ran concurrently: the World Casio Quartet, Echoes of God, the Joy Buzzers. Much of these groups' music centered around free improvisation, but the World Casio Quartet experimented with changing beats caused by the friction between slowly glissandoing drones. Interestingly, given First's rock background, he is one of the few New York totalists to avoid using explicit rock materials—most specifically, a backbeat—in his music. Most of his pieces from the late eighties take the form of sound continuums, slowly changing streams of drones whose acoustic beating grows more active during the slow slides from one consonant sonority to another.

In the early 1990s, though, he began adding drumbeats to his continuums in arithmetical ratios analogous to those of his harmonic consonances. A beautiful milestone in this respect was *Jade Screen Test Dreams of Renting Wings* (1993)—First has a wry penchant for circuitous titles, and this one refers to a mythical figure who wishes she could fly. The work's drummer sets the rhythmic pace by listening to a clicktrack over headphones against which two more drummers play complex cross-rhythms. Meanwhile, violin, cello, English horn, bassoon, and no fewer than five electric guitars slide their pitches through tones emitted by a computer module. The resulting buzz glows and sizzles with acoustic phenomena, and the listener can't identify where the pitches are coming from.

First's most ambitious work to date has been *The Manhattan Book of the Dead* (1995), an opera with solo vocalist, dancers, video, and his own idiosyncratic orchestra with electronic keyboards and guitar. Conceived as a response to the AIDS epidemic, this was the first work in which all sides of his music converged smoothly, including massive drone textures, some free improvisation, and even a couple of pop songs in a fairly minimalist rock style. Despite such diversity, the work grows from a drone and dissolves back into it, with all style changes smooth and gradual.

Bernadette Speach

Morton Feldman was one of the late century's best composition teachers, and his concern for timbre, for the physical immediacy of the way each note breathes, left its mark on a whole school of composers. There are many composers touched by the Feldman heritage—besides Peter Gena, Nils Vigeland, Bunita Marcus, Barbara Monk—but the most visible (or audible) has been Bernadette Speach. Though a little older than the other composers here, Speach got off to a late start as a composer, and one aspect of her music is typical of the nineties: with one foot in the classical avant-garde and the other in jazz, Speach has led a split career of string quartets on one hand and improvisations on the other, often fusing the two.

Bernadette Speach.

Speach was born on New Year's Day, 1948, and at her first piano recital four years later she refused to play the classical piece she had prepared unless she could also play a work of her own. Despite such early musical determination, at the age of eighteen she joined the order of the Sisters of St. Joseph of Corondelet, and she was a nun until 1977. As such, she taught music at parochial schools and continued to write music, some of it religious, much of it folk music for voice and guitar. In 1977 she left the order and enrolled at Columbia University. She met Feldman on a summer session in Siena, Italy. She found his concern for sonic physicality more inviting than the religion of pitch complexity at Columbia, so she went to SUNY at Buffalo to study with him and Lejaren Hiller. In Buffalo Speach met and married Jeffrey Schanzer (b. 1954), a composer and jazz guitarist whose political music is marked by Marxist sympathies. In 1984 the two returned to New York, where Speach has since been active as a new-music administrator and presenter.

While Speach's music doesn't sound like Feldman's, it is reminiscent of his in a couple of important respects: she tends to limit some aspect of her materials such as dynamics or rhythm (a Feldmanesque tendency that has crept into much postminimalism as well), and she relies on musical images, note complexes that return over and over without being literally repeated. A good example is the series of waves built up over and over again, from the cello to the viola to the second violin to the first violin, in the opening measures of her string quartet *Les Ondes pour Quatre* (Waves for Four, 1988, example 13.8).

As a presenter of such A.A.C.M. figures as Cecil Taylor and Muhal Richard Abrams, as well as through her marriage to Schanzer, Speach became greatly affected by free jazz and incorporates some improvisation into almost all her music, at least at a detail level. The level to which Speach can erase the lines between improvisation and composition is brilliantly demonstrated in her piano concerto *Within* (1990). Near the end, the pianist improvises a cadenza, which flows smoothly into notated but still free-sounding material. The orchestra then starts echoing the notated gestures and sounds as though they are freely riffing off of the pianist's improvisation, a theatrical achievement Mozart might have envied.

Among Speach's finest works have been her collaborations with the poet and novelist Thulani Davis, especially *Telepathy Suite* (1987), in which Davis reads her vernacular poems about black life in her own inimitable rhythm while Speach's ensemble provides a notated but jazzy background. Though Speach's nonverbal works tend toward postminimalism, they are almost always complex in pitch; her piano piece *When It Rains, Llueve* (1995), for example, intercuts from one image to another in an accessible but cinematic strategy rare among postminimalists.

EXAMPLE 13.8 Bernadette Speach, *Les Ondes pour Quatre.*

Larry Polansky

If Peter Garland embodies the melodic and rhythmic side of American experimentalism for his generation, then Larry Polansky does the same for the intellectual and mathematical side. Like James Tenney, Polansky is a composer fascinated by musical form and process, and many of his works set up a gradual transformation through which an initial musical image metamorphoses into something very different. Of the composers highlighted in this chapter, he is the least concerned with audience response or accessibility, but his overtone-based processes nevertheless often result in forms of ravishing beauty.

Polansky (born 1954, in New York City) grew up playing jazz, bluegrass, and rock guitar, and he nearly became a professional jazz guitarist. A wandering academic career took him to the University of California at Santa Cruz, where he took composition and electronic music with Tenney and Mumma, while becoming friends with Lou Harrison; all three became important personal influences. When Tenney took a job at York University, Polansky followed and worked there with David Rosenboom. He left to get his masters at the University of Illinois, studying with Johnston, Martirano, and Herbert Brün and working with the Partch archives there. Subsequently, Polansky taught at Mills College from 1980 to 1990, and more recently at Dartmouth.

Polansky's interest in computer-controlled formal process found its initial expression in the first of his *Four Voice Canons* from 1975–1976. The *Four Voice Canons* are Nancarrovian-style tempo canons; No. 5 (1983) is a two-against-three-against-five-against-eight canon for percussion sounds and is performable live, and No. 6 (1986) uses four different timbres, including a Javanese *rebab* and croaking frogs. Much of Polansky's work is concerned with pure tunings, and his tuning pieces are based on overtone series in various relationships. For instance, *Psaltery (for Lou Harrison)* (1978–1979) runs a bowed psaltery sample through a transformation from one harmonic series to another. Transformation—or, as he puts it, mutation—is a seminal Polansky idea, given perhaps its clearest form in *51 Melodies* for two guitars (1990–1991), in which an energetic, rock-style melody is repeated with cumulative variations that gradually transform it into a very different melody. Like Tenney's works, Polansky's invite the ear to follow complex gradual processes.

The extreme and multidimensional literalness of some of Polansky's mutations often requires a computer, and he was one of the designers, along with Burke and Rosenboom, of the computer-music language HMSL. *B'rey'sheet (Cantillation Study No. 1)* (1985) uses HMSL to transform a sung Hebrew cantillation (sung by Jody Diamond, Polansky's wife and one of America's leading gamelan musicians) into a complex texture in seventeen-limit tuning, slowly moving from disorder to

greater order as the computerized melodies become more clearly related
to the singer's line.

One of Polansky's most extraordinary works is atypical: *Lonesome
Road (The Crawford Variations)* (1988–1989). Written while he was on
leave in Surakarta, Java, it is a sprawling, ninety-minute set of fifty-one
variations on Ruth Crawford's arrangement of the folk song "Lonesome
Road," dazzling in its pianistic complexity and kaleidoscopic variety.
After a gentle opening, the theme disappears into myriad complexities
that bring together serial technique, jazz, blues, and Ivesian sound-lay-
ering, the theme occasionally reappearing, splendidly and suddenly, like
a sunset glimpsed after rounding a mountain curve. Example 13.9 gives

EXAMPLE 13.9 Larry Polansky, *Lonesome Road,* Variation III.

EXAMPLE 13.10 Larry Polansky, *Lonesome Road,* beginnings of Variations VI and
XXXVIII.

most of Variation III, one of the simplest variations by far and the first
point at which the swirls of arpeggios subside to allow the theme (present in the top notes) to be heard. Example 13.10 gives the more typically virtuosic openings of Variations VI and XXXVIII. The piece is an
even larger and worthy successor to that other great set of American
piano variations, Rzewski's *The People United.*

Other Totalists

For all the dazzling variety of the current music scene, the most typical
manifestations of 1990s activity fall into two broadly defined trends. One
is the tendency toward ensemble music, usually for groups of from five
to twenty players, often rhythmically complex. Many composers of such
music have been associated with the Bang on a Can festival: Evan
Ziporyn, Art Jarvinen, Julia Wolfe, and David Lang. This music differs
from the older style of classical chamber music in that it is usually not
soloistically written, but written to achieve powerful ensemble effects,
and with a steady, articulated beat. In effect, the mixed ensemble of eight
to twelve players has replaced the conventional orchestra, both for economic reasons and internal reasons of musical style. Furthermore, this
music has been a needed release from the limitations of the seventies
conceptualist school, who out of economic necessity had concentrated on
solo performance. The other major trend, discussed below, is still mostly
solo: a tendency toward performance art incorporating music and multimedia into a theatrical setting.

To list composers who have borrowed techniques from some brand of non-Western music would virtually be to name every young composer active in the 1990s. Evan Ziporyn (b. 1959 in Chicago) is a particularly intense case, since he is active both as a jazz clarinetist and director of Balinese-style ensemble, Gamelan Galactica, at the Massachusetts Institute of Technology. Between attending Yale and Berkeley he studied in Bali with Made Lebah, the same teacher Colin McPhee had studied with five decades earlier. As a result, his music unapologetically inhabits two worlds at once, though his rhythms still possess a totalist tendency of shifting back and forth between tempos. His first piece in this style to receive wide public attention was *Luv Time* (1984), whose piano chords and nipple gong, marking out clocklike beats at different tempos, have a Balinese flavor, even as its saxophones shifting among different pentatonic scales bring John Coltrane to mind.

Though more episodic than Gordon's, Ziporyn's works similarly contain long passages based on different tempos marked off by different instruments; *Tree Frog* (1990) is a particularly ambitious example, its mellow beginning of ornate, elaborately ornamented wind solos over a shimmering synthesizer chord giving way to energetically pounding tempo clashes and wild solos. Ziporyn has written music for gamelan (*Aneh Tapi Nyata* of 1992, for example), and in *Tire Fire* (1994) he took the audacious step of combining gamelan and electric guitars in one large, sprawling work, each playing in more or less their accustomed styles.

Julia Wolfe (born 1958 in Philadelphia) started out writing theater music for the Wild Swan Theater she helped found in Ann Arbor, Michigan; when she met Michael Gordon in 1982, he persuaded her to study with Bresnick at Yale, and in 1987 they founded Bang on a Can. Her music emerges organically from irregular repetition; "I'll just sit and play one chord until I start to hear a melody come from it," she has explained,[8] and you can almost hear this process occur at the beginning of a piece like *Tell Me Everything* (1994) for chamber orchestra. Much of Wolfe's music has an impulse of rock energy behind it, evinced through relentless reiteration of sonorities. This is obvious in a work like *Lick* (1994), with its rock riffs irregularly repeated and built up additively, but also true of her calmer orchestra work *Windows of Vulnerability* (1991), with its interplay of rich, colorful chords. Her music is among the most coloristic of her generation, moving from lush consonance to harsh dissonance but within a postminimally circumscribed set of harmonies.

The third composer in the Bang on a Can trio, David Lang was born in 1957 in Los Angeles and studied with Lou Harrison, Jacob Druckman, and the German symphonist Hans Werner Henze. Lang's music is less systematic and rhythmically complex than that of his totalist colleagues; he opts instead for a sense of theatrical gesture. Perhaps more than anyone else he straddles the uptown and downtown worlds of New York music. A few of his works evince minimalist roots, notably

Orpheus Over and Under (1989), for two pianos, a poignant meditation first in quickly repeated single notes, then in minor-key tremolos. Many are notable for disconcerting titles, such as *Spud* (1986) and *Eating Living Monkeys* (1985) for orchestra. *Are You Experienced?* (1987) for narrator, tuba, and ensemble, its title taken from a Jimi Hendrix song, begins with Lang as narrator dealing one of the more effective sucker punches in recent music:

> "Hello. I'm David Lang. I know you were looking forward to hear-
> ing this piece, but something terrible has just happened. While we
> were busy setting up, someone crept up silently behind you and
> dealt a quick blow to the side of your head. As you fell towards the
> floor and began losing consciousness, a number of disconnected
> thoughts crowded into your head. Here are a few of them. . . ."

The music then launches into rhythmically punchy sonorities that could indeed sound like something throbbing inside your head. The Hendrix connection is cleverly driven home by the amplified tuba achieving the same sort of feedback that Hendrix popularized on guitar.

While totalism has been mostly an East Coast phenomenon, the music of Arthur Jarvinen of Los Angeles (b. 1956, a student of Subotnick at CalArts) has a totalist rhythmic complexity, combined with a whimsi-cal sonic imagination. Like Rouse and Gordon, Jarvinen phase-shifts loops of different durations. A delightful example is his *Murphy-Nights* (1989), based on the philosophical idea that a lecturer who spoke every night for infinity would eventually have nights in which every member of the audience was coincidentally named Murphy. The idea is carried out by an electric bass playing in 33/16 meter and an electric keyboard in 8/2 (32/16), so that the bass gets a sixteenth-note behind the keyboard with each measure. Most striking is Jarvinen's uninhibited timbral imag-ination: his *Egyptian Two-Step* (1986) is punctuated by the hissing of aerosol spray cans. The textures of his *The Paces of Yu* (1990) emanate from flicked window shutters, grinding pencil sharpeners, a reeling fish-ing reel, and eight mousetraps snapped at once, deployed in subtle tempo shifts and with an elegant sense of composition.

Ben Neill (born 1957 in North Carolina) is the leading composer among those who have moved in the direction of ambient music. A trum-pet player and Rhys Chatham protégé, Neill studied, like Chatham, with La Monte Young, and in 1992 he took up Chatham's old job as music director of the Kitchen. Neill nurtures a totalist fascination for complex rhythms, but instead of synchronizing them in ensemble performance like Rouse or Gordon he sets them loose in computerized sound-fields that operate as ambient sound installations. His *678 Streams* (1993) allows him a solo on his mutantrumpet—a three-belled trumpet attached to a computer, whose valves signal changes in computer logic somewhat as in

David Berhman's music—over rhythms spelling out tempos of 6 against 7 against 8. *Green Machine* (1994) is a larger installation based on the numbers 6, 7, 8, and 9, a verdant aural jungle of drumbeats, atmospheric chords, and sampled thunder. Neill has also written less rock-oriented pieces such as *Money Talk* (1987), in which he cleverly plays trumpet over the incessant patter of an auctioneer used as a drone. As an ambient rocker who sometimes works with disc-spinning DJs like DJ Spooky (Paul D. Miller), Neill has become something of a crossover artist with a rock following.

Jerome Kitzke exemplifies the young composers so immersed in both jazz and classical worlds that they cease to make a distinction. A virtuoso pianist, Kitzke (born 1955 in Wisconsin) incorporates elements of American Indian chanting into his music, often playing the piano with one hand while chanting vocally and shaking a rattle with the other. He performs his works with his group Mad Coyote, who play both improvised and notated music that is sometimes atonal, often jazzy, but always rooted in an earthy, tribal aesthetic. His works such as *We Need to Dream All This Again* (1992–1993) weave narration into the music, often with Native American or political texts. Kitzke's major work to date has been *The Paha Sapa Give-back* (1995), a huge theatrical piece for thirteen instrumentalists (including six percussionists), four singers, and actor narrator. In a drumming ritual with the players moving among different positions in the space, the piece urges a restoration of the Black Hills to the Sioux people.

Another composer heavily influenced by American Indian music is Kyle Gann (the author, born 1955 in Dallas, Texas), whose works are also drum-driven; specifically, he has developed a rhythmic language of changing tempos from the beat-shifting music of the Hopi, Zuni, and Pueblo Indians. In this respect his ensemble music (such as *Astrological Studies*, 1994) is similar to Michael Gordon's, but smoother, more consonant, and more melodic, in a style once referred to by the *New York Times* as "naive pictorialism." Oddly (since postminimalism provides such a clear context for microtonal perception), Gann is the only totalist or postminimal composer working in just-intonation tuning; his electronic works use purely tuned pitch systems of up to thirty-seven pitches per octave. An example is *Custer's Ghost to Sitting Bull* (1995), on a text imagined as spoken by General George Custer after the Little Bighorn debacle.

Nick Didkovsky is one of the most unusual composers of his generation, with a computer-generated complexity to his ensemble music that goes beyond totalism. Though Didkovsky (born 1958), a virtuoso guitarist, studied with Christian Wolff at Dartmouth, he took his degree in mathematics and until recently made his living teaching math and computer science. Didkovsky composes most of his music via computer, setting up probabilities and letting the software compose according to Myhill distributions, Markoff chains, recursive systems, and other mathematical algorithms. This all sounds very complex and cerebral; what makes it astonishing is that Didkovsky's ensemble since 1984, Doctor Nerve, is a jazz-rock band with a hard-hitting beat, blaring brass, and the ability to turn on a dime. As a result, Doctor Nerve's music sounds like big-band jazz from Mars, with odd-shaped phrases repeated over and over and peculiarly off-balance rhythmic phrases. Didkovsky generates his titles via some of the same software processes he uses on notes, so that his pieces include *Take Your Ears As the Bones of Their Queen, Their Eyes Bulged with Sparkling Pockets,* and *Don't Call Too Late My Husband's a Baker.*

Like Didkovsky, Diana Meckley (born 1954 in Denver) uses algorithms to write ensemble music, derived in her case from fractals. In *Strange Attractors* (1989) for string quartet, percussion, and sampler keyboard and *The Evolving Artifact* (1991–1992) for brass and keyboard sampler, she has made forms in which the same material gets presented both acoustically and electronically, played live and then stretched and folded by the samper for challenging perceptual effects. By contrast, Bunita Marcus, a Feldman protégé, writes quintessentially intuitive music of reiterated sonorities. Her *Adam and Eve* (1989) is a gorgeous continuum of recurring chromatic motifs, with a lithe sense of angularly leaping melody. A new breed of ensemble composers is represented by the composers of the bicoastal collective Common Sense, including Dan Becker, Belinda Reynolds, Carolyn Yarnell, John Halle, Ed Harsh, Randall Woolf, and Marc Mellits. Becker's chamber works such as *Gridlock* and *S.T.I.C.* are marked by a playful postminimal rigor, while Woolf uses vernacular elements to comment on society. Yarnell's music is more highly emotive, typified by her piano concerto *Arrow through Heart* (1996), whose relentless textures of running eighth-notes accumulate in cathartic energy.

Performance Artists

While many young composers have turned to rock sources and rhythmic complexity, others experiment instead with unusual modes of performance, working with low-tech performance systems or moving in the direction of theater. Examples are Brenda Hutchinson, Laetitia de Compiegne Sonami, Linda Fisher, Joshua Fried, and Phil Kline.

Like Janice Giteck, Brenda Hutchinson (born 1954 in Trenton, New Jersey) has worked with mental patients, and she uses their stories in her music. In *EEEYAH!* (1989), a sampled recording of a Thai farmer's pig call (transcribed in the title) becomes the frame for a meditation on the names of people who have died of AIDS, punctuated by the beat of a bass drum. In her *Apple Etudes,* Hutchinson overlays the recorded stories of mental asylum patients with the tinkle of a giant, three-foot-diameter music box she built. The personal intensity of

Hutchinson's pieces can be eerily compelling; in *Every Dream Has Its Number* (1996) she interviewed her dying mother about her gambling compulsion. Hutchinson's strategy is often to focus our attention on some aspect of the acoustics or physics of a performance, meanwhile slipping in a real-life monologue by some unfortunate victim whose story hits us all the harder for catching us off guard.

Laetitia de Compiegne Sonami (born 1957) is a French-born composer of interactive electronic music who has lived in San Francisco since 1978. Her early works, written while studying at Mills with Ashley, Behrman, and Terry Riley, were mostly for tape with simple, homemade electronics, but she has increasingly turned toward live theatrical work. In pieces such as *What Happened* (1987), she tells a story by the brilliant West Coast novelist Melody Sumner Carnahan, as her voice triggers the electronic environment around her. In *Pie Jesu—Sounds from Empty Spaces* (1990), that environment includes sound samples such as Moslem songs and a section of the Fauré Requiem. Sonami performs more recent pieces such as . . . *and she keeps coming back for more* (1995–1996) with her invention the Lady's Glove, a pressure- and direction-sensitive glove with which she can control sixteen computerized functions at once. Her work is always mysterious, inscrutable as to electronic process, but seductive in its emotional narrative.

Linda Fisher (born 1949) has also moved from homemade electronics into a theatrical direction; she started out as a David Tudor protégé, performing in his *Rainforest*. Her *Girlfriends* (1990) for keyboard sampler offers a different sound complex on each note; *Big Mouth* (1991) employs samples from a Porky Pig cartoon for a witty satire on Freudian psychoanalysis. Her more ambitious recent works, though, are a series of electronic pieces about women scientists, in which Fisher sings over her live electronics in textures alternately noisy and postminimal. In this series, *The Scientist* (1990) alludes to the life of Margaret Mead, and *Girl Devil Dancing* to that of Alexandra David-Neel.

One of the most inventive performance-artist-type composers is Joshua Fried (born 1959 in Los Angeles), a rock-influenced postconceptualist with a steady stream of startling ideas. In 1981 he started performing in New York clubs with an act in which he would run several tape loops at a time and control which ones were heard through a mixer. After awhile he implanted piezoelectric discs in everyday objects (usually old shoes) and drummed them with drumsticks to trigger noise from the loops, so that while the content was prerecorded, he could control the results improvisatorily. Next, in 1991 he started an ongoing work called *Travelogue*, in which he made tape collages of pop songs, noises, and poetry and asked various singers and actors to listen to the tape over headphones and imitate it as closely and as quickly as possible. The audience hears not the tape the singer hears, but a different background tape, plus the singer's hysterical attempt. *Travelogue* became so successful that Fried expanded the technique to a chorus of six singer-actors at once in *Headset Sextet* (1995), employing complex tempo canons and stunning effects of theatrical simultaneity.

Equally inventive is Pamela Z, a San Francisco performance artist and songwriter. Born Pamela Ruth Brooks in Buffalo in 1956, she went from playing guitar and singing her songs in clubs and coffee houses to being one of San Francisco's most inventive and popular performance artists. She frequently performs solo with a large rack of electronic equipment used to make loops of her voice and to create digital delays. Her pieces are as delightful as Laurie Anderson's and have the same irreverent, technological spirit. In "Cultured Pearls," her sampled voice repeats on the sliding word "pearl" as she details their activities: "They go to the opera, they support the ballet." In "You," Z uses as lyrics a long list of phrases all beginning with the word "you"; it turns out to be a page from a catalogue of popular song titles. Since 1991 Z has performed with her trio The Qube Chix in songs such as "I Want a Bald Boyfriend," a rock song with only drums and clarinet as accompaniment: "I want a man who's well-behaved / Who's neat and clean, whose head is shaved."

Phil Kline, a guitarist in Glenn Branca's symphonic ensemble, has delighted New York audiences with his performance pieces for multiple ghetto blasters or boom boxes (cheap tape recorders). In works such as *Bachman's Warbler* (1990), he plays a harmonica tone into a recording tape loop, plays it back and records the loop with a new tone on another loop, and so on for twelve tape players, gradually building up impressive masses of sound. He has also, as a Christmas season tradition since 1991, enacted living sound sculptures in which a large number of people carry ghetto blasters through the streets, all playing tapes that have been computer-sequenced to create echoes and scintillating quasi-minimalist phase patterns.

Another of the fastest-growing movements among younger composers is the movement toward alternative tunings. Whereas, earlier in the century, alternate tunings generally meant quarter-tones, sixth-tones, or some other equal-tempered system of more than twelve, for the current generation it more often means just-intonation systems of pure tuning. Often these composers do not receive much exposure, because of both the difficulty of getting their microtonal music performed well and, in many cases, their tendency to emphasize theory over performance. On the East Coast, the leader of this movement is Johnny Reinhart, composer, bassoonist, and director of the perennial American Festival of Microtonal Music. Skip LaPlante, another microtonalist active in New York, specializes in home-made instruments fashioned from cast-off objects. Dean Drummond is well-known for directing the Newband Ensemble, which plays and maintains some of Harry Partch's original instruments as well as a few replicas. And Erling Wold of San Francisco is a microtonal composer of brief, enigmatic works, who has also had some success with scores for independent films.

Postlude: The Road from *4' 33"*

So many music writers today are pessimistic about the future and present state of music. Does this chapter sound pessimistic? It is true that the audiences for classical music are falling off, that more and more young people don't attend live concerts, that symphony orchestras are folding, that university departments are increasingly forced to cater to rock and commercial music to attract students. But such oft-quoted statistics have primarily to do with the decline of interest in *European* music. How about *American* music? Are the fates of the two continents chained together? Or does the death of the prestige of European music offer American music an opportunity it has been yearning for since the influx of immigrants before World War II?

If it were possible to kill off American music through lack of audience, lack of funding, and lack of institutional support, American music would have died a thousand deaths over the last 150 years. American composers are accustomed to surviving on virtually nothing. One European's book of interviews with American composers was entitled *Desert Plants,* acknowledging that they can get by on infinitesimal amounts of support that European artists would consider starvation rations. Our educational institutions have barely tried to expose students to American music to find whether they are attracted to it or not. How can the impending death of European music's support system in America possibly hurt any American composers except those tied in to European performance practice? Aside from their constitutional rights as citizens and the occasional small grant, what do most American composers possess that can be taken away?

Were I forced to choose the decades that I thought were the most fertile in American music, in terms of excellence and beauty, I would quickly pick the 1920s and 1990s, less certainly the 1930s and 1980s. John Cage himself named 1952 as the low point in American culture[9]— significantly, the year he composed *4' 33"*. Since that year—if *4' 33"* can be considered a kind of death of music that renders a rebirth possible— American music has been reforming itself, building up a new, firmer, more solidly indigenous tradition. That frustrating gap between composers and audiences? It's gone, or else kept alive only by virtue of an artificial life support system that our institutions keep it on. There is nothing complicated or off-putting or opaque about the musics of Eve Beglarian, Mikel Rouse, Glenn Branca, John Luther Adams, Peter Garland, William Duckworth, Pamela Z, Joshua Fried. Anyone who's

curious can comprehend their musics *more* easily than they can understand Mozart.

It is true that, as the classical music establishment sinks, American
composers will have to fight in order not to sink with it. But the fight
cannot be more difficult than the struggle already has been to be
included and well represented within the Euro-classical world in the first
place. The battleground is shifting—American composers have established a much stronger foothold on the Internet than they possessed in
orchestra programs or classical record stores, and much of their music is
more easily available via the Web than it has been through standard
retail outlets. In order to survive, composers and their slim support system will have to create a public perception that classical (European)
music is one thing, and the world of American composition something
else altogether, unhampered by the elitist and class associations that
make Mozart and Brahms seem more irrelevant with each passing year.

The problem is that, as the theorist Mihaly Csikszentmihalyi has
written,[10] a creative culture is a triangle requiring three points: individual artists, a tradition to work within and against, and a public with an
adequate amount of disposable attention. The third variable is what is
lacking today. As corporate control over the economy necessitates ever
more work and income to keep up with technology and ahead of infla-
tion, people have less time than ever to explore the art springing up
around them. And, paradoxically, just as disposable attention plummets
toward zero, there has never been so much exciting music, there have
never been so many imaginative composers. Our music scene is collaps-
ing under the weight of more good work than our current stressed-out
and distracted audiences can assimilate.

Art cannot solve the problems of society—at least, most of us reflex-
ively assume that it can't. In recent years, politicians and administrators
have attempted to use art to ameliorate social ills, mostly by increasing
the programming of art by members of designated minorities so that
those minorities will feel included by our cultural institutions. Whether
this strategy really does improve collective self-esteem, or whether it is a
sop thrown to minorities in lieu of political change that would materially
benefit them, remains to be decided. But can't Thelonious Monk's music
uplift and inspire a white person, and couldn't Copland's music have the
same effect on an African- or Asian-American? Doesn't the enormous
impact of gamelan and Indian ragas on late twentieth-century American
music prove that art's meaning isn't limited by ethnic categories?

Say for a minute that artists are, as they have so often been
described, the antennae of the race, the first people to register and
reflect undercurrents of collective psychological change. If so, then the
composers of the 1990s, in once again creating music in which intellectual, physical, and emotional appeal are no longer separated, may be
pointing toward an upcoming rebirth in American society. Perhaps the

road from *4'33"* to Monk's *Atlas* and Rouse's *Dennis Cleveland* and Adams's *Dream of White on White* is a road that society itself is slowly and belatedly traversing, a road that starts with the simple, egoless act of stopping to listen, and that points toward a reintegration of personality, toward restoring playfulness and emotiveness to creativity. If any of this is true, isn't it possible that the music of these 1990s might be indeed supremely useful, if nothing more, as a psychological model, operating on deeper terms than any orchestra-sponsored questionnaire would be able to measure?

I believe so. I further believe that composers and audiences alike have forgotten how crucially important music can be to nonmusicians and that they, composers and audiences both, are resisting remembering because of the tremendous responsibility that importance entails on both sides. However, every few years bring a new crop of composers whose music has wide and lasting appeal, each crop larger than the last. As Cage said so often, "We need not fear for the future of music." This book ends in the middle of a crescendo. And if the music described here falls into disuse in the twenty-first century, it will be because twenty-first-century composers stood on our shoulders to create a music so heavenly that there was no longer any need for the past.

Notes

1. John Cage, "Overpopulation and Art," in *John Cage: Composed in America,* Marjorie Perloff and Charles Junkerman, eds. (Chicago: University of Chicago Press, 1994), pp. 14–17.
2. Robert Ashley, "Just One Complaint," in the program catalogue for New Music American '82.
3. Quoted in Kyle Gann, "Shadowing Capote," *Village Voice,* February 7, 1995, p. 63.
4. Interview with the author, October 15, 1996.
5. Interview with the author, July 22, 1996.
6. Ibid.
7. David First, liner notes for *The Good Book's (Accurate) Jail of Escape Dust Coordinates Part 2,* O.O. Discs 0023, 1995.
8. Interview with the author, October 15, 1996.
9. Quoted in *Conversing with Cage,* Richard Kostelanetz, ed. (New York: Limelight Editions, 1988), p. 206.
10. Mihaly Csikszentmihalyi, "Society, culture, and person: a systems view of creativity," in *The Nature of Creativity: Contemporary Psychological Perspectives,* Robert J. Sternberg, ed. (Cambridge University Press, 1988), p. 325.

Index

Boldface indicates musical examples or photographs